# BATTLE
## SURFACE!

## OTHER BOOKS BY STEPHEN L. MOORE

*Relic Quest: A Guide to Responsible Relic Recovery Techniques with Metal Detectors.*
Garland, TX: RAM Books, 2011.

*Savage Frontier: Rangers, Riflemen, and Indian Wars in Texas. Volume IV: 1842–1845.*
Denton: University of North Texas Press, 2010.

*European Metal Detecting Guide: Techniques, Tips and Treasures.*
Garland, TX: RAM Books, 2009.

*Presumed Lost: The Incredible Ordeal of America's Submarine Veteran
POWs of World War II.* Annapolis, MD: Naval Institute Press, 2009.

*Last Stand of the Texas Cherokees: Chief Bowles and the 1839 Cherokee War in Texas.*
Garland, TX: RAM Books, 2009.

*War of the Wolf: Texas' Memorial Submarine, World War II's Famous USS* Seawolf.
Dallas, TX: Atriad Press, 2008.

*Savage Frontier: Rangers, Riflemen, and Indian Wars in Texas. Volume III: 1840–1841.*
Denton: University of North Texas Press, 2007.

*Spadefish: On Patrol With a Top-Scoring World War II Submarine.* Dallas, TX: Atriad
Press, 2006.

*Savage Frontier: Rangers, Riflemen, and Indian Wars in Texas. Volume II: 1838–1839.*
Denton: University of North Texas Press, 2006.

*Eighteen Minutes: The Battle of San Jacinto and the Texas Independence Campaign.*
Plano, TX: Republic of Texas Press, 2004.

*Savage Frontier: Rangers, Riflemen, and Indian Wars in Texas. Volume I: 1835–1837.*
Plano, TX: Republic of Texas Press, 2002.

*Taming Texas: Captain William T. Sadler's Lone Star Service.*
Austin, TX: State House Press, 2000.

*The Buzzard Brigade: Torpedo Squadron Ten at War.* With William J. Shinneman and
Robert W. Gruebel. Missoula, MT: Pictorial Histories Publishing, 1996.

**For more information, visit www.stephenlmoore.com**

# BATTLE SURFACE!

Lawson P. "Red" Ramage and the
War Patrols of the USS *Parche*

**STEPHEN L. MOORE**

Foreword by Vice Adm. Albert H. Konetzni Jr., USN (Ret.)

NAVAL INSTITUTE PRESS

*Annapolis, Maryland*

Naval Institute Press
291 Wood Road
Annapolis, MD 21402

Library of Congress Cataloging-in-Publication Data

Moore, Stephen L.
  Battle surface! : Lawson P. "Red" Ramage and the war patrols of the USS
Parche / Stephen L. Moore ; foreword by Albert Konetzni Jr.
    p. cm.
  Includes bibliographical references and index.
  ISBN 978-1-59114-532-5 (hardcover)
  1. Parche (Submarine) 2. World War, 1939–1945—Naval operations—
Submarine. 3. World War, 1939–1945—Naval operations, American. 4. World
War, 1939–1945—Campaigns—Pacific Ocean. 5. Ramage, Lawson Paterson,
1909–1990. 6. Submariners—United States—Biography. I. Title.
  D783.5.P34M66 2011
  940.54'510973—dc22
                                    2011000487


Printed in the United States of America on acid-free paper

15 14  13  12  11        9 8 7 6 5 4 3 2 1
First printing

# Contents

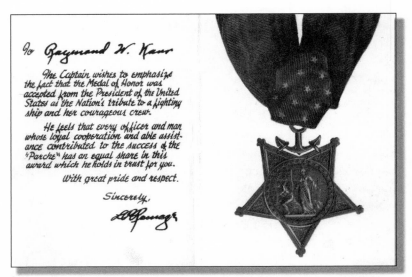

Cdr. Lawson P. Ramage, upon being awarded the Congressional Medal of Honor for *Parche*'s second war patrol, created this certificate for each man who was on board his submarine. Ramage wrote that he felt "every officer and man whose loyal cooperation and able assistance contributed to the success of the *Parche* has an equal share in this award," which he held in trust for them. *Image courtesy of Ray Karr.*

# Foreword

History tells us that the Japanese surprise attack on the United States in December 1941 was a grave miscalculation for Japan. Clearly the attack amassed much damage and death at Pearl Harbor, but the sneak attack's limited objectives resulted in little damage to the ship repair facilities, no damage to the above-ground fuel tanks, and little damage to the Submarine Base. This series of non-events led to wartime scenarios not expected in prewar planning.

The attack certainly "awakened a sleeping giant"; it enabled the former "scouting force" of submarines to take on a completely new role. Immediately after the commencement of hostilities our submarines were ordered to begin unsupported operations against the enemy. As the commander of the U.S. Pacific Fleet, Adm. Chester W. Nimitz stated: "It was to the Submarine Force that I looked to carry the load until our great industrial activity could produce the weapons we so surely needed to carry the war to the enemy."

The Submarine Force accorded itself proudly during the three year, eight month duration of the war. Japan entered the war with 6 million tons of merchant shipping. At the conclusion of hostilities only 300,000 tons of merchant shipping remained. The American Submarine Force was responsible for sinking 5 million tons (1,178 ships) of Japanese shipping as well as 600,000 tons (214 ships) of naval vessels. These losses strangled Japan. Its dependence on oil from the south and the loss of its tankers sealed its fate by the end of 1943.

The achievements above are more noteworthy when one considers that the United States Submarine Force consisted of less than 2 percent of the U.S. Navy's personnel. As important as the Submarine Force accomplishments are, it is also necessary to review our submarine losses. Fifty-two out of 228 American submarines were lost in the war—almost one in five!

The thumbnail sketch that I've drawn here provides a short history of the impact of the American Submarine Force on hostilities with Japan in World War II. The ability to achieve such success in less than four years is a tribute to the men who manned and supported our submarines. In order to truly understand the overall achievements of the Force one must know the men who volunteered for submarine duty.

*Battle Surface!* tells their story in their words. USS *Parche* and its skipper, Cdr. Red Ramage, were the epitome of operational success during the war. *Battle Surface!* clearly points to the highs and lows a commanding officer of a naval vessel experiences and the reaction of individual crew members to these swings in attitude. *Battle Surface!* describes the lack of physiological and psychological privacy on our submarines and how these deficits enabled camaraderie to flourish.

I was lucky to have known Red Ramage and many of his crew members, including Frank Allcorn, his torpedo officer. One encounter with any of these fine sailors allows the listener to truly understand how the American Submarine Force accomplished so much in World War II. *Battle Surface!* is a must-read for all who want to understand what the "Greatest Generation" gave us in World War II.

—Albert H. Konetzni Jr., Vice Admiral, USN (Ret.)
Former Commander, United States Submarine Force,
U.S. Pacific Fleet

# Preface

AT AGE 92, BOB ERWIN LOOKS healthier than many people I've seen who are decades his junior. Sporting a dark tan from playing golf five days a week, he is eager to look over the latest revisions to the manuscript. The walls of his southern Florida apartment are adorned with evidence of his past handiwork as an officer of the United States Submarine Service of World War II—a combat insignia pin representing four successful war patrols, a copy of his boat's Presidential Unit Citation, the Silver Star, and the Bronze Star.

Bob produces photo albums, patrol reports, and various memorabilia from days on board the USS *Parche*. As we review the details of various attacks made by his submarine, he is quick to clarify the fine points and steer credit where credit is due.

More than 65 years have passed since his warship entered the annals of submarine history on 31 July 1944, and yet he remembers the fine details as if it happened last year. Bob relates how he was hunched over his little plotting table in *Parche*'s conning tower that night, penciling in ever twist and turn his boat made. Above him on the bridge stood Cdr. Lawson Paterson Ramage, a resilient warrior who was in his element that day.

Known to his contemporaries as "Red" for his hair color, Ramage coolly conned his boat in, around, and through the large Japanese convoy MI-11 during the predawn hours of 31 July with little regard for his own safety. In the span of a half hour, he dispatched 19 of his submarine's two dozen torpedoes against tankers and transports with deadly effect. Twice *Parche* passed within a stone's throw of an enemy ship, close enough that the American and Japanese could actually shout insults at each other.

Wartime doctrine generally called for calculated approaches by submarine, in order to release war fish in spreads at distances far enough to enable a silent escape into the depths afterward but close enough to guarantee a high percentage of hits. Few skippers dared to charge directly into the midst of an enemy convoy while surfaced and sustaining gunfire from all directions. None had ever attempted the tricky tactic of reloading torpedo tubes while bouncing around on the surface in the midst of deadly combat. Only seven U.S. submariners would earn the nation's highest honor, the Congressional Medal of Honor, during World War II. *Parche*'s Red Ramage was the third man so honored and the first one to do so who had not perished in the course of earning his medal.

The veterans of the Silent Service of World War II accounted for some 55 percent of all Japanese vessels sunk in the war, although the submarine force only accounted for 1.5 percent of the U.S. Navy. They paid dearly for this success rate: one in five U.S. submariners of World War II did not return from patrol.

The wartime media clamp kept much of their exploits silent. *Parche* was one of only a handful of submarines whose name made the newspapers in 1945 after skipper Red Ramage was awarded the Medal of Honor. *Parche*'s men were true warriors, fighting submerged and slipping away as the bombs and depth charges rained down. Yet they also fought it out on the surface, engaging enemy craft with their deck guns. One opponent placed a shot through her hull and machine-gun bullets richocted off *Parche*'s structures on more than one occasion. On another occasion, a Japanese merchant ship was hit by a 40-mm round from *Parche*'s forward gun and the vessel literally disintegrated in a violent explosion.

In recent years, many of the more decorated submarine crews of World War II have been chronicled in books about the Silent Service. The story of the war patrols of the USS *Parche* is long overdue. *Parche* was later honored by having a nuclear submarine named for her and another warship, USS *Ramage*, named for her Medal of Honor–recipient skipper. Today her bridge structure, periscope shears, and upper deck gun are on display at the submarine base in Pearl Harbor. In addition, visitors to the USS *Bowfin* Museum and Park at Pearl Harbor can climb inside *Parche*'s original conning tower.

The wartime accomplishments of the USS *Parche* are related through the eyes of both her senior officers and the teenage sailors, electricians, motor machinist's mates, yeomen, cooks, and torpedomen who went to war on this proud vessel. Her battle flag sports the motto "Par Excellence," and excellence in combat they did certainly achieve. Analysis conducted immediately postwar by the Joint Army-Navy Assessment Committee stops short of recognizing many of the Japanese ships that should be properly credited to these submariners. JANAC, for instance, did not acknowledge ships smaller than 500 tons that were destroyed by deck gun actions. Other vessels could not be counted due to an absence of proper Japanese records. For the historic surface action during the night of 31 July 1944, questions will forever linger concerning which ships were truly destroyed by *Parche* or by her wolf pack mate *Steelhead*. Admiral Ramage would feel slighted by some of the ships that were officially listed as "shared" credits.

More recent analysis of Japanese records that were not available in the 1940s to JANAC's team led submariner John Alden to reassess the true totals of the U.S. Silent Service boats of World War II. His work would suggest that *Parche*'s total kills amounted to 22 ships of all types destroyed by her torpedoes and guns, plus another nine vessels damaged to varying degrees for a total of more than 88,000 tons of Japanese shipping destroyed or damaged. Skippers Red Ramage and Woodrow Wilson "Mac" McCrory were both highly decorated for their boat's achievements, but credit is certainly due equally to every man who did his duty to make their boat successful.

The *Parche* story could not be told as fully without the close relationship these proud veterans still share. Fred Richards, who falsified his birth certificate in order to join the Navy at age 15, was the youngest man to serve on *Parche*. In later years, he was the man instrumental in organizing his *Parche* shipmates to attend the first reunions. Bob Hall, the baker from New Hampshire, later served as the ship's unofficial historian, cranking out periodic newsletters to keep his shipmates informed. His son Dave Hall, an Air Force veteran, partnered with his father in recent years to produce a photographic tribute to the war years of the *Parche* crew. The volumes of photos and *Parche* data collected by Richards and the Halls proved to be invaluable source material.

Former *Parche* officers Bob Erwin and Jim Campbell fielded dozens of e-mail and telephone queries regarding events both large and small relating to *Parche*'s history. Dozens of other *Parche* veterans generously shared their stories, their photos, and their memories, namely: Roland Burker, Lowell Burton, Nicholas Casassa, Hurschel Chambers, William Coleman, David Forbes, Richard Frank, Henry Gay, Paul Gilcher, Ralph Giordano, Charles Gooden, Myron Grover, Eugene Haba, Thornton Hamlin, Benjamin Harrison, David Hussey, Raymond Karr, Carl Kimmons, Gus Kulick, Alden Lawrence, Joseph Leiching, Corwin Maupin, Charles McNutt, Glenn Meise, Carl Meyer, Edward Mokos, Ozro Payne, Edward Rauscher, Samuel Roberts, Robert Silvis, Harold Staggs, Robert Swanson, George Tubb, Carl Vozniak, Donald Walters, Charles Welton, Ronald Williams, and Carl Zeller.

Special thanks to Jim Morriss for helping me to track down Loni Martin, daughter of the late William "Lonnie" Hughes, who kept an illegal wartime diary aboard *Parche*. Maury and Don Martin, grandsons of the late Carl Schmelzer, were the catalysts who drove me to look deeper into the *Parche* story. Maury produced photos and papers from his grandfather's *Parche* files, interviewed several veterans, and assisted in tracking down others who contributed to this project.

Additional material was furnished by the widows and children of many other *Parche* veterans, including: Frank W. "Skip" Allcorn IV, Stephen Barnett, Grace Buckner, William Christy, Joseph DeSola, Mary Dillon, Robert Ernest, Howard G. Ernest, Genny Fournier, Mike Gadd, Rex and Wahneta Goon, Emme Hawn, Ruth Holleran, Richard Kuter, David Kuter, Donald Larsen, Claude Lutz Jr., Norma Manns, Eugene Payne, Margaret Satterfield, Pat St. Denny, and Cecile Vogedes. Several people deserve acknowledgement for their hours of checking *Parche* facts and reviewing various sections of this manuscript as it progressed: Bob Hall, Dave Hall, Bob Erwin, Fred Richards, Jim Campbell, Charles Mc-Nutt, Dave Hussey, Ray Karr, and Jim Ramage.

Charles Hinman of the USS *Bowfin* Museum once again came to my assistance by digging up a copy of Quartermaster Dale Mielke's wartime diary that was kept on board *Parche* during two of her runs. Special thanks to Capt. Paul Hunt, USN, for putting me in contact with Vice Adm. Al Konetzni Jr. (USN, Ret.). The former commander of the U.S. Submarine Force, U.S. Pacific Fleet, kindly offered to write a foreword for this book to pay tribute to his friend Red Ramage and the entire *Parche* crew.

This book is dedicated to the proud diesel boat sailors who took *Parche* in harm's way to help speed the war's end with Japan. They served elbow to elbow in tight quarters during tense actions both submerged and surfaced and often sweated out counterattacks at silent running. Through the combined efforts of this family of silent warriors, *Parche* became one of only seven submarines whose skipper earned the nation's highest honor, the Congressional Medal of Honor. *Parche*'s crew earned the Presidential Unit Citation for "extraordinary heroism in action" as they displayed "valor and gallantry" in earning a well-deserved place in the annals of the Silent Service history of World War II.

# BATTLE
## SURFACE!

# CHAPTER ONE

# Red Ramage's Return

Few men were happier to be heading back on war patrol than steward's mate second class Carl Eugene Kimmons. The war against Japan in the Pacific was more than two years old but he was still just as eager to seek revenge against the enemy as he had been when he witnessed the war erupt before his eyes one Sunday morning years before.

Carl Kimmons was one of only two African American sailors on board one of the Navy's newest fleet submarines this day. He was serving at a time when the Navy still had heavy restrictions on the combat roles that could be held by a man of color. Such limitations were mere formalities for he knew that every man on board his vessel served an equal role in maintaining the fighting ability of an underseas boat.

Kimmons had recently helped commission the submarine USS *Parche* (SS-384) and had been involved since the earliest days in preparing his vessel for war. It was only fitting that his *Parche* would set sail into the Pacific War on 29 March 1944 from Pearl Harbor, where the young steward's mate had been so violently thrust into World War II some 27 months prior.

The deck trembled lightly beneath Kimmons' feet as two of *Parche*'s four powerful diesel engines rumbled to life. His boat—more than 311 feet in length—was still moored to Berth Sail-4 at the Pearl Harbor Submarine Base as eager deck hands stood ready topside to cast off her securing lines. She sported a fresh multi-color paint scheme and all necessary provisions for patrol had long since been stored below decks.

In anticipation of getting under way, Kimmons was in the stewards' pantry in the forward battery compartment just outside the officers' wardroom. With a freshly brewed pot of coffee, he started forward to offer some to the officers on the bridge.

Raised in Hamilton, Ohio, Kimmons had joined the Navy in 1940. He was serving aboard the old four-stack destroyer *McFarland* on 7 December 1941, when the Japanese attacked Pearl Harbor. "While on the *McFarland*, I used to hang around the yeoman's shack in my off time because I could type and want-ed to be a yeoman instead of a mess attendant," he recalled. His destroyer was at sea in the Hawaiian Islands on the "day of infamy," and thus escaped damage from the attacking Japanese warplanes. Kimmons quickly requested submarine duty and he was transferred to the USS *Plunger* in April 1942, where he would be advanced to officer's cook, third class.[1]

Aboard *Plunger*, Kimmons bunked in the forward torpedo room, and was on the reload gang during torpedo attacks. He also volunteered as part of the gun crew for battle surface actions and trained as the .50-caliber machine gunner. Kimmons saw no action on the .50-caliber during his four patrols on *Plunger* but did exert plenty of sweat manhandling 3,000-pound torpedoes into their tubes while on the reload gang. A fellow officer's cook on *Plunger*, CK2c James Thomas McGuire, was a muscular man who had enlisted in the Navy from Louisville, Kentucky. McGuire had been part of the ammunition handling crew aboard *Plunger* during her sixth war patrol and was rated officer's cook second class at the end of this run, partially because of his devotion to keeping the ammunition line moving swiftly during gun actions.[2]

McGuire joined Kimmons again as an officer's cook on board *Parche* on 8 March 1944, just three weeks prior to the boat's departure on her first war patrol. McGuire, a seasoned submariner, was a late replacement for a steward's mate who was put ashore because of a sexually transmitted disease he had contracted. *Parche* had spent several days in Balboa in the Panama Canal Zone during February en route to Pearl Harbor. There, some of the crew took the opportunity to visit the bordellos for rum and Coke drinks and "visits" with Colombian ladies.

Several days out from Balboa, a special "short arm inspection" was ordered in which *Parche*'s pharmacist's mate, Quentin Brown, discovered a half dozen cases of venereal disease. One of the "victims" was an officer's orderly, who was assigned other duties away from food until he could be transferred at Pearl—thus paving the path for McGuire and Kimmons to be reunited before *Parche*'s first patrol.[3]

Kimmons and McGuire had become friends aboard *Plunger* and they continued as an efficient team on *Parche,* where they bunked in the forward torpedo room. Both men had more feathers in their respective war bonnets than three-quarters of their new comrades aboard *Parche*. To Carl Kimmons, color and his specific role on board ship mattered less than the fact that he was once again holding a position he loved: serving on a wartime fleet submarine head-ing into action. Carl's four war patrols on the *Plunger* were more than any of *Parche*'s officers except the skipper.

Steward's mate Carl Eugene Kimmons had made four war patrols aboard *Plunger* before joining *Parche*. He became close with his new skipper and after the war, Carl Kimmons would be the first black submariner to be promoted into an officer's rank who had started his naval service as an officer's cook. *Courtesy of Bob Hall.*

When he was finally approved to return to submarines after months of trying, Kimmons found that his Exec on the destroyer *Scott* was not pleased. He had Kimmons' bag inspected and any items not issued by the *Scott* were confiscated. The destroyer was preparing to leave New York Harbor on a new convoy assignment when the paperwork was shown to the executive officer. Unwilling to delay his ship's departure, *Scott*'s second in command put Kimmons on a motor launch back to the docks. The young mess attendant was unphased, however. "I was so glad to be returning to submarine duty that I would have walked," he recalled.[4]

After months of training and breaking in his new boat, Kimmons' USS *Parche* was now preparing to get under way. He passed through the control room with his coffee en route to the bridge. The control room was the heart of operations for *Parche*, whether she was surfaced or submerged. In the control room, Kimmons carefully balanced his load of hot beverages as he climbed the steel rungs of the ladder leading up into the conning tower, the small watertight compartment from which the periscopes were operated. During an attack, this area would be packed elbow-to-elbow with officers and men directing the fire control of *Parche*'s torpedoes. Another ladder led directly to the sunlight beaming down from the bridge through the open hatch.

On the bridge, Kimmons delivered the coffee to a small group of his officers including his executive officer and a wolf pack commander who had just reported aboard. Ens. John Henry Parks, a stout, congenial mustang officer, quickly accepted his cup, thanked Kimmons and returned to scanning the action on deck as *Parche*'s lines were taken in.

Ensign Parks was a busy man this day. As the boat's first lieutenant, his responsibilities included the deck detail who were busily hauling in the lines that had secured *Parche* to her berth. Parks was also the duty officer of the deck

(OOD) as his skipper conned their submarine away from the sub base. Like all of *Parche*'s officers, Parks was married and the Navy was his life. He had been in longer than most of his seven fellow officers. He was a mustang, having been promoted up through the ranks as a chief boatswain's mate aboard surface ships.

Pearl Harbor's beautiful waters sparkled in the bright afternoon sunlight. War was evident and oil continued to trickle to the surface near Ford Island from the twisted hulk of the once-proud battleship *Arizona*. Parks alternately called out orders to enlisted men on the deck and directed the helmsman in the conning tower below in backing the boat away from the pier. Most of the 81 officers and men aboard *Parche* felt a keen sense of pride as they finally were getting under way for their call to duty, submarine warfare in the Pacific.

As always, Kimmons was pleased to catch his skipper's eye, a tall, thin man who offered a nod of assurance and a courteous greeting as he accepted his coffee from the officer's cook. The captain was thoughtfully tugging on an ever-present tobacco pipe as he chatted with the wolf pack commander. Carl Kimmons already felt a connection with his skipper from their frequent chats in the wardroom during the past four months of training. He knew that Cdr. Lawson Paterson Ramage was eager to return to the war and that his skipper's past command experiences left little concern that he was a man destined to lead *Parche*'s crew to great achievements.

---

Lawson Ramage had been born in Monroe Bridge, Massachusetts, on 19 January 1909. His father was an adventurous Scotsman who had journeyed to America to join other members of the Ramage family who were engaged in the papermaking business. Young Lawson had acquired a taste for sea life at the early age of four, when he accompanied his father on a voyage across the ocean on a Cunard liner to visit his grandparents in Scotland. "It grew to be a passion and a very important part of my life," he recalled. "The reason being, I guess, was that I was about the only youngster aboard and had the run of both ships, coming and going. The captain and the officers made a great deal over me, giving me the opportunity to visit all parts of the ship."[5]

From that point on, Ramage had a desire to go to sea. He attended high school in the small town of Beaver Falls in northern New York, where his father was general manager of a paper company in the Adirondaks. He graduated from high school in three years at the age of 15 due to the regents system. When his father moved to Vermont to take another paper mill job, Ramage attended the Williston Academy prep school in Easthampton, Massachusetts.

*Parche*'s first skipper was Cdr. Lawson Paterson Ramage. Known to his peers of the Silent Service as "Red" for his hair color, this bold Scotsman had previously earned the Navy Cross for his success as skipper of the submarine *Trout* in the Pacific War. *Official U.S. Navy photo, courtesy of Jim Ramage.*

After attending the Army-Navy football game in Chicago in 1926—a famous game that ended in a 21-all tie—Ramage wrote to the Naval Academy to find out how he could enroll. With his father's help, he was able to obtain the necessary congressional appointment from a Vermont legislator. "With five boys to educate, it was a real acceptable solution" for his father.[6]

Lawson Ramage entered the Naval Academy at Annapolis in 1927, where he managed to stay in the top 20 percent of his class throughout his four years. His wavy red hair earned him the obvious nickname "Red," and he would always be known as Red Ramage by his friends and fellow officers. "I played soccer in the fall and wrestled in the winter and [played] lacrosse in the spring," he recalled. During a cruise in his freshman year, he was thrilled to visit Europe and even see his relatives in Edinburgh, Scotland.[7]

Ramage injured his right eye while wrestling at the Academy, a mishap that affected his vision so that he failed the aviation physical. Upon graduation from the Academy in 1931, he was thus assigned to surface duty on the old four-stacker destroyer *Dickerson*. His first skipper assigned Ensign Ramage to the duties of navigation because of his Academy training. "So, I stood no watches at sea much to the distress and horror of these other officers who were much senior." Ramage was next assigned as engineering officer of another new destroyer, *Lawrence*.[8]

After a year on *Lawrence*, he became the radio officer for the heavy cruiser *Louisville*. During his two years on this surface ship, Ramage became interested in submarines. He was unable to pass the physical, however, due to his old eye injury. He worked with one of the Navy's eye specialists but could not pass the eye exam during his first two tries. "I took the opportunity to memorize the eye chart so that when I returned I had no problem reading off the chart and getting his approval," Ramage recalled. He thus "passed" the eye exam and was given approval for submarine duty.[9]

In sub school, he was again faced with a required eye test. "This time I managed to pass the eye exam by just exchanging the card before my right eye and reading with my left eye in both instances," he admitted. The examiner missed the fact that Ramage had covered the same bad eye each time. When he left *Louisville* to report to New London for submarine school, the cruiser's executive officer, Cdr. Olaf Mandt Hustvedt, told him to look up his niece Barbara Alice Pine, whom he eventually met three months later. "From that point on, I believe I had a date with her every day for three months until the day we were married," he said.[10]

Lawson and Barbara Ramage were married on 2 November 1935. Because she had been born and raised in Honolulu, the couple was anxious for duty in Hawaii. At Pearl Harbor in January 1936, Lieutenant (jg) Ramage was assigned to an older S-boat, the *S-29*. The couple had many close friends and family in the Hawaiian Islands because Barbara's grandfather, Henry E. Cooper, had been a federal judge there since 1893. He had been involved in the annexation efforts that made Hawaii a territory of the United States.[11]

In 1938, Ramage started postgraduate school back at the Academy but the war in Europe disrupted his schooling in 1939. In September he joined the destroyer *Sands* as her executive officer through February 1941. His next orders sent him happily back to Hawaii, where Lieutenant Ramage was assigned as the force communications and sound officer for Adm. Thomas Withers, commander, Submarines Pacific Fleet (ComSubPac).[12]

Ramage's wife Barbara and their young children Barbara Joan and James Lawson reached Pearl Harbor in November 1941. Red Ramage worked on a number of communications projects during 1941, including efforts that allowed submarines to receive radio communications while submerged via direction finder coils mounted in their conning towers. "This is what we were working on about the time the blitz came," Ramage related. Admiral Withers' flagship was the cruiser *Richmond* but Ramage and his fellow staff members were based ashore on Oahu at the time of the Japanese surprise attack on 7 December 1941.[13]

Ramage was due to go on duty at the base at 1000 but his telephone began ringing promptly at 0800 that Sunday morning. It was his friend, Cdr. Edwin R. Swindburne, the ComSubPac flag secretary.

"Get out here right away!" exclaimed Swindburne. "The Japs are attacking Pearl Harbor!"[14]

Figuring his buddy was pulling his leg, Ramage casually retorted, "Oh, yes, Ed. I know you can handle that situation. You can take care of it in due time."

Ramage thought the phone call was a joke until a bomb exploded nearby in his neighborhood. En route to Pearl Harbor from his family's home in Pacific Heights, Ramage saw the rising smoke and soon saw the slowly circling Japanese aircraft making their dives on the plentiful American shipping in the harbor. Soon, from the second floor windows of his office at the base, Lieutenant Ramage had a grandstand view of the greatest disaster to befall the U.S. Navy to date. "It was just incredible to see this whole line of battleships just engulfed in thick, black smoke and fires blazing up," he recalled. "We were all just dumbfounded that this could happen. They said it couldn't happen here. But here it was not only in technicolor but with sound effects and all."[15]

Ramage survived the Japanese attack without injury, as did two of his brothers who were also stationed at Pearl Harbor on that date. Red Ramage made his first war patrol on the submarine *Grenadier* when he went aboard her in April 1942 as her navigator and executive officer to make his prospective commanding officer (PCO) cruise under Willis Ashford "Pilly" Lent. When *Grenadier* torpedoed and sank her first ship, Ramage was admittedly "a little bit" shaken up by the torpedo explosions. "I had never heard a torpedo go off before," he recalled. "In due time, of course, that got to be the sweetest music I ever heard."[16]

*Grenadier* survived heavy depth charging on this run and Ramage emerged a bloodied fighter. He was awarded the Silver Star for his role in helping to destroy two Japanese ships while on board *Grenadier* and he was given command of the submarine *Trout*. As the skipper and attack coordinator on *Trout*, Ramage did not let his poor sight in his right eye affect his performance. In fact, he later believed that this turned out to be an advantage. "I didn't have to fool around with the focus knob on the periscope," he explained. "Before I raised it,

I turned the knob all the way to the stop [extreme focus]. When the scope came up, I put my bad eye to the periscope and could see perfectly."[17]

During his first patrol (*Trout*'s fifth) in August 1942, Lieutenant Commander Ramage sank an 863-ton merchant vessel and then had the torpedo setup of a lifetime. On 28 August, *Trout* encountered an important convoy that included the 19,000-ton Japanese aircraft carrier *Taiyo*. At this point in the war, only one crippled Japanese carrier had been hit by American torpedoes, during the battle of Midway—and these had been duds.

Ramage fired five torpedoes at this prize, and at least one of them exploded, damaging *Taiyo*'s stern and killing 13 sailors. This was the first time that a U.S. submarine had scored a hit on a Japanese aircraft carrier. "The last I saw of her was that she was on fire and listing and the destroyers were moving around in position," recalled Ramage.[18]

Days later, *Trout* was attacked by a Japanese aircraft while at periscope depth. With his periscopes wrecked, Ramage was forced to retire to Brisbane for repairs. After a hasty overhaul period in which Ramage was promoted to commander, *Trout* was sent toward the Solomon Islands on her next patrol to support the Guadalcanal campaign. On 12 November 1942, Ramage received an Ultra dispatch—specific classified data obtained by U.S. codebreakers—that ordered him to intercept a Japanese combat force bound for Guadalcanal which included the battleship *Kirishima*. Ramage closed to 1,800 yards and fired five torpedoes at the battleship, a rare submarine target. Although Ramage's war fish failed to conect on this occasion, he had become only the fourth U.S. skipper to fire on a battleship. He returned his boat to Brisbane after this short patrol to complete a proper overhaul.[19]

On his third command patrol in December 1942, Ramage was given another Ultra to intercept the 17,000-ton tanker *Kyokuyo Maru* on the west coast of Borneo. Finding this large ship at anchor, he slipped into the channel and fired four torpedoes on the surface. Two hit with brilliant explosions but one prematured and one was a dud. "We tore out of there on all four engines," he recalled. "It was amazing how quickly all the lights in that place went out, immediately."[20]

*Trout* sank two schooners with gunfire near Camranh Bay on 18 January and a 3,000-ton freighter with torpedoes three days later. Ramage then engaged a Japanese destroyer from the point-blank range of 900 yards. He watched them run straight and true toward the enemy warship but angrily wrote that his missiles were "DUDS!" in his patrol report.[21]

Targets were plentiful on this patrol and *Trout* was soon chasing another Ultra dispatch along the Singapore-Manila sea lanes. *Trout* was unable to reach a firing position on these tankers, but Ramage received a third Ultra in early February that directed him to return to Miri for another supertanker. On 7 February, he found the 17,000-ton *Nisshin Maru* at anchor and boldly attacked submerged in the daylight. Ramage fired two torpedoes from the long range of 5,000 yards and then battle surfaced. *Nisshin Maru* opened fire with her own guns, driving Ramage under. He claimed damage to this ship from at least one torpedo that caused smoke to rise from her stern.[22]

During the next week, *Trout* was given two new Ultras. On 14 February, Ramage had his boat in position to intercept the 1,911-ton converted gunboat *Hirotama Maru* off Balikpapan. He fired two torpedoes from a mere 700 yards. The first blew off *Hirotama*'s bow but the second was another dud—Ramage's fifth of the patrol. Furious, he called for a battle surface and his gunners took to the deck to polish off the wildly maneuvering Japanese ship. His gunners began raking the Japanese ship but were unable to slow it down. From her stern, the merchant ship opened up on *Trout* with a machine gun. "It didn't seem to be causing any trouble until all of a sudden I discovered that there was blood all over the deck and some of our people had been hit."[23]

Seven crewmen were wounded by .25-caliber machine-gun bullets and shrapnel in their legs, feet, thighs, or forearms. Another three members of the gun crew had suffered ruptured eardrums during the action. Ramage turned *Trout*'s stern to the freighter and fired another torpedo from 700 yards. This one worked and *Hirotama Maru* sank quickly with no survivors. He returned to Fremantle to get medical care for his crew and was furious to be ordered to remain outside of the port's torpedo nets overnight. He became more irate when he noted that five large merchant liners loaded with Australian troops were also forced to anchor for the night outside the harbor. "Here were the five greatest targets in the world sitting right there at anchor and they wouldn't open the gate to let us in."[24]

He was bitter when he returned to Fremantle, claiming one premature explosion and five duds of the 14 torpedoes he had fired. He angrily condemned the performance of the fish and estimated he had endured a 43-percent failure rate. Codebreakers confirmed that both *Nisshin Maru* and *Kyokuyo Maru* had been damaged but *Kyokuyo* was later salvaged. He was given wartime credit for sinking two schooners and four ships totaling more than 45,000 tons, but postwar analysis trimmed this tonnage to only 4,900.[25]

He did not take the dissapointment quietly, however, opting to stand toe to toe with Rear Adm. Ralph Waldo Christie, commander of submarines, Southwest Pacific, and voice his opinion. As *Trout* prepared to go out on her next patrol, Ramage visited Admiral Christie. The admiral had once worked at the Newport, Rhode Island, torpedo station where he helped develop the Mark 6 magnetic exploder for the Navy's torpedoes. When U.S. sub skippers began criticizing the failures of these torpedoes in 1943, Christie was defiant. "Many remarks made in patrol reports are absurd," he wrote to Adm. Charles Lockwood. "A great deal can be done in improving torpedo performance in the overhaul shop and in the forward and after torpedo rooms."[26]

When Red Ramage visited Admiral Christie, his *Trout* had just been loaded with mines to place off Borneo to disrupt the passage of Japanese tankers.

Christie asked him, "How many torpedoes have you got?"[27]

"I've got 16 torpedoes and 23 mines on board," Ramage replied.

"Well, I want you to get 16 ships with those torpedoes."

Ramage did not hesitate to attack Christie's pet torpedoes. He told the admiral in no uncertain terms that he would be happy if he scored only 25 percent hits with these faulty torpedoes. "This was, of course, a deliberate needle because it was his torpedo. He had been the project officer and he considered this torpedo was his and any disparaging remarks about it were not countenanced at all," Ramage later reflected.[28]

Ralph Christie snapped that many people were making "snide remarks" about his torpedoes. At this point, the *Trout* skipper felt that "things were getting a little bit strained" at best. The admiral's operations officer, Capt. Heber "Tex" McLean grabbed Ramage by the neck and snapped, "It's time to leave."[29]

Outside of the admiral's office, McLean informed Ramage, "You're goddamned lucky to be going to sea."[30]

Ramage quipped right back, "I think you've got that turned around a little bit. I think what you mean to say is we are goddamned lucky to be *coming back* from sea." He boldly invited his superior to grab his sea bag and come along on patrol to see just how these torpedoes truly functioned.[31]

"That stopped all conversation for the time being for the rest of the trip to Fremantle," recalled Ramage.

Commander Ramage's fourth command patrol aboard *Trout* in March 1943 was disappointing all around. At one point, his boat came close to being grounded off Australia. He did successfully lay his mines off the Natuna Islands but his torpedoes failed to create damage. Ramage fired 15 of his 16 torpedoes without a hit; all missed their mark except for one dud that produced only a low-order detonation. Once back in Fremantle, he complained again about poor torpedo performance but Admiral Christie blamed Ramage's failure on shooting errors against wildly maneuvering ships. Christie noted in his diary, "Red had a miss last patrol—many chances and many failures. He is due for a relief and will be sent back to the U.S. for a new boat and rest at the same time."[32]

After leaving *Trout* in Australia, Ramage flew back to Pearl Harbor and found that he was being sent to new construction at the Portsmouth Navy Yard. "This disappointed me considerably because the family was all set up in New London," he later admitted. He had thus hoped to get new construction out of General Dynamics at the Electric Boat yards in New London.[33]

Ramage's friends soon convinced him that the Portsmouth assignment was not a bad thing. The new boats coming out of the ways there were of the new thick hull design and would be far more durable than his *Trout* had been. "So, I held quiet and got back and had some leave with the family and made arrangements to move to Portsmouth," he recalled. "This turned out to be one of the happiest times in our lives. We thoroughly enjoyed that six months in Portsmouth."[34]

---

Red Ramage's new command was something of a second lease on life in terms of his naval career. He had dared to speak out in the face of Admiral Christie against his faulty torpedoes. He had not been reprimanded but had earned a trip back Stateside to cool off while commissioning a new boat. Perhaps Christie silently accepted the fact that there may be a little truth behind this brash commander's words. Perhaps he held respect for the bold attacks Ramage had carried out. Or perhaps he was a little relieved to let the fiery red-headed skipper become someone else's concern for a while.

In any event, Ramage was determined to make the most of his new opportunity and prove his capabilities once again. Shortly after his arrival at the Portsmouth Navy Yard, he began to assemble the exceptional officers and seasoned enlisted men who would form the nucleus of his new crew. The first officer to join him was Lt. Woodrow Wilson McCrory, a capable Texan who would serve as his executive officer, second-in-command, during *Parche*'s finishing-out period.

Born in rural Waelder, Texas, in 1914, McCrory had always shown a knack for intelligence and leadership. He had been valedictorian of both his high school class and at the Schreiner Institute, where he worked his way through school. At the Naval Academy, he had been on the pole-vault team and finished sixth in a class of 648 cadets in 1938. He spent two years on the cruiser *Concord*, flagship for Rear Adm. Harold R. Stark, before volunteering for submarine duty.

McCrory's first assignment in 1941 was on board the old boat *S-48*, where he learned and then taught submarine battle tactics. To some, he was "Will" but to most he was known as "Mac." Ramage was happy to receive McCrory, whom he considered to be "one of the smartest officers you could ever hope to find." He soon learned that McCrory had been aboard the *S-48*, a boat that "never dove twice the same and was a thrill every time they submerged."[35]

Shortly after meeting his new Exec, Ramage told him, "Well, I'm sure there's nothing we can do on this ship that's going to disturb you or frighten you after all the experiences you must have had on your previous assignment."

Mac McCrory was described by one of his crewmen as "an athletically built, square-jawed, tough-looking officer. He presented a very serious, no-nonsense demeanor. We were all afraid of him at first, but got to respect and admire him for his strength, integrity and courage as we worked together as shipmates through many tough experiences."[36]

McCrory and his new skipper were tasked with organizing the other officers and crew who would man their new boat that was finishing its construction at the Portsmouth Navy Yard. Her hull number was SS-384 and her name was USS *Parche*. This submarine, like its sister boats, was named for an ocean fish. The parche is a small, colorful, four-eyed butterfly fish found on tropical reefs around the world but concentrated in the Indo-Pacific oceanic region. Butterfly fishes are deep-bodied and thin from side to side, with a single dorsal fin and a small mouth with tiny, bristle-like teeth. The parche is unique for the large, dark spot on the rear portion of its body that acts as a false eye to confuse its attackers.

*Parche* was among the newer *Balao*-class submarines, which sported a thicker hull than the Navy's previous *Gato*-class boats. Her pressure hull was made of ⅞" thick high-tensile steel and her test depth was listed at 412 feet, meaning that she had a 100 percent safety factor at that depth. In theory, the thick-skinned *Balao*-class boats were strong enough to descend a couple hundred feet beyond this depth before the tremendous pressures of the sea imploded their hulls. Few wartime skippers opted to test these limits except under extreme circumstances.

*Parche*'s keel had been laid on 9 April 1943 and she had been launched on 24 July. Miss Betty Russell smashed the traditional bottle of champagne across the bow on that date as the boat slid into the water for the first time. Miss Russell was the daughter of the U.S. District Judge Robert Lee Russell, formerly Judge Advocate General of the Navy.

Yard workers then proceeded to install the electrical equipment and main machinery that would drive this underseas war vessel. Her power plant consisted of four 1600-horsepower Fairbanks Morse 10-cylinder piston-opposed diesel engines which were connected to four 110-kilowatt direct current generators. These generators could be connected directly to the main electric drive

*Parche* is put into commission. Left side, first sailor is CEM Verlin Peterson, who would later serve as *Parche*'s chief of the boat. Beside him is CMoMM Montgomery Oliver. Officers standing in background are, left–right: Bill Bergen, John Parks, Bob Erwin, Admiral Thomas Withers, Red Ramage reading his orders, Captain Roper, Dave Green (partially obscured), Captain Lew Parks, and Mac McCrory. *Courtesy of Bob Erwin.*

motors or could be used to charge the two huge banks of 126 cell batteries. These batteries could drive the boat at up to 8.5 knots while submerged. Her four diesels were capable of propelling *Parche* at a surfaced speed of slightly better than 20 knots.

 *Parche*'s wardroom began taking shape as the yard work proceeded. In addition to Lieutenant McCrory, Ramage had received two officers with war patrol experience, two lieutenants, David Hepburn Green and Frank Walter Allcorn III. Green, the carefree and casual-natured son of a senior naval commander, was the only other Naval Academy graduate aboard. Whereas Mac McCrory was seen by his new crewmen as a strict officer with little time for idle chitchat, Dave Green was more congenial and more apt to ignore the formalities of his rank. As *Parche*'s third most senior officer, Lieutenant Green was assigned the duties of engineering and diving officer.

USS *Parche* is launched on 24 July 1943 at the Portsmouth Navy Yard in Kittery, Maine. *Courtesy of Bob Erwin and Jim Campbell.*

By the time Green graduated the Naval Academy in 1941, he felt "it must have been very obvious that we would be in the war soon." He felt that his curriculum did not properly train him for the departmental record keeping, crew training, and other key duties "a young division officer should know. Most of that I learned the hard way." Instead of presenting Ramage with the best training and experience, Green felt that his engineering department "got by mostly because I had good troopers backing me up."[37]

Ramage's fourth officer was tall, slim Reservist Frank Allcorn, who officially became the boat's torpedo and gunnery officer. Born and raised in Atlanta, Allcorn had recently turned 24 in June 1943. He was a former Eagle Scout who had graduated from the Boys High School and the Georgia Institute of Technology in Atlanta. While at Georgia Tech he was president of the Sigma Alpha Epsilon fraternity, and a member of the student council and many honor societies. He was also a part of the Navy ROTC program and competed on the Georgia Tech swim team. Upon graduation in 1941, Allcorn served on *S-25* for two months before assisting in the commissioning of *Finback*. He completed four patrols on *Finback*, where he earned the Silver Star for his work on the torpedo data computer (TDC) in the conning tower during torpedo attacks. Red Ramage was pleased to have Allcorn as his torpedo officer because "he was the only one" with real war patrol experience of his new *Parche* wardroom.[38]

*Parche*'s fifth officer was Lt. (jg) Churchill James Campbell, who assumed the role of communications officer. Campbell had volunteered for the Navy after the war broke out. He was a Reservist at the time, working for Standard Oil after graduating from the University of California at Berkeley in 1938 with an electrical engineering degree. He had served on surface ships during 1942 out of San Diego before a mustang officer convinced him to volunteer for the submarine service for better pay. In the interim of waiting for an assignment, Campbell completed a semester at Northwestern and at Purdue. From there he had been sent to Texas to help commission the *LCI L-83*.

"We were taking her out and had gotten as far as the Sabine River in Orange, Texas, when I got my orders to sub school," he recalled. Campbell went through the New London Submarine School but was found to have wax buildup in his ears during a medical exam. "The medic who scraped it out scratched my eardrum, so I wasn't able to do the 100-foot ascent in the diving tank," Campbell said. He was then assigned to the old *S-48* for temporary duty as her assistant engineer and communications officer.

On board *S-48*, the Exec was Lt. Mac McCrory, who would also later move on to join the *Parche*'s construction. He was in the wardroom when Campbell first reported aboard.

"What's your name?" he asked.

"Churchill Campbell," replied the eager young officer.

McCrory appeared to sample the name before he replied, "That's too long. We need something shorter. What's your middle name?"

"James," answered Campbell.

McCrory then decided, "We'll call you Jim." And so Jim Campbell it was from that moment on in his Navy career. On board submarines, officers and men alike generally were referred to by short nicknames or their last name.

As fate would have it, McCrory and Campbell would spend a considerable amount of time on board submarines together. The old S-boat operated in the North Atlantic during the spring of 1943 and Campbell had ample time to brush up on his skills as diving officer. He was finally able to complete sub school after his scratched eardrum had healed. Campbell achieved good grades in his class and earned the honor of requesting his new assignment. "I had been on an old training boat long enough with only one stern tube, four bow tubes and lousy engines, so I wanted a modern boat," he recalled. By this time, Mac McCrory had become the new Exec on *Parche* during her construction period. "We got along well and he was a whale of a smart guy,"

*Parche*'s officers for the first patrol, seen at the boat's commissioning in November 1943. Left–right are Lt. (jg) Bob Erwin, Ens. John Parks, Ens. Bill Bergen, Lt. (jg) Jim Campbell, Cdr. Lawson Ramage, Lt. Dave Green, Lt. Frank Allcorn, and Lt. Woodrow McCrory. *Courtesy of Bob Erwin.*

according to Campbell, who accepted McCrory's offer to join him again on a new fleet boat.

The sixth officer aboard *Parche* was Lt. (jg) Robert Lee Erwin, who had been assigned the duties of commissary and assistant gunnery officer. Bob Erwin had finished his Bachelor of Agricultural Engineering degree from Ohio State University in June 1941 when he went to the Navy recruiting office in Columbus to apply to become an officer. He began working in Ohio State's Agricultural Engineering department in the fall while planning his wedding to his sweetheart Mary Campbell. The couple was married in December 1941, just two weeks after the Japanese attack on Pearl Harbor.[39]

Erwin was commissioned as an ensign in the Navy in March 1942 and he completed his officers' indoctrination program at Notre Dame. He then completed Torpedo School in Newport, Rhode Island, and was assigned to the Sub Base Torpedo Shop at New London through the spring of 1943. He became intimately familiar with the Navy's torpedoes and eventually volunteered for submarine duty, hoping to "not return home wounded." Submarine pay offered him a 70 percent increase over the $125 per month he was drawing as an ensign. Erwin was promoted to lieutenant, junior grade, in May and he was trained on the old *O-8* at New London before completing submarine school in the fall and finishing second in his class. In October

1943 he and Jim Campbell were both assigned to the *Parche* construction at the Portsmouth Navy Yard.[40]

"The training had started before Jim and I arrived and continued without a break," Erwin recalled. The pair immediately immersed themselves in finishing out their new boat and in training the crew. Both were quick to tackle any and all odd jobs. When skipper Red Ramage wanted an extra cable cleat mounted forward that the yard would not allow, Erwin and fellow officer Bill Bergen found an extra cleat and literally manhandled the 150-pound chunk of metal back to *Parche* to be welded on.[41]

The final officers of *Parche*'s eight-man wardroom were two ensigns, Bergen and John Henry Parks, both mustangs—veteran submariners who had been promoted up from enlisted status. Parks became the first lieutenant and Bergen worked as Lieutenant Green's assistant engineering officer. Commander Ramage soon found that he had full confidence in his seven fellow officers who would help him achieve his goal of returning to the war zone.

———————

On 15 November 1943, a commissioning party was held for the new officers and crew of the *Parche*. The alcohol was financed by a ten-cent slot machine that had been installed on board the *Parche*'s work barge some time after launching. The married men were allowed to bring their wives and the dance floor was quite active. By the end of the evening, the dance floor was coated with a layer of beer and many a sailor was in rare form. Young motor machinist's mate Nick Casassa would long remember stumbling back on board ship "feeling no pain." Casassa slipped on the ladder leading from the deck into the after battery, "hitting every rung on the ladder with my chin. What a hangover!"

Five days later, *Parche* was commissioned a vessel of the United States Navy by Rear Adm. Tommy Withers, commandant of the Portsmouth Navy Yard on 20 November. The officers and crew donned their dress uniforms and lined either side of the afterdeck. Withers pinned Commander Ramage with a Navy Cross that he had earned as skipper of *Trout* before Ramage proceeded to read his orders to take official command of his boat. Ramage's crew truly took over the ship on 1 December, on which date *Parche*'s daily log book commenced.

*Parche* was longer than a football field, stretching 311 feet and 8 inches from stem to stern. She measured 27 feet in diameter and could carry a full

*Parche*'s commissioning party in November 1943. The officer seated at the far left on the front left is Bill Bergen. Moving to the right are Chief of the Boat Luke Parker, John Parks (holding *Parche* life ring), Bob Erwin, Red Ramage, Mac McCrory, Frank Allcorn (holding life ring), Dave Green, and Jim Campbell. The wives seated on the second row are (left–right): Mrs. Parker, Jennie Bergen, Blanche Parks, Mary Erwin, Barbara Ramage, Dorothy McCrory, Dee Allcorn, Nancy Green (leaning forward), and Alma Campbell. *Courtesy of Bob Erwin and Bob Hall.*

load of two dozen torpedoes, which were fired from her four after tubes and six forward torpedo tubes. The new crewmen who reported to the Navy Yard in the winter months began learning every inch of their submarine.

On 11 December, *Parche* was officially completed and signed over to the United States Navy. As the supply officer, Lieutenant (jg) Erwin signed the Navy receipt for $3,000,000 for the new boat. "We all had a chuckle about the Navy paperwork and wondered who paid if we lost the *Parche*," he recalled.[42]

Two days later *Parche* commenced her first operations by conducting various drills, dives, and exercises while anchored in the lower harbor at Portsmouth, New Hampshire. The original *Gato*-class boats had a test depth of 300 feet but *Parche* reached her 420-foot test depth on 14 December under the supervision of shipyard personnel. This was carefully made and only minor leaks that could be repaired were noted. She then began a 39-day training period operating out of the Portsmouth Navy Yard around Gould Island, Newport, Rhode Island, and the Submarine Base, New London, Connecticut.

Ramage was fortunate to have Rear Admiral Withers available in Portsmouth during this period. He had perviously served on Withers' staff and the two were old friends, thus making it easier to incorporate new ideas into the final work completed on *Parche*. Capt. Lewis Parks came aboard to supervise *Parche*'s shakedown cruise in late December in the North Atlantic off Greenland. The seas were rough and the bridge personnel endured the spray of waters so cold that it froze on the rigging. *Parche* spent Christmas Day 1943 submerged off the Isle of Shoals on maneuvers. "Lew Parks, our division commander, was told by Adm. Freeland Daubin not to have any ships at sea during Christmas, but that didn't bother him," recalled Ramage. "We were at sea on Christmas running trials." Ironically, Ramage could actually see his family's little cottage on Cutts Island through the periscope this day and could only imagine them sitting around their dinner table enjoying a Christmas meal without him.[43]

The trials and training continued in the New London area during January and this practice period was not without incident. On one dive, someone forgot to open the No. 8 most aft ballast tank, thereby creating a large air bubble aft that held *Parche*'s stern up during the dive. The bow took a 20-degree down-angle as she went under at full speed. *Parche*'s bow was buried in the mud of Long Island Sound, creating some embarrassment for the duty diving officer until the boat could be reversed out of this situation.[44]

Ramage was impressed with his crew from the start. He wrote his wife Barbara during the early days of training at sea, "In four days we made 33 dives, fired all the guns and worked out all the machinery. Right now I feel we could go right out on patrol." He praised his crew, the food on board ship, and the zeal of his second-in-command. "Of course, Mac is everywhere like he was at the commissioning party and so we never make the same mistake twice."[45]

The training wrapped up at New London and before heading out toward the war zone, Red Ramage took the opportunity to address his crew. "The skipper told us that we would be an aggressive boat that would go into harm's way," recalled Torpedoman Ray Karr. "He said that anyone who wanted off could request a transfer now and nothing would ever be said about their decision." By and large, everyone on board was eager for the fight. Only one older chief petty officer opted for a transfer after Ramage's talk at New London on 21 January 1944. Yeoman Warren Dingman handled the paperwork and a replacement senior electrician's mate, William Alonzo Hughes, jumped at the chance to join *Parche*.

Ramage and his crew departed New London the following day, 22 January, en route to the Naval Ordinance Base, Key West, Florida. Junior officer Bob Erwin, granted a temporary leave by Red Ramage to see his new daughter Sandy in the hospital at Gallipolis, Ohio, narrowly made the return trip in time for *Parche*'s departure. "When we left New London the eighty percent of us

USS *Parche* viewed under way arriving in port. Note that her hull number 384 was not visible during wartime. *U.S. Navy photo, courtesy of Bob Hall.*

who had never been in a war zone began to realize we were going to a war that was up to this point 'over there,' " Erwin recalled. "We were well aware that the *Dorado* had been lost on this same trip in October by friendly fire and we trusted no planes."[46]

German U-boats often frequented the East Coast waters and Ramage exercised due caution with his watchstanders en route to Key West. She arrived on 28 January and commenced additional combat training exercises with surface ships. The crew was also given a taste of depth charging when a destroyer dropped several ash cans at a "safe" distance. The resulting explosions were still close enough to make the lights flicker, chip paint from the bulkheads, and make all on board realize what they could soon expect from the Japanese.[47]

Submarine sailors, by nature, lived for their off-duty time and some of *Parche*'s enlisted men made the most of their nightly liberties in Key West. Red Ramage had his first true discipline incident when four of his sailors were delivered back on board on the morning of 11 February 1944 by the shore patrol. Sub sailors had no love for the shore patrol, who had largely served as professional police officers in peacetime.

"I rolled out of my bunk to see what was going on," Ramage recalled of Exec Mac McCrory shaking him awake with news of trouble. The shore patrol was at the gangway requesting permission to come on board and identify other *Parche* crewmen who had been involved in the overnight melee. Ramage "had no use" for such shore patrolmen who were not involved in fighting the war and he resented their demands. Electrician's mate Joe Caruso recalled, "The captain wasn't going to let the shore patrol come on board to identify them."[48]

Ramage and McCrory met with the angry SPs to sort out details of the previous night's encounter. He learned that several of his men had been late returning to the boat for the midnight curfew. Some of his men had tried hitching a ride with the shore patrol to make curfew in time, but they were instead driven to the base brig. Chief Motor Machinist's Mate Montgomery Oliver and one of his enginemen, Charles Satterfield, were charged with cursing the shore patrol after a drunken brawl. Even worse, TM2c Marion Taylor had assaulted one of the officers with his own nightstick. Torpedoman Harold Staggs was close friends with two of the men who bunked in his forward torpedo room who were involved in the caper. "Swettenam and Mo Taylor mixed it up a little with the shore patrol. Mo, who was a big guy, took away one of their night sticks and used it on the shore patrolmen," Staggs recalled.

In addition to Taylor, several others involved in the drunken melee—MoMM3c "Freddy" Frederick, GM2c Leroy Swettenam, EM2c Dixie Howell, and RM2c Alfred Rick—were put on restrictions upon their return to the boat. Several others involved in shore brawls—TM3c Ray Karr, MoMM3c John Nania, MoMM1c Orvail Buckner, and MoMM1c Zach Vogedes—somehow escaped attention from the authorities. The crew had nonetheless, according to Karr, achieved "a fighting reputation."[49]

The base patrol officers and their commanders wanted to charge more of the *Parche* sailors and court-martial those involved in the fight. Ramage consented to a certain degree. Chief of the Boat Luke Parker had the entire crew mustered on deck in the warm Key West sun while the SPs tried to identify the other guilty men. "We took testimony from 1 o'clock in the afternoon until 9 o'clock at night and we kept those SPs standing there," Ramage related. "It became apparent that the charges didn't fit the individuals' stories." He had his torpedo officer, Frank Allcorn, standing by with his sidearm to maintain order. "We made Christians out of those buggers for sure," added Ramage.[50]

*Parche* was due to sail from Key West for the war zone and Ramage finally decided he would deal with his rebellious crewmen in his own way. "I told the captain of the yard that we were sailing and to hell with his goddamned court-martial and that was the end of that," Ramage said. He, of course, could not simply dismiss the incident and thus a captain's mast was held the next day after *Parche* was under way. Ramage and McCrory heard evidence of the infractions while two other junior officers assisted with the penalty hearings. In the end, penalties were handed out to the worst offenders to serve as a lesson for future conduct. Chief Oliver was docked $15 per month in pay for two months and Satterfield was docked $10 per month for two months. Taylor was later docked $15 per month for two months and was assigned extra duties.

*Parche* moved from Key West across the Gulf of Mexico and passed through the Panama Canal en route to her new home port, the Submarine Base at Pearl Harbor, Hawaii. She moored at Balboa in the Canal Zone on 15 February for a few days to take on provisions for the Pacific. The leading cook, Charlie Johnson, found that he could take on all the Argentina beef he wanted so he loaded *Parche*'s freezers with steaks and roasts. Red Ramage, who took on board several cases of scotch for his friends and superiors at Pearl, recalled, "We had steaks all the way to Pearl and throughout our first patrol." Several rounds of 4-inch shells for the deck gun were left behind in order to store the booze in the ammunition lockers. "The discrepancy was covered by gun drills held on our way to Hawaii, necessary since ammunition was always inventoried and accounted for," Bob Erwin recalled.[51]

Mess attendant Carl Kimmons had his first encounter with segregated water fountains in Panama. One was labeled "gold" and the other was labeled "silver." Never shy to a challenge, Kimmons "took a drink from both of them. The water tasted the same!"[52]

The crew took advantage of their liberty options and the inexpensive rum and Coke drinks in Balboa. Once again, Red Ramage was quickly faced with another incident involving one of his crewmen. Charlie Satterfield, recently disciplined for his brush with the shore patrol at Key West, beat up a couple of Balboa's shore patrol officers but escaped and returned to the boat. *Parche*'s crew was lined up on deck the next morning so the shore patrol could pick out their man. Satterfield escaped attention when the officers picked a torpedoman with a swollen face who had fallen asleep against some hard object on the ship. Sometimes a good sailor's good performance on board ship outweighed his bad conduct ashore.[53]

After clearing the Panama Canal on 19 February, *Parche* spent 16 days at sea en route to the Hawaiian Islands. Commander Ramage put his crew through the paces, conducting gunfire drills and emergency crash dives. He often spent time on the bridge to relax and smoke. One of the skipper's phobias was the sight of smoke emmanating from his boat's diesel engines on the surface which might be spotted by Japanese lookouts or pilots. Dave Green's engineering department was specifically taxed with preventing such telltale smoke. Officer of the deck Bob Erwin recalled that Ramage "would always look back at the exhausts. If he saw any smoke, his next words were, 'Send for Mr. Green.' "

While smoking his pipe on the bridge one evening, Commander Ramage suddenly shouted, "Plane at 10 o'clock!" When OOD Erwin did not immediately respond, he snapped, "Don't stand there with your finger up your ass! Do something!" The young officer knew that *Parche* was 1,000 miles from any aviator's base but realized his skipper's intentions and ordered a crash dive. Erwin later realized that such training "paid off later when there were enemy planes."[54]

Mac McCrory conned *Parche* into Pearl Harbor on the afternoon of 5 March 1944 and moored her to the starboard side of USS *Finback* at Pier Sail 5 at the U.S. Submarine Base. "Most of us new to Pearl were impressed by the Naval activity and awed by the still-visible destruction on Battleship Row," recalled Erwin.

Other evidence of the December 1941 surprise attack lingered. Fire controlman Sam Roberts and a few of his shipmates found out that the harbor was still heavily polluted with diesel fuel leaking from the sunken battleships. "Several of us decided to go swimming in Pearl Harbor one night," Roberts related. "We dove in and we came up coated with diesel oil." The fuel was difficult to scrub away and Roberts found that scissors were the best remedy to remove some of the residue from his hair. "We did that once but we didn't do it again."

As demanding as he was on his junior officers, Red Ramage still found time to enjoy the practical jokes his crew played on the green hands. Young seaman Bob Gubaney, a torpedoman striker, was often tasked with running coffee to the senior petty officers in his torpedo room. "Every time he did well, they 'promoted' him and every time he didn't do well they demoted him," Ramage recalled. "When we pulled into Pearl, Gubaney came up on deck with a crow on his sleeve."[55]

Ramage hollered down to the young sailor, "Where the hell did you get that rating?"

Gubaney explained that one of the chiefs had just rated him that morning. "Poor old Gubaney," Ramage laughed. "He really got the works down there from those guys!"

The crew then spent the next three weeks in intensive training and reprovisioning the boat in final preparations for their first war patrol. The conning tower fire control team trained with simulated torpedo attacks on Japanese convoys and senior staff officers accompanied *Parche* on training exercises at sea to gauge the crew's readiness for real war conditions.

Whereas Red Ramage had found Admiral Christie quite difficult to work with in the southwestern Pacific, he found Vice Adm. Charlie Lockwood to be first-rate. In his role as the new ComSubPac, Lockwood had been instrumental in pushing for improvements in his fleet boats and in addressing the serious torpedo problems that had plagued his skippers during the previous year. The admiral became affectionately known to many of his submariners as "Uncle Charlie."

Two captains, John "Babe" Brown and Charles "Swede" Momsen, of Admiral Lockwood's staff developed wolf pack doctrine that included extensive training by those who would participate in the action on patrol. In the rear of the Pearl Harbor Submarine Base's Bachelor Officer Quarters was a covered lanai that had been used prewar as a dance floor. Brown and Momsen had converted the checkered black and white tile floor of the dance hall into a war games board. War college training was not new to naval officers, but the Silent Service's new "Convoy College" included more than just the senior sub commanders.[56]

The Convoy College war games at Pearl Harbor were played by the entire fire control parties from the subs. From *Parche*, this included skipper Red Ramage, Exec Mac McCrory, torpedo officer Frank Allcorn, TDC assistant operator Sam Roberts, plotting officer Bob Erwin, senior Quartermaster Wilbur Sprague, radar operator John Gray, senior sonar operator Percy Barnett, and conning tower battle talker Bob Daufenbach. Model ships were laid out on the dance floor in a convoy arrangement, hidden from view from each of several fire control parties by screens. At times, one screen would be lifted for two seconds to allow one group of officers to catch a quick glimpse of the convoy arrangement.[57]

*Parche* was scheduled to operate with USS *Tinosa* and USS *Bang* on her first run as the fourth-ever U.S. wolf pack sent into combat. "Communications was one of the biggest problems working with wolf packs," Bob Erwin recalled. "Each of our three fire control crews was separated from the others and we communicated by telephone like we would by radio if we were at sea. Sometimes the trainers would allow us to see certain things. Other times we weren't allowed to see certain things. We practiced communicating to the other fire control teams what we were allowed to see."

Jim Campbell, *Parche*'s communications officer, and his radio gang went through extensive communications drills to simulate conditions that would exist as their boat was operating in a wolf pack. Torpedo officer Frank Allcorn took his torpedo reload crews ashore to the training base at Pearl, where they had a mock torpedo room with real tubes. Allcorn had conceived a new rapid reloading technique for the torpedo tubes and he drilled his men incessantly in this new procedure until they had it perfected. In short time, his vision would be put to the test when Commander Ramage allowed Allcorn to use his new reload technique in the war zone.[58]

The three boats also put to sea for more realistic wolf pack training exercises against an incoming convoy during late March under the close supervision of base staff officers. *Parche* was declared ready for sea on 29 March 1944, the date of her departure for her first war patrol.

During *Parche*'s final day at Pearl Harbor, Exec Mac McCrory and his chief of the boat, Luke Parker, were busy with last-minute crew details. Chief Torpedoman Parker, a veteran of previous war patrols, had been selected as *Parche*'s chief of the boat to help train the new hands during the fitting out period Stateside. This key position, equivalent to an Army top sergeant, was usually filled by the most senior enlisted man on board ship. He set the watch schedules and served as a go-between with the skipper and Exec. Parker had joined the Navy in September 1938 and he had considerable experience with torpedoes with his background at the torpedo shop at Pearl Harbor.

Several new men had been received on board at Pearl and in return a few others had been shuffled off to the base relief crew. The last of these transfers was Chief Oliver, who had gotten into trouble at Key West weeks before and had since been disciplined by a Captain's Mast. Oliver was upset with his sentence and shortly before *Parche* had reached Pearl Harbor he had threatened junior officer Jim Campbell. Just six hours before their boat was to depart on patrol, McCrory and Parker had Oliver transferred.

Fortunately for the chief petty officer (CPO) watch schedule and the engine-room gangs, an able replacement in the form of three-year Navy veteran CMoMM Mark Goding had been received on board. New Yorker Warren Dingman, the boat's yeoman, sorted out the required paperwork and typed up a final sailing list to be passed over to the sub base before *Parche* was under way. Dingman's list included the names of all on board ship and the addresses of their next of kin in case *Parche* failed to return. Just thirty minutes before *Parche* departed, Dingman added the name and address of the wolf pack commander who came on board at 1530.

*Parche* was finally under way at 1600 with the two other boats of her wolf pack. Frank Allcorn and Bill Bergen had the watch as their boat moved through Pearl Harbor's channel and they steered her through the anti-submarine net. Shortly after the entrance buoys had passed abeam, the signal lights flashed from the ships as orders were passed. *PC 578* took the lead and *Tinosa* fell in 1000 yards abeam of the escort ship. *Parche* and *Bang* quickly took their respective positions in column astern of the first two ships.

On the bridge, skipper Red Ramage kept a watchful eye on his duty officers and lookouts. He tugged on his ever-present pipe, the smoke drifting astern with the breeze as *Parche* twisted through Pearl Harbor. Ten months had passed since he had brought *Trout* in from a luckless patrol and been sent home by Admiral Christie to "cool off."

Lawson Ramage was anything but cooled off. He was eager to prove his merits once again in the war zone, a place where the shenanigans of some of his more wild-hearted sailors could be left behind. *Parche* was playing for keeps now.

# CHAPTER TWO

# The *Parche* Crew

P*arche*'s maiden war patrol would be made as part of America's fourth-ever coordinated attack group or wolf pack. The U.S. Navy adopted this method from the German U-boat wolf packs in late 1943 and placed their first pack under the command of staff officer Swede Momsen. While this coordinated unit only destroyed three ships that were confirmed in postwar analysis, its wartime claims of five ships sunk and another eight damaged was enough to make the brass authorize more wolf packs.

Cdr. Freddy Warder led the second wolf pack, which accounted for seven confirmed sinkings. The third pack was dispatched in December 1943, with new tactics in place such as having the three boats rendezvous at sea on patrol for more effective communications. By the time Admiral Lockwood's staff was preparing to send out another wolf pack, *Parche* had arrived on the scene at Pearl Harbor.

Cdr. Red Ramage's boat would serve as the flagship of the three-boat coordinated attack group that included *Parche*, *Tinosa* (SS-283), and *Bang* (SS-385). Although he was skipper of a new boat, Ramage had five war patrols under his belt, four in a commanding role. *Tinosa* had made five prior war patrols but her skipper, Lt. Cdr. Donald Frederick Weiss, was making his first in a senior role. *Bang*, under Lt. Cdr. Anton Renki "Tony" Gallaher, was also making his first run on a fleet submarine.

Overall direction of this fourth wolf pack was given to Capt. George Edmund Peterson, the commander of Submarine Division 141 from the Academy class of 1924. Peterson, who had spent most of his war with boats operating out of Scotland in the Atlantic, had never made a Pacific war patrol.[1]

Ramage was in command of 81 men aboard his ship although only 32 of them were qualified in submarines. His men were eager to learn of their new assignment. Prior to departure, only Ramage and his Exec Mac

McCrory had been privy to *Parche*'s destination as the commanding officer and navigator. Once safely out from Pearl Harbor, Ramage gathered his junior officers in the wardroom and opened his sealed orders. He read aloud the typed instructions that *Parche* was to operate as a wolf pack in the Luzon Strait and the South China Sea with *Bang* and *Tinosa*.

Captain Peterson's wolf pack was assigned to Area Eleven, an expanse of the Pacific Ocean between southern Formosa (present-day Taiwan) and northern Luzon in the Philippines. This area was a busy passage for Japanese merchant shipping to and from Japan, the Philippines, the Malay Peninsula, and the oil fields of the Netherland East Indies. Peterson's search plan for Area Eleven was to divide it into squares of 60 miles per side—one degree latitude by one degree longitude.[2]

Outbound from Pearl Harbor, Commander Ramage was still trying to adjust to the new lighter paint scheme his boat had been painted at Pearl Harbor. He had been initially upset because he "wanted to be the blackest cat out there." The base camouflage experts, however, had deemed that solid black was not the best color for a wartime submarine. The new multi-colored paint scheme had proven effective during *Parche*'s convoy exercises off Oahu. "It didn't take any time to convince me that they were right," Ramage admitted. "I was amazed by the effect of these different shades of grey on the hull—it just painted you completely into oblivion."[3]

The wolf pack maintained a steady 16.5-knot speed through the night and into the morning hours of 30 March as the boats ran on three-engine speed. Shortly after dawn, Red Ramage passed the word to his OOD to conduct a trim dive. Lt. Dave Green cupped his hands at 0652 and barked, "Clear the bridge!"

Green, Ramage, the quartermaster, and the lookouts quickly dropped down the conning tower hatch as the Pacific was already covering *Parche*'s bow. The lookouts knew that time mattered during a real emergency dive. Fireman Dave Hussey recalled, "When we made practice emergency dives, they were timed. The target goal was to get the boat down to periscope depth at 62 feet in 26 seconds. As lookouts, we had to do our part to make it happen or we would be moved out."

Down below in the control room, the reassuring thump of valves slamming shut indicated that the main induction was properly sealed, shutting off the oxygen supply to the big diesels that drove the boat. Chief Torpedoman Parker watched the hull opening indicator light panel known as the "Christmas tree" to see that all lights had changed from red to green to indicate that all hull openings on the submarine were properly closed.

Clarence Allard, operating the air manifold, blew a blast of compressed air into the boat. The barometer rose, a good sign that *Parche* was indeed watertight throughout her nine key compartments from bow to stern.

"Green board," called Parker. "Pressure in the boat."

Lt. (jg) Jim Campbell, the duty diving officer, had already directed the bow and stern planesmen to maneuver the giant flippers to put the boat into a dive. Thousands of gallons of seawater pouring into the open ballast tanks quickly made the boat negatively buoyant and pulled her down. In about 40 seconds, *Parche* was beneath the waves and Green was coaching his men into leveling off their submarine at the prescribed depth.

This process had become almost routine to *Parche*'s crew but it was never taken lightly. One error in the process could make the difference between life and death. The boat remained down only 15 minutes before she resurfaced and rejoined her pack mates for the run into Midway.

Red Ramage maintained a casual approach to letting his officers handle their duties. Lieutenant Green had the duty as OOD as the noon hour approached on 30 March. The officer of the deck stood four-hour watches with a junior officer of the deck (JOD). His replacement team at noon was Lt. (jg) Bob Erwin and Ens. John Parks. This duo had been alternating as JOD and OOD since *Parche*'s commissioning. Parks, as an old-school enlisted man turned mustang officer, lived by the motto "never volunteer for anything and never be early." On this particular day, however, Parks had arrived 20 minutes early for his scheduled watch as officer of the deck. He had relieved Green's JOD and not the OOD as he was supposed to. When Erwin, senior in rank to Parks but with less Navy experience, arrived just before noon, he simply took over as officer of the deck as if it were normal.[4]

Ramage and McCrory noted this casual switching occur on two consecutive days and Erwin finally felt compelled to explain. Ramage only smiled and nodded, "Let it go that way." Erwin recalled, "As a result I may have been the only submarine officer of the deck without previous sea duty to stand deck watches on his first war patrol."[5]

———

Ramage had equal faith in all of his departments, each of which was run by an able chief petty officer or leading petty officer. As chief of the boat, Luke Parker and his small group of CPOs each rotated watches in the control room throughout a 24-hour period to monitor the Christmas tree and

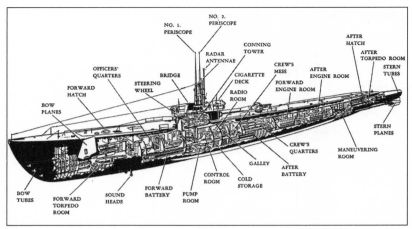

Cutaway of the compartments of a typical U.S. diesel fleet boat of World War II.

oversee the sailors going on to watch as helmsmen, sonar operators, and lookouts. The non-rated seamen on board ship would spend many hours training or "striking" for a rating within one of *Parche*'s various departments. Those men who did not stand topside watches on patrol would spend the majority of their time within their respective areas.

Every inch of *Parche* was designed for the maximum use of space. Starting forward, the first watertight compartment was the forward torpedo room, which contained bunks for 15 men. Beneath and around these bunks 16 torpedoes had been loaded. The senior petty officer in charge of this room was TM1c Don Walters from Iowa, who had enlisted in the Navy in 1939.

He started his service as a yeoman striker on board the cruiser *Richmond* on the East Coast. He soon found that he was not the most organized person to be handling important papers for the senior command, and Walters volunteered for submarines. His first year was on board the old *O-3* in New London before he helped commission *Guardfish* in 1942. Walters made *Guardfish*'s first two patrols and then another aboard *Whale* in 1943 before being ordered to *Parche*'s construction. With three successful war patrols under his belt and a first class rating, he had seniority over his other forward room companions. In his spare time, Walters also doubled as the ship's unofficial barber, cutting hair for a quarter in his forward torpedo room.

Next in seniority to Walters was TM2c Harold Staggs, a 20-year-old from Pasadena, California. Staggs had joined the submarine *Tambor* in

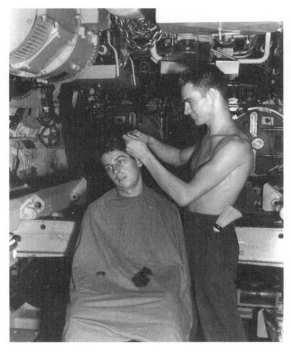

Signalman Claude Lutz receives a haircut in the forward torpedo room from senior Torpedoman Don Walters, who later became *Parche*'s chief of the boat. *Courtesy of Bob Hall.*

October 1941 and had completed six patrols on her before being assigned to *Parche*. Two other second class torpedomen in the forward room had previous patrol experience, Marion "Mo" Taylor from New Orleans and Chuck Gooden from Kansas City. Both men looked the part of submarine sailors, Mo Taylor with his trademark bushy beard and Gooden with his tattoos. "I had one of a pinup girl and another was of the Seven Dwarfs," Gooden said. Born in Chicago, he had been living in Missouri at the time the Japanese bombed Pearl Harbor. Gooden joined the service in January 1942 in the hopes of being a real Pearl Harbor avenger. Following boot camp in the Great Lakes, he completed submarine school and was shipped to Hawaii, where he made his first patrols in 1943 aboard the *Gato*, namesake boat of her submarine class.

Two of the third-class torpedomen, Ray Karr and Jim Hawkey, were old friends before joining Don Walters' forward torpedo room. Karr's grandmother, father, and three uncles had immigrated to Chicago from Denmark in 1898. Ray Karr was an energetic, athletic youth who worked numerous odd jobs for spare money in a Scandinavian neighborhood of Forest Park in west Chicago. "I was somewhat rebellious, often in trouble in school, in church or with my parents and on several occasions with the police," he admitted.

Ray and his brother Bill bought a junk Model A Ford for $12 in 1937 and learned how to rebuild it from junkyard parts. He was working at a filling station in a town called Melrose Park near Chicago when the Sunday morning radio in December 1941 delivered the news of the Japanese bombing of Pearl Harbor. He and his older brother Bill were eager to enlist but their father insisted they wait until Ray turned 18. "Dad had been a U.S. cavalry master sergeant in World War I and he wanted me to finish high school," Karr recalled. "He didn't want us taken for 'cannon fodder' as young volunteers with no skills. He said that he would rather we went Navy."

Ray Karr was at the Navy recruiting office in Chicago on his 18th birthday on 4 November 1942. He was assigned to boot camp at the Great Lakes Naval Station in Illinois, where he soon became good friends with another 18-year-old enlistee, Robert James Hawkey from Minnesota. Hawkey and Karr then attended torpedo school together at Great Lakes. In the spring of 1943, they both went through submarine schooling at New London in "Spritz's Navy."

Chief Torpedoman Charlie Spritz was a former Bronx policeman, a veteran master diver, and the Navy's version of a Marine master sergeant. Spritz did not drink or smoke and never married. He drilled the new recruits hard at New London's submarine school and came down hard on anyone who failed to perform. Although he was hated by many new submarine sailors, those who survived "Spritz's Navy" would often later respect the teamwork and discipline this taskmaster had instilled in them.[6]

Following New London, Ray Karr was detailed to the World War I–era training boat *R-4* in July for four months of operation off Key West. In November 1943, he was assigned to help commission the new *Parche*. He was reunited with his buddy Jim Hawkey, who had been involved with the commissioning and early training of the new *Billfish* in Portsmouth but had remained at the dockyard due to an illness.[7]

Hawkey and Karr had been instrumental in bringing on board a little Buddha statue for good luck. Using Chief of the Boat Luke Parker's former ties with the base torpedo shop at Pearl Harbor, they swapped some items to have the Buddha made. "We thought we needed a belly to rub for good luck," Karr recalled.

Another veteran sailor of the forward room was TM3c Jasper Hill, who had joined the Navy three years earlier in January 1941. The other two members of the forward torpedo room were strikers, Seaman First Class Johnny Barnes and Corwin "Cory" Maupin. Barnes, a native of New Jersey, had attended torpedo school in Rhode Island and New London's Submarine School before being assigned to *Parche*'s construction. Cory Maupin, eager to join the war, enlisted in the Navy at age 17 during his senior year of high school in Denver.[8]

At sea, Walters and his gang made sure that *Parche*'s Mark 14 steam torpedoes were always in ready service. The 1944 model Mark 14s, equipped with Mark 16 exploders, were an upgrade to the previous models that had so troubled the early skippers of the Silent Service. This gas-steam war fish used compressed air to supply the oxygen required for combustion of its alcohol fuel. Each Mark 14 torpedo cost the Navy $10,000, or about $150,000 each in 2010 dollars, adjusted for inflation. At the low speed setting of 31.1 knots, each torpedo had a range of 9,000 yards or a 4,500-yard effective range at the higher speed of 45 knots. *Parche* also carried a supply of Mark 23 torpedoes, a newer model identical to the Mark 14 with the exception of the slower 31-knot setting.

Chief Parks implemented special maintenance procedures to insure that *Parche*'s torpedoes were always in good functioning order. "The torpedoes as manufactured had had some problems," recalled Ray Karr. "They tended to run defectively and might or might not explode when they hit a target. Ramage had Chief of the Boat Luke Parker teach us torpedomen how to modify the magnetic exploders into contact exploders. This was against Navy regulations and was kept quiet. Some other skippers must have been doing the same thing, since we got the materials for modification from the Sub Base Torpedo Shop at Pearl Harbor."[9]

Aft of the forward torpedo room was *Parche*'s forward battery compartment, below which were 126 Edison-type batteries from which the boat drew its power while submerged. The forward battery also contained the high pressure air tanks needed for blowing the ballast tanks when surfacing the boat. *Parche*'s hull contained four tanks for trimming the boat for a level, neutral buoyancy—the forward trim, after trim, safety tank, and negative tank. The negative tank was used to create negative buoyancy for a quick dive and was used to blow excess water once a desired depth was reached.

Within this watertight compartment was located four spaces on the starboard side: the yeoman's office, the captain's cabin, the Exec's cabin, and a two-bunk cabin for officers. Per Bob Erwin, the port side contained the officers' wardroom, the steward's pantry, a three-bunk officers'

Auxiliaryman Henry
Bougetz operating the
valves of the air manifold
in *Parche*'s control room.
*U.S. Navy photo, courtesy
of Bob Hall.*

quarters, and a six-bunk chiefs' quarters. The normal arrangements were
shuffled once a wolf pack commander came on board, who took over the
Exec's cabin and forced Mac McCrory to move in with third officer Dave
Green in the two-bunk officers' quarters. The three-bunk cabin to starboard
was then filled by Erwin, Jim Campbell, and Frank Allcorn. The two junior
officers, Bill Bergen and John Parks, both slept in the nearby chiefs' quarters when a wolf pack commander was on board, forcing one or more CPOs
into torpedo room bunk areas.

The third watertight compartment aft of the forward battery was the
control room, which was the heart of operations aboard *Parche* for diving
and surfacing. Near the base of the steel ladder leading up to the conning
tower was the hydraulic manifold, which opened and closed the vents on
the ballast tanks and fuel ballast tanks. Once opened, the vents allowed
air to escape and be replaced by tons of water, which rushed in through
flood ports in the bottom. Above the hydraulic manifold was the Christmas
tree, the panel of red and green lights that showed the status of every hull
opening.

Another key instrument in the control room was the trim manifold,
which controlled the amount of water in the trim tanks to keep *Parche*
level. In contrast, the air manifold regulated the amount of high-pressure

CGM Jim Plumley, seen in 1945, operates the hydraulic manifold in the control room which opened and closed *Parche*'s ballast tank vents and air induction valves. The Christmas tree—the red and green indicator lights that detailed whether all watertight hatches and ballast tanks were open or closed—is located in front of Plumley's face. *U.S. Navy photo, courtesy of Bob Hall.*

air used to empty the tanks when surfacing. Just below the control room was the pump room, a tight compartment filled with machinery for the compressed-air, hydraulic refrigeration, and air-conditioning systems. The manifolds and pump room equipment were maintained and monitored by a special four-man group of engineers known as the auxiliary gang.

The leading auxiliaryman on *Parche* was MoMM1c Clarence Allard, a man of Salish Indian ancestry who had been born with an identical twin in Montana. His gang included MoMM2c Ralph Van Eperen, a popular Wisconsin native who had joined the Navy in October 1941 and F1c Henry Bougetz from Minneapolis, the most junior of *Parche*'s auxiliarymen.

The fourth member of Allard's auxiliary gang was MoMM2c Philip Bukowski, a New Yorker with more than four years of experience including previous patrols on board *Grayback*. Phil and his twin brother Thaddeus Bukowski had served together on *Grayback* until the five Sullivan brothers were all killed together during the Guadalcanal campaign when their cruiser *Juneau* was lost. The Navy began splitting up any siblings who were serving on the same ship to prevent such future tragedies. By doing so, Phil was spared his brother's fate. Phil went to *Parche*'s construction while his brother Thaddeus continued to make all ten runs aboard *Grayback*. He and all hands were lost when *Grayback* was sunk by an aircraft bomb

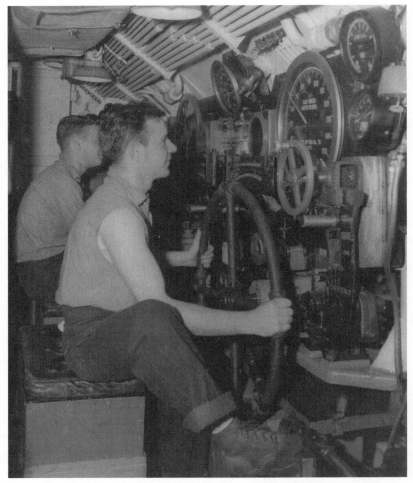

Ed "the Greek" Mokos (right) and Charlie McNutt operate the bow and stern planes in *Parche*'s control room during the second patrol. *Courtesy of Jim Campbell.*

in February 1944, just as *Parche* was preparing to depart on her first war patrol.

Just aft of the conning tower ladder in the control room was *Parche*'s diving station, where two sailors continually manned the bow and stern planes while submerged. The bow planes were like 12-foot aircraft wings that jutted out from either side of *Parche*'s bow to control the angle of a dive. When the boat was surfaced, these large flippers were hydraulically folded up against the superstructure. When *Parche* prepared to dive, the bow planesman was responsible for pushing a lever to bring the bow planes down to a horizontal position.

The stern planes, similar fins, did not fold up but instead remained in a horizontal position at all times. The stern planesman was able to tilt the stern planes to the desired angle to help control the boat's depth. The bow and stern planesmen sat before giant steel wheels they turned to maneuver their planes to make the boat dive, go deeper, surface, or hold the ship level at a prescribed depth. The duty diving officer kept a ready eye on these men and the inclinometer in front of them. Its indicator included a bubble like a level that showed the angle of the boat forward and aft. The diving officer often coached his men to "keep a zero bubble," meaning that *Parche* was level both fore and aft while submerged.[10]

In the after corner of the control room on the boat's port side was the small communications department known to all as the radio shack. In this tight cubicle was the ship's radio transmitters and receivers, a safe to store coded messages that were received, and just enough room for two radiomen to squeeze in to monitor their gear and copy daily dispatches from Pearl Harbor and other bases. The radio shack would normally carry the ECM (electronic coding machine) but because *Parche* would be operating in relatively shallow waters, this device was not carried on her first patrol.

Directly above the control room was the conning tower, from which the skipper or the officer on duty operated the two periscopes, usually one at a time. The conning tower also contained the helmsman's wheel, sonar gear, and significant torpedo fire control room equipment including the torpedo data computer (TDC), the torpedo firing keys panel, a plotting table, and radar scopes. The skipper or duty officers were assisted by the quartermasters and signalmen, who helped man the helm, keep the logbooks, operate the periscope controls, and serve as battle stations talkers to the other compartments throughout the ship. Chief Quartermaster Wilbur Sprague, who had joined the Navy in 1940 and was now *Parche*'s assistant navigator, had four others in his gang to round out the watch schedule. Seaman First Class John O'Brien, a husky New Yorker striking for his quartermaster rating, was the most junior of his group, followed by another towering New Yorker, QM3c Bob Daufenbach.

Twenty-four-year-old SM3c Courtland Chester Stanton was a high school honor student who had previously attended the Cornell defense course in engineering and was employed prewar by Ingersoll-Rand making the Navy drawings for the ships' service air compressors. He joined the Navy in 1942, attending both the Quartermaster Signalman School at the

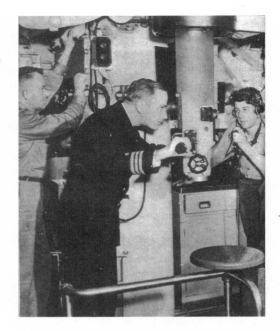

*Parche*'s conning tower was packed during torpedo attacks. This early 1943 view was taken on board the submarine *Haddo*. The skipper manning the periscope is Cdr. Willis Lent, who was commander of *Grenadier* in 1942 for Red Ramage's first war patrol. The battle talker in the right of the photo is SM1c Claude Lutz, who was one of Ramage's senior signalmen for *Parche*'s first three patrols. *Courtesy of Claude Lutz Jr.*

University of Chicago and the Submarine School at New London before being assigned to *Parche*'s construction. "Chet" Stanton's sixth sense on the helm had earned him the roll of battle stations helmsman in *Parche*'s conning tower.[11]

Twenty-three-year-old SM1c Claude Lutz, whose wife lived in Connecticut, had spent nearly six years in the Navy, three of which had been on board subs. As a youth, Lutz ran away from home and traveled to Nevada where he worked for the Western Pacific Railroad for four months. He did not return to high school, opting to join the Navy in 1938. After more than two years on board the cruiser *Richmond* (CL-9), he had been on board the *O-2* (SS-63) when Pearl Harbor was attacked.

Lutz helped commission *Haddo* (SS-255) in 1942. On her first patrol, *Haddo* dived with her main induction open and the boat reached 650 feet before she was saved. "We took on over 44 tons of water," Lutz recorded. "It took 30 hours on the surface to get the water out." Lutz made *Haddo*'s first two runs and the third patrol of *Herring*. Months after reporting aboard *Parche*, he would find that *Herring* had been lost with all hands in 1944.

Lying just beyond the radio shack were the tiny 6-by-11-foot ship's galley and the much larger crew's mess, where 80-odd sailors were fed three

The boat's original baker, Howard McMahon (left), removes cream-puffs from the galley oven during the second patrol. McMahon's brightest trainee, Seaman Bob Hall (below), soon took over as *Parche*'s baker for the remainder of the war. *Courtesy of Bob Hall.*

times daily. Below the galley were a freezer compartment, food storage areas, and ammunition lockers for the topside guns. During battle stations surface, ammunition was passed up from the galley through a hatch to the main deck. Ship's Cook First Class Charlie "Johnny" Johnson was already an "old man" among the *Parche* crew at age 25. He was a graduate of the school of hard knocks; he had joined the Navy in 1936 and was married before the war started. He had served on board the destroyers *Chandler* and *Litchfield* before volunteering for submarines and joining *Shark I* in 1939. Johnson then joined the *S-12* and spent nearly four years on her before reporting to *Parche* as her senior ship's cook.[12]

During the early days of *Parche*'s training, Johnson was stressed with the challenges of feeding 80 hands three meals a day without going into the red. When the skipper stopped by the galley one day to see how everything was going, Johnson confessed to being worried about the necessary book work on food expenditures and running his mess in the hole. Red Ramage just smiled and told him, "You feed them and I will do the worrying." Johnson was much relieved to have the captain's confidence and, in fact, he would soon be rated as a chief petty officer.[13]

Commissary officer Bob Erwin trusted Johnson enough to let him handle all of the ordering of supplies with one exception. "I did have to go down to the customs house to pick up cigarettes for the crew," recalled Erwin. "It had to be an officer to do that. I left most everything else up to Johnson and spent my time keeping track of how much we spent per person."

One of the brightest mess cooks was Seaman Robert Ames Hall, who had never attended Navy cook school but was hoping to bake his way into a galley rating. A 19-year-old from the little town of Castine, Maine, Bob Hall was armed with no baking experience and only a few recipes from his mother. On board ship, Hall slept in the after battery compartment on a middle bunk where he was always just a few steps away from the galley. He was typical of many young sailors aboard *Parche*. After boot camp, Hall had volunteered for submarine service because he had heard about the good food on submarines and the extra 50 percent hazard pay that was allocated. "Growing up on the coast of Maine, I've always joked about having salt water in my veins," he recalled. "I had not done any cooking prewar at home but I loved to eat. My mother was an excellent cook and I grew up a little bit overweight."

Hall took advantage of the experience of senior cook Johnson, baker Howard McMahon from New York, and 30-year-old SC2c Dan Hayes, who had enlisted in the Navy in September 1942. "Dan Hayes from Greenwich, Connecticut, was the one who could really put the final touches on the food and he made everything super," recalled Red Ramage. Hall started at the bottom of the ladder as mess cook, and his eagerness was noticed early on. Johnson—seeing his mess cook work tirelessly loading provisions onto their boat one evening well into the early morning hours without taking a break—recommended Hall be advanced in rating to seaman first class. Johnny Johnson would continue to pay attention to his bright trainee in the ensuing months.[14]

As *Parche* headed out on her first war patrol, Hall felt no special apprehension about the approach of combat. "All of us had jobs to do and we just did them," he related. "We had heard what had happened to other subs. We were losing about one out of five boats that went on patrol, but we didn't have time to let it bother us."

Just aft of the crew's mess was the after battery compartment, located above another 126 battery cells and additional high-pressure air tanks. This was the main sleeping quarters and washroom area for three dozen of the enlisted men. Aft of the crew's quarters were the forward and after engine rooms, each of which housed two of the powerful Fairbanks Morse diesels that drove *Parche* on the surface.

Due to the last-minute transfer of Chief Oliver at Pearl, the senior motormac on *Parche* was newly reported CMoMM Mark Goding. He had joined the Navy in July 1940 and had been shipmates with electrician Lonnie Hughes on board the sub tender *Beaver* before serving on the submarines *Argonaut* and *S-32*. Goding was fortunate in having veteran motor machinists in each engine room who had been with *Parche* since her commissioning, such as MoMM1c Ken Mathews, an Ohio man with two years of submarines under his belt. MoMM1c Charlie Satterfield, a 26-year-old from Oklahoma, had six years of experience in the Navy, including previous war patrols on *Tambor*.

Another veteran motormac aboard *Parche* was MoMM1c Dana Jensen, a 24-year-old Wisconsin man. Jensen had left the Wisconsin farms at age 18 to join the Civilian Conservation Corps, where he heard about the life of sailing the Pacific and all that San Diego had to offer. He joined the Navy in 1940 and had already completed six patrols aboard the *S-35* before joining *Parche*. Jensen took charge of *Parche*'s after engine room.[15]

MoMM1c Dick Hawn joined the Navy before finishing high school and served early on in the old P-boats. His parents had passed away when he was young, leaving his uncle to raise the rebellious youth. His uncle finally gave Dick an ultimatum: either join the military or go to reform school. Hawn chose the Navy in 1937 and he cut his teeth on the P-boats. After graduating with the highest grades in his submarine and diesel school, Hawn and his buddy Clabe Legget chose to be assigned in early 1940 to the new construction of *Trout* (SS-202) in Portsmouth, New Hampshire. "We had heard there were lots of girls in Portsmouth," he recalled.[16]

Hawn made seven war patrols on *Trout*, including three under Red Ramage, who would award Hawn the Silver Star for gallantry in action. "Shortly after I left her, the *Trout* was lost and I still remember the names of many of the men who went down with her," he recalled. Hawn spent some time in the relief crews at Perth, Australia, before being shipped back to the States to help commission *Parche*. "When I put the *Trout* in commission in 1940, I and about four or five others were the only ones who had never been through submarine school. All others were old timers," he wrote. "By contrast, in 1943, I put the *Parche* in commission and I and four or five others were the only experienced men."[17]

Commander Ramage was elated to find that at least one of his former crewmen was available to help put *Parche* into commission. "He was one

Motor machinist's mates
Phil Mackey (left) and
Bob Silvis share the close
quarters of one of *Parche*'s
engine rooms. The intake
air ducts are beside the two
men. *Courtesy of Bob Hall.*

of the finest diesel men ever," Ramage admitted of Hawn. "I was extremely lucky to get him. He was the only guy that grumbled for the sake of grumbling but he was a real jewel with those engines."[18]

Hawn found each of the four 10-cylinder, 1600-horsepower Fairbanks Morse engines to have an "unusual configuration. It had no cylinder heads; it had two pistons in each cylinder, one above the other. The upper pistons were connected to the upper crankshaft by connecting rods as were the lower pistons connected to the lower crankshaft." At her top surface speed, *Parche* could make 21 knots under this power.

Twenty-three-year-old Dick Hawn was put in charge of *Parche*'s forward engine room. One of his brightest motormacs was MoMM2c Orvail Buckner, who had been born in Salem, Oregon, and grew up working on a farm in central Oregon. His two older brothers left farming behind to serve on aircraft carriers earlier in the war. Curly-haired farmboy Orvail had followed in his brothers' footsteps, volunteering for subs and joining *Parche* for her commissioning.

MoMM3c Nick Casassa, who would serve as Hawn's battle stations fireman in the forward room, was a jack-of-all-trades with a knack for repair work. There was also MoMM2c Frederick Zacharias "Zach" Vogedes, a 24-year-old from Baltimore who had joined the Navy in 1939.

Although Vogedes had recently volunteered for the boats and completed sub school, he was an experienced hand among the black gangs on surface ships. He was stationed at Pearl Harbor in 1941 when the Japanese attacked and he recalled Japanese aircraft flying over so low toward Battleship Row that he could see the pilots' faces. He had served on board the destroyer *Morris* during the early part of the war, taking part in the carrier battles of Coral Sea and Midway. Zach Vogedes was a lively sailor who had earned the nickname of "the Baron" during *Parche*'s early training cruises.

During one East Coast liberty in New London, Vogedes and his buddy Ray Karr had indulged in more than their fair share of liquor at a local roller rink. The sailors had a 2000 curfew to be back on board *Parche* but they found it difficult to obtain a cab back to the base in time. When the next cab arrived, the driver told them that he had a fare to pick up in the bar. As the driver went into the bar to find his fare, Vogedes slid into the driver's seat and Karr jumped in beside him.

When Vogedes and Karr reached the sub base at Groton in their stolen taxi, they found the base guards were waiting for them. "We were hauled away to the New London jail for a sleepless night in one of their foul-smelling cells," Karr recalled. The *Parche* sailors were brought before a tough local judge the next morning for sentencing. When they were asked to state their name, age, and rank to the court, Vogedes—still feeling the effects of his liquor—smartly announced, "I'm the Baron von Vogedes, motormac second class."[19]

*Parche*'s Exec, Lieutenant McCrory, was present in the courtroom and listened to the charges against his sailors who were accused of unlawful use of a private taxi. Vogedes and Karr pleaded no contest and were ultimately released to the custody of their senior officer for due consequences. Karr recalled that their demeanor was "pretty subdued" as they rode back to *Parche* with their Exec in a jeep. As they pulled up to their boat, McCrory announced to Vogedes, "Baron, you and the Kid better behave yourselves from now on. Your ass belongs to me!"

Silent Service nicknames were hard to erase and these troublemakers were thereafter tagged "the Baron" and "the Kid" by their shipmates. For Karr, the potentially serious situation turned out to be the first time he had seen his tough executive officer crack a smile. In the wardroom, McCrory jestingly announced to Red Ramage that the judge had set the *Parche* sailors free because he had a poor case.

"We ought to torpedo the whole no-good town!" Ramage laughed. Karr and Vogedes, figuring "we were heading for a Navy court-martial," were

(Above) EM1c William "Snuffy" Vukovcan.
(Left) The electrician's mates were often called upon to crawl through tight spaces to check and service the boat's batteries. *Courtesy of Bob Hall.*

much relieved to find that their commanding officers had elected to write off the whole episode as a humorous mistake.[20]

Another young man with experience in the Navy was 21-year-old F2 Dave Hussey. He had joined the Merchant Marines during peacetime before joining the Navy. He knew that he could count on his engine room boss, Dick Hawn, when things got tough. "The skipper didn't want to have to bother with the engine rooms," said Hussey. "He knew he could count on Hawn for any damn thing."

Aft from the engine rooms was *Parche*'s eighth main watertight compartment, the maneuvering room. In this tight space, thick electric cables converged behind rows of massive switches, breakers, and buss bars that controlled currents between batteries, generators, and motors. Directly below the maneuvering room was the motor room, which housed the motors and reduction gears that drove the propellers.

Forty percent of *Parche*'s crewmen were motormacs, electricians, or firemen who were striking for either an electrician's or motor machinist's mate rating. The electrical gang was presided over by the three most senior petty officers, including EM1c Verlin Peterson—a heavyset, three-year Navy veteran—and EM1c William "Snuffy" Vukovcan, a tough Pittsburgh native of Russian ancestry and veteran of the prewar Asiatic fleet who was five months junior to Peterson in Navy time. Vukovcan, known for his constant tobacco-chewing, was also one of *Parche*'s more wild-hearted souls on liberty. While the boat was finishing out in Portsmouth, skipper Ramage had discovered a disassembled bicycle in the after torpedo room that Vukovcan had swiped while ashore. "How he ever got it down the

Torpedomen Ray Karr and Bill Hilditch buying supplies in Honolulu before *Parche* departs on her first patrol. *Courtesy of Ray Karr.*

hatch I'll never know," Ramage later laughed, "but he managed to get it reassembled and back up."[21]

In addition to shifting power source from batteries to engines in the maneuvering room, the electricians took periodic readings of specific gravity, cell temperature, and battery acid levels. To take such readings, the duty electrician had to go below the decks of the forward battery compartment in officers' country or the after battery compartment in the crew's quarters. The crawl space was approximately 30 inches in height and temperatures in the battery wells could well reach 110–120 degrees after a long battery charge on the surface at night.

Like most submarine sailors, the men of Pete Peterson and Snuffy Vukovcan's department had quickly acquired nicknames. EM3c Howard Ernest of Philadelphia was dubbed "Hose Nose" for his facial features. Ernest had joined the Navy right out of high school once the war had started, attended electrical school in Rhode Island and submarine school, and then joined *Parche*'s construction.[22]

EM2c Joseph Ray Howell, born in rural Keokuk, Iowa, was orphaned as an infant. He was raised by his maternal aunt Beulah Jackson and his uncle "Boss" with their family on a farm in Missouri. Joe had no love for farm work and he joined the Navy shortly after graduating high school. Due to his southern roots and the slight accent he developed, Howell became known to all as "Dixie." He was originally assigned to the construction of the new boat *Blueback* at Groton, but Dixie Howell was transferred to *Parche* before her commissioning.

The electrician's mate with the longest Navy tenure was EM1c William Alonzo Hughes, a 26-year-old who had joined the service in 1936 from the Big Hole country of Montana. "I went to China in 1936 at 18 years of age and was in Shanghai when the Japs captured it in July 1937," he recalled. Hughes later served on board the sub tender *Beaver* in 1939 and was among the P-class boats that returned to China in 1941 before the start of the war. He joined *Parche* at New London after her commissioning and would become one of the senior chiefs of the watch. Aboard *PC 548* in 1943, he had been nicknamed "Buckwheat" by his buddies, but on board *Parche* he became known as "Lonnie" for his middle name Alonzo. Hughes always kept a small bound journal in the maneuvering room entitled "Signs of My Friends," in which his closest friends signed their autographs and home addresses, particularly as they were transferred on to new assignments.[23]

The final watertight compartment aboard *Parche* was her after torpedo room, which contained four torpedo tubes and eight wakeless, electric Mark 18 torpedoes. This room was under the charge of TM1 Carroll Edward Kinkel, a seasoned patrol veteran from Philadelphia who had been in the service for four years. His crew included veteran TM1c Carl Dilley and others who were making their first war patrol, such as TM3c Joe Nichols, TM3c Bill Hilditch, and striker S1c Bob Gubaney. The after torpedo room had bunks for 16 crewmen nestled above and between the torpedoes and rows of lockers for the personal belongings of half the crew.

*Parche* was a fighting ship of the finest design from stem to stern. Her officers were blessed to have a crew, with few exceptions, that had become especially tight during their training period. One reason the men bonded so well early on was that at least 18 men who would soon serve on *Parche*—Johnny Barnes, Adolph Russel, Freddy Frederick, Dave Hussey, Joe Nichols, Dave Frank, Snuffy Vukovcan, Walt Ekelund, Chet Stanton, Bob Daufenbach, Bill Hilditch, John Nania, Howie Ernest, J. G. Hill, Harold Staggs, Joe Sheppard, Orvail Buckner, and Bob Hall—had graduated from submarine school together on 4 November 1943. Each of the 81 crew members departing with the wolf pack in March 1944 would play an integral part in whether the team as a whole was successful or not on patrol.

It did not take long for wolf pack commander George Peterson's lack of combat experience to present itself. Lt. (jg) Jim Campbell was standing watch as the JOD one night as *Parche* headed across the Pacific.

Captain Peterson asked permission to come onto the bridge to observe. The OOD, Lt. Dave Green, acknowledged the request. Peterson clambered up the ladder with a lit cigarette in hand. Campbell, aware that even the light of a glowing cigarette could be spotted by a lurking enemy submarine, immediately grabbed it and snubbed it out. Peterson, realizing his mistake, muttered, "Oh, my God."[24]

Peterson was a rather quiet man who did not go out of his way to engage his fellow officers in conversation. Campbell felt that the division commander possessed a fair amount of nervous energy, however, and he felt that there was some tension between the big boss and skipper Red Ramage. "But, I was just a junior officer," Campbell recalled. "What went on between a skipper and a pack commander was not my concern."

The officers' watches switched every four hours and a new JOD and OOD came on duty whether surfaced or submerged. Frank Allcorn, Dave Green, and Bob Erwin were the designated deck officers while Bill Bergen, Jim Campbell, and John Parks, respectively, rotated watches as their normal junior deck officers. When he was not on duty, Lieutenant Allcorn often checked up on his torpedomen in the forward and after rooms.

On 1 April, he and Commander Ramage held simulated battle surface gun drills to test fire *Parche*'s weapons. The main deck gun was a 4-inch, .50-caliber dual purpose cannon. With a muzzle velocity of 2,700 feet per second, it was equally effective against both surface and aerial targets. *Parche* also had two manually operated Oerlikon 20-mm guns permanently mounted on the cigarette decks, one forward and one aft, each capable of firing up to 450 rounds per minute. Spare 20-mm barrels were kept in lockers near the guns in case of overheating. There were also side mounts on the bridge for portable .50-caliber machine guns that were hustled topside and mounted for firing. In the event of close action, other crewmen might be asked to bring up Thompson submachine guns or M1 30-06 rifles.

The gun drills gave gunnery officer Frank Allcorn and his two veteran gunner's mates the chance to evaluate personnel for each key position. Twenty-year-old GM2c Leroy Swettenam from Indiana had been serving on board the sub tender *Pelias* in Pearl Harbor when the Japanese attacked on December 7. Swettenam thereafter made five war patrols on the *Grampus* before being assigned to *Parche*'s new construction. His timing was impeccable because *Grampus* was lost with all hands on her next run. Gunner's mate Reno Ussin from Seattle was outstanding on *Parche*'s 4-inch gun; he was already a veteran of four war patrols on the old *Nautilus*.[25]

Torpedoman Chuck Gooden tried his hand for the position of hot shell-man. "I had to wear these oversized asbestos gloves and catch the 4-inch casings as they were ejected from the breech," he said. "But those things were hotter than hell." Gooden opted out of the gun crew, preferring to let someone else toss the hot cartridges into the sea. Mess cook Bob Hall also spent some time on *Parche*'s gun crew during his first run, but his efforts to permanently join the galley gang would soon take priority over any topside action.

Pack commander Peterson and skipper Ramage put together wolf pack instructions en route to Midway, where they would be shared with the other two boats. The skipper also conducted daily trim dives and had his communications gang exercise wolf pack tactics, including shifts of frequency to throw off potential eavesdroppers.

During the morning of 2 April, *Parche* entered the main channel at Midway to top off her fuel and provisions. Midway was an advanced base in the Pacific for submarines to refuel and make post-patrol repairs. The sandy atoll was surrounded by a coral reef. Prior to the war, Midway had served as a refueling stop for Pan-Am's Trans Pacific air route. The airline had a building that once served as a hotel for passengers while planes were refueled. Now the building served as an officers' quarters and other Quonset huts had been built for the enlisted men who worked the island. A sub tender or two were always in the lagoon.

Red Ramage and the commanding officers of *Tinosa* and *Bang* had a conference in which they were given their Detailed Plan of Coordinated Patrol and Attack for the group. Ramage and Captain Peterson had figured out some basic attack procedures involving the three boats. "Two submarines would try to get themselves in position ahead on either bow of the target and the third submarine would be the trailer and he would take station astern in case the target was damaged, then he could pick her off," Ramage recalled. "Or if she turned or reversed course or eluded the two advance submarines, he would be in a position to attack."[26]

*Parche* remained at Midway little more than 24 hours before her war patrol resumed. In addition to fuel, she took aboard one additional enlisted man, RT2c Desmond Albert Christy, who joined the radio gang. *Parche*'s leading radio operator was RM1c Percy Barnett, a 22-year-old who hailed from Alabama. Known to his buddies as Barney, he had made several war patrols before joining *Parche* as the most senior of the radio gang.

On patrol, other non-rated sailors would train on the radio gear, stand sonar watches and work toward achieving their rating. During the boat's early months of training, Barnett had five other rated radio, sonar, and radar operators under his charge—RT1c John Gray, RM2c Alfred Rick, RM3c Myron Grover, RM3c John Folse, and RM3c Nelson Fournier. *Parche* contained a dual-head JK-QC sonar head that was trained hydraulically and could be retracted into protective trunks in the forward torpedo room when not in use to prevent damage. The JK gear was used for listening and for echo-ranging to determine a target ship's distance. *Parche*'s JP sonar contained a T-shaped hydrophone that was sonic and manually trained for listening. As senior radioman, Barnett was responsible for manning the JK sonar gear in the conning tower for target approaches.

An Iowa native, Myron Grover had completed radio school at Northwestern before moving on to sub school at New London. He felt welcome on his new boat from the first moment. Exec Mac McCrory made a habit in the wardroom of scrutinizing the transfer papers of each new man reporting on board. Grover was pleased when the second-in-command found him to be sufficiently qualified. "I see that you graduated number 12 out of a battalion of 250," McCrory had announced. "Welcome aboard the *Parche*, young man."

The little extra boost of recognition was just enough to make the new sailor feel right at home. His little circle of the radio gang soon became tight. "Rick used to cut our hair sometimes, but he was not much of a barber," said Grover. "After he got through cutting my hair the first time, he had scalped me so bad that people starting calling me 'Forehead.'"

Fournier, like Grover, had no war patrols under his belt yet. Rick, a veteran of the old *Dolphin* and *Narwhal,* was quick to grow a long beard on patrol. He was a husky man who had joined the deck gun crew to help pass the heavy 4-inch shells for battle surface actions. Radio technician John Gray, a native of Maryland with extensive radar training, would be *Parche*'s lead SJ radar operator during attacks. The oldest of four brothers, Gray had worked for Westinghouse before entering the Navy and he was something of an electronics whiz kid. Barnett and Red Ramage, seeking a seasoned conning tower attack team, had jumped at the chance to add another experienced sound operator when the chance presented itself at Midway.

Desmond Christy—often called Chris by his buddies—had attack experience on the sound gear and radar from his previous patrols on

*Tambor.* Born in Clifton, Arizona, Christy had spent the first year of the war as a riveter on aircraft at the Northrup Aircraft Corporation in California following his graduation from high school. He enlisted in the Navy in November 1942 and had subsequently attended nine months of sonar and radar schooling in Houston, Texas, and at Treasure Island before being assigned to *Tambor.* He left *Tambor* following her successful ninth patrol and joined *Parche* on 2 April from Midway's relief crew. Quiet, confident, and book-smart, 22-year-old Desmond Christy would help round out Percy Barnett's six-man radio gang.

 *Parche, Tinosa,* and *Bang* departed Midway at 1230 on 3 April and steamed in formation at 8-mile intervals to the 180th Meridian. Once the pack had cleared the 30-mile circle from Midway, they proceeded in line for the next two weeks toward their assigned patrol area. During daylight, the boats zigzagged along their base course at an economical 10- to 11-knot speed to conserve fuel. The officers and crew stood four-hour watches and then used their off time to read, play acey-deucy or cribbage, study their qualification notebooks, or watch movies in the torpedo rooms. In the wardroom there was a turntable with records for idle time and the crew had a radio in the crew's mess that had been purchased at Portsmouth for entertainment. The radio could generally be tuned to some station for music while at sea and, closer to Japanese waters, Radio Hanoi was picked up as the boat neared its patrol area.[27]

 As the wolf pack moved toward the sea lanes south of Formosa, its skippers conducted routine drills, dives, and training each day. The three skippers exchanged information on the surface each evening. Jim Campbell and his radio gang received a good workout, employing the use of wolf pack code in their daily transmissions. *Parche, Bang,* and *Tinosa* remained surfaced during the first week en route to station, zigzagging along their base course at 10 knots.

 The deck officers and their lookouts remained vigilant, anticipating the first sightings that might finally bring action for their boat.

# CHAPTER THREE

# First Action

L t. Frank Allcorn had seen his fair share of action as the TDC operator on board *Finback* on his previous war patrols. By August 1943, *Finback* had destroyed at least nine Japanese ships and achieved a reputation as an efficient fighting ship. Like most of *Parche*'s crew, Allcorn was eager for the fight once again. He had no doubts about his new boat or his shipmates.

"We knew the ship had the ability," Allcorn later wrote. "It had taken us well below test depth on the second dive out of the Portsmouth Navy Yard. The crew had been selected with the special skills required to do the job and had drilled, drilled, drilled and was eager."[1]

It was only fitting that Allcorn had the deck when *Parche*'s first wartime target sighting was made at 1815 on 12 April.

"I've got a mast on the horizon," announced one of his lookouts.

Lieutenant Allcorn quickly studied the small mast dead ahead on the horizon through his binoculars and called for the skipper. Red Ramage arrived on the bridge promptly as *Parche* ran up flank speed of 21 knots to close the enemy vessel. The radio gang dashed off a contact report to pack mates *Tinosa* and *Bang*. As the range decreased, the lookouts announced that the small ship ahead was nothing more than the drifting hulk of an abandoned trawler that had apparently been shot up by another submarine.

"Battle stations, gun!" The call went out over the 1MC shipboard announcing system as Ramage decided that this drifting hulk would make an ideal gunnery target to sharpen his gunners' skills. Reno Ussin and Leroy Swettenam led their teams out on deck to man the 4-inch, .50-caliber cannon, the 20-mm bridge guns, and the .50-caliber machine guns. *Parche* made a run on the trawler, whose decks were awash from previous gun damage. *Parche*'s 20-mm gunners expended three magazines (305 rounds) on the hulk before Ramage let *Tinosa* move in to give her gunners some practice.

Japanese antisubmarine efforts became more evident the next day as *Parche*'s radar made three different aerial contacts during the early hours. John Parks and Bob Erwin had the watch at 0915 when the first airplane was contacted by radar. Fifteen minutes later, another bogey appeared on the screen. Fortunately, none of the planes came within 16 miles of his boat, so Ramage had his duty officers keep the boat surfaced. Contacts that came within 10 miles were a different story. During the early morning hours of 14 April, Erwin and Parks again had the deck when the SJ showed a radar contact at 1900 yards and approaching. "A few seconds later contact was 1150 yards, typical of a low flying airplane," recalled Erwin.[2]

The lookouts had not seen or heard anything but the officers opted to make an emergency dive just to be safe. While submerged, the sonar operator picked up *Tinosa* passing to starboard. *Parche* surfaced again after *Tinosa* had safely passed and was seen on radar at 9800 yards. The SJ radar was not able to tell if the reported contact was on the surface or submerged but merely gave the bearing and distance. "In any case it was better to dive than be sorry," said Erwin.[3]

Ramage conducted tests of his other equipment on 15 April en route to station. *Parche* fired false target shells while submerged. These shells were fired out of the underwater signal tube from the after torpedo room so that the resulting fizzy bubble masses could be tracked by the boat's listening gear. Ramage noted that he was "not impressed. Nothing was heard on the JK/JP, nor was it possible to get an echo range with the QB/QC." Ray Karr, who had been trained in such anti-tactic equipment, knew that the intended effect of these false shells "was to make false noises in the water that were supposed to sound like a submarine to mislead enemy destroyers."

The wolf pack reached its assigned patrol area in Luzon Strait on 16 April and *Parche* rendezvoused with her pack mates to exchange patrol instructions from Captain Peterson. The pack commander did not otherwise supervise skipper Ramage's daily command. Junior officer Bob Erwin found that the wardroom relationship with wolf pack commander Peterson was generally good. "He was not very outgoing but he was cordial and did not interfere with the ship's people or activities," he recalled.[4]

*Parche*'s first full day on station passed uneventfully, save for a pesky leak in the bow buoyancy blow valve, which kept Clarence Allard's auxiliarymen busy. By midafternoon on the following day, Ramage became bored by the lack of targets, as evidenced by his patrol report notes. At 1500, he logged: "Picked up sky lookout—bird (genus: unknown; sex: undetermined; habits: not altogether proper), which took station on [the

No.] 1 periscope, going round and round and up and down, hanging on with dogged determination for over 4 hours." When *Parche* surfaced for the evening to charge her batteries at 1900, Ramage noted that the bird was still "perched high up on #1 scope."

The periscope watches during the day and evening lookouts had little else to pique their interest during the ensuing days. "We divided our patrol area up into 60-mile squares, which is one degree on a side and each submarine was assigned to a 20-mile-lane 60 miles long," related Ramage. "As soon as somebody made contact they would relay the word to the other two and they would close in."[5]

*Parche*'s radar gang tracked rain squalls on 19 April and were able to detect the high mountain peaks of Formosa at a distance of 70 to 80 miles. John Gray, the radar technician, figured out that the SJ was picking up pulses sent out on one sweep and getting the echo the second or third time around, thus doubling or tripling the indicated range. The SJ contact may also have been a "skip contact," per Bob Erwin. "We later found that the radar would pick up distant objects if they were big and then record them on the second pulse."[6]

The routine of war patrolling set in as the days passed without enemy contacts. Mac McCrory, as the ship's navigator, went topside at first light and at dusk each day to take a star sighting. He and his senior quartermaster, Wilbur Sprague, used their sextant to shoot the stars and fix the boat's position. *Parche* remained submerged during the daylight hours as she conducted periscope watches. The OOD manned the periscope with one of the junior quartermasters or signalmen assisting. The JOD handling the diving officer duties kept the boat at a constant depth while the OOD exposed five to seven feet of periscope above the surface to sweep the horizon for targets. The hours passed slowly. "We often felt like we were wearing a periscope," Lieutenant (jg) Erwin recalled.[7]

Six of *Parche*'s eight officers stood the deck watches around the clock. They each stood four-hour watches, had eight hours off, and then stood another four-hour watch during the course of 24 hours. In between watches, they were required to handle their various departmental duties and also assist with deciphering incoming radio traffic, thus leaving little time for actual sleep. Ramage decided that he would not make another patrol with only eight officers.[8]

Peterson had *Parche* move from the east coast of Formosa on to a new patrol station on 21 April, where she dived on station at 0600 the next day off the eastern entrance to Bashi Channel. Jim Campbell, standing the

This was a typical view for the officer of the deck and his lookouts at dawn on board *Parche*. *U.S. Navy photo, courtesy of Jim Campbell and Bob Erwin.*

afternoon periscope watch, sighted the mast of a small vessel but *Parche* was unable to close this ship. After another fruitless day off Bashi Channel, *Parche* moved to an area south of Takao on 24 April.

During the early morning hours, radar picked up another vessel and tracking commenced, but Ramage soon became convinced that he and another wolf pack mate were actually tracking each other. The watch was at least more eventful this day as fifteen Japanese aircraft were tracked at various times by the periscope watch. *Parche* remained undetected and no bombs were dropped. The constant threat of aircraft attacks and occasional Japanese fishing vessels at least made the watch routine seem less boring during the next four days.

---

*Parche*'s luck took a turn for the better on 29 April when Tony Gallaher's *Bang* reported at 2020 that she had located a large convoy hours before some 50 miles away. Ramage set course to intercept this convoy and rang up full speed. He was rewarded three hours later with an SJ radar contact on a large ship with an escort 19,000 yards away. *Parche* commenced tracking these ships and sent contact reports to *Bang* and *Tinosa*. There was a bright half moon in the west as *Parche* made an end around on the surface during the early minutes of 30 April. By 0200, Frank Allcorn and Bill Bergen's lookouts had sighted a second escort, a *Chidori*-type torpedo boat.

*Parche* was silhouetted by the moon, however, and the escort quickly spied the American submarine. The Japanese vessel picked up steam and began chasing *Parche*. Red Ramage elected to stay on the surface and pour on the power. There were several tense moments for those topside, but *Parche* soon began to outdistance her opponent with a half-knot speed advantage. Ramage shook off the escort in 20 minutes but he lost contact with the convoy in the process.

The radar gang continued to track surface targets during the next two hours but Ramage could not be certain of which were Japanese and which might be his pack mates. By 0355 an escort ship was sighted at 7000 yards and plotting officer Bob Erwin soon figured that he was making 14 knots on various courses. *Parche* passed this vessel at a three-mile distance in the dark without being sighted. A short time later, an explosion and flames visible on the horizon were clear indicators that *Bang* was working over this convoy.

Rookie skipper Tony Gallaher would soon share the news of his handiwork via the wolf pack network. Gallaher's *Bang* had doggedly attacked the convoy—officially labeled TAMA-17 by Japanese command—during the night. By dawn of 30 April, *Bang* had fired 20 of her 24 torpedoes. Less than one-third of these connected, but Gallaher succeeded in damaging two Japanese merchant ships and sinking the 2,859-ton tanker *Nittatsu Maru*.[9]

Red Ramage had great faith in the abilities of John Gray, his lean, energetic leading radarman. According to shipmate Dick Hawn, Gray "weighed only 100 pounds soaking wet." He and his new assistant Chris Christy had already been monitoring Convoy TAMA-17 all night. Shortly after 0500, Gray had locked his SJ radar onto ships of Convoy TAMA-17 and *Parche* was on the hunt again. During the ensuing minutes, at least ten ships proceeding at 6 knots could be counted.[10]

The approach of dawn prevented Ramage from reaching a proper attack position, so he commenced an end around as *Bang* continued to work over the Japanese ships. By 0624, *Parche's* lookouts had *Tinosa* in sight closing from the west. The boats closed each other so that Captain Peterson could pass instructions. He told Don Weiss that Ramage's *Parche* would go in first on the convoy's port flank while Weiss' *Tinosa* should follow to starboard.

Eleven minutes later, *Parche's* lookouts had the tops of the enemy ships' masts in sight and Ramage pulled the plug to prepare for a submerged attack. Bob Erwin, John Parks, and their lookouts scrambled below as *Parche* went to 90 feet. Ramage eased up to periscope for peeks as he maneuvered to reach a spot ahead of the convoy. He noted a Mavis four-engine flying boat and a Nell two-engine bomber patrolling over the convoy in the bright sun and slick sea of the early morning.

By mid-morning, it was already 14 hours into the pursuit of this convoy and *Parche* had yet to attack. By 0957, Commander Ramage had his ship at battle stations submerged and a column of merchant ships in his crosshairs with *Parche* 20 degrees on the port bow of the center column. *Parche*'s conning tower was tightly packed as her fire control team prepared to put their hours of battle stations training to good use.

Chief Quartermaster Sprague stood ready as the periscope jockey to call out the relative bearings from the ring above and surrounding the scope while his skipper made observations. At the wheel, forward of the scope, was SM2c Chet Stanton, who as battle helmsman handled speed changes and called out the log speeds. QM3c Bob Daufenbach entered all commands, course changes, and relevant data in the Quartermaster's Notebook. Daufenbach was also wearing the sound-powered headset as the battle stations talker, responsible for relaying orders to other compartments throughout the boat.

Moving aft, Frank Allcorn was at the TDC with Fire Controlman Sam Roberts assisting and standing by the centrally located firing panel. The TDC was Roberts' "beast." According to him, "we were elbow to elbow in the conning tower during attacks." Bob Erwin stood back-to-back with Allcorn at the little plotting table to plot the enemy convoy's course. John Gray was vigilantly monitoring the blips on his SJ radar's small PPI scope, while senior Radioman Percy Barnett intently tracked the screws of the target ships on his sonar gear.

Lt. Mac McCrory had dropped below into the control room to oversee the men on duty there. Chief of the Boat Luke Parker was standing sentry over the Christmas tree while auxiliarymen Phil Bukowski and Clarence Allard handled the hydraulic air manifold and trim manifold. Diving officer Dave Green oversaw the sailors on the bow and stern planes who brought their boat up to periscope depth on command. Jim Campbell stood by to take over the diving duties when Green ducked back aft to check on his engineers.

At 1003 Ramage maneuvered to fire his forward tubes on the convoy's center column and his after tubes on the port column. "Make ready all tubes," talker Daufenbach called to Don Walters and Carroll Kinkel in their two torpedo rooms. Four minutes later, Ramage motioned with his thumb up and Chief Sprague pressed the white button that engaged the cables to raise the No. 2 attack periscope from its well. Its larger night lens helped to compensate for the lower visibility after sunset and could optically measure ranges. The only downside to this scope was its much larger upper column, which created more of a wake for alert Japanese lookouts to spot.

This is *Parche*'s tight conning tower as it now stands at the Submarine Base
Museum in Pearl Harbor. During torpedo attacks, it was crowded with the fire control
party. Forward of the periscope is the helmsman's wheel and the engine order
control displays. To the left of the periscope is the TDC. Just across to the right is the
small PPI scope for *Parche*'s radar and the ship's sonar gear. *Courtesy of Bob Hall.*

As the periscope rose from the deep well in the center of the conning
tower deck, Sprague turned the housing tube and folded down the handles
for the skipper to grasp. This enabled the skipper to be right on the target's
known bearing without having to search for the ship when he peered into
the scope. Ramage had his face pressed to the rubber cushion around the
glass before the scope was fully raised.

The night scope's cross wires were right on the target vessel as the
skipper made a quick observation. "Dammit, they're zigging to the left!"
he snapped. Ramage immediately ordered Chet Stanton to wheel *Parche*
around to bring the stern tubes to bear, as the convoy's course change had
spoiled the chance for a good shot from the forward tubes.

"Stand by for a setup," Ramage ordered as the stern tubes came to bear.
"Range, mark!"

Sprague, reading the dials on the side of the scope, called out,
"Eighteen hundred yards."

"Bearing, mark!" called Ramage.

Sprague replied with, "Bearing one seven oh."

From the TDC, Frank Allcorn confirmed, "TDC checks."

The TDC was essentially an analog computer driven by gears that
automatically received the boat's speed from the pit log, a seagoing speed-

ometer of sorts, and the sub's heading from her master gyrocompass. Lieutenant Allcorn input the target ship's observed bearing and range as given by the skipper and radar operator John Gray. As the observations continued, Allcorn could deduce the actual speed and course of the target vessel. His call of "check" indicated that his data on the TDC perfectly matched Ramage's observations.

During these observations, plotting officer Bob Erwin used the same called bearings and ranges to help accurately determine the course and speed of the target. Ramage reported the target ship's course by estimating the angle on the bow during his periscope observations. "A zero degree angle indicates the target is heading directly toward you," related Erwin. "A ninety-degree angle indicates it is broadside. These are fairly easy to estimate but those in between are difficult."[11]

The chances of obtaining a hit were improved by the degree of accuracy of these estimations. Any miscalculations were generally overcome by firing a spread of torpedoes on target and slightly ahead of and behind the target ship to allow for any slight errors or changes in speed or course. All was in readiness for *Parche*'s first war shots.

In the darkened conning tower, only the glow of a few red lights enabled the attack team to complete the final steps. "Make ready the after tubes," said Ramage. "Set depth on the fish at nine feet."

Senior Torpedoman Kinkel readied his after tubes by flooding them with sea water and then blowing air pressure into each tube to equalize it with the outside sea pressure. Carl Dilley opened the hydraulically controlled outer torpedo tube doors while the other members of the after gang stood ready to verify the final firing angles being transmitted electrically by the TDC in the conning tower. Talker Daufenbach relayed back to the skipper that Kinkel's tubes were flooded and the depth settings were as prescribed. JK sonarman Barnett continued to make reports on the target ship's bearings when the periscope was down while Desmond Christy on the JP sound gear set kept tabs on the convoy's escort ships.

"Up scope," the skipper called again as he jerked his thumb in the up signal to Sprague. With one last check of the target's bearing and range, Ramage then barked, "Fire one!"

Daufenbach repeated the order to the after room as Sam Roberts punched the firing key. *Parche* jerked as a huge rush of compressed air blasted the first torpedo from its tube. Roberts turned the selective switch on the firing panel to the No. 8 tube and waited the standard eight-second interval before firing the next torpedo at a 1750-yard distance. *Parche* lurched again and then Ramage called for the firing of the last two after torpedoes at the next leading ship in the convoy.

Below in the control room, leading auxiliaryman Allard quickly adjusted the boat's trim at the trim manifold to compensate for the 12,000-plus pounds of weight that had been ejected from the after room. It was 1010 as the four war fish churned away in a cloud of bubbles, two each en route to the two leading ships of the convoy. The distance to the second target was 2250 yards.

Fate was not in Red Ramage's favor this day, however, for the Japanese apparently spotted *Parche*'s raised periscope as she fired. He spotted the convoy raising a two-pennant signal and making a hard turn to avoid the torpedoes heading their way. Cook Johnny Johnson, listening to the action from the galley, later felt his greatest disappointment aboard *Parche* was "when the first two torpedoes missed."

"They spotted us and they're turning away," Ramage snapped. "Take her to 200 feet. Rig for depth-charge attack," he ordered.

The planesmen immediately put a down angle on the boat and all hands responded to the call by shutting down any unnecessary equipment in anticipation of a depth charging. Ramage knew that an airplane had been circling above the convoy and he fully expected bombs to be dropped at any moment.

At 1014, three minutes and 55 seconds after firing the fourth torpedo, a heavy explosion was heard. Since the ships had all turned it was believed to have been one of the torpedoes striking home in a distant ship. *Tinosa* reported that one of *Parche*'s torpedoes went on past the target and hit a ship in the other column. A stick of aircraft bombs—four to six of them—exploded above as *Parche* clawed for depth. A number of distant depth charges were heard during the next hour and a half, all thankfully distant.

Erwin wrote, "We counted fifty aircraft bombs plus numerous depth charges. None were very close but the aircraft bombs made us hold our breath. We could easily hear them hit the water as the noise wave hit our hull. Then we would hold our breath until the explosion. We always figured if we could hear the explosion we were going to be OK."[12]

This was the real baptism of fire for two-thirds of the *Parche* crew. Everyone performed admirably. This Japanese tactic of slow and persistent bombing was designed to keep a single boat down and thus prevent further attacks. The planes and escorts did manage to keep *Parche* down until noon. Silent running and deep submergence was the standard protocol for evading depth charge attacks. Some skippers took their boats even deeper than their designed test depth to throw off the Japanese attackers. One of Red Ramage's fellow 1944 skippers, Dick O'Kane, had even tested his boat *Tang*'s ability to withstand the pressures of 600-plus feet—a test that for his ship and crew admittedly "did cause some uneasiness." As for *Parche*, Ramage felt, "Our test depth was 412 feet. I never thought there was any future in going any deeper than we needed to. When the time came I had to do it, that would be soon enough. There was no use putting extra strain on the boat and its hull fittings."[13]

Ramage returned to periscope depth at 1208 and observed the smoke of the convoy in the distance as well as the two-engine bomber some two miles distant. Ramage tried to pursue at periscope depth but his only satisfaction was hearing other explosions during the afternoon as *Tinosa* attacked the convoy. Contact was lost with the convoy in late afternoon. After surfacing that evening, *Tinosa* reported sinking one freighter and damaging two other ships. The wolf pack continued to search for the Japanese ships through the night but without luck. *Bang* reported having been depth charged for seven hours. The convoy apparently closed the coast of Luzon and then headed south during the night.

Peterson directed the wolf pack to resume their patrol stations on 1 May if they could not reconnect with the convoy. The pack had been in constant pursuit or attack against the convoy for 28 hours and the crew was tired. "It was a let down to have been so close with virtually no results," Erwin admitted.[14]

The pack continued its westerly movement the following day and rendezvoused on the surface late in the evening of 2 May. At 0001 on 3 May, *Parche* shot over a line and passed across a bottle containing group instructions from Peterson for *Bang*. Minutes later, *Tinosa* maneuvered alongside and the line-throwing gun was again used to pass over a bottle with instructions for *Tinosa*'s skipper.

At this point in the war, submarines were routinely sent to chase convoys based upon intelligence reports. Ultra dispatches were sent out with a very secure coding system. This required Jim Campbell and the other officers to use coding strips to decipher the special code. Because the wolf pack operated so close to enemy soil in shallow waters, *Parche* was not allowed to carry an ECM for this run. The manual method was a slower process of lining up the coded Ultra on a clipboard to figure the correct letters using strip charts. Hours later at 0715, *Tinosa* reported a seven-ship convoy making 8 knots some 20 miles away.

Ramage changed course to the north and rang up full speed to intercept. He hoped his luck would be better this time.

# CHAPTER FOUR

# Convoy Killers

It did not take *Parche* long to pick up this convoy as it moved through Luzon Strait. By 0800 on 3 May, her lookouts had sighted smoke 15 miles away. The tops of these ships came into view within a half hour and Ramage commenced an end around. Aircraft contacts became present on the SD air search radar, forcing OOD Dave Green to take the boat under to avoid contact.

The convoy continued moving east as its planes kept *Parche* submerged throughout the day. She surfaced at 1537 and went ahead at full speed to regain contact. Distant smoke and eventually the tops of the enemy ships came into view again and Ramage commenced another end around at 1700.

Lt. (jg) Jim Campbell was called to the deck because his battle station for surface approaches was that of manning the target bearing transmitters (TBTs). "This was my first surface attack and I was a little surprised at Captain Ramage's procedure," admitted Campbell. "The skipper had us take off running and he headed us away from the convoy. I couldn't understand what he was doing at first." Campbell soon realized that his experienced commander was keeping the convoy at a safe distance while completing his run to get into attack position before driving back in again well ahead of the approaching ships. "His techniques surprised me but they proved to be effective in putting us into attack position."

This time a *Chidori*-class patrol boat eventually sighted *Parche* and took up chase for an hour and a half. By 1940, the escort was still pursuing but was a good nine miles distant thanks to *Parche*'s half-knot surface speed advantage. Thirty minutes later, Ramage felt he had lost the escort and he turned *Parche* around to regain radar contact. At 2051, radar picked up these ships again at 29,000 yards. During the next two hours, Ramage narrowed the range but had to contend with keeping a careful distance due to a bright three-quarter moon. "The end around is fast becoming a run around," he wryly logged at 2300.

The night passed into 4 May as *Parche* continued to doggedly pursue these ships. "The sky was becoming overcast with heavy rainstorms and lightning to the northwest, the direction the convoy was traveling, and this was to our advantage," recalled plotting officer Bob Erwin.[1]

Ensign Bill Bergen reported at 0022 that the SJ picked up a small ship at 6,600 yards that had an escort vessel. Ramage analyzed the situation and figured it was worthy of attacking this ship. He reasoned that after an 18-hour chase, "there was little improvement in our position relative to the convoy." He also knew that the convoy was soon due to make a base course change back toward Takao and the sky was overcast with scattered rain squalls. Ramage therefore "decided to close the convoy and make the best of any situation that developed."

At 0044, *Parche* went ahead to full speed, changing course to intercept as Ramage rang up battle stations. The tracking crew had stayed at or near their posts during the long pursuit. Six large ships in line came into view and a convoy course change at 0052 put them on *Parche*'s port bow. This was Convoy TE-04 consisting of six ore carriers and three escorts—escort ship *CD-1*, auxiliary gunboat *Kazan Maru,* and the minelayer *Maeshima.* They had departed Yawata on 3 May. The big ships—all in the 5,000- to 6,000-ton range—were *Toyohi Maru, Shoryu Maru, Taiyoku Maru, Kinrei Maru, Taibu Maru,* and *Yulin Maru.*[2]

Skipper Don Weiss' *Tinosa* was first to strike. He fired six torpedoes into Convoy TE-04 and believed he had sunk two ships and damaged a third. Postwar evidence showed that he sunk the 6,436-ton freighter *Toyohi Mau.* Angry escort vessels forced *Tinosa* down and pounded her with depth charges, leaving the door wide open for *Parche* to strike.

Ray Karr to starboard and Joe Nichols to port were topside as two of the battle lookouts for this surface attack. Communications officer Jim Campbell felt that pack commander George Peterson and Red Ramage seemed to have some tension between them. Campbell recalled that Peterson "was present in the conning tower to observe our torpedo attacks but he didn't get involved in them."

Fortunately for *Parche*, Convoy TE-04's escort vessels had gone after *Tinosa* following her torpedo attack, believing that only one American submarine was present. This careless tactic left the remainder of the convoy unprotected and wide open for *Parche*'s attack.[3]

Ramage quickly crossed ahead of their column and commenced swinging to the right to create a starboard firing track on the leading freighter. Ramage used Gray's radar ranges and Campbell's TBT bearings to help

*Parche*'s torpedoes sunk at least two Japanese merchant ships during the night of 4 May 1944 and damaged a third ship. This World War II periscope view shows a merchant ship beginning to sink from torpedo damage as another explosion rips her after section. *Author's collection.*

Allcorn generate the final firing solution. Campbell, who had excellent night vision, manned the target bearing transmitter while Ramage studied the convoy with his 7x50 binoculars to decide which ship to attack first. During the approach, Ramage remained on the bridge but occasionally dropped down into the conning tower to look at Gray's SJ radar screen to analyze the pips.

By 0106, the range had narrowed to 1,900 yards and torpedo officer Frank Allcorn announced that he had a good firing solution on the TDC. Ramage commenced firing four torpedoes from Don Walters' forward room toward the leading merchant vessel. Cory Maupin stood by the firing key and hit the plunger for each torpedo just in case the electrical system didn't work. J. G. Hill and Chuck Gooden were in position to check the torpedoes' depth settings. The torpedo course settings were fed directly from the TDC into each torpedo as the data developed in the conning tower.

Walters recalled, "My station was to time the flooding of the sea water coming back aft after the torpedoes went out. It was always a bit of guess-work on timing to keep the proper trim on the boat and taking in the right amount of water to compensate for the lost weight of the torpedoes we had fired." Walters and his torpedo jockeys quickly prepared the next two war fish for firing as their skipper took aim above.

Ramage then coached helmsman Chet Stanton to swing *Parche* to port to bring the remaining two tubes to bear on the second maru in the line. Two minutes after firing the first fish, *Parche* belched forth two more Mark 16s from the No. 5 and No. 6 tubes from a range of 2,200 yards. As she did, the bridge watch observed three hits on the first target, which was later identified as the 5,949-ton freighter *Kinrei Maru*. Ramage wrote that the ship "appeared to blow up, breaking in two" and sinking almost immediately.

Japanese records would show that *Taibu Maru* had fired at a surfaced submarine on the night of 4 May shortly before she was hit in the stern by at least one torpedo. *Taibu* broke in two although enough remained of her forward section for gunboat *Kazan Maru* to take the hulk in tow. *Kazan*'s skipper, however, abandoned *Taibu*'s remnants as a total loss on 6 May.[4]

*Parche* continued swinging left to allow her stern tubes to fire their four fish at the third ship in column. At 0110 as *Parche* was completing her turn, two hits were observed on the second freighter, "which began settling rapidly by the stern." This ship was later identified as the 5,949-ton freighter *Kinrei Maru*. Japanese records would show that *Kinrei* was hit in her starboard No. 3 hold at 0106 and sank by stern with the loss of six lives.[5]

Numerous explosions were heard during this period, most assumed to be depth charges. All hell had broken loose in the convoy and the third target began zigging wildly and opening up the range before *Parche* could fire again to unleash her after room war fish. By 0120, the second freighter *Taiyoku Maru* had sunk and the remaining convoy vessels were firing their deck guns wildly into the night. Ramage's plotting team struggled to line up the evading ships during the next eight minutes. Ramage found that every time he tried to bring his stern tubes to bear "this fellow would open up with machine-gun fire."[6]

His torpedo officer, Frank Allcorn, sensed the skipper's desire to strike the convoy again and asked for permission to reload the bow tubes with Mark 14 steam torpedoes.

"This was something that was absolutely unheard-of," Ramage related. "No one had ever considered reloading the torpedoes with the submarine on the surface charging around at 20 knots in contact with the enemy and subject to dive without notice. Once you get those torpedoes out of the rack, they're just like a greased pig. You could lose control of them and they would really mash people up."[7]

Lieutenant Allcorn insisted that his men were prepared for the dangers involved. Don Walters' forward gang, in fact, had already cleared the bunks

Extra hands pitch in to prepare a celebration cake in *Parche*'s galley. Left–right are: Francis Stammen, baker Howard McMahon, Don Green, Walter Ekelund, Philip Bukowski and "LB" Frederick. *Courtesy of Bob Hall.*

out of the way and Allcorn assured his skipper that his men could safely effect the reload on the surface.

"All right, then, go ahead," Ramage allowed.

Walters' crew quickly manhandled more 3,000-pound torpedoes into the tubes during the 15 minutes following their first firing. The torpedomen had to carefully align the gyro, depth setting, and aiming mechanisms on each while their boat pitched and rolled on the surface in pursuit of the convoy.

Ramage finally settled on the largest remaining freighter, the 6,400-ton *Taibu Maru*, and *Parche* fired four more torpedoes at 0127. She fired all four forward tubes. One minute later, two torpedoes hit, one amidships and one aft, blowing out the after mast. The target freighter opened fire with her 20-mms down the torpedoes' track. Ramage noted that her fire came "close aboard over our stern." Two minutes after the hits, this freighter was settling by the stern and listing to port, apparently dead in the water.

*Parche* continued to circle the area until 0140, when her radar picked up another submarine to port. This was *Bang* closing in to attack, so Ramage hauled clear of the convoy to give her room and to reload her own torpedo tubes. By 0150, the radar pip for *Parche*'s third victim had disappeared from the scope. "Target last seen listing heavily to port with deck awash," Ramage wrote. *Parche* reloaded and then turned back at 0220, but within five minutes the sounds of more explosions could be heard as *Bang* made another attack on the convoy. John Gray soon had the convoy on his radar at 13,000 yards, but luck was not with *Parche* this time.

"At 0245 our gyrocompass failed, effectively neutralizing our fire control system," plotting officer Bob Erwin recalled. To further complicate matters, the moon came out from behind the clouds and made *Parche* quite visible. One of the Japanese escorts spotted her and turned to pursue. Ramage took evasive action and headed his boat toward the nearest rain squall to shake his attacker. The gyro was soon brought back into service but the good ships of the convoy were hard to find. Radar and sighting reports were all small ships, likely escorts. Ramage was forced to dodge another pesky escort as he continued to maneuver about the fleeing ships in the predawn hours.[8]

More torpedo explosions were heard at 0515 as *Tinosa* attacked. *Tinosa* radioed at 0550 that she had sunk two ships and damaged two others. The convoy had certainly taken a beating, as Ramage took in the scene: "All the escorts seemed to be searching the area aimlessly for their ships that were not there."

Dawn was beginning to break so Ramage was forced to dive while still searching for any remaining targets. Distant depth charging was heard through the morning as the escorts flailed about to exact revenge. Post-war records credited the trio of submarines with five ships sunk for 30,542 tons, *Parche* getting credit for three cargo ships. Of the six major freighters of this convoy, five had gone down and only *Yulin Maru* arrived safely in Takeo.

At 2025 on 4 May, Commander Peterson directed *Bang* and *Tinosa* to head for home, as they were both out of torpedoes. *Parche* sent a detailed dispatch that night describing her attacks. Skipper Ramage made a tour through the boat to congratulate his men. Cory Maupin found it interesting that the skipper even stopped to rub the little Buddha's belly for good luck and thank him for their success. Ray Karr found the skipper to be outgoing with the crew after attacks while Exec Mac McCrory was "straight-laced and strictly business with his enlisted men."

*Parche* remained on station on 5 May, watching Japanese aircraft while submerged. She surfaced that evening and picked up a small ship with her

SJ radar at 2113. Ramage stationed his tracking party and commenced an end around to pursue the ship, which had been picked up at 21,000 yards. The Japanese ship was making 14 knots, meaning overtaking her would be a slow process as the evening passed into 6 May. The range dropped to 14,000 yards and Ramage called his crew to battle stations. When the range had decreased to 10,000 yards ten minutes later, he submerged to prepare for an attack.

By 0024, the range had closed to 6,000 yards. Radar indicated interference from a sweeping type radar. "By this time we were suspicious of a trap but continued our approach," recalled Bob Erwin. The skipper was soon able to identify this small ship as a patrol boat or sub chaser and pinging was heard. At this inopportune moment, diving officer Dave Green allowed *Parche* to broach as the boat came up to periscope depth. She rose to 30 feet with her decks awash. The patrol boat suddenly stopped sweeping with his radar and locked onto the submarine. "Looked like a trap as target had slowed to eight knots," Ramage wrote.[9]

He broke off the attack and took his boat to 200 feet to evade the pinging escort. *Parche* stayed down for an hour to open up the distance. When she returned to the surface the escort was still pinging but had fallen back to a safer 12,000-yard distance.

*Parche* moved south of Takao during the next days, which proved to be long hours of fruitless searching along the Bashi Channel lanes off Formosa. Her efforts were rewarded with only sightings of sampans and small trawlers.

Carl Kimmons and James McGuire, the steward's mates, kept fresh coffee brewing for the duty officers. When called upon, they were often able to visit the bridge to deliver coffee. "It was always a pleasure going to the bridge because it would give the steward a chance to breathe some fresh air—and maybe spend a few moments there gazing at the scenery," recalled Kimmons.[10]

When the ship was not at battle stations, McGuire and Kimmons carried out their daily routines. "Lunch and dinner were prepared by the ship's cook in the galley, and we just transported them to the pantry," Kimmons related. "After breakfast, we cleaned the wardroom, the pantry, the officers' rooms (including making the beds), and the forward battery."

Mess cook Bob Hall put in many hours in the galley as he worked with Johnny Johnson, Dan Hayes, and Howard McMahon to become a baker. "I didn't do any real baking on my first patrol," he recalled. "As a mess cook, I washed dishes, peeled potatoes and set tables. If they needed flour in the galley, the mess cook had to fetch a 25-pound square tin of flour." Hall had to crawl behind the engines in the after engine room to retrieve the heavy tub of flour. "Those engines were damn hot," he recalled.

*Parche* passed through the Bashi Channel, spotting only three fishing vessels to the north as she did. During the night of 13 May, those topside could see the navigation light of Kasho To Island. One sampan and two small trawlers were seen close to the beach during the morning as *Parche* ran submerged about six miles off the coast of Formosa.

Captain Peterson opted to make a thorough photo reconnaissance of military installations on the island of Ishi Gaki Jima on 14 May. Throughout the day, heavy air traffic was noted over the island and the watch observed a bombing practice. *Parche*'s officers watched aircraft land and take off throughout the day and plotted the position of two radio towers. "Considerable truck traffic was noted along the dusty dirt roads," Ramage logged. Periscope photos were taken of the entire island and its installations before *Parche* surfaced that evening to retire from the area.

Ramage ran his boat on the surface during the next 48 hours. On the afternoon of 16 May, the boat was running on the surface at 14.5 knots when one of the lookouts spotted a periscope and shears that appeared to be American. Jim Campbell alerted the skipper and kept a cautious eye on the other submarine's movements. "The other boat apparently was not sure of us as she reversed course and followed us astern," recalled Bob Erwin. "We also reversed course and exchanged calls by using sound gear." The other submarine was identified as the *Perch II* and they proceeded on their way.[11]

*Parche* sent a message late on 16 May that she was departing her patrol area and she passed between Kita Iwo Jima and Iwo Jima the next day. The SD radar picked up an aircraft contact at eight miles at 1011 on 19 May. Bob Erwin, who was sharing the OOD duties with John Parks, recalled, "Since we could not see him we assumed he was low." Erwin pulled the diving alarm and the lookouts scrambled down from the shears to drop through the hatch. "Before we cleared the bridge we could clearly see the plane coming in low on our beam," said Erwin.[12]

Within a minute, *Parche* was submerged and clawing for 200-foot depth. At 1014, one light aircraft bomb exploded above fairly close.

*Parche* resurfaced 20 minutes later and continued to clear the area at 17 knots. Lookouts sighted an enemy trawler a mere 1,000 yards away that night at 2010. Ramage decided to give his rapid-fire gun crews some action and he changed course to close this vessel three minutes later. Bob Erwin had the deck for this action. The bridge gunners manned the 20-mms and the .50-caliber guns as the ammunition was hoisted to the bridge.

*Parche* opened fire with her automatic weapons at 2023. Visibility was poor and Ramage made three runs on the little trawler. The small guns were ineffective and suffered several stoppages. The Japanese on board their vessel began returning fire with .25-caliber guns. "The night was so dark that the target could not be seen at 500 yards while firing," Ramage logged. "This prevented spotting and precluded the use of the deck gun." During the exchange of fire, the trawler got in two good bursts, obtaining numerous hits on *Parche*'s superstructure and conning tower fairwater. "By the grace of God, no casualties resulted."

At 2100, Ramage opted to break off the attack to avoid any further damage to his boat. "When we heard the Jap .25-caliber bullets cracking like firecrackers around our ears, we cleared the bridge," related Erwin. "The Japanese .25-cal bullet velocity is supersonic thus there is a distinct sonic crack as the bullets pass." Ramage had seven of his crewmen on *Trout* wounded during such a gun exchange and he was not willing to suffer a repeat. "One of the reasons I chose the Navy over the Army and submarine duty over DDs was to avoid being shot at," thought Erwin. "I wondered about that decision on this occasion."[13]

Larry Lawrence, one of the radiomen on duty in the control room at the time, recalled Lieutenant (jg) Erwin pounding down the ladder in his excitement and exclaiming, "The little bastards are shooting at us!"

Ramage had had orders to clear this sea lane by 0600 as the area was restricted for U.S. surface vessels in the area. *Parche* rang up her best speed in order to clear the area. She had cleared the restricted area by 0900 on 20 May and she slowed to 17 knots while en route to Midway.

The remainder of her run into Midway was uneventful. Ramage and his officers worked with Yeoman Warren Dingman on writing up the patrol report. Ramage wrote that this run did "demonstrate the advantages of the wolf pack and prove that they can be effectively employed" to more fully exploit every contact. He felt without the spread of *Parche*, *Tinosa*, and *Bang* over a larger area that "neither convoy would have been sighted." With larger and more heavily guarded convoys, Ramage thought "the odds against the lone wolf are manifestly increased."

Ramage felt "communication between all boats was excellent and the frequencies were shifted daily without difficulty. However, on both occasions once contact had been made, a continuous exchange of information could and should have been maintained between all boats."

The wardroom found humor in some of the small things. On board a submarine, even the use of the head was not without its dangers. Waste from the toilets and washbasins drained into two sanitary waste tanks that were flushed out into the ocean each night by an auxiliaryman. The intake was closed and high pressure air blew the waste out through a valve opening.

"After the tank was emptied he would close the opening to the sea and vent the air pressure in the tank," related Bob Erwin. "At least twice I remember the last step was not done or was only partially done." During *Parche*'s first patrol, Ens. Bill Bergen was the first victim as he used the same forward torpedo room head. When he flushed the toilet, "the effluent went up instead of down." There were no serious consequences to Bergen's mishap other than an unscheduled shower to remove the filth.[14]

During the return run, Johnny Johnson and his cooks notified the officers that *Parche*'s stores still included an ample supply of the Argentina steak picked up in Balboa during the boat's Panama Canal transit months before. Knowing that this meat would be removed during the refit at Midway, Johnson was given the go-ahead to use it all up. The crew enjoyed steaks for lunch, dinner, and even breakfast during the next few days.

Commissary officer Bob Erwin had to come up with some creative accounting to justify such an expense of red meat. He was only allotted so many dollars per day per man for food and his crew was far surpassing his quotas. "We had a lot of unusual 'spoilage' that we wrote off as unusable even though we had eaten it," he admitted. Ramage worked with Erwin to "survey" enough meat—declaring it "bad"—that the commissary report worked out just fine.[15]

She crossed the international date line at 2340 on 23 May and gained a day. On her second 23 May, she entered Midway's lagoon, Ramage docking her at 1057 along the port side of *Bang*, nested with *Proteus*, and ended her first war patrol. The crew was given a grand welcome at the sub base, with all of the brass on dock to greet them. Even better was the bag of mail and fresh milk and ice cream. Each man was allowed to send a brief radiogram home to his family. "The messages we were allowed to send consisted of three numbers that designated three phrases," Erwin related. "The numbers only we radioed to Western Union, where the words were added and sent on to the proper addresses. The message might come out as, 'I am back to base well. The letters were welcome. I love you.' "

*Parche* had made 16 shipping contacts and sighted 31 Japanese planes. She had departed on patrol with 81 men aboard, 43 of whom had been unqualified for submarine duty. During the patrol, 34 of these men had successfully passed their exams by knowing every inch of the boat and how each part of the boat was operated. Of the officers, mustangs Bill Bergen and John Parks had previously qualified while enlisted men. Jim Campbell and Bob Erwin, the only unqualified officers to start the run, both earned their coveted dolphins but it had been a physically trying first run for both. "I left Midway for patrol weighing 160 pounds and returned weighing 145 in spite of good food and no seasickness," recalled Erwin.[16]

Total tonnage of enemy shipping damaged or destroyed for *Parche*'s first war patrol was more than 25,000 tons. The Submarine Combat Insignia was awarded for her highly successful maiden patrol. The patrol endorsements were good. Of Ramage, Lew Parks noted, "The skill of a veteran Commanding Officer is evident in the highly proficient manner in which the attacks were conducted." Parks also felt it "was desirable to continue the practice of sending out these organized attack groups." He credited *Parche*'s crew with sinking three ships for 23,900 tons. Capt. Leo L. Pace, group commander of Submarine Squadron Twenty, added his blessing to Parks' endorsement, writing the crew had made an "exceptionally well-conducted patrol."

The *Parche* would also later be awarded the Presidential Unit Citation for her first and second patrols on 25 August 1945. Red Ramage was recommended for his second Navy Cross. He was therefore authorized to recommend two Silver Stars and three Bronze Stars to his crew. The actual approval and presentation of these awards would take several months but Ramage recommended the Silver Stars to assistant approach officer Mac McCrory and to radar operator John Gray. Bronze Stars would later be presented to fire controlman Sam Roberts, Ens. John Parks, Torpedoman Don Walters, and battle helmsman Chet Stanton.

Ramage listed torpedo performance and equipment issues in his report. He also cited the good food available on this run. "We are extremely fortunate in having two cooks who possess the rare faculty of being able to make the average dishes appear to be blue plate specials in both taste and appearance." He also praised his crew, saying that "all hands met every situation and emergency like seasoned veterans." He specifically cited Lieutenant Commander McCrory for perfectly coordinating the fire control parties and Lieutenant Allcorn for his fire control solutions and torpedo direction. RT1c Gray was commended for his excellent work on tracking ships with the radar and for keeping the key electronic equipment running.

The ship sinkings made by U.S. submarines were assessed postwar by the Joint Army-Navy Assessment Committee (JANAC). They cut *Parche*'s claims to two ships sunk plus others damaged. John Alden, who published two books on the submarine sinkings of World War II, had access to the declassified Ultra information for his second book, plus a number of Japanese sources not available to JANAC. In his credits to *Parche*, he found that she had certainly destroyed two ships and that *Bang* and *Tinosa* likely polished off at least one other ship that *Parche* had already damaged.

Pack commander Peterson was glowing with pride following the return of America's fourth-ever wolf pack. In his reports, he claimed eleven Japanese ships sunk and six more damaged for a total tonnage of 116,250. Although these figures were obviously overestimated, Adm. Charles Lockwood was thoroughly impressed with how *Parche* and her packmates had carried out their coordinated attacks so well. "In the second convoy attack," wrote Lockwood, "the *Tinosa* made the initial contact and all three were able to make a series of running attacks at night, which practically eliminated the convoy."

### USS *Parche* First War Patrol Summary

| | |
|---|---|
| Departure From: | Pearl Harbor/Midway |
| Patrol Area: | Formosa area |
| Time Period: | 29 March–23 May 1944 |
| Number of Men On Board: | 81: 73 enlisted and 8 officers |
| Total Days on Patrol: | 55 |
| Miles Steamed: | 11,090 |
| Number of Torpedoes Fired: | 14 |
| Wartime Ships Sunk Credit: | 3/23,900 tons |
| JANAC Postwar Credit: | 2/11,700 tons |
| John Alden Postwar Credit: | 2/12,389 tons |
| Shipping Damage Claimed: | 2/12,940 tons |
| Return To: | Midway |

# CHAPTER FIVE

# Parks' Pirates

There were three great pleasures in being a submarine man," according to motormac Dick Hawn. One of these pleasures was "the quality and abundance" of good food aboard the boats. Another was the rest and recuperation period following a war patrol. But first on Hawn's list of three great pleasures "was arriving back in port at the conclusion of a war patrol. At the beginning of the patrol we lived off the fresh food we had brought with us but towards the end of the patrol we ran out of fresh food and lived on canned, dried and frozen food."[1]

Hawn enjoyed the Navy band playing to greet them dockside and the customary visit from the base commander and his staff who came on board to congratulate them. Better yet for Hawn were the bags of mail awaiting the men and the "case after case of fresh fruit and containers of fresh milk. I can remember sitting on deck and eating four fresh cantaloupes one right after the other, washing them down with fresh milk."

Signalman Claude Lutz, finding himself with nothing better to do after *Parche* docked, volunteered to pass out the mail to the crew. "There were 53 letters and two packages waiting for me," recalled Lt. (jg) Bob Erwin. "I remember that the packages contained, among other things, crushed cookies and a lock of [his daughter] Sandy's hair." Electrician Lonnie Hughes read a letter from his wife Nancy in which he "got the best news of my life"—he was soon due to become a father.[2]

Top receiver among the enlisted men was Johnny Barnes with 15 pieces of mail, followed by cook Dan Hayes with 10 and Bill Fisk with "God only knows." Lutz had written a letter to his wife every five days but found that in return she had only sent two to him. Feeling a little down on his own luck, he decided that he would have to read them more than once.

Submarine Division 202's relief crew began the process of refitting *Parche* upon her arrival at Midway on 23 May. Most of the crew was relieved of duty at 0900 and they were allowed to go ashore for rest and recuperation (R&R). The officers moved into the little hotel that had once served passengers of the Pan Am Trans Pacific's flights. By this time in 1944, the atoll was largely a submarine refueling and refitting post for boats heading out or returning from patrol. Only a small faction of Marines remained on the island as base guards.

The submarine tender *Proteus* and her relief crew handled most of the minor voyage repairs that were required following *Parche*'s first war run. During the next two weeks, minor improvements were made to the boat. Among these was the installation of an air-conditioning unit with a booster blower in the control room to alleviate the excessive heat. *Parche* also received a preamplifier for her SD aircraft-detecting radar, an APR-1 radar detector to pick up signals from friendly and enemy aircraft, and IFF (Identification Friend or Foe) equipment. Although the crew was not required to participate in this work, many of the officers and chiefs made frequent visits during their R&R to check the progress and to help alleviate their own boredom with Midway.

Many found little to do but drink beer, gamble, sleep, write letters, and relax. Torpedoman Chuck Gooden was familiar with the boredom of Midway from prior liberties during his service on *Gato*. "I wasn't much of a gambler," he recalled. "Any time I got into a game, I lost my money pretty quickly and then had to find other ways to pass the time." Some of Gooden's buddies tried feeding beer to the ever-present gooney birds but even this sport was only interesting for so long. Swimming and soft-ball games helped to pass the time. Others took the chance to pass their submarine qualifications exams and earn their coveted dolphin pins. The officers had their own club to visit for mixed drinks in the evenings while the enlisted men enjoyed their daily beer rations.

Bob Erwin found that some of his fellow officers were eager to try and beat the "Midway Special" drink contest. "The bartender had a stand-ing offer," he recalled. "Anyone who could sit at the bar, consume two Midway Specials in a half hour and walk unaided out the door about 20 feet away could drink free for his stay. Many tried and failed." The enlisted men found their own forms of dark humor. "One crew member took the opportunity to be circumcised and when there were complications he provided a few laughs by walking around with his bandage showing and eating a pickle," Erwin wrote. "Lt. Green as designated Medical Officer had stopped the pharmacist's mate [Quentin Brown] from performing this operation as we were coming home from patrol, so he had it done at the base infirmary."[3]

One of Midway's ever-present gooney birds. *Courtesy of Bob Hall.*  Chiefs Clarence Allard and Mark Goding at Midway. *Courtesy of Ray Karr.*

Ray Karr and his buddies found additional recreational activity in the form of deep sea fishing. Using whaleboats acquired from the Navy rest camp staff, "we spent several hours rod and reel fishing for albacore tuna with no luck. So we took out some hand grenades from our lunch pack and tried them," said Karr. "A couple of *boom*s underwater brought up enough fish to feed the whole Rest Camp mess hall. The cooks couldn't believe it. They were used to a few or no fish coming in off these fishing trips. We never told them 'the rest of the story,' as Paul Harvey would say."

During this liberty period, *Parche*'s crew went through the normal process of transferring veteran sailors on to other duties, often back to the States to help commission new boats. Fifteen members of the crew were transferred to new assignments including Chief of the Boat Luther Parker. Chief Electrician's Mate Verlin Peterson, by virtue of experience, was tapped to move into the key role of chief of the boat prior to *Parche*'s second run. His watch schedule remained intact thanks to Dick Hawn's promotion to chief motor machinist's mate. Notable among the key replacements were new senior signalman George Plume to replace CQM Sprague, ship's cook Lamar Brown to replace Dan Hayes, and veteran gunner's mate James Plumley for Leroy Swettenam.

Electrician Lonnie Hughes collected autographs and notes from several of his departing shipmates, including Harold Staggs, Ed Gubaney, Chester Loveless, and Leroy Swettenam. Fellow electrician Loveless wrote, "I haven't known you very long so I hope it is just the beginning of a long friendship. We are parting now but may we meet again through the years to come." Tragically, Loveless would be lost several months later when the USS *Tang* was sunk by her own circling torpedo and only nine men survived to be picked up by the Japanese as POWs.

Red Ramage's wardroom endured its fair share of changes. Mustang officers Bill Bergen and John Parks were transferred. In return, *Parche* received two new officers, Ens. Bob Ashe, a Reservist from New York, and Lt. (jg) Edward Rauscher—both making their first war patrols. Following his graduation from Vanderbilt, Ed Rauscher had attended midshipman school at Notre Dame and then three months of additional schooling at Northwestern. He returned as an instructor at the midshipman school at Notre Dame for eight months while awaiting his request for submarine duty to go through. Finally able to get in, Rauscher went through pre–submarine training at San Diego and then New London before being sent to the relief crews in the Pacific. Commander Ramage, intent upon adding an extra watchstander to his wardroom, secured a third new officer on 8 June in the form of Lt. (jg) Robert Thompson Stevenson, a bachelor Reservist from South Carolina who was also new to submarines.

*Parche*'s crew returned on board on 7 June and started loading stores in preparation for her next war patrol. Work was paused long enough this day for Capt. Leo Pace to come on board for a presentation of the combat insignia pins to commemorate the boat's first successful war patrol. *Parche* then proceeded to conduct three days of independent training in the form of collision drills, fire drills, and crash dives. The drills took on a note of authenticity on the first day when a real fire broke out in the No. 2 air-conditioning unit panel. Alert leading electrician Lonnie Hughes and his companions stopped this fire within two minutes, but not before many among the crew experienced the anxiety of a true emergency at sea.[4]

Mark 14 practice torpedoes were fired during the next three days and new gun captain Jim Plumley had the chance to drill his men on battle surface action with the 20-mm, the 4-inch deck gun, and the .50-caliber machine guns. *Parche* also participated in coordinated attack training exercises with the submarines *Hammerhead* (SS-364) and *Steelhead* (SS-280). *Parche* practiced end-around radar approaches and fired six training torpedoes in concert with training vessels *Litchfield*, *PC 603*, and *Greenlet*.

The training days were long and intense but the training and direction of senior officers Red Ramage and Mac McCrory made them successful. Many of the crew idolized their skipper while a few felt that their XO (Executive Officer) was less appealing due to his willingness to crack the whip for discipline when it was called for. Junior officer Bob Erwin

Capt. Leo Pace hands out combat insignia pins to the *Parche* crew following the first patrol. Chief Commissary Steward Charlie "Johnny" Johnson is receiving his pin. Moving to the right from Pace are Red Ramage, Frank Allcorn, Jim Campbell (partially obscured), and Mac McCrory. S1c Bob Gubaney is behind Johnson. *Courtesy of Jim Campbell and Bob Erwin.*

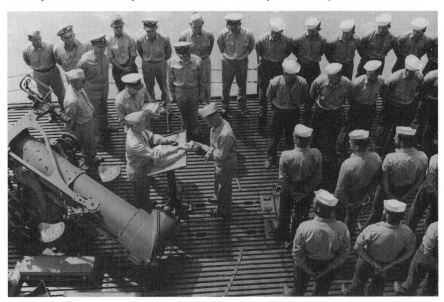

Awards presentation at Midway on 7 June 1944. Capt. Pace presents Lt. Cdr. Mac McCrory with combat pin. Officers seen in background (left–right) are: Bob Erwin, John Parks, Cdr. Lew Parks, Bill Bergen, Dave Green, Cdr. Ramage, Frank Allcorn (behind Ramage), and Jim Campbell. *Submarine Force Museum, New London, Connecticut.*

*Parche*'s crew after the first war patrol on 7 June. Officers, front row (left–right): Bob Erwin, John Parks, Bill Bergen, Mac McCrory, Red Ramage, Dave Green, Frank Allcorn, and Jim Campbell. Second row (left–right): CMoMM Allard, CMoMM Hawn, CCS Johnson, CQM Sprague, CMoMM Goding, CEM Peterson, CTM Parker, CMoMM Mathews (in green cap behind Allcorn), TM2c Mo Taylor, and QM3c John O'Brien. *Courtesy of Bob Hall.*

recalled that McCrory and Ramage's training bordered at times "on slave driving but they were both generally liked and respected."[5]

*Parche* took on a fresh load of Mark 14 steam torpedoes. Ramage was at least convinced now that Frank Allcorn's torpedomen could safely and successfully effect reloads on the surface in case that tactic might be required again.[6]

*Parche* was deemed ready for sea again on 17 June and Commander Ramage mustered his crew at quarters at 0750. All hands were accounted for and preparations commenced to head to sea once again on war patrol. Officer's cook Chiriaco Sanchez, a Filipino attendant, came aboard at 0755 from the Submarine Division 202's staff, a move that sparked some scuttlebutt from those not in the know. Any questions concerning the new attendant were quickly relieved when Commander Lew Parks stepped on board at 0915 to take command of a new wolf pack with *Parche* as his flagship.

Parks was the most combat-experienced pack commander to date to take a coordinated submarine group on patrol. He had made three war patrols in command of *Pompano* and had earned two Navy Crosses for his successes in 1942. Parks had then been assigned to the staff of Commander

Submarines, Atlantic Fleet Tommy Withers and had helped to check out *Parche* at New London during her shakedown cruise. He returned to Pearl Harbor in November 1943 as a full commander to assume the supervision of Submarine Division 202.[7]

Lew Parks was an advocate of periscope photography and even carried his own movie camera equipment aboard *Parche*. A husky, six-foot-tall 42-year-old, Commander Parks had wavy, black hair and thick, black eyebrows that made some *Parche* sailors think that he looked like actor Fred MacMurray. He was somewhat familiar to the crew, as well. "Parks had been with us in the cold North Atlantic on our shakedown cruise as well as the trials in New London," Bob Erwin related. The crew was somewhat relieved at the pack commander's casual nature on board their boat, where Parks was prone to wear sandals with loose-fitting polo shirts tucked into his khakis. Red Ramage was a little relieved that his new senior passenger at least had more combat experience than his last division leader.[8]

---

*Parche* was once again slated to head to sea as part of a wolf pack or coordinated attack group—the Navy's eleventh ever organized. Red Ramage's second patrol area was again to be south of Formosa in company with the submarines *Hammerhead* and *Steelhead*, with Commander Parks as the group commander of Coordinated Attack Group 17.15. *Hammerhead*, under Cdr. John Croysdale Martin, was a new boat and Cdr. David Lee Whelchel had the *Steelhead*.

The new wolf pack was called "Parks' Pirates." Red Ramage's other pack name idea had gone unused. "I was more or less inclined to refer to it as the 'Head Hunters' because they had the *Steelhead*, the *Hammerhead*, and the red head," he later related.[9]

Ramage immediately perceived a difference with his division commander. George Peterson, his pack commander on the previous patrol, had no combat experience and "was going to go along with anything and take any suggestions." Lew Parks, however, had a true feel for attacks as a former skipper and "was pretty much a stickler for detail," Ramage said.[10]

Frank Allcorn recalled that Ramage made it clear to Parks early on that he was the skipper. "Red established that early. Parks contributed *to*, rather than *made*, decisions." Some of Ramage's officers had become aware of the fact that the division commander would be making a run on the *Parche* a few days before he actually reported on board. Bob Erwin was still the commissary officer at the time of the boat's provisioning. "I had been advised to have scrapple for breakfasts and avocet (stabilized cream) for his desserts," he recalled. "This caused my early impressions of him to be not too good. As it turned out I enjoyed both him and his cook."[11]

With the wardroom changes, Commander Ramage shuffled the duties of some of his junior officers before leaving Midway. Erwin was promoted to first lieutenant. He was in charge of the quartermaster gang, unattached seamen, and was generally responsible for the boat's cleanliness, topside gear, navigation systems, anchors, ropes, and exterior lights. He felt that as commissary officer he had been the "chief cook" and that his "promotion" was akin to becoming the boat's "chief janitor." Erwin retained his additional role as assistant gunnery officer and battle stations plotting officer. Bob Ashe stepped into his former position of commissary officer for the second patrol.[12]

By 0930 on 17 June, *Parche*'s diesels were rumbling. Yeoman Dingman passed the official sailing list over to division command on *Proteus* shortly before *Parche* backed away from her berth and steered for Midway's channel entrance buoys. Packmate *Steelhead* steamed in the lead and *Hammerhead* brought up the rear seven miles astern of *Parche* as the pack headed for their assigned patrol area.

Chief Johnny Johnson and his two cooks, Howard McMahon and Lamar Brown, settled into their daily routine of turning out hot meals for 83 officers and men. They were assisted by Bob Hall, the mess cook who was beginning to take on more duties in his effort to become *Parche*'s baker. Hall was pleased any time he found willing hands to pitch in with the galley work at night. Glenn Meise, a newly reported radioman who had once worked as a mailman before joining the Navy, was one of them. Meise enjoyed peanut butter, which required a strong arm to mix the oily top layer of the large containers to create a consistent blend. "Glenn became the official peanut butter mixer," Hall related. "We had the stuff in number ten cans and it wasn't getting mixed to go on the tables so Glenn volunteered his time and muscle to help us out."

Meise, a man of Scottish ancestry who hailed from Akron, Ohio, was working in the blacksmith and welding shop at the Goodyear apprentice school in 1942 when his best friend Bob Burgoon convinced him that they should enlist in the Navy to avoid an Army draft. "I agreed that it would be better sailing on the sea than trudging somewhere in the mud," Meise recalled. Upon completing boot camp at the Great Lakes Naval Training Center, he was sent to radio operators' school at Miami University in

Oxford, Ohio. One day, the instructor sent around a paper asking for volunteers for submarine service.[13]

"I immediately passed the paper to the guy on my left without even thinking of volunteering," wrote Meise. When the other man explained that the Silent Service offered 50 percent extra pay, Meise quickly snatched the sheet back and signed it. At the New London sub school, the young radioman—a poor swimmer—narrowly passed his swimming test one evening with an instructor who was more preoccupied by missing his own liberty than verifying that Meise was a good swimmer.

Meise may have questioned his own desire for the Navy over the Army as he rode the sub tender *Proteus* from San Francisco to Pearl Harbor. He could not keep his food down in the rolling seas during his first day. Forced to go on duty at midnight in the radio shack, Meise sat at the operator's position "with a bucket between my legs and each time the ship rolled, I was throwing up."[14]

Eight of the fifteen new hands aboard were third class or lower in rating. The officers and senior petty officers spent several days a week training their new submariners for their duties and helping them to strike for a proper rating in various departments. Three of *Parche*'s new enlisted men—S2 Paul William "Bill" Gilcher, F1 Ed Mokos, and F2 Charlie McNutt—became close friends.

Fireman Second Class Charlie McNutt had registered for the draft against his mother's wishes in October 1942 in Chicago after he turned 18. He wanted to make it into submarines so much that he had endured two attempts in the 100-foot escape tower at New London. On his first try, he was unable to equalize ("crack") his ears and he was put on mess cooking for a week without liberty. When his next attempt came to escape the tower, McNutt was determined despite the pain he began feeling. He had made up his mind that he would "crack my ears or bust same" in the process. Chief Charlie Spritz was a tough teacher and McNutt was not about to fail a second time.[15]

He passed and completed schooling and joined the tender *Proteus* as part of the relief crew. His lucky break in getting aboard a combat submarine came when he ran into senior electrician Verlin Peterson, who had been one of his trainers during electrical school.

"Do you want to come on board?" Peterson asked.

"I'd love to," replied McNutt. Exec Mac McCrory soon welcomed him into the crew. McNutt was teamed up with two other unqualified new hands, Bill Gilcher from the little town of Freeport, Ohio, and Ed Mokos from his own hometown of Chicago. He found that Mokos was an easy-going guy who had once sung in his church choir but was not afraid to live it up a little while on liberty. Due to the limited number of bunks on board, Gilcher found that he had to hot-bunk with another new shipmate, Charles Welton.

"When we came onboard ship, we didn't know anything," McNutt admitted. "You weren't allowed to touch the valves or anything until you were fully qualified, so they put the three of us on mess-cooking duty." Gilcher, McNutt, and Mokos reported to senior cook Charlie Johnson in the galley where they soon found that preparing meals for a crew of more than 80 was an endless routine.

*Parche, Steelhead,* and *Hammerhead* conducted exercises and training dives en route to station. Jim Campbell felt that Ramage and Exec McCrory "trained, trained, trained" their new men on their duties until "they could do it in the dark. Training made all the difference." *Parche* proceeded to her station with her pack mates for the first few days while running mainly on the surface, zigzagging at 14.5 knots. The deck officer teams rotated every four hours to keep them alert.[16]

Navigator Mac McCrory went to the bridge shortly before the morning dive and after *Parche* had surfaced each night in order to take a navigational fix. SM1c George Plume had become his navigational assistant for this patrol. As the Exec and Plume were taking their star sights one night, McCrory was surprised to find that one of his new lookouts knew exactly what he was doing.

Seaman First Class Charlie Welton, who had come on board during the refit at Midway, had taken a course on celestial navigation while he was attending high school in Nantucket. "I always had a fascination with the sea and had a vision that I would end up there one day," he recalled. Welton had attended torpedo school and had made a run on *Kingfish* as a torpedoman striker before joining *Parche*. Assigned to Carroll Kinkel's after torpedo room, he was also among the usual evening rotation for topside lookout watches. As he chatted with Lieutenant Commander McCrory on the bridge, he realized his schooling in navigation was more formal education that his Exec had been given in his own on-the-job training. "So, here I was this young kid who knew about as much as this officer who was doing our star sights for navigation," Welton mused.

During the early evening of 21 June, pack commander Lew Parks rendezvoused his flagship *Parche* with *Steelhead* and *Hammerhead* for a brief update on patrol instructions while cruising at eight knots. Parks

F1c Ed Mokos from Chicago was nearly lost overboard during his fifth day on board *Parche*. Mokos is seen here atop the shoulder of shipmate Tony Herman at a ship's party in 1945. *Courtesy of Charles McNutt.*

had deck hands fire over a line to each boat with his instructions for their daily operations upon reaching their patrol area. The three boats quickly resumed a 12-knot speed toward station.

---

For fireman Ed Mokos, his fifth day on submarines was almost his last. Just two hours after the wolf pack had completed its rendezvous on 21 June, Mokos proceeded to carry out a seemingly mundane topside task. As one of the galley's mess cooks, he and buddies Bill Gilcher and Charlie McNutt were often in charge of disposing of the daily garbage that accumulated in the course of feeding 83 sailors.

New Radioman Glenn Meise had been amused watching this garbage detail during one of his first nights on JP sonar watch in the conning tower. Several new sailors were hauling the day's garbage up the conning tower ladder in burlap bags. "One of the guys was having trouble getting the weighted sack through the hatch up to the bridge," wrote Miese. The sailor tugged on the pants leg of the guy in front of him and asked if he could lend a hand with the bags. "Little did he know that he was pulling on the pant leg of the skipper!" Meise recalled.[17]

The garbage detail took a more serious turn on the night of 21 June, however. McNutt was in the control room passing the weighted bags up to Paul Gilcher in the conning tower. "Gilcher, Mokos, and I took turns on who would go up and toss the bags at night," said McNutt. Mokos asked

OOD Bob Erwin for permission to come on deck to toss the bags. Erwin gave his approval and Gilcher passed the bags to Mokos on the ladder. As Mokos came topside, he could see the seas were pretty rough this night.

"Here you go," said Gilcher as he passed the trash up to Mokos.

Mokos noted how dark it was as he headed to toss the trash. He picked the wrong side of the bridge, to the starboard side where the rough seas were slapping at *Parche*. Suddenly a large swell smacked heavily against *Parche*'s side at 2055 and Mokos felt the water rising up above his knees. The seas suddenly lifted him right off the conning tower and he was pulled from the ship.[18]

As he was washed overboard, gut instinct took over and he clawed to fight his way back. In the rush of the current, his right arm slammed against a stanchion of the after ladder and he grasped it amid the pain of his battered arm. "Man overboard!" shouted one of the lookouts.

Lieutenant (jg) Erwin immediately commenced the man overboard drill as he shouted orders to go all back emergency, flip on the searchlights, and make ready the life preservers. He was much relieved within a moment to hear the after lookout's call, "Mr. Campbell has him on the after deck."[19]

The alert junior officer of the deck, Jim Campbell, saw Mokos being swept away and he raced aft to help. Finding the mess cook clinging to a pipe column supporting the stairs to the bridge, Campbell grasped Mokos and helped haul him back up the ladder.

Cold and soaking wet, Mokos was assisted back down through the conning tower. Pharmacist's mate Quentin Brown gave him a shot of medicinal brandy and the skipper allowed him to hit the shower to warm up. The first thing Red Ramage said to Mokos when he found him in the shower was, "What the hell happened up there?"

Frank Allcorn, keeping the deck log in the conning tower, made the brief entry for the night of 21 June: "Mokos, Charles Edward, F1c, while dumping garbage sustained injuries on the right forearm when he was thrown from his feet by a swell." Mokos had little memory of what happened to him during the rush of the ocean but would later feel that "I was always kinda lucky for that boat."

Lieutenant (jg) Erwin recalled, "We were all scared but relieved. The chances of picking up a man that goes overboard at night are not good. If Mokos had not been rescued there would automatically have been a Navy Court of Inquiry and I would have, in all possibility, been held responsible."[20]

---

Commander Ramage exercised his gun crews on 22 June in test-firing the .50-caliber and 20-mm guns. Pack commander Parks made another running rendezvous with *Steelhead* and *Hammerhead* the following day to fire over new written instructions with a throwing line.

*Parche*'s first enemy ship sighting came at 0543 on 24 June, when Jim Campbell sighted an unidentified small vessel at ten miles. Course was changed and the lookouts found it to be a patrol vessel with a radio antenna. Ramage would later classify this ship as a 170-foot, 300-ton, newly built steel hull ship "similar to [a] net tender." The patrol vessel had a modern pilot house rounded in the front with ports instead of windows, was armed with machine guns, and was equipped with a radio. She had two masts and a well deck forward with a short funnel aft of the pilot house.

Battle stations were called at 0605 and the 20-mm and 4-inch gun crews swarmed out onto the deck from the gun access trunk at 0618. Gunnery officer Frank Allcorn helped spot for his 4-inch crew while GM1c Jim Plumley served as the gun captain. MoMM1c Dana Jensen took his seat on the left side of the gun to serve as pointer while TM3c Ray Karr jumped into the right seat in his role as the trainer. TM3c Joe Nichols assisted Plumley as the sight setter. The heavy 4-inch shells were hustled toward the gun by a group of the stronger men on board. There was MoMM1c Charlie Satterfield and MoMM3c Red Williams, the latter a red-haired youth who had just joined *Parche* at Midway. Williams had been raised in western Pennsylvania and joined the Navy in 1940 because the Army would not take him at 17 years of age. Williams first served on board the destroyer *Stack* in the Atlantic and later in the South Pacific before volunteering for subs. Third shellman Mo Taylor sported a heavy beard that gave him the look of an eighteenth-century pirate. GM2c Reno Ussin took his post close to the gun to set the fuses on each shell before first loader Cory Maupin pushed the shells into the breech.

Ussin had assumed the duty of setting the fuses after finding that some of his newer hands were unwilling to do so. Charlie McNutt, one of the new hands, was in the galley passing the heavy shells topside during gun drills. During one of the practice drills, Ussin had gone below and quizzed the sailors, "Who is setting the fuses on this armor?"

"We all looked at each other and nobody knew what the hell he was talking about because we weren't very bright," admitted McNutt. Ussin pointed out the wrench that was to be used to line up and set the shells for firing.

"What happens when you do that?" asked McNutt.

"Well, when the shell is hit, then it fires," replied Ussin.

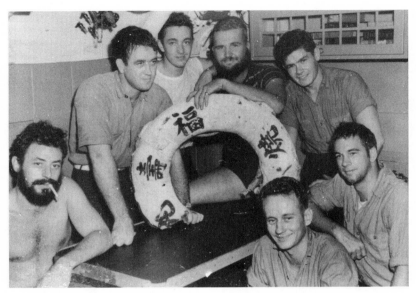

Some of the gun crews pose after a deck gun action on the second patrol. Clockwise from lower left are: Alfred Rick (bearded with cigarette), Charlie Satterfield, John Barnes, John O'Brien, Bill Hilditch, Jim Hawkey, and Reno Ussin. *Courtesy of Bob Erwin.*

McNutt thought for a moment and then blurted, "We're not gonna do that down here. If we drop that son of a bitch, it'll blow us all to pieces!"

With that, Ussin had given up on the notion of trusting his below decks help to properly set the shells. From that moment on, he carried the wrench topside for gun actions and took care of this business himself.

The bridge area was equally crowded with officers, the duty quartermaster, battle lookouts, and the smaller caliber gunners. Forward and aft standing by to man the 20-mm cannons and the .50-caliber machine guns were motormac John Nania, torpedomen Jim Hawkey, Bill Hilditch, and John Barnes, Quartermaster striker John O'Brien, and Radioman Al Rick, the latter also sporting a heavy beard for the patrol. Assistant gunnery officer Bob Erwin was on the bridge to help direct their efforts. Wolf pack commander Lew Parks took position on the bridge with his home movie camera to record the whole action.[21]

Below decks, those not needed for other duty joined the shell handlers from the galley locker to topside. The 4-inch, .50-caliber deck gun opened fire from a range of 3,600 yards. The shots were spotted onto the target and their third shot hit deck house and brought down the antenna and after mast. The patrol craft was maneuvering wildly at top speed until a round

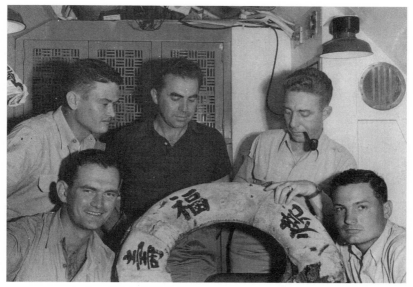

*Parche* officers who were topside for the sampan action pose with a captured Japanese life ring. Left–right are Frank Allcorn, Mac McCrory, wolf pack commander Lew Parks, Red Ramage, and Bob Erwin. *Courtesy of Bob Hall.*

hit and jammed the rudder full left. The big gun scored one hit out of every three into 2,000-yard range and then scored three out of every four shots as the distance narrowed.

The patrol craft was now running in circles to port and *Parche* circled wildly to keep it in range. Two attempts by the Japanese to man their deck guns were ended when their gunners were "blown sky high." In his patrol report, Ramage noted that the Japanese gunners "paid the supreme penalty." Cory Maupin, loading the shells, saw a direct hit where the Japanese gun was taking his fellow crewmen under fire and then "it was gone." Trainer Ray Karr added, "We took their guns away from them pretty fast."

Dana Jensen, serving as the 4-inch gun's pointer, detailed the end of one of these two gunners. "They had us stop firing as the top area had been destroyed. Through the sight, I saw a man go up to the bridge where there was a machine gun swinging around," Jensen wrote. "The man raised the gun and pointed it in our direction. I knew we would not want him to fire at us so I kicked off a round without permission. It hit the area where the gun was mounted and he went flying, arms and legs outstretched. I will never forget the scene as it was spectacular."

Finally, a well-placed shot in the PC's stern brought it to a halt. Ramage then closed the target and his 20-mm crews went to work. They fired 1,240 rounds at close range before they were able to set the ship afire. Ramage felt that the 20-mms needed incendiary shells in the future. The firing was excellent in spite of moderate sea conditions. At least 50 percent hits were scored out of the 61 rounds of 4-inch, .50-caliber shells fired. The steel hull took ten good hits and the topside "was a complete wreck." The target still showed no signs of giving up until she had been burning furiously for ten minutes. At 0717, the vessel sank stern first with her bow sticking up in the air while five survivors scrambled out of the forward hold very much alive. *Parche* investigated the debris but found nothing of interest.

"We were trying to see if we could pick any of them up," recalled Ramage. He and Parks were not overly enthusiastic about the prospects of guarding prisoners "because we were still just on our way to our patrol area. But none of these people in the water showed any inclination to come aboard. As a matter of fact, they were just the opposite: they swam away from us."[22]

Junior officer of the deck Ed Rauscher was standing just a few feet away from Red Ramage, relaying the skipper's orders to the bridge machine-gun crews. He was feeling "a little queasy" about the prospects of whether his skipper would order his gunners to shoot up the survivors in the water. Rauscher was more than a little relieved when Ramage muttered, "To hell with them. Let them swim."

Six survivors were counted after the boat went down but one was soon lost to the sight of the lookouts. "To our great surprise we found that this fellow had pulled a bucket over his head and he was sighting out through the bung-hole and trying to keep from being picked up," Ramage related.[23]

The only item of interest in the water was part of a ruined life ring fished on board for identification purposes. It had likely been retrieved from the ocean by the patrol boat crew from the wreck of another Japanese vessel. Ramage and Parks felt that it would make a fitting souvenir for Admiral Lockwood upon their return to Pearl Harbor. This ring was hauled below and *Parche* cleared the area, leaving the six survivors in the water as Ramage secured the crew from battle stations at 0750. The life ring was later determined to have come from *Fukuju Maru No. 3*, a 150-ton coastal freighter.[24]

---

*Parche* ducked two aircraft contacts the following day and was due north of the Bonins on 26 June. *Parche* slowed per Commander Parks' orders the next day to conserve fuel. The pack commander also used his personal camera to take photos of himself and the officers involved in the gun action holding the life preserver, and of a group of the *Parche* gunners also holding their prize. The gunners were ordered topside this day to swab out the 4-inch gun while auxiliarymen converted the No. 4 forward fuel ballast tank to a main ballast tank.

*Parche* proceeded through the southern Bonins, 30 miles south of Sofu Gan on her way to the South China Sea. The sea was glassy slick and an occasional floating mine could be seen at several miles distance. *Steelhead* remained in radio contact with *Parche* during this time but *Hammerhead*'s skipper was remiss in making his reports on a regular basis. "Commander Parks was heard to make a comment that he was sure he knew how John Martin, skipper of the *Hammerhead*, had previously received his nickname 'Hammerhead' during his Naval Academy days," recalled Bob Erwin.[25]

Torpedo officer Frank Allcorn found that wolf pack commander Parks confronted any off-duty officer with the query, "How 'bout a game of cribbage?" any time of day or night. Allcorn and Mac McCrory had given up their stateroom to Captain Parks and moved into the CPO quarters for the cruise. Allcorn had then been faced with finding a bunk for Parks' steward, Sanchez, with whom he had previously served on *S-25*. He quickly figured how to get Sanchez a bunk in the after torpedo room, knowing that Sanchez "wanted to be a torpedoman anyway. But at that time in the world, stewards could only be stewards." Allcorn decided that with *Parche*'s innovative torpedo reload system, "we needed that extra body in the after room for reloads."[26]

A low fog created zero visibility on the morning of 28 June, forcing the bridge watch to maintain a conservative speed and alert lookouts. *Steelhead* was spotted twice over the next two days almost dead ahead through low visibility. Commander Ramage finally received a report from *Hammerhead* by the 29th and was relieved to find that his pack mate was still bringing up the rear of the pack.

*Parche* entered her patrol area during the night on 30 June and Dave Green dived on station at 0547 on 1 July. The boat was just south of the area of her first patrol, running in the Luzon Strait along the known path of Japanese ships supplying the Philippines. She surfaced at 1250 on 2 July for Mac McCrory to shoot a quick sun line to make a good navigational fix.

She was on the surface again that evening to transit the Balintang Channel just north of the tip of Luzon during a bright moonlit night. On the evening of 3 July, a contact reported from *Seahorse* placed an enemy

KOREA

EAST CHINA SEA

FORMOSA
(Taiwan)

SOUTH CHINA SEA

Bashi
Channel

4 May 1944:
*Kinrei Maru, Taibu
Maru* sunk by *Parche*

LUZON
STRAIT

24 June 1944:
300-ton patrol craft
sunk with deck guns

31 July 1944:
*Koei Maru, Ogura Maru,
Dakar Maru, Yoshina
Maru* sunk by *Parche*

Babuyan Channel

30 April 1944:
*Parche*'s first
torpedo attack

Luzon

PHILIPPINE
SEA

**USS *Parche* First and Second Patrol Areas
April–July 1944**

convoy about 200 miles to the westward, well out of range. Aside from the deck gun action ten days prior, *Parche*'s crew had not sighted anything worth attacking.

"It was pretty discouraging," Commander Ramage later admitted.[27]

# CHAPTER SIX

# "A Perfect Dream"

P*arche*'s Fourth of July 1944 started with explosive action and ended with a fire. In between intermittent rain showers, radio technician Desmond Christy was able to pick up the solid pip of a ship at 0024 on his radar's Position Plan Indicator (PPI) scope. Officer of the deck Bob Erwin called for the skipper as the SJ contact quickly developed into three good pips at 21,000 yards. Upon reaching the bridge, Red Ramage increased speed to 15 knots and stationed his tracking party. Sending contact reports to *Steelhead* and *Hammerhead*, he went ahead on four main engines to commence an end around. By 0035, two larger ships and a smaller vessel were plainly in sight in the moonlight.

Christy, who had been manning the radar, asked one of the new radiomen, Glenn Meise, to take over watching the PPI scope in the conning tower for a few minutes while he ran to the head. Meise slid over from his spot on the JP sonar gear and took Christy's place without even bothering to ask in which direction he had been reporting the range and distance of the Japanese ships. "When I took over the radar I started sweeping the opposite from what he had been sweeping," Meise related. "Our very observant skipper saw that and got on the intercom."[1]

Ramage called down to the conning tower from the bridge, "Who the hell is running the radar?"

"Meise," came the reply.

Not understanding the new sailor's name and thinking he had heard a wise remark, Ramage hollered back, "Who the hell is ME?" As Meise admitted, "That was a conversation piece for a while."

Bob Erwin felt a rush of adrenaline on the bridge as he studied the first Japanese warships that he had ever seen. "Range decreasing and bearing drawing ahead indicated we had some fast customers," Ramage noted in his patrol report. Erwin's hopes that something good might develop from this contact evaporated when a large destroyer suddenly swung to starboard toward *Parche* at 0056. This tin can was plotted as making 30 knots at a range of 9,000 yards. One minute later, the destroyer opened fire, followed by one of the heavy cruisers from the long range of 16,000 yards. Ramage logged, "Our Fourth of July was then officially recognized with the Nips providing the fireworks."[2]

The wolf pack commander, Lew Parks, had joined Red Ramage on the bridge as *Parche* drove in toward these warships. As the first flashes lit the distant horizon, Parks queried, "What was that?"[3]

"They're shooting at us," Ramage replied rather matter-of-factly.

The mighty *kaboom! kaboom!* from the sound followed the flashes that had been seen on the horizon. A large splash of water fountained off *Parche*'s starboard quarter while three more erupted to her port side. All of the shells hit the ocean within 100 yards of the submarine. "At that range they had us on radar obviously and their gunnery was damned good, far better than I would have ever believed possible on an opening salvo," Ramage thought.[4]

As quickly as the shells ripped into the water near *Parche*, Lew Parks was on his way toward the conning tower. "Where are you going?" Ramage called to his senior officer.

"I'm going below!" said Parks as he slid down the ladder. "You can do whatever you want."

Ramage did not contemplate the situation long, figuring discretion to be the better part of valor. Bob Erwin pulled the diving alarm at 0102 and *Parche* initiated a crash dive. "There was an immediate scramble to clear the bridge and the second salvo arrived as our conning tower hatch went under water so we are not sure how close the shells were to us," recalled Erwin.[5]

*Parche* went to silent running and all non-essential machinery was shut down. As they quietly awaited the destroyers racing toward them, some reflected on their odds. Torpedoman Cory Maupin was typical of most of the younger hands. At age 18, he felt more a sense of adventure than he felt a danger. He figured the older sailors, the chief petty officers, and those who had wives and children, looked the most concerned.

Four depth charges were dropped at 0105; none were close enough to cause damage. Screws were heard overhead during the next 20 minutes as the destroyer evidently made one pass and then proceeded on with the heavier warships. When *Parche* surfaced more than an hour later, Parks directed the pack to break off the search for this swift-moving group of warships. Radar contact was soon made with *Steelhead* and *Hammerhead* as contact reports were sent off to ComSubPac.

*Parche* continued her routine patrolling during the next three days without shipping contacts. Japanese aircraft were a constant threat and Charlie McNutt on his first patrol learned a healthy respect for the enemy. On 7 July, he stood his first lookout watch from 0400 to 0800 and it was one he would never forget. After two weeks of mess cooking and hauling garbage topside, he was anxious to try his hand topside. "Boy, what an improvement, I thought, getting onto the bridge and into the control room where all of the action will be," he recalled. "I was a fired-up kid never having been away from home and very gung-ho."[6]

The first two hours of his watch on the after lookout station had passed without event. As daybreak was beginning to arrive, McNutt enjoyed the view of a beautiful dawn off the northwestern tip of Luzon near Cape Bojeador. He knew the boat would be diving soon for another day of submerged patrolling. He noted the skipper had come topside to confer with OOD Dave Green prior to the dive. McNutt continued to sweep the after horizon excitedly in anticipation of his first dive topside.

After a few minutes, he glanced around and suddenly found that the port and starboard lookouts were gone. He was oblivious to the fact that one of his fellow lookouts had spotted a Sally bomber ten miles out on the horizon. Lieutenant Green had cupped his hands and shouted, "Clear the bridge!" but McNutt missed the call due to a strong wind that was blowing across the bridge.

At 0643, the engines were cut and those below rigged *Parche* for a dive as the first two lookouts dropped below. McNutt turned and looked forward only to see Red Ramage waving his arms excitedly and shouting at him. He immediately realized that his submarine was going into a dive. "The fastest I have ever moved in my life was from the after lookout station to the hatch," he recalled.

Ramage sidestepped the fleeing lookout and allowed him down the hatch ahead of him. McNutt leaped down through the opening without even touching the rungs, landing squarely on JOD Bob Ashe's shoulders in the process. "I hit him with my Marine boots, picked up on Midway, and knocked him to the deck in the conning tower," McNutt recalled.

Ensign Ashe scrambled down the control room hatch and McNutt leaped down behind him, knocking the officer to the deck once again. McNutt was relieved that Ashe did not reprimand him, but he did not stick around to give him the chance. Advised to go to the forward torpedo room to operate the sound gear, he sprinted forward.

*Parche* clawed for depth as the Japanese plane began a bombing run. McNutt donned the headset just as the airplane released its two bombs over the diving submarine. "The last guy wearing the headset had cranked up the volume to full," he recalled. "So, when the bombs went off the explosions just about blew me out of the boat." Wolf pack commander Lew Parks happened to be emerging from the officer's head in the forward room as two bomb explosions rocked the boat at 0646. Unshaken, he grinned at the sight of the young sailor who was shaking as he held onto his sound gear. "What did it sound like, son?" Parks asked.

McNutt, still rattled from narrowly escaping the bridge and from the explosions, erupted in the most colorful "sailor language" as he offered his thoughts to the division commander.

The Japanese plane hovered about the area for two more hours to keep *Parche* down. By 0859 a *Wakatake*-class destroyer was sighted approaching. A Mavis flying boat joined the party and prevented *Parche* from attempting to close the tin can. Charlie McNutt, recovered from his trying moments on the bridge, went aft toward the control room after being relieved in the forward room. En route, he noticed Commander Ramage in the wardroom.

"McNutt, come here," the skipper called. "When we surface again later, I want you to take a bucket with a mop and clean up the deck where you were standing topside, got it? By the way, I'll never get in your way when you're clearing the bridge!"

The young sailor was much relieved that his first real brush with the enemy had not been more severe and that his skipper at least had a good sense of humor. McNutt was also certain that he would never again be caught off guard for a crash dive. "I must say, you learned very quickly," Ramage told him later.[7]

Frank Allcorn had the deck when *Parche* surfaced at 2007 and some activity soon ensued. A fire broke out in the maneuvering room at 2038. A short circuit across leads to the No. 4 generator occurred in the battery group of the main control cubicle. The two port leads had shorted at the terminal block, burned loose and then grounded on an angle iron in the cubicle. Electrician Lonnie Hughes and several others had the fire controlled within two minutes. Such quick action resulted in only superficial damage, which the crew set to work repairing. The electrical gang's quick action prevented a major fire and serious threat to the ship. Jim Campbell passed on praise for Hughes to Exec Mac McCrory. "Lonnie never hesitated," Campbell recalled. "He stepped into the cubicle—which was extremely hazardous in itself—spotted the trouble and took the proper corrective action."[8]

*Parche* sighted only a sampan, trawler, and an occasional Japanese aircraft during the next week of patrolling on station. Percy Barnett's radio gang was able to pipe in American music from Hanoi during this time and the crew was often entertained by the threats broadcast by Tokyo Rose. "We had been informed that many American mothers were going to be sad when their sons on the *Parche* did not return home from this patrol," recalled Bob Erwin. "I believe we were identified by radio messages between our wolf pack, as these were not very secure." Radioman striker Paul Gilcher "loved her music and laughed at her other stuff." Aside from Tokyo Rose, some atmospheric fluke allowed the radiomen to occasionally pick up a radio station from Minneapolis during the night while the boat was surfaced.[9]

Lew Parks ordered a pack rendezvous in the early hours of 14 July. *Steelhead* and *Hammerhead* each eased up close to *Parche* in spite of heavy seas so that a line could be fired across with new patrol instructions from the pack commander. The seas increased this day and the barometer began dropping steadily. The stormy weather continued to increase during the night as the outer effects of a nearby typhoon were felt. Mac McCrory and his senior quartermaster, George Plume, were unable to shoot a sun line during this time due to the heavy weather.

At 0022 on 15 July, PhM1c Brown was noted to be suffering from what he self-diagnosed as an acute case of appendicitis. A message was sent to ComSubPac and Brown was confined to his bunk with a liquid diet, ice packs and sulfasthiazol. "The pharmacist's mates of three boats had performed successful appendectomies early in the war and had received much publicity," recalled junior officer Erwin. "We were not ready for an amateur operation especially as the prospective patient was our doctor."[10]

Visibility was zero this day with rough seas and heavy rain. Depth control was difficult to maintain due to the swells. The rough weather continued for another 24 hours before beginning to abate. After six failed attempts on 17 July, the other two boats finally acknowledged receipt of Commander Parks' new assigned stations. To further the frustration, *Parche*'s SJ radar went out of commission that night and the radar gang spent four tense hours trying to repair it as the weather worsened again.

The boat was hard to operate on the surface and rolled heavily even at periscope depth. Charlie Welton, who chose to spend his time reading while off-duty versus gambling in the mess hall, felt the ship rolling even at depth as he flipped the pages in his book in his rack above the torpedoes in the after room.

*Parche* surfaced at 1855 on 18 July "in heavy storm weather again with all the general appearances of an approaching typhoon." Within 30 minutes however, the radio gang picked up a contact report from

The 19,500-ton Japanese escort carrier *Taiyo*, seen above, was one of three escort carriers at sea near Formosa on 19 July 1944. *Taiyo* or one of her sister carriers, *Kaiyo* and *Jinyo,* was sighted and chased by *Parche. Author's collection.*

another wolf pack of a convoy of transports, naval auxiliaries, and at least one carrier. *Parche* bent on full speed to the west and relayed the contact report to *Hammerhead* and *Steelhead*. All three boats submerged on the morning of 19 July and continued to close the convoy's route. Aircraft were buzzing about the area of Parks' wolf pack as they drove in. At 1000, *Hammerhead* reported that a plane had attacked her while she had radar contact with four ships heading south. *Parche* was unable to close during the rough seas in the daylight so Lew Parks ordered his boats to keep a regular, hourly radio guard for updates.

Monitoring the radio guard required *Parche*'s diving officers to bring the boat to very shallow depths once an hour to expose the radio antenna above the waves. Just after 1300, *Parche* broached while attempting to keep regular hourly radio guard in the rough seas. In the resulting increased periscope height, Lt. Frank Allcorn reported a welcome surprise. He spotted a Japanese aircraft carrier with no island at 16,000 yards. Five or six planes were circling overhead but no other ships were in sight. It was a submariner's dream come true and Red Ramage raced to the conning tower.

This was either *Kaiyo*, *Taiyo*, or *Jinyo*, three escort carriers that had departed the port of Mutsure in Japan on 13 July. Their warplanes were charged with escorting convoy HI-69 to Manila. This important convoy was additionally escorted by a light cruiser and four antisubmarine vessels. Sightings of Japanese carriers by U.S. submarines was fairly rare and *Parche*'s skipper was eager to make his torpedoes count.[11]

*Parche* went to battle stations at 1305 and commenced a full speed approach. Within six minutes, the range had been narrowed to 12,000 yards and Ramage was thrilled: the carrier was in sight with no escorting destroyers and no planes noted overhead. The flattop zigged toward *Parche* and the range dropped to 8,000 yards by 1318.

At 1326, the carrier turned into the wind and was observed to launch an aircraft. "But the cat was out of the bag—the end of a perfect dream," Ramage wrote. Moving away at 18 to 20 knots, the carrier quickly opened up the distance from the submerged *Parche*, which came to radar depth and began sending contact reports.

Electrician Lonnie Hughes wrote in his diary that the carrier was "taking off planes and steaming zig zag. One more zig our way and we would have had him." Sonar operator Glenn Meise would never forget the anger and despair Red Ramage felt in seeing this carrier escape: "The skipper was on the periscope when we had to quit and all he could say—with his arms resting on the periscope side bars—was, 'God damn. God damn. God damn.' We lost a biggie that day."[12]

By the time *Parche* resurfaced at 1457, the seas were very rough as 50-mph winds whipped the whitecaps. The topside watch took a beating as their boat plowed through the waves at 13 knots in the direction of the departed carrier. *Parche* tried to close the convoy's anticipated route but OOD Bob Erwin was forced to dive at 1716 when one of the carrier's aircraft was spotted coming in low on the water. "These Japs apparently fly in any kind of weather, even the worst," Ramage wrote. After 16 days of patrolling with no shipping targets, Erwin found this missed carrier chance to be bitterly disappointing. "We had this plum close enough to taste but not close enough to eat."[13]

Lew Parks assigned patrol stations that evening and his three boats patrolled on station the next day as the weather worsened. By 1245 on 20 July, the boat was rolling 13 degrees to each side even at 150 feet in the height of the typhoon conditions. The typhoon reached its peak on 21 July when its center was estimated to be about 100 miles to the south. The wind reached Force 12 and the seas were 35 to 40 feet high. On the surface it was necessary to run with the seas to prevent water from coming down the open hatch. Stretching more than 300 feet in length, *Parche* rested on the front of an oncoming wave with her stern in the trough and her bow not yet reaching the oncoming crest. The lookouts and officers topside were unable to see over the top of the wave while *Parche* was in the trough.

"We figured the speed of the typhoon's winds was 140 miles per hour," recalled Lt. (jg) Ed Rauscher. He was one of at least several aboard *Parche* who wished that their skipper would just keep the boat down. Standing watch on the bridge was rough. "We had 40-foot waves coming over us and it was tough to keep your footing." Some of the swells would literally engulf the bridge and force the officers and lookouts to hang on tight. "We had a three-sides shield with a roof over it that offered us some protection," Rauscher recalled. The shield helped some against the force of the seas but Rauscher and his companions found themselves taking a deep breath before a big wave momentarily swamped the bridge. The water was cold and once the drenched men had recovered from its blasting effects they found themselves waiting for the next one.

Bob Erwin and Jim Campbell had the 1600 to 2000 watch during the height of this typhoon. At 1952 *Parche* surfaced in the rough ocean. To do so, the tank vents were closed and high-pressure air was blown into the ballast tanks to displace the water and force the boat to the surface. "This particular surfacing we had used more high pressure blowing than normal to get as high out of the water as possible so we could open the main induction and start the low-pressure blowers," recalled Erwin.[14]

Erwin scrambled topside and took station forward near the bridge cowling while Campbell went to the after bridge deck. The duty quartermaster, Bob Daufenbach, stood by the conning tower hatch in case the rough seas necessitated its closing. "I was trying to decide if it was safe enough to open the main induction and start the low-pressure blowers when we were completely swamped by a huge rogue wave rolling over us from aft," wrote Erwin. An alert Daufenbach, a tall, powerfully built good-natured man, managed to force the hatch shut before the ocean poured into the conning tower below.[15]

The giant wave pushed *Parche* down deep and the conning tower deck was suddenly about 20 feet underwater. Daufenbach was pinned under the cowling by the water pressure. Erwin, who had been yelling into the speaker tube, found his face pinned flat against the speaker for what seemed to be an eternity. Below decks, duty chief Lonnie Hughes continued blowing high-pressure air into the ballast tanks to get the boat higher on the surface.

When *Parche* regained the surface, Daufenbach and Erwin were unharmed, although Erwin had a cut lip and cheek from the side of the speaker tube. They immediately checked aft, not expecing to find Jim Campbell still on the bridge. "He saved himself by clamping his hands to the deck pipe railing," Erwin recalled. "I tell him to this day that he bent the rail and his handprints are still on the pipe."[16]

---

The storm began to abate on 22 July and McCrory took his first sights in three days to fix the navigation. 23 July passed with the sighting of a patrol boat and two aircraft contacts but no worthwhile shipping. The patrol boat was radar-equipped and he turned toward *Parche* for 20 minutes before finally breaking off. The weather increased again to a full gale force wind blowing at 50 to 60 knots on 24 July.

In spite of the weather, Red Ramage was itching to find action. His enthusiasm was piqued when ComSubPac sent an Ultra to Convoy College. Lockwood alerted his wolf packs that the Japanese submarine *I-29* was en route from Germany to Japan with a cargo of prototypes and blueprints of advanced German weapons. According to ComSubPac's Ultra, the Japanese I-boat would pass through Balintang Channel around noon on 26 July.[17]

Communications officer Jim Campbell was tasked with decoding the special Ultra messages. "Only the officer decoding these messages, plus the skipper and Exec were privileged to read them," he recalled. "Command was very particular about us destroying the messages after they were read." Having taken classes in decoding while aboard *S-48* in 1943, Campbell quickly took the little strips of paper and worked out the code of the day for the top-secret dispatch.

The Ultra was actually directed toward the nearest wolf pack, under Cdr. Warren Dudley Wilkins. Consisting of *Tilefish, Sawfish,* and *Rock,* "Wilkins' Wildcats" was stationed in this area. Ramage consulted with Lew Parks on 25 July, suggesting that the Pirates should join the Wildcats in Balintang Channel. Six boats were better than three "to be damned sure we got this submarine," Ramage offered.[18]

Parks concurred and Jim Campbell's radiomen soon had Commander Wilkins' approval via radio for Parks' Pirates to enter the patrol area of his own wolf pack. Wilkins laid out plans for all six submarines to take up stations in the channel. *Parche* entered Balintang Channel late that evening and moved toward her assigned station. Mac McCrory and Chief Peterson gave strict instructions to their topside lookouts as to the importance of their alert watchstanding this night. "We were told that this sub was bringing out secret information from Germany and that our mission was to sink it," recalled Charlie Welton. "It was so dark as we went through the Balintang Channel that we couldn't really make out the nearby land. We could just see a dark mass on the horizon and tell that it wasn't water."

Jim Campbell took the boat down for the day at 0541 on 26 July. The Ultra intelligence said that *I-29* would pass right through the channel around noon, so *Parche* took her position to wait.

"At noon we were just holding our breath expecting to see this submarine any minute and nothing happened," Ramage recalled. The noon hour passed without a word. By 1500, "we were getting very discouraged," he said.[19]

Frank Allcorn had taken his duty watch at 1200 with the expectation that he might be the first to spot the important Japanese submarine. To his chagrin, his watch ended at 1600 without even the sight of an enemy aircraft. Bob Erwin assumed the periscope watch and just over an hour later there was a loud explosion heard in the distance.

Commander Ramage had Dave Green trim the boat up so that he could expose more of the periscope for a longer look-see. Ramage spotted a "big column of smoke going up. So we knew that one of other submarines in the other pack had gotten that submarine. If that fellow had gotten by them, we'd have been next in line. We just missed out on it."[20]

Wilkins' Wildcats had indeed claimed the glory this day. *I-29* was hours late but right on course and *Sawfish* fired a spread of torpedoes as the big Japanese submarine cruised through Balintang Channel on the surface in broad daylight. Captain Alan Banister noted in his patrol report: "Noted no periscope shears, which was a relief since one of our boats might have been passing through at that time." He also saw a "big rising sun on conning tower fairwater" and opened fire on the I-boat from 1,850 yards with four torpedoes. Banister watched as three of his four torpedoes hit home and *I-29* disintegrated in a pillar of flame and smoke that rose more than 300 feet. *I-29* took all hands and her German secret information to the bottom of the channel.[21]

The night of 27 July, Parks sent word to all boats to continue patrolling to the north at ten knots. *Hammerhead* sent a report that night of contact with two patrol boats.

Ramage was particularly frustrated for his *Parche* crew. They had spent nearly a month in their patrol area without firing a single torpedo. He felt certain that the Japanese patrol planes had been doing their part in spotting the wolf packs and helping to divert shipping traffic away from them. Commander Parks, knowing that he had run out of time, radioed ComSubPac to request permission to extend the patrol since all boats had full loads of torpedoes.

Admiral Lockwood sent an affirmative reply to Parks on 28 July. *Parche*'s lookouts spotted a lone Mavis flying boat during midday on 29 July but no shipping targets. Ramage dreaded the prospect of a "dry run" in an area that had normally been a very productive target area.

"We certainly didn't want to go home empty-handed after all this," he recalled. "I had vowed before we ever left that if we got into a convoy I was going to get my swag, regardless of the others, and get out. I wasn't going to get left behind like I had been on the first patrol."[22]

# CHAPTER SEVEN

# Red's Rampage: "I Got Mad"

The extension of patrol days for Parks' Pirates quickly proved to be a smart move. Cdr. Jack Martin's *Hammerhead* was the first to attack Japanese shipping after the period had been extended. During the morning of 29 July, Martin fired three torpedoes at a 900-ton coastal tanker escorted by two patrol boats in Bashi Channel. All missed and *Hammerhead* was forced down for the remainder of the day.

Martin's boat was in the right position again the following day, for her radar picked up a group of pips at 0352 at a position about 60 miles south of Formosa. *Hammerhead* had happened upon an important convoy, MI-11, which had sailed from the port of Moji in Japan for Miri on the coast of Borneo. Convoy MI-11 had refueled at the port city of Takao on Formosa before departing again for Miri on 27 July. By the time *Hammerhead* made contact with this large convoy on 30 July, it consisted of eleven Army-laden merchantmen and six escorts.[1]

MI-11 included tankers whose job was to pick up raw crude from Borneo to return to Japan for refining. Flagship *Ogura Maru No. 1* carried the commander of Maritime Transportation Unit No. 6. *Fuso Maru* and *Yoshino Maru* were passenger ships officially designated by Japan during 1944 as protected hospital ships that could not be attacked. By international convention, *Fuso Maru* and *Yoshino Maru* should have been clearly marked with red crosses. In reality, these two Convoy MI-11 vessels carried nearly 10,000 Japanese Army troops, plus their equipment and supplies. Other ships of this convoy carried Japanese soldiers, army engineers, and civilians, plus cargoes of construction equipment for building new airfields in the Philippines. One freighter had turned back with engine problems on 29 July, leaving eleven merchant vessels and six armed escorts—two destroyers, two minesweepers, a coastal defense ship, a sub chaser, and an armed converted merchantman. The escort ships were heavily armed with guns, depth charges, and they possessed radar.[2]

Jack Martin hurried off a contact report of seven ships and three escorts making eight knots at 0420 before commencing his attacks. The only trouble was that his navigation was so much in error that neither this report nor his later follow-up reports offered anything resembling his boat's true coordinates. Bob Erwin and Jim Campbell had the deck when *Hammerhead* transmitted the first position, course, and speed of the Japanese convoy. Captain Lew Parks was duly informed that *Hammerhead*'s contact was 20 miles *south* of *Parche*—although events would soon show that this reported position was completely off base.

Based on the given coordinates, Red Ramage set course to 180T at full speed to intercept. With good surface speed, *Parche* and her pack mate *Steelhead* should reach the convoy's area within the hour. In the meantime, Martin headed his boat in to attack. Within 20 minutes of the first contact report, Captain Parks was becoming very frustrated. He ordered Percy Barnett's radiomen to ask *Hammerhead* for a verification of the convoy's plot, for *Parche*'s own plot showed that these ships should have passed directly over her position three hours before.

At 0450 Myron Grover picked up *Hammerhead*'s second contact report, one that offered a clarifying position of the convoy. This position "bore little relation to the previous one," an angry Lew Parks would later write in his post-patrol report. This time, the confused Commander Martin radioed that *Hammerhead* was 30 miles to the *north* of *Parche* instead of 20 miles to the south.

Ramage angrily swung his boat around and headed *Parche* off at full speed surfaced in the other direction. Parks had also grown angry by this time and he asked for another location update from *Hammerhead* at 0455. This time, Martin sent word that his boat was preparing to attack from a new set of coordinates northeast of *Parche*. Parks decided to use this latest bearing and he ordered *Parche* and *Steelhead*'s skippers to make their third radical change of course in thirty-seven minutes.[3]

While his pack mates raced about in frustration with erroneous position reports, Martin took his *Hammerhead* in to attack. He fired all six bow tubes at 0532 and then turned to fire all four stern tubes. Martin would claim one ship sunk and two damaged, although all of these claims were disallowed, possibly because of his own errant position plotting. As dawn began to break, *Hammerhead* sent another contact report to Parks' Pirates to announce the torpedo attacks she had made. The enemy convoy was now scattering. *Hammerhead* then proceeded toward Fremantle per her previous orders.

"It was probably well that she did not come back to Pearl with us," *Parche* junior officer Bob Erwin later wrote. Lew Parks and Red Ramage were absolutely furious. They had spent the entire night chasing phantom position reports that were all way off the convoy's true bearing. Parks would write in his post-patrol report that "the reports from Martin were confused, erroneous, and niggardly." Ramage, cursing bitterly about his bridge and conning tower, calmed enough when he penned his patrol report days later to be diplomatic: "As the sun came up, it finally dawned on us that we were the victims of another snipe [hunt]. That was bad enough but we never expected to be left holding the well known burlap by one of our own team-mates."[4]

Jack Martin learned later that his inexperienced communications officer had been misinterpreting the wolf pack code letters while encoding messages. When Martin learned on 30 July that his junior officer had erred three times in reporting the position of *Hammerhead* and the Japanese convoy, he asked that this man be relieved of further submarine combat duty.[5]

Unfortunately, this move came too late to help *Steelhead* or *Parche* during the first day's encounter with convoy MI-11. *Parche* was forced to dive after dawn on 30 July and await further news. Nothing further was heard from *Hammerhead* so Parks directed *Steelhead* to continue searching submerged. *Parche's* periscope watch avoided a patrol boat and several aircraft contacts throughout the morning. At 1025, Lieutenant (jg) Stevenson picked up smoke on the horizon. Shortly after changing course, the scope watch had five columns of smoke in view but three circling aircraft prevented *Parche* from surfacing to pursue.

The distant smoke was lost in the afternoon's squally seas. *Parche* surfaced at 2014 with Dave Green and Ed Rauscher on deck and soon received a report that *Steelhead* had sighted the convoy, and gave its location, track, and speed. Ramage calculated the convoy was 35 miles southwest of his position and would not be reached before daylight.

Pack commander Parks differed in opinion. "Red, we're going after that convoy."[6]

"You can't get it," Ramage protested. "There aren't enough hours left in the night for you to get it. You're going to run us out of fuel. Then we'll go home without any targets."

Captain Parks was insistent, however, that *Parche* would indeed make contact if she chased the convoy. "Sometimes you feel lucky," Parks would later relate. "I just felt as if we were going to do it. I was going to take the chance."[7]

Ramage thus called his plotting team to their battle stations long before midnight and headed *Parche* in pursuit on four main engines. Frustrated, Ramage retired to his cabin for a nap, leaving Lew Parks hunkered over the chart table to formulate an attack plan.[8]

*Parche*'s battle plotting team would remain at their posts for eight hours—hours that would make *Parche*'s name one of the most recognized in the fleet.

———

Japanese convoy MI-11 changed course early on the morning of 31 July as *Steelhead* continued to help direct *Parche* in for the kill. *Parche* raced at full speed around the convoy's west side to get into a position ahead. Lt. Dave Green took over the middle watch and he soon found tensions simmering between his skipper and the pack commander.

Ramage, now in the conning tower following his quick nap, felt that *Parche* should have intercepted the convoy after running several hours at high speed in their direction. He asked Parks to call *Steelhead* for an updated position report but Parks refused to break radio silence at this crucial time. Ramage was "greatly agitated" with this reluctance. "I was quite convinced that probably the convoy had changed course."[9]

He felt that MI-11 may have shifted from a southwesterly course to a more southeasterly course to run around the northern end of Luzon closer to the land. Ramage continued to request the pack commander to call for a new report until a compromise was finally reached. "If we haven't heard anything from them by twelve-thirty, we'll go ahead and ask," Parks said.[10]

The awaited report did not come and at 0030 Ramage had his radio gang contact *Steelhead*. Dave Whelchel's new position placed Convoy MI-11 about 30 miles southeast of *Parche*. Just as Ramage had suspected, the convoy had made a course change. "We were way off in right field," he reflected. "So we swung around and started heading in."[11]

Ramage stood sentry on the bridge with Lieutenant Green and his lookouts as *Parche* raced toward the new position. Thirty-five minutes later, John Gray called toward the bridge with welcome news. "Radar contact on several ships!" he announced as his SJ finally picked up radar interference from the Japanese.

By 0240, the convoy was on Gray's SJ radar screen at 34,000 yards just as the moon was setting. At his position on the plotting table in the conning tower, Lieutenant (jg) Erwin found that "the convoy was now southeast of us heading roughly south."

Six minutes later, *Parche* went to battle stations as the bells from the 1MC chimed throughout the ship. All compartments reported that they were properly manned as their boat commenced closing the convoy's track. Dave Green dropped below to handle the diving duties while Jim Campbell

## Japanese Convoy MI-11: 31 July 1944

| Merchant Ships: | Taketoyo Maru |
|---|---|
| Akakumo Maru | Teiritsu Maru |
| Ayayuki Maru | Yoshino Maru* |
| Dakar Maru* | |
| Enoshima Maru | **Escort Ships:** |
| Fukuju Maru | Shimushu |
| Fuso Maru* | Shiokaze |
| Hachijin Maru | W-28 |
| Harima Maru | W-39 |
| Koei Maru* | CH-55 |
| Kokura Maru No. 1* | Kazan Maru |
| Miho Maru | |
| Manko Maru* | *   Sunk by *Parche* or *Steelhead*. |
| Ogura Maru No. 1** | ** Torpedoed by *Parche*. |
| Shichiyo Maru | |

took over the TBT on the bridge. Erwin on plot and torpedo officer Frank Allcorn on the TDC had six different enemy ships they were tracking. Other pips—escort ships or possibly *Steelhead*—soon appeared on Gray's SJ radar at closer range. By 0316, radar reported ten ships ahead at 18,000 yards.

"My role as fire control officer was to man the TDC, which gave me a complete picture of the attack problem," Allcorn related. "At my shoulder was the executive officer, Mac McCrory."[12]

Ramage had his best night vision battle lookouts on the periscope shears for this attack. Fireman Dave Hussey was on the after platform with his 7x50 binoculars. Torpedoman Ray Karr had the starboard side and Radioman Glenn Meise had the port station on the shears. The enemy ships were all running without lights on a southeasterly course.

Three escorts were sighted as *Parche* drove in closer. The convoy skippers were nervous and several ships began firing flares at 0340. *Steelhead* had made an attack moments before, firing ten torpedoes. Skipper Dave Whelchel believed that he had sunk at least one ship but his torpedoes had merely damaged two Japanese ships, transport *Yoshino Maru* and tanker *Koei Maru*.[13]

By this time, *Parche* was abreast of the convoy, which was directly to the east on a southwest course. On the plotting table, Bob Erwin listened to the radar reports from RT1c Gray and from the lookouts on the bridge. One of the escort vessels ahead to port had either spotted *Parche* or by chance maneuvered radically to remain ahead of the convoy. "In any case he was coming straight towards the *Parche*," recalled Erwin.[14]

"We were coming more or less straight up from the stern or off their quarter," Ramage later detailed. "They had an escort on their beam and one a little further forward on their bow on the starboard side. We had no idea where the *Steelhead* was but we presumed that she was over on the port hand, where she should have been according to the regular patrol doctrine."[15]

*Parche* was moving in unnoticed but another of the escorts was seen to be moving out in her direction from the head of the convoy. With three escorts formed behind and ahead of MI-11, Ramage decided he would maneuver to get inside of the escort screen before making his first attack. The convoy was maneuvering radically at a distance of less than 5,000 yards. He immediately called to his battle stations helmsman Chet Stanton at 0342, "Right full rudder!"

*Parche* swung hard to starboard to pull a reverse maneuver against the charging escort ship. After a 270-degree circle to starboard, *Parche* was heading directly toward the convoy, which had apparently made a 90-degree right turn. "We were right in the middle of them and they were sending off flares and rockets to communicate," lookout Ray Karr related. By reversing the field, Ramage suddenly found himself *within* the convoy's screen in prime position. "All of a sudden, we were right in the middle of the convoy," recalled junior officer Jim Campbell. "Luck is better than skill sometimes."

*Parche*'s charge into the heart of the convoy was the start of what would be the wildest hour of Red Ramage's career. He stood fast on the bridge, surveying the setup that was changing rapidly before him. Ed Rauscher was on the port side of the bridge scanning the scene directly ahead while Jim Campbell tracked targets on the TBT.

To his delight, Ramage found that the Japanese convoy was dead ahead at 6,000 yards and was steaming directly toward *Parche*. Erwin's plot showed that the convoy had turned right, putting *Parche* on their opposite, or port, flank. At 0354, Ramage commenced a surface approach on the nearest target, a medium-sized freighter.

"Make ready all tubes," talker Bob Daufenbach relayed over the sound-powered phones to the torpedo rooms.

"Everybody on the boat was trembling with excitement," recalled torpedo officer Frank Allcorn. "Since our attack was to be on the surface, torpedo wakes would be no problem but their 40-knot speed was every-

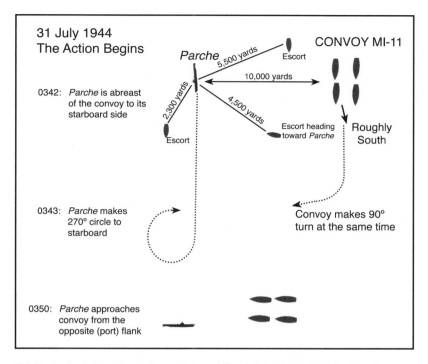

31 July 1944
The Action Begins

CONVOY MI-11

Parche

5,500 yards

Escort

10,000 yards

0342: *Parche* is abreast
of the convoy to its
starboard side

2,300 yards

4,500 yards

Escort heading
toward *Parche*

Roughly
South

Escort

0343: *Parche* makes
270° circle to
starboard

Convoy makes 90°
turn at the same time

0350: *Parche* approaches
convoy from the
opposite (port) flank

This illustration is based upon the sketches of *Parche*'s battle stations plotting officer
Bob Erwin depicting the opening moments of the 31 July action. Following mutual course
changes, *Parche* was suddenly charging headlong into the midst of Convoy MI-11.

thing. To be certain there would be no problems, the torpedoes had been serviced on the way to the area. They had been individually checked by the torpedo gang in both the forward and after rooms. We planned to shoot as fast as possible. In their racks, the torpedoes were lined up with the tubes so, unless orders were given to cease fire, the empty tubes would be loaded as soon as they were empty with no delay to reload."[16]

Within minutes, Ramage suddenly found that his team had greatly overestimated the range to the enemy ship. Before he could get a setup, radarman John Gray announced that he had lost the target ship from his PPI screen at a mere 450 yards. The range was too close for *Parche*'s torpedoes to properly arm themselves. The Mark 14 had a complex gear mechanism that held its exploder inert until the torpedo had traveled more than 400 yards.

"Right full rudder!" Ramage hollered as *Parche* passed dangerously close to the freighter ahead. "Before we could do anything we were alongside them and going by at [a combined] 20 knots," he recalled. *Parche* slid down the side of this merchant ship at a 200-yard distance. "We were so close that we could hear people shouting on the decks of the Japanese ship," Campbell related. Lookout Glenn Meise recalled, "As they passed through our wake, Skipper Ramage hollered, 'Hirohito's horseshit!' to the sailors who were at the aft end of their ship." As soon as *Parche* was clear astern, Ramage continued to swing his ship to starboard to make another pass at this ship.[17]

As the range opened to a proper distance on this freighter, Frank Allcorn called out that he had a good firing solution on his TDC.

"Fire one!" barked Ramage.

The range had opened to 480 yards as *Parche* fired her No. 1 and No. 2 bow tubes at this ship. These torpex-loaded Mark 14s were set at ten feet with contact detonators. Ramage quickly noted that the Japanese skipper was fully alerted and had already started swinging to the left.

"The torpedoes are passing astern of the target!" port lookout Meise announced.

Ramage watched as his first two fish bubbled harmlessly past the rear of the Japanese freighter so he quickly checked fire on the other two tubes. Fortunately, the freighter had effectively blocked off an alert escort vessel that was racing in to intercept the American submarine.

One minute later, lookout Ray Karr spotted what first appeared to be two Japanese flattops off the starboard bow. "Carriers!" he called.

Other binoculars quickly surveyed Karr's "aircraft carriers" and determined that these two ships were actually large oil tankers. The larger one was the 10,238-ton *Koei Maru*, which had already been damaged by *Steelhead*, and the other was the 7,000-ton *Ogura Maru No. 1*. "To hell with this guy," Ramage hollered toward the freighter he had just missed. "Let's go over and get these big ones."[18]

*Parche* was making 18.5 knots on the surface as Ramage ordered Stanton to make another hard right rudder to approach the two large tankers. As the boat clawed for flank speed, Lieutenant Allcorn continued to track the freighter that had just been missed with the first two torpedoes. Erwin's plot and Allcorn's TDC solutions were both good for another chance at the ship, so Ramage had Daufenbach call back to the after torpedo room, "Make ready the stern tubes."

At 0402, Ramage ordered Carroll Kinkel's after gang to fire the No. 7 tube at the original freighter from a range of 2,000 yards. Charlie Welton quickly set the prescribed depth on his torpedo. *Parche* shuddered as a rush of compressed air expelled her third war fish of the young action.

There was little time to track the results of this firing. An explosion was heard two minutes later but the source could not be confirmed. This torpedo was thus officially believed to have been a miss as well. In the wild action that ensued, *Parche*'s bridge team had completely lost sight of this first freighter target.

Red Ramage had his sights set on the two Japanese tankers dead ahead, the already damaged *Koei Maru* and the convoy flagship *Ogura Maru*. Closing the leading tanker, *Parche* opened fire at 0407 with four bow tubes, 3, 4, 5, and 6, at *Koei Maru*. The distance was a mere 1,500 yards with a 110 port track. According to Ramage, the first torpedo "disintegrated" this three-masted tanker's bow. The other three torpedoes were witnessed to pile into the tanker's bridge, quarter, and stern, respectively. This tanker was seen to sink rapidly, leaving only a small pool of burning oil on the surface. "The leading tanker collected the full salvo and sank immediately," Allcorn recalled. By some hand of fate, the majority of the soldiers on board her survived the sinking.[19]

"Right full rudder!" Ramage called as he set up on the next target.

*Parche* swung to starboard to bring her stern tubes to bear on the second tanker. At 0410, she fired her remaining three loaded stern tubes at the other tanker, the flagship *Ogura Maru*, from a distance of 1,200 yards. The first was seen to miss ahead. The second and third torpedoes exploded forward on *Ogura*, slowing him down to about two knots but not stopping him.

"The escorts now began to become a problem with their indiscriminate machine-gun fire and flares," logged Ramage. Lookout Dave Hussey found it increasingly difficult to keep track of all the enemy ships among the explosions, flares, and gunfire. "There were ships all over the place. We were mainly concerned with dodging the ships that were intent upon sinking us," he recalled. Glenn Meise recalled, "Mixed in with their regular shells were tracer bullets and they had our deck lit up like it was daylight. I kept trying to squeeze further into the indentation between the two periscope wells until I felt like I was part of them."[20]

According to Ray Karr, the skipper became concerned with the tracers zipping by above the bridge and ordered his lookouts down from the upper shears. "The lower sections of the bridge were protected by armored plates," he said. "The Japanese were overshooting us toward each other, so Ramage told us to get down off the shears for our own protection. The tracers looked like they were going to hit you right between the eyes until they got close and appeared to veer off."

*Parche* had spent all ten of her loaded torpedoes but Jim Campbell continued to monitor the situation on the TBT for skipper Ramage. Gray's

One of *Parche*'s 31 July torpedo victims was the 7,169-ton freighter *Dakar Maru*. ONI-208-J Revised.

radar scope in the conning tower indicated the size of the various large and small ships of the convoy. The skipper occasionally dropped down to the open hatch leading into the conning tower to question Gray on the size of these pips before returning to Campbell on the TBT. Ramage would return with the bearing of a prime target and then coach his TBT operator to lock onto that target. "Once I got centered on the target I couldn't get off it to look at anything else," Campbell related. "I had to stay with that ship."[21]

Radar man John Gray maintained a steady stream of data to the skipper's constant queries on target distances. Radioman Bill Gilcher would long remember one exchange between Gray and their skipper that night. Ramage called down to ask if anything was on the PPI screen to port. Gray's matter-of-fact reply from the conning tower was, "If they're closer than 50 yards, I can't pick them up."

Sixteen minutes had passed since *Parche* had commenced her approach on the first freighter. In spite of the escorts' wild firing, another target of opportunity presented itself immediately. A medium-sized merchantman with a sizable superstructure came into sight. The convoy had apparently changed course in an effort to escape the oncoming *Steelhead*. The new target that turned into *Parche*'s path was "just asking for trouble," Ramage logged. This ship was later determined to be the 7,000-ton freighter *Dakar Maru*.[22]

Submarines normally submerged after an attack so that the crews could safely reload their tubes. On this night, it was not an option and Frank Allcorn's surface reload plan was put into motion once again.

In Don Walters' forward room and in Carroll Kinkel's after room, the reload gangs labored to swing new torpedoes into the tubes. Red Williams, a new hand assigned to the after reload gang, recalled, "It was kinda hectic reloading those tubes because we were maneuvering all around on the surface." Williams worked with an efficient team in Walters' forward room that included Mo Taylor, Jasper Hill, Bill Hilditch, Jim Hawkey, Chuck Gooden, Charlie McNutt, and Johnny Barnes.

McNutt, one of the new hands for this run, had been assigned to Walters' forward room as part of the reload crew. Their bunks had already been

Entitled ". . . *I Got Mad! . . .* ," this painting by British artist John Meeks depicts *Parche's* 31 July 1944 surface attack on Japanese convoy MI-11. Red Ramage ably conned his boat past enemy ships that attempted to ram *Parche* as tracers and flares lit the skies. *Original painting by artist John Meeks courtesy of www.SubArt.net.*

cleared out of the way to move the 3,000-pound fish from their ready racks into the tubes as McNutt and his comrades began reloading. Each torpedo was secured with a metal belly band. "Special quick-release straps had been made at Portsmouth Navy Yard so the torpedoes could be locked in place for quick safety," recalled Lieutenant Allcorn. Before the bands were removed, lines were secured to a dog on the back of the Mark 14 that helped the men swing the heavy warheads from the racks toward the tubes. Gooden found the reloading experience on the surface "a little more hectic than normal" with all of the pitching and rolling as *Parche* twisted.[23]

In their zeal to speed the reload, McNutt and Williams had quickly removed the quick-release straps before the lines were attached to the dogs. Jasper Hill, a veteran second class torpedoman from New York, barked, "Don't take the belly bands off the torpedoes!"

The unsecured torpedoes could easily bounce loose as the submarine pitched and rolled on the surface during her wild ride through the Japanese convoy. But Hill's admonitions went unheeded. "We already had the first belly band off and it was gone," McNutt recalled later. "I'll never forget him yelling at us."

The scene was equally fast-paced in the after torpedo room where senior Torpedoman Kinkel oversaw the labors of Carl Dilley, Ray McMahon,

Joe Nichols, Cory Maupin—who had joined the after room for the second patrol—Charlie Welton, Ed Mokos, and Ralph St. Denny, the latter a new hand who hailed from Niagara Falls, New York. Mokos, the young sailor who had been nearly washed overboard earlier in the patrol, recalled, "I didn't have time to be scared. We were firing our torpedoes as fast as we could get them in the tubes."

Torpedo officer Frank Allcorn remained at his TDC in the conning tower but periodically checked the progress of his reload crews during this hiatus from firing. "I have never been so busy or so concentrated on anything in all my life," Allcorn later said of his efforts to direct *Parche*'s war fish this night.[24]

---

*Parche*'s frantic romp through the Japanese convoy was little more than a quarter-hour old when Red Ramage received word topside that his able torpedomen had completed the reload on forward tubes 1 and 2. He commenced an approach on his fourth target at 0412. Almost as soon as the hydraulic tube doors had been opened, he called for the firing of these two war fish.

*Parche* shuddered slightly as two more Mark 14s raced ahead toward the nearest freighter, *Dakar Maru*. This vessel was only 800 yards away on a starboard track but the distance quickly narrowed to 500 yards. Both torpedoes were seen to hit the ship directly amidships. The heavy freighter broke in two and sank within minutes according to those watching topside from the bridge. Japanese post-action reports, how-ever, would indicate that *Parche*'s torpedoes ripped a hole in *Dakar*'s port side 40 feet long by 20 feet high, flooding the engine room and killing her power. The freighter remained stubbornly afloat, drifting through the currents of Balintang Channel.[25]

*Parche* had thus far led a charmed life in dodging and weaving through this convoy handing out deadly violence. But Red Ramage was not finished yet. The next minutes, in fact, were ones that had not been equaled by any U.S. boat thus far in the Pacific War. The red-haired skipper remained on the bridge throughout, conning his boat like a poised quarterback leading his team on a desperate come-from-behind offensive drive in the closing moments of a championship game. In football, a mistake meant an interception, a fumble, or an expired time clock that ended the game and unfairly branded the valiant quarterback as the loser. For *Parche*, a mistake at this point by her leader would mean the loss of the boat and 83 lives.

Just like that quarterback who achieves the incredible last-minute victory, Ramage needed good luck and coordinated teamwork.

This night, he had plenty of both.

Frank Allcorn felt that Ramage "was in his element" this night as he calmly picked targets and dodged others. Bob Erwin, noting his plotted squiggles of the boat's maneuvers through MI-11, recalled that *Parche* "made at least two full circles inside the convoy."[26]

At 0417, one minute after firing on this last ship, Ramage came right to avoid the nearest escort and headed back to finish off his second crippled tanker, *Ogura Maru*. "As we closed, we could see lights on his stern indicating he was manning his guns," he wrote. *Parche* crossed the tanker's track only 200 yards astern at 0419 while opening up the range to bring the stern tubes to bear—which the after gang had been furiously reloading.

As the distance opened up to about 500 yards, *Ogura*'s gun crew opened up on *Parche* with everything they had. Shells estimated at 4- or 5-inch caliber whistled overhead and landed well ahead of the submarine. "Apparently his trim down by the bow did not permit depressing his gun sufficiently to get on us," Ramage noted. The tanker's 20-mm, 40-mm, and small fire, however, was "too hot to handle."

Small arms fire clattered around *Parche*'s superstructure. Fortunately, no one was hit as bullets clanged off the sub's upper works. Just after 0419, the skipper sent all lookouts below for their own safety. "There just wasn't room for everybody up there, so I said, 'Clear the bridge,'" Ramage would later relate.[27]

Ramage did not want excess hands topside in the face of the hot gunfire. Lookouts Karr, Meise, and Hussey cleared the bridge as *Parche* tore through the convoy. Hussey quickly took his normal submerged station at the bow planes to prepare for the dive he expected any moment. For the moment, Ramage had only three other men with him topside—battle stations OOD Jim Campbell, JOD Ed Rauscher, and the duty quartermaster, George Plume. Per his log, "the quartermaster stuck to the after TBT until we had the setup" while Campbell manned the forward TBT. The minutes that followed were hectic at best and Ramage would find even this small number topside to be too many.[28]

"The whole place was alight with gunfire," the determined skipper recalled. "Everybody was shooting at everybody and anything. But nobody, I felt, could see us except for this rooster tail that we were laying out there, going through at 20 knots."[29]

Lieutenant Allcorn on the TDC wrote that this tanker "was shooting at us from a stern gun. Red called down and said, 'You've got to hit this guy.'"

This 1949 illustration depicts skipper Red Ramage on the bridge of *Parche* during his Congressional Medal of Honor–awarded romp through the Japanese convoy. He sent his lookouts below due to the heavy gunfire, leaving only one officer and a quartermaster to help man the bridge TBTs. *Painting by Fred Freeman.*

Allcorn acknowledged his skipper's request by hollering back, "I can hear the gunfire!"[30]

By 0421, Carroll Kinkel's after gang had three more torpedo tubes loaded and ready. Commander Ramage did not hesitate to use them. The crippled tanker, having just crossed astern of *Parche*'s track, had opened up the range to 700 yards when Ramage decided to fire "at this menace."

Three more torpedoes bubbled away from *Parche*'s stern and in short order three powerful explosions ripped the oiler and effectively silenced any gunfire coming from that quarter. With as many as five solid torpedo hits, this vessel finally gave up the fight and went down, leaving only a small oil fire on the surface like the first tanker.[31]

At 0423, two escorts on the port quarter were concentrating their machine-gun fire on *Parche*. Ramage was about to come right to put them astern and "head for the prize of the evening, a huge AP." This was the large transport *Yoshino Maru*, already damaged by *Steelhead*'s torpedoes earlier in the night. But another ship had been spotted, a small converted gunboat. *Kazan Maru* approached in the darkness, coming in sharp on the starboard bow apparently intent upon ramming *Parche*.[32]

Junior officer of the deck Ed Rauscher picked up this angry ship and called to Ramage, "Captain, we're going to be rammed."

Ramage, focused on his next target ship, ignored the call and said that he was busy trying to fire torpedoes.

As the Japanese ship surged closer, a nervous Rauscher called louder, "Captain, we're going to be rammed!"

"I'm firing torpedoes!" Ramage snapped without looking. He had a good setup and did not want to lose it. With each second, gunboat *Kazan Maru* was coming closer to slicing right through *Parche*. In the midst of the battle and all of the maneuvers to line up on target ships, *Parche* had actually come to a stop at this point. Electrician Dixie Howell called up from the maneuvering room to inform the skipper that his boat was on all stop, a fact that Ramage had completely lost track of. Jim Campbell, aware from helmsman Stanton's announcement of "all stop" that their boat had stopped, later recalled, "I think we were all trying to get his attention." Rauscher finally called to the skipper a third time in a much louder tone to announce the danger.

Ramage finally shot a glance in the direction his nervous junior officer was indicating and exclaimed loudly, "Jesus Christ, we're being rammed!"

"All ahead flank!" the skipper yelled down. "Give me all you've got!" Ramage made no mention in his log of these desperate seconds. "The other fellow had the right of way, but we were in a hurry," he casually noted. Fortunately for *Parche*, battle helmsman Chet Stanton had already anticipated the captain's orders. Hearing the shouts of the freighter driving in to ram, he rang up all ahead full even before the order came down from Ramage seconds later. "Stanton saved all of our lives that night," Ray Karr recalled.[33]

*Parche*'s screws dug in deep as senior controller Howell and his maneuvering room assistant, Joe Caruso, pushed her to all ahead flank speed.

On the bridge, Ed Rauscher hung on for the inevitable collision as *Kazan Maru* came in dangerously close. *Parche* surged forward and when she was halfway across the oncoming ship's bow, Ramage ordered hard right rudder to swing his stern clear of the charging ship.

"The Japs were screaming like a bunch of wild pigs as we cleared all around by less than 50 feet. Mutual cheers and jeers were exchanged by all hands," Ramage wrote. Karr, now below in the control room, remembered that even "Ramage was screaming at them like a mad-man," with language appropriate for his disdain for his enemy skipper. Jim Campbell later recalled, "I think one report said she missed us by 50 feet. If she missed us by 50 inches, I'd be amazed."[34]

"I think they didn't bother shooting us because they were so sure that they had us rammed," thought Rauscher. He noted the angry enemy sailors screaming and shaking their fists as the two ships passed "damned close" to each other. Like the lookouts before him, Rauscher was ordered below so Ramage could concentrate on the large transport *Yoshino Maru* dead ahead.

Those in the control room could only imagine what kind of chaos was going on topside. Nick Casassa, tapped to join the auxiliary gang for the second patrol, was standing watch at the air manifold station throughout the rampage. With the *Parche* surfaced and maneuvering wildly, he listened to the exchanges between the bridge and conning tower since the mikes were kept open. "You could hear the whole thing that was going on and it sounded like we were pretty well boxed in," said Casassa. "I was wondering how the hell we were going to get out of this one." Under these circumstances, Casassa also couldn't help but wish he was still back in his little cubbyhole down in the forward engine room.

Steward's mate Carl Kimmons listened to the action on his headset in the forward battery compartment, where he was stationed as a talker. "During that historic battle, those of us below only knew that the skipper sent the lookouts he didn't need below," he recalled. "We only had a vague idea what was going on."[35]

Bob Hall kept busy in the galley through the night as he worked with baker Howard McMahon. "It was probably just as well that I wasn't wearing the battle phones to hear all the action up above," he recalled when he learned of the near ramming.

In the after torpedo room, Cory Maupin recalled hearing the skipper shout a personal insult to Hirohito in his best "Navy language" as the sub and Japanese ship passed within spitting range of each other.

In the forward torpedo room, Don Walters was concerned with the hard turns being made by *Parche* as his men continued reloading the tubes. "At one point, I heard a call for hard right rudder and we had to lock down one of the torpedoes we were moving until we got through the turn," Walters recalled.

*Parche* found herself boxed in on both sides by several small craft. The big transport was dead ahead with a zero angle. This left no choice but to fire at it down the throat. Thirty minutes after firing his first torpedoes this night, Ramage commenced firing his reloaded bow tubes at 0429 from an 1,800-yard distance. The first torpedo from tube 3 started off target to the right so Ramage checked fire. After respotting back on target, he fired two more torpedoes from tubes 4 and 5 as the transport continued to bear directly down upon his submarine. These were right in the groove and both hit with violent explosions that stopped *Yoshino Maru*. *Parche* closed in on the transport's starboard bow and then swung hard left to bring the last loaded stern tube to bear.

At 0433, she fired her last stern tube at *Yoshino* from 1,100 yards on a starboard 90 track. As the distance narrowed, the run to target was only 800 yards. "It was a bull's-eye, hitting squarely amidships," Ramage recorded. Taking a moment to survey the scene of chaos before him, he found that the Japanese escorts "were still busy firing at us and at each other." Gray's SJ radar gave a count of eight ships now. By the light of flares and gunfire, Ramage, Plume, and Campbell could see that their big transport target was dead in the water and was down by the bow.

Still, *Yoshino Maru* showed no sign of sinking so Ramage decided he would swing *Parche* back around to deliver the coup-de-grace. As he lined up on the maru, *Yoshino* suddenly disappeared from sight and from radar at 0442 as her stern came up and went straight down. *Yoshino Maru* took 2,442 Army soldiers—half of those she was carrying—down to the bottom with all of their equipment and another 53 sailors. By 0445, radar reported only seven pips remaining. All were smaller pips, offering no side lobes that usually indicated larger ships, with ranges varying from 2,000 to 12,000 yards.[36]

The entire attack had lasted 46 minutes from the time *Parche* commenced her romp through the Japanese convoy, but the thick of the torpedo action had actually taken place in only 34 minutes.

Further attacks were hampered by a mishap in the forward torpedo room that had occurred during the reloads. As the new torpedoes were being jammed into the tubes, gyro setter operator Johnny Barnes was just starting to match the settings when the spindle on the No. 5 tube was engaged. Don Walters, whose station was to handle the incoming flood of seawater, recalled, "*Parche* lurched a bit as we were preparing one of the torpedoes.

The torpedo went forward with a little more speed because of the lurch and since we had a slight down angle it hit the end of the tube door."

The spindle that Barnes was inserting was bent and Walters' crew had to clear the torpedo from the tube. The result placed the gyro setting gear for the entire tube nest out of commission until the crew could pull the torpedo from the tube to correct the bent spindle and housing. "We had to report back to the bridge that due to this slight damage, this last torpedo would have to be fired on a zero angle if it was needed," recalled Walters. Five forward torpedoes remained at this point.

*Parche*'s forward nest was effectively disabled for the time being. At 0447, Red Ramage thus called for course 330 degrees True to put a little distance "between us and this hornet's nest." Dawn was breaking as *Parche* began her egress from the convoy's vicinity. Rockets and gunfire continued to play around the brightening skies.

Bob Erwin remained at this plotting table as *Parche* began pulling clear of the convoy. Exec Mac McCrory, who had been supervising the men in the control room through much of the action, popped back into the conning tower. "What a two-hour adventure that was!" McCrory exclaimed.

Erwin, glancing at his plot, noticed that the entire attack had lasted only 34 minutes between the time the first and last torpedoes had been fired. "It was as if time stood still," he later reflected. "Most people had no idea how long this action had truly gone on."

TDC officer Frank Allcorn had been thoroughly consumed with his duties throughout the attack. Sonarman Bill Gilcher, just behind the TDC, had been lighting the lieutenant's cigarettes and passing them to him during the frantic action. At one point, Allcorn had called for another cigarette. "You've smoked them all!" Gilcher announced. "The whole pack!"[37]

Signalman Chet Stanton came topside to relieve Quartermaster George Plume. One of the escorts challenged *Parche* with the signals AA, AA, AA via searchlight, obviously unaware of what ship they were challenging. This was international code meaning, "Who are you?"

Stanton turned to the skipper and said, "Captain, that destroyer wants to know who we are!"

Ramage found it amusing that the enemy escort was hoping to find the name of this unknown submarine. Stanton, also finding the humor in this query in the wake of the destruction that had been inflicted on Convoy MI-11, quipped, "Those Japs probably have a lot of forms to fill out, too."[38]

# CHAPTER EIGHT

# "The Good Lord Had Been With Us"

Flares and explosions continued to blend with the dawn's first light as *Parche* hauled clear of the tattered Japanese convoy for an hour before submerging for the day at 0554. An hour later, a tremendous explosion was heard in the distance and other explosions were heard into the early afternoon.

Escort ship *Shimushu* charged about looking for the American submarines while three of the merchant ships began hauling on board Japanese survivors from the ocean. *Coastal Defense Ship No. 28* found one of *Parche*'s victims, *Dakar Maru*, drifting in Balintang Channel and she transferred her crew over. *Dakar* was ordered to be taken under tow to Calayan Island, 35 miles to the east, to save her cargo of valuable construction equipment. Admiral Lockwood's codebreakers in Hawaii picked up a flurry of Japanese communications on 31 July and soon knew the names of four ships that had been lost to Parks' Pirates this night: *Yoshino Maru, Koei Maru, Fuso Maru,* and *Manko Maru.* They also learned that *Dakar Maru* and *Ogura Maru No. 1* had been badly damaged by torpedoes; *Dakar*'s damage had actually been fatal.[1]

Two of these ships, *Yoshino Maru* and *Fuso Maru*, were technically listed as hospital ships by the Japanese. Lockwood's codebreakers for the Silent Service's Ultra system, in fact, had collected enough intelligence to know that many of the 22 officially recognized Japanese "hospital ships" frequently operated in miltiary fashion. They knew that Convoy MI-11's two protected ships were crammed with soldiers and equipment when they sailed in July.[2]

*Parche*'s historic romp through Convoy MI-11—often referred to as "Ramage's Rampage"—would become noteworthy to other skippers because of its technique. *Parche* had remained on the surface throughout the battle, charging in and around escorts and marus while continuing to fire her torpedoes and reload on the surface. Following this patrol,

*Parche* Torpedoman Bill Hilditch paints a Japanese Rising Sun flag on one of the torpedo tubes that had scored a hit. Note the little Buddha statue that Hilditch is clutching with his left hand. *U.S. Navy photo, courtesy of Bob Hall.*

Lockwood would credit *Parche* with sinking five ships for 34,000 tons and *Steelhead* with two ships for 14,000 tons.

Ramage was later unclear exactly how much damage *Steelhead* had done that night since most of her firing had been from much longer ranges than that of his *Parche*. "He got credit for a couple but I think they gave him credit for two of the ones we got," Ramage reflected. "But at least according to the book they gave us credit for the same ships."[3]

After the torpedo rooms had been secured after dawn on 31 July, Ed Mokos made his way to the after battery and tried to unwind on his bunk by playing cards with some buddies. He was impressed when Red Ramage passed through congratulating his crew. "The skipper told me later that he had to walk through his boat and pat each of the engines," Mokos recalled. "He said he had to do it because all night they had been going ahead all full, then all back, then all ahead full again. The engines and the guys in the maneuvering room had really done a job. The Good Lord had certainly been with us this day."

Lt. Frank Allcorn adds another Rising Sun flag to the merchant ship kills recorded on the wardroom bulkhead. *Courtesy of Bob Hall.*

*Parche* surfaced that evening and set course for Balintang Channel. Thirty minutes into charging the batteries, the SD radar announced that an aircraft was at 11,000 yards and closing rapidly. One minute later, a lookout sighted a four-engine Mavis flying boat at 7,300 yards. Frank Allcorn and Ed Rauscher made a crash dive to avoid it.

As *Parche* cleared Balintang Channel that night, the radiomen picked up reports that *Steelhead* had six torpedoes remaining. At 0513 on 1 August, she exchanged recognition signals with *Steelhead* via SJ radar. Warren Dingman spread the welcome news from the radio gang of advancements effective this date, including his own from yeoman first to chief yeoman. John Gray had been rated chief radio technician and Don Walters became a chief torpedoman.

That night, Lew Parks sent departure information to ComSubPac reporting the results of the patrol. Doc Brown, suffering from his appendicitis symptoms for two weeks now, was "growing steadily weaker from successive and severe attacks of appendicitis," per *Parche*'s patrol report. Brown had been on a liquid diet with an ice pack and sulfathiazole treatment. During the worst attack, which occurred about every third day, it was necessary to administer morphine to bring him relief.

Brown's condition had threatened to end *Parche*'s patrol early. "The wolf pack commander and I felt that a lot of it was just being put on, so we decided to stay," Ramage recalled. One of Brown's bunkmates in the after battery felt that the attacks were real. "I thought for sure he would die," Lonnie Hughes wrote in his little diary. After the convoy attack, the skipper checked on his ailing pharmacist's mate. Ramage asked Brown how he was feeling and "whether he wanted us then to take him into Saipan directly or all the way back to Pearl Harbor. He said he felt better and he thought he could make it all the way into Pearl; he wasn't too sick after all."[4]

*Parche* had cleared her patrol area by midday on 2 August and made course for Midway to refuel. That evening, Admiral Lockwood sent revised orders, directing Ramage to instead take his ill crewman into Saipan for treatment. Two hours later, Ramage logged, "Pharmacist's mate appeared greatly improved, mentally at least, since we were headed for home. Sent message to ComSubPac that we were continuing to Midway."

At 1500 the next day, however, Brown's ever-changing condition took another turn as he claimed to be stricken with another acute attack. Ramage set course for Saipan one hour later and sent word to ComSubPac that evening of his intentions. At 0715 on 4 August, ComSubPac ordered Ramage to go alongside the tender *Holland* at Saipan to transfer his patient. *Parche* entered the safety zone near Saipan at 1645, but hours later Ramage had still received no word on what escort ship he was to meet to guide him into the island. He radioed at 2330 that he wanted information on his escort ship "as time was getting short and was afraid we might have missed his answer."

The welcome escort news was finally received at 0600 on 5 August and a PBM patrol plane appeared on the horizon within two hours. At 0824, recognition signals were exchanged with the PBM, which circled *Parche* twice. *Parche* soon rendezvoused with the destroyer *Bagley* and arrived off the entrance to Tanapag Harbor at 1448. Within an hour, *Parche* was moored alongside *Holland*'s starboard side in Saipan's Tanapag Harbor. "*Holland* treated us royally with fresh fruit, ice cream, a new lot of magazines—even had the band out," Ramage noted.

Quentin Brown was transferred over to the tender shortly after mooring. Aboard *Holland*, her medical officer "found no indication of peritonitis and decided to feed the patient intravenously for a few days to build up his strength prior to attempting an operation," Ramage's report detailed. A replacement pharmacist's mate, PhM1c Rex Shaw from Michigan, was received on board late that afternoon. Before leaving the boat, Brown wrote in Lonnie Hughes' autograph book, "So long, Hughes." Brown assured his after battery bunkmate that they would both long remember *Parche*'s second patrol and he offered Hughes a casual apology for "my assorted disturbances waking you all the way into Saipan."

Pharmacist's Mate Rex "Doc" Shaw (right) joined *Parche* at Saipan when PhM1c Quentin Brown was transferred due to an attack of appendicitis that had threatened to cut *Parche*'s famous second patrol short. *Courtesy of Bob Hall.*

Ramage decided to spend the night alongside the tender since he had to fuel and get off his submarine notice. "After listening awhile to all the sniping going on over the beach, all hands were willing to forego liberty." A few of the officers, including division commander Lew Parks, did manage to make it ashore. "There was warm beer in a tent set up by the British and we talked to a couple of intelligence officers who were making forays into the brush at night to try and capture some Japanese to get some information," recalled Bob Erwin. "Sub duty sounded tame compared to their stories. My worst experience there was kicking a shoe on the beach that still had a foot in it."[5]

At 0725, *Parche* eased away from *Holland* and headed out of the harbor. She rendezvoused with *Bagley* again outside the torpedo nets and proceeded through the safety lane. The SJ radar picked up a large pip that night. *Parche* came within sight of a large U.S. task force in the early hours of 7 August that consisted of five battleships and three destroyers. Signalman Claude Lutz fired a green recognition flare toward the warships and the task force crossed ahead without incident. Ironically, this task force was under the command of Vice Adm.Olaf Hustvedt, the uncle of Ramage's wife Barbara. Once recognition was established, Ramage felt relieved that Hustvedt was aware that his nephew-in-law commanded *Parche*. "Eventually, the task force changed course and let us go by," he recalled.[6]

New pharmacist's mate Doc Shaw had his first patient on 12 August when TM3c Jasper Hill fell through the deck into the pit in the forward torpedo room, lacerating his calf on a deck plate. Lonnie Hughes noted that the wound was "clear to the bone." He watched as Phil Bukowski held a light on Hill's leg while Shaw applied five stitches to close the gash. Regarding the new pharmacist, Hughes wrote, "He is swell so I don't worry about getting hurt because he will fix me up."[7]

Bob Hall spent his nights working alongside Howard McMahon in the galley as he continued to earn his baker's rating. "I tried to think of dishes that might be interesting to the men or homemade," he said. Some worked better than others. One evening, he decided to make his mother's fried cornmeal mush, a hot breakfast dish served with syrup. After mixing up the batter, Hall let it solidify in a pan before slicing it up and frying it in fat.

"This was all well and good except for the fact that frying up the mush created a lot of smoke," he recalled. "There was so much smoke that they had to surface the boat to air it out." Ramage made his way back to the galley to determine the source of all the smoke.

The skipper told his new baker that Lew Parks would have personally come back to chew him out except for the fact that "he had tears in his eyes as big as horse turds from all the smoke." The wolf pack commander took the incident in stride but, said Hall, "we obviously crossed fried cornmeal mush off the menu!"

During the return trip, *Parche*'s quartermaster gang busied themselves with creating a battle flag. The boat had not designed one during its first war run. Ramage's wardroom had been kicking around ideas for a flag. The engineering officer, Dave Green, finally approached one of his firemen, Dave Hussey, and said, "You're always making sketches in the engine room. Why don't you take these ideas out of the wardroom and design our flag?"

Hussey, who bunked in the forward torpedo room, had a knack for the graphic arts. "Carl Kimmons, one of the officer's stewards, bunked right beside me and he was something of a poet," Hussey recalled. "I helped illustrate his book of poetry with some of my sketches." When Lieutenant Green asked him to sketch some of the design ideas, Hussey took on the challenge and penned several options.

The one that was selected stemmed from an idea from the Exec, Mac McCrory. Submarine battle flags often depicted the namesake fish of the boat riding a torpedo but they were not allowed to display the name of the warship. *Parche*'s new battle flag included her name in a roundabout way.

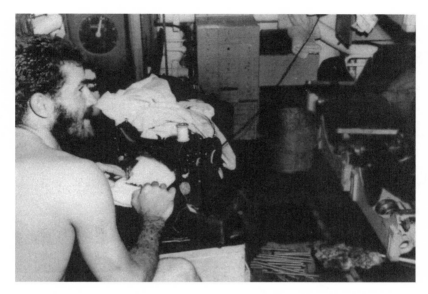

Electrician's mate Francis Stammen sews the Submarine Service dolphin on the upper portion of the new *Parche* flag. *Courtesy of Bob Erwin.*

In the upper left was the letter "P" and in the bottom right was the letter "E." In between, McCrory suggested that Hussey draw in the Arche de Triomph from Paris as an icon. The resulting "arch" in between the letters P and E symbolically spelled out "*Parche*" for those in the know. "On either side of this shield, I originally had two stars to indicate our two successful patrols," said Hussey. Above the *Parche* shield was the Submarine Service dolphin insignia and below it was a scrolled banner with the words "Par Excellence."

"The details on the dolphins, the volutes, and scroll work on the arch columns and capitals—as well as the cornice and frieze—were stitched by a very patient bridge crew, signalmen, and quartermasters, who also supplied the flag bunting and sewing machine," Dave Green related. "The 'sweat shop' for the seamsters was the crew's galley, between meals of course, but immediately behind the coffee pot."

*Parche* headed toward Pearl and made the passage without incident during the next week. One of the best kept secrets on board ship during the return run was a small still that had been constructed near the after engine and after torpedo rooms. TM1c Carl Dilley, who had made previous war runs before joining *Parche*, was one of the masterminds behind the still in partnership with motormac Charlie Satterfield.

Signalman George Plume sews the new *Parche* battle flag on the second patrol while Quartermaster striker John O'Brien (left) and Radioman Alfred Rick (rear) look on. *Courtesy of Bob Hall.*

Satterfield and some of his machinists had acquired enough sheet copper and necessary parts to actually build two stills. "Making two stills enabled the captain to find one during inspection of the ship and destroy it before we docked," explained Charlie McNutt. Fortunately for *Parche*'s bootleggers, the skipper never found out about the contraption. Dilley's torpedomen were responsible for acquiring the extra torpedo alcohol for the still. Chief Johnson made sure to order an extra case of grapefruit, pineapple, or tomato juice for mixers that other willing volunteers helped to hide until *Parche* came into port.[8]

Torpedoman Cory Maupin helped run the still in the bilges of the after engine room. He and several others used some of the excess torpedo alcohol and obtained fresh water from the Very gun. "We had our own system," Maupin said. "We would be warned if an officer was coming our way and we'd shut it down very quickly."

Don Walters and some of his forward torpedo room gang were not even aware of the gilley brewing. "I found out about it later from one of the firemen, Nick Casassa," Walter recalled. "Casassa told me he was on duty one night in the control room when Lieutenant McCrory, the Exec, happened to comment, 'It smells like alcohol.' Luckily, he didn't suspect anything but Satterfield was actually down below cooking a batch in the pump room at the time! If McCrory suspected anything at the time, he never let on."

The illegal brew was not enjoyed on board the boat but rather was brewed and collected by the gallon to be taken ashore at Pearl Harbor. "We had a deal with the engineers," admitted Torpedoman Ray Karr. "They ran it at night when we were on the surface so the smell of it would go out with the exhaust. The diesel guys would get half of it when we got into port and the other half was split between the electricians and torpedomen. Chief Allard from Montana was in on our system, too." The electricians stored their share of the gilley juice in the bilge under the main switch gear.

Many of the new hands spent their time studying the boat and drawing all of the systems in order to pass their qualification exams. Officers Dave Green or Mac McCrory handled many of these qualification tests during the return to Pearl Harbor. "If you didn't qualify, they put you off the boat on the relief crew on the sub tenders," recalled Charlie McNutt. "When you took your exam, you had to know your answers because you got a demerit every time you answered wrong." For most of the newer crewmen, their learning time in between actions on the second run had been productive, as McNutt and his buddies Ed Mokos and Bill Gilcher each earned their coveted dolphins.

*Parche* exchanged recognition and call signals with *Steelhead* at 0200 on 15 August as the pack mates approached the Hawaiian Islands. Two outbound submarines, *Gar* and *Grouper*, were also sighted later that morning. With the division commander on board, Ramage had his officers in presentation attire as *Parche* entered Pearl Harbor. "I can remember Jim Campbell and I being dressed in clean uniforms playing acey-deucy in the wardroom until we passed the entrance net," Bob Erwin wrote. "We seldom wore a full uniform while on patrol. Cut-off dungarees and a T-shirt was usual garb in the warm weather."[9]

*Parche* was flying her new war flag as she entered port and nine small Japanese flags trailed from her periscope shears to represent the nine enemy merchant vessels she had claims for destroying in two patrols. Dave Green had the watch with Mac McCrory on the bridge as Captain Parks strolled out on deck to record the proud homecoming with his personal camera. At 1030 on 16 August, *Parche*'s second war patrol came to an end as she moored at Pier S5 at the Submarine Base, Pearl Harbor.

Admiral Lockwood, his staff, and the base band were on hand to greet *Parche*. For the crew, an even more welcome sight was the bags of mail, fresh fruit, and other goodies waiting for them. Lew Parks and his personal assistant, Ciriaco Sanchez, were quick to end their temporary duty on board *Parche* as ComSubPac's staff swarmed on board to congratulate Red Ramage and his men.

Jim Campbell and Frank Allcorn were more than a little surprised to see one of the sailors who helped take in *Parche*'s lines. It was their old pharmacist's mate, Quentin Brown. "Not only had he survived the ordeal but he met us at the dock at Pearl Harbor to take our lines as we tied up," recalled Allcorn. Commander Ramage and Captain Parks were less than pleased to see Brown on the dock to greet his shipmates "in high glee." Ramage would later state, "That convinced us that he had been putting on quite a show and could well have caused us to abort the whole patrol."[10]

---

In reviewing Ramage's patrol report, Cdr. Charles Frederick Erck wrote that "the *Parche* hit the jackpot with a vengeance." He credited her with 14 or 15 hits out of 19 torpedoes fired on the night of 31 July. "The *Parche* took all wind out of their sails while taking the buoyancy from their largest ships." Admiral Lockwood congratulated *Parche*'s officers and crewmen "for this fighting, outstanding war patrol, the second successful patrol for this excellent representative of Submarine Squadron Twenty."

Ramage found that not all of his superiors looked highly upon the actions he had taken on the surface during his romp through convoy MI-11 on the night of 31 July. Cdr. Merrill Comstock, Admiral Lockwood's chief of staff, wrote in his notes that the action had been dangerous, foolhardy, and of too much risk. Ramage's actions had been against approved procedures, but Comstock relented in the fact that *Parche* had at least gotten away with it.

Although his own intelligence at the time did not bear out as many confirmed sinkings, Lockwood credited Dave Whelchel's *Steelhead* with two ships sunk for 14,500 tons and Red Ramage's *Parche* with five ships sunk for 34,300 tons. The postwar Joint Army-Navy Assessment Committee would later slash these totals to two ships for *Parche* totalling 14,700 tons and two to *Steelhead* for 15,400. Additionally, JANAC gave half credit to each skipper for sinking the 9,000-ton transport *Yoshino Maru*, giving *Parche* a final tally of 2.5 ships for 19,200 tons.[11]

Commander Ramage, for one, would believe that *Steelhead*, firing from greater distances, had unfairly been given credit for some of *Parche*'s maru victims during the frenzied night attacks against Convoy MI-11. Many years later, Navy commander John Alden would make his own independent assessment of the work done by *Parche* and her pack mate *Steelhead* on the night of 31 July 1944. He credited two ships to *Steelhead* directly and another four ships either destroyed by *Parche* or torpedoed by both submarines:[12]

| Ship Name | Type | Tonnage | Sunk By |
|---|---|---|---|
| *Koei Maru* | AO | 10,238 | shared credit |
| *Ogura (Kokura) Maru No. 1* | AK | 7,270* | *Parche* |
| *Manko Maru* | XAP | 4,471 | *Steelhead* |
| *Yoshino Maru* | AP | 8,990 | shared credit |
| *Fuso Maru* | AP | 8,195 | *Steelhead* |
| *Dakar Maru* | AP | 7,169 | *Parche* |
| | Totals | 46,333 | |

* Badly damaged but towed to Manila; considered a loss.

The *Parche* crew had performed admirably in action and all hands were authorized to receive the Submarine Force's combat insignia pin. Prior to the second patrol, 58 of 74 men were qualified for submarines. By the end of the run, four more had qualified and ten men were advanced in rating during the patrol.

The accomplishments of Commander Ramage easily qualified him for the Navy Cross. Earlier in the war, this medal was handed out to sub skippers who had conducted particulary aggressive patrols that had inflicted severe losses on the enemy. By July 1944, a new Submarine Board of Awards had been created and the Navy Cross standards had been tightened so that a skipper would need to sink four enemy ships, sink a capital warship or display "outstanding aggressiveness or heroic action on a special mission" to earn it.[13]

In Ramage's case, Lockwood credited him with enough kills on *Parche*'s second run. The scuttlebutt around Pearl Harbor was all about Red's surfaced romp through the Japanese convoy for 34 minutes in which he was credited with 15 hits out of 19 torpedoes fired. Talk turned to him deserving the Congressional Medal of Honor and the awards board did indeed recommend Ramage for the nation's next highest award above the Navy Cross. The endorsement would require a climb through the Navy's chain of command—including Adm. Ernest King's chief of staff, Dickey Edwards—before it reached the political grounds of Washington in late 1944 for further approval.[14]

Ramage, notified by Lockwood that he would be receiving the Navy Cross and possibly an even higher award, made his own recommenda-

*Parche* returns to Pearl Harbor following her successful second patrol flying her new battle flag. Henry Bougetz is in the foreground with binoculars below the flag as Exec Mac McCrory keeps watch. *Official U.S. Navy photo, courtesy of Bob Hall and Ray Karr.*

tions for *Parche* officers and men he wished to single out for their special actions. Although he truly believed that *Parche*'s survival on the night of 31 July was only possible due to the teamwork of 83 men, he could only hand out so many awards.

Wolf pack commander Lew Parks earned a Gold Star in lieu of his third Navy Cross. To his Exec and assistant approach officer Mac McCrory, Ramage would recommend the Silver Star. Silver Stars would in due time also be approved for the TDC work of Frank Allcorn and the bridge fire control work of Jim Campbell and George Plume. Bronze Stars would also be awarded to battle stations plotting officer Bob Erwin, radar operator John Gray, and to torpedomen Carroll Kinkel and Don Walters. With insufficient awards to pass out for the other men who had played key rolls in *Parche*'s greatest success, the skipper opted to write Navy Letters of Commendation with Medal awards for others, including Dixie Howell, Percy Barnett, Chet Stanton, Dana Jensen, and Reno Ussin.

Two previous submariners had been awarded the Congressional Medal of Honor and both gave their lives in service. John Phillip Cromwell was a division commander aboard *Sculpin* in November 1943 when the boat was badly damaged by depth charges. *Sculpin* surfaced and fought a one-sided battle against a Japanese destroyer. The submarine's conning tower was quickly riddled with heavy shells which killed most of *Sculpin*'s senior officers. The diving officer passed the word to abandon ship before he ordered two men to scuttle the boat. Cromwell, who had been briefed

---

### USS *Parche* Second War Patrol Summary

| | |
|---|---|
| Departure From: | Midway |
| Patrol Area: | South of Formosa |
| Time Period: | 17 June–16 August 1944 |
| Number of Men On Board: | 83: 74 enlisted and 9 officers |
| Total Days on Patrol: | 61 |
| Miles Steamed: | 13,873 |
| Number of Torpedoes Fired: | 19 |
| Ships Credited as Sunk: | 5/34,300 tons |
| JANAC Postwar Credit: | 2.5/19,200 tons |
| John Alden Credit: | 3.5/26,474 (plus 300-ton patrol craft destroyed by gunfire) |
| Shipping Damage Claimed: | 1/4,000 tons |
| Return To: | Pearl Harbor via Saipan |

on the upcoming invasion of the Gilbert Islands and knew of the Silent Service's Ultra secrets, opted to ride *Sculpin* to the bottom versus the possibility that he might give up such secrets under torture. He was posthumously awarded the first Medal of Honor for a U.S. submariner.

Cdr. Howard Walter Gilmore received the second posthumously awarded honor for his command of *Growler* on her fourth patrol. *Growler* charged in for a surface gun action on 16 January 1944 against the 900-ton provision ship *Hayasaki*, which turned to ram the charging American submarine. There was a frightening crunch as the warships collided and 18 feet of *Growler*'s bow was bent sideways. *Hayasaki*'s gunners then swept *Growler* with machine-gun fire that killed two men on the sub's conning tower and mowed down three others, including Gilmore. Mortally wounded and unable to get below, Gilmore uttered the famous call, "Take her down!" His executive officer carried out the order and enabled his boat to escape. Commander Gilmore was swept away to become part of the Silent Service's colorful history of valor.

The third such recipient from the Silent Service—and the first not awarded posthumously—would be Lawson Paterson Ramage, although several months would pass before the recommendation received the necessary approvals in Washington. After a long patrol that had thus far been void of torpedo attacks and full of bickering with his heavy-handed pack commander, the night of 31 July 1944 had been one in which Red Ramage vented some of his frustrations against the Japanese. As he would later explain his own "heroism" to President Roosevelt, "I got mad."

To a fellow submarine veteran who was writing a history of the Silent Service in World War II years later, Ramage was more succinct: "I just got pissed off."[15]

# CHAPTER NINE

# "A Calculated Risk"

Foremost on our minds when we got ashore was, of course, girls and booze," admitted leading motormac Dick Hawn. With months of pay fresh in hand, including the 50 percent premium for sub duty, the *Parche* sailors were prepared to pay well for both pleasures. After arriving at Pearl Harbor on 16 August, *Parche*'s refit was conducted by Submarine Division 44's relief crew and the Submarine Base. The crew boarded a bus with their personal gear and extra clothing for transportation to the Royal Hawaiian Hotel.[1]

Outgoing mail was subject to censoring by fellow crewmen and officers to prevent classified details of the boat's operations from being distributed back to the States. "It was a tedious and unpleasant chore but it had to be done," recalled Lieutenant Green. Once the mail was received, many men shared their letters with their friends. Fireman Ed Mokos picked up his new nickname "Greek" during this mail session. One of his buddies was reading over a letter from his sister describing how their mailman had delivered a Greek war effort letter to their home because he felt they had a Greek name. "I wasn't at all Greek," Mokos related. "I was actually of Slavic descent but after this my shipmates began calling me 'the Greek,' and the name just stuck."[2]

Pearl Harbor was a whole different ball game for submariners. At Midway, there was no bourbon unless the officers gave some of their allotment to the enlisted men. At Pearl, bourbon and all kinds of liquor were available. "Four men were assigned to a room where there were two double bunks, a couple of dressers and cushioned chairs," recalled Charlie McNutt.

Cory Maupin, Ray Karr, Chuck Gooden, McNutt, and others helped still masters Carl Dilley, Charlie Satterfield, and Freddy Frederick smuggle their illegal still ashore for parties at the Pink Palace with the "pink lady." Once the crew was settled in, they set up their little still on the commode

Liberty at Pearl Harbor. (Top) The Royal Hawaiian Hotel, known as the Pink Palace, and Waikiki Beach, seen prewar. (Bottom, left) Electrician Adolph "Pop" Russell and Radioman Glenn Meise during R&R. (Bottom, right) Radioman Myron Grover on the balcony of his room. *Photos courtesy of Bob Hall.*

and ran the coiled tubing into the bottom of the bathtub. The end of the tubing came over the top of the tub to run into a glass sitting atop a little stool. Willing volunteers hauled in buckets of ice to fill the tub and complete their little bar.[3]

"We cut it down with grapefruit juice," Maupin said. In the Royal Hawaiian, the juice was diluted in a bathtub with a mixture of one gallon of gilley to several gallons of water. A favorite drink was to mix the gilley with powdered Tang crystals and ice cubes to cut it down. Radioman Myron Grover and one of his roommates, Henry Bougetz, joined their shipmates to partake in the gilley. "All I know is that stuff could make you go blind," recalled Grover. "It was enough to make you feel like jumping out of the Royal Hawaiian."

One *Parche* sailor, in fact, did drink enough of the juice to do just that. "Zach Vogedes bailed out of a third floor window at the Royal Hawaiian because he thought he could fly," recalled Ray Karr. Fortunately for the high-spirited engineman, a lower-level canopy broke his fall and Vogedes returned to *Parche* after only a short stay at the base infirmary to tend to his cuts and bruises.

*Parche*'s new baker, Bob Hall, chose not to partake in the gilley juice. "I wasn't much of a drinker because I had done a year and a half of college before joining the Navy," he recalled. "I had seen plenty of young freshmen drinking too much and throwing up all over the floor. I wanted no part of that." His stay at the Royal Hawaiian Hotel made Hall feel like he was reliving his college days. Instead of enjoying the drunken frenzy, he instead helped his inebriated shipmates stumble back into their hotel rooms and find their beds.

Marine guards patrolled the floors to keep things from getting too out of hand. Some of the *Parche* crewmen really felt the lack of air-conditioning. They kept their windows open and busted out some of the slats on the louvered doors for ventilation. "When we checked out, they charged us a dollar for each busted slat," recalled Maupin. "For us, that was a lot of money, more than the cost of renting the rooms!"

Radioman Bill Gilcher recalled that Quartermaster Chuck Breckenridge and another sailor "paid $95 for a bottle of Vat 69 scotch. We told Breck to take it back to the hotel and we'd grab a cab and get some mix. Just as we started to get in the cab we heard glass break." To their horror, Gilcher and his buddy saw that Breckenridge had tripped on the curb. "He was stretched out flat with only the neck of the bottle in his hand. Ninty-five dollars down the drain!"

The officers enjoyed rooms with only one roommate each and a view of the beach out their back doors. They wandered through the local shops in Honolulu or attempted to bodysurf on Waikiki Beach. Curfew was at 2000 and most found the food at the Royal Hawaiian to be superior to the chow served at the local restaurants. "The bordellos in downtown Honolulu opened at 8:00 AM and if one passed through that part of downtown before 0800, it was usual to see a line of sailors waiting for the doors to open," recalled Bob Erwin.[4]

The officers were well stocked with alcohol for their two weeks of leave and could buy all the drinks they wanted in the officers' bar at the hotel. Each was given two bottles of liquor, two cases of beer, and one case of champagne. Erwin, newly promoted to full lieutenant, decided to offer a quart of whiskey from his allotment to one of his favorite enlisted men,

The first showing of the *Parche* battle flag post–second patrol at Pearl Harbor at the home of Dave Green's cousin. Visible officers left to right are: Bob Erwin, Dave Green, Green's cousin, Frank Allcorn, Red Ramage, and Mac McCrory. *Courtesy of Jim Campbell.*

Lonnie Hughes. Erwin and Hughes were the same age, spent time together on watch each night and often talked of their families. Erwin had a young daughter and Hughes was an expectant father. Hughes and his companions would benefit from Erwin's liquor donations during this and upcoming leaves.[5]

Red Ramage borrowed a Navy car one afternoon and treated five of his senior officers—Mac McCrory, Frank Allcorn, Dave Green, Jim Campbell, and Erwin—to a trip over Pali Pass and around Oahu. "I remember passing through the extensive sugar cane fields and several miles of pineapple fields," Erwin wrote. The officers were invited to a picnic at the home of Lieutenant Green's cousin. They brought their new battle flag and posed for pictures with the young lady. It was certainly a treat to be relaxing in a private home in Hawaii.[6]

———

The crew reported back aboard *Parche* early on 31 August after a much-enjoyed two weeks at Waikiki Beach. It had been exactly one month since the wild night attack on the convoy. The crew made an inspection of the relief crew's work, and at 1135 Admiral Lockwood came aboard with his staff. The ComSubPac flag was hoisted as "Uncle Charlie" proceeded to award Commander Ramage a Gold Star in lieu of another Navy Cross. The crewmen were also called forward to receive their combat insignia pins for having completed another successful war patrol.

Lieutenant Commander McCrory and his Chief Yeoman Warren Dingman processed paperwork to handle the obligatory shuffling of per-

(Left image) The *Parche* crew enjoys a beer bust following the second patrol at a ship's picnic at Waikiki Park in Honolulu. Top row (left–right): Dave Hussey, Ray McMahon, Johnny Barnes, and Cory Maupin. Bottom row (left–right): Don Green, Doc Shaw, and Ray Van Eperen. *Courtesy of Jim Campbell.* (Right image) Standing (left–right): Sam Roberts, Cory Maupin, and Reno Ussin. Kneeling is James McGuire.

(Left image) Carl "Gilley" Dilley. (Right image, left–right) Sam Roberts, Ray Karr, Cory Maupin, Chet Stanton, Ralph St. Denny, and Johnny Barnes. *All images, unless otherwise noted, courtesy of Ray Karr.*

sonnel. Among those being shipped out was Chief Clarence Allard, *Parche*'s senior auxiliaryman.

Allard had gotten himself into trouble during the refit period. He was charged with stealing Navy property, namely a base typewriter. One of the base guards had taken the senior motor machinist in for questioning regarding the theft. The charges against Allard hit him hard and he believed Chief of the Boat Verlin Peterson was responsible for ratting him out. "The borrowed item was returned to its original location but Allard was accused of theft of government property," recalled Torpedoman Jim Hawkey.[7]

Allard was confined to the boat overnight while the charges against him were being debated. A Captain's Mast was held on 30 August, in which

Red Ramage (left) and his executive officer Mac Mc-Crory pose with *Parche*'s new battle flag. *Courtesy of Fred Richards.*

Allard was charged with being "irresponsible and failure to safeguard government property entrusted to him." As punishment, Commander Ramage had his chief auxiliaryman busted down to first class. Infuriated with the turn of events, Allard was put on duty at the gangway as the deck watch night guard while his shipmates were ashore enjoying liberty. Things turned ugly when Peterson came back aboard that night. Allard threatened his fellow chief, brandished his .45 pistol and chased the older, heavyset chief about the deck until duty officer Bob Ashe could separate the two.

Perhaps in an effort to put the whole ugly event behind them, Red Ramage and Mac McCrory put both Allard and Peterson on the transfer list on 31 August. Chief motor machinist's mate Mark Goding was tapped to take over the duties of chief of the boat. Torpedoman Don Walters, promoted to chief petty officer, would help fill out the CPO watch schedule. Walters' shipmates had followed an age-old submarine custom of tossing him off the pier at Pearl Harbor to celebrate his promotion. Lonnie Hughes, promoted 1 September to chief electrician's mate, joined Walters on the CPO watch schedule. Electrician Joe Caruso was pleased, as he had recently written in Hughes' autograph book, "I hope like hell you make chief as fast as Snuffy the mad Russian [Vukovcan] as he and I don't jive."

Hughes had served with new Chief of the Boat Mark Goding on the sub tender *Beaver* before the war and had helped convince Goding to join *Parche* before her first patrol. "He bought my cap when I made chief," recalled Hughes. "I never got to wear it because we were leaving on a patrol run. My bunk was in the after battery right by the medical locker, which had a mirror on the door. I put the cap up on the battery vent motors

Among the new officers received was Ens. George "Gib" Tubb (left), seen on liberty. *Courtesy of George Tubb.* Right image: Chief Don Walters (left) and Lonnie Hughes, who made chief before the third run, on liberty. *Courtesy of Glenn Meise.*

and the kids used to take it down and try it on and look at themselves in the mirror as they cocked it all angles. The bill on the cap was broken and mutilated to the extent that I never got to wear it."[8]

While on liberty at the Royal Hawaiian, Hughes had roomed with Don Walters, Blackie Nania, and Phil Bukowski. As a father-to-be, Hughes had lived it up on liberty as his wife Nancy was expecting their first daughter within months. Walters autographed Hughes' little journal with the following note, "At the end of two of the fastest and most pleasant weeks we've had in a long time, Ski is still bitching."

With the promotion of Walters and with TM1c Carl Dilley being sent to new construction at Mare Island, there was a necessary shuffling of torpedo room personnel. Carroll Kinkel took charge of the forward room and Mo Taylor and Charlie Gooden took over the after room. Ray Karr, who had been schooled in electric torpedoes during *Parche*'s construction, moved to the after room to help with the new electric, wakeless Mark 18 fish taken on board for this run.

*Parche*'s refit work had included the installation of a DRT and duplex charging panels in both torpedo rooms. Both screws were replaced and the tail shafts were repacked during routine docking. From 4–7 September, *Parche* conducted sound tests and training exercises which included the firing of all guns and three practice torpedoes.

Gunner Jim Plumley was pleased that *Parche*'s firepower had been enhanced. One 20-mm gun remained aft of the conning tower but on the forward cigarette deck a new Bofars rapid-fire 40-mm antiaircraft gun mount had been installed. The single-barrel, manually loaded 40-mm was capable of delivering 160 rounds per minute at ranges to 2,800 yards.

Plumley evaluated new hands on the various guns during battle surface drills to find qualified backups for surface actions. Charlie McNutt and new Torpedoman Harold "Pinky" Pannell from Ohio volunteered to try out on the 20-mm gun as a secondary crew. The ocean was a little choppy but gunnery officer Bob Erwin had two five-gallon cans lashed together and thrown overboard.

McNutt was ordered to serve as Pannell's spotter. His job was to yell, "Mark! Mark! Mark!" when he had the bobbing cans lined up in the gun's sight. Each time Pannell fired the gun, however, McNutt jumped in antici-pation of the blast. "It kinda got to me," he admitted. "The officer beside us kept pushing me back down. I never did make it as a gun man." After a half dozen misses caused by McNutt's flinching, the pair was relieved on the 40-mm by the first team. "They knocked that can out of the water with their first shot," McNutt admitted.

Motormac Zach Vogedes bunked in the after torpedo room beside his buddy Bill Hilditch. "I thought after the war I was going to have to listen to all his battle stories, so I asked for the .50-caliber," Vogedes recalled. When Lieutenant Erwin asked him if he knew how to shoot one, Vogedes replied, "I'm the best shot in the Navy."

Erwin thus put the engineman to the test by asking him to blast the five-gallon cans with the machine gun. "I pulled the trigger but nothing happened," wrote Vogedes. "I pulled again, nothing. I looked up at him and he was shaking his head. About then the loader reached over and cocked the gun." All went well at that point and Vogedes was allowed to be the .50-caliber gunner.

*Parche*'s wardroom had its share of shuffling prior to the third war patrol. Lt. (jg) Ed Rauscher, quizzed enough by Red Ramage during the second patrol to know that he was not in the skipper's good favor, asked for a transfer upon his return to Pearl. "In submarines, men could actually ask to be transferred, unlike on surface ships," he related. Ramage was less than pleased with his junior officer's transfer request and Rauscher was passed over for awards for the second patrol even though he had been on the bridge with the skipper through the early action on 31 July.

Scheduled to go on board another submarine, Rauscher instead drew the fortunate assignment to join Capt. Babe Brown's staff at Pearl Harbor as his flag lieutenant. "It was a great position," he admitted, one in which he would eventually follow Brown on board a light cruiser for a tour of the Aleutians that would stretch to the end of the war.

Fourth officer Frank Allcorn also had new orders and Bob Erwin stepped into his job as the new torpedo and gunnery officer. Commander Ramage was fortunate in finding a willing replacement for his first lieutenant in the form of Lt. (jg) John Parks, who had commissioned *Parche* and made the first run. "Parks was an old Navy man doing things by the books and we took a full inventory before he signed off to relieve me as first lieutenant," Erwin recalled. "I probably still owe him one valve that was missing when we took inventory." Among items Erwin found to be missing was a .45 handgun that had been assigned to Allcorn as the gunnery officer. "This was one of the few times I can remember when we really followed Navy procedures and had a formal sign off when we assumed responsibility over a new department," Erwin wrote.[9]

Ensign George Gilbert Tubb, who was raised in a small northern Texas town near Amarillo, was received on board *Parche* one day before the start of her third war patrol by winning a coin toss. He had been a junior at the University of Texas when the Japanese attacked Hawaii in 1941. He casually stopped in a campus bookstore on Guadalupe Street and noticed the store clerk listening to a radio announcement about the bombing of Pearl Harbor. At that moment, Tubb did not even know where in the world Pearl Harbor was, but he would soon know it well.[10]

In the spring of 1942, Tubb hitchhiked from Austin to Houston to enlist in the Navy's V-7 program for officer candidates. "The ocean was a long way from the dry, flat plains of my hometown in White Deer, Texas, and I suppose that contrast gave me a special interest to join the Navy and see the world," he recalled.[11]

While completing his Midshipman School at Notre Dame in the fall of 1943, Tubb volunteered for the submarine service and was one of seven men from 286 volunteers to pass the entrance exam and physical. His submarine schooling at New London had commenced in January of 1944 with training aboard the old *S-17*. "There I was, a 'dry lander' maneuvering this huge mass of iron away from the dock, down the river, under the New London bridge and out to our exercise area," he recalled. "Somehow the docks, the bridge and shoreline managed to survive my inexperience."[12]

Soon after graduation in July, Ensign Tubb was shipped out to Pearl Harbor for further training and to help supervise Navy repair crews installing new equipment on submarines. While waiting for a ship assignment, he was working in the office when Commander Ramage stopped by looking for a junior officer to fill a vacancy on his officer's list. "He was unable to establish a preference between myself and another ensign, so he flipped a coin," Tubb recalled.[13]

Tubb called "heads" and won the toss. Within an hour, he was shuffling across *Parche*'s gangplank with his seabag as sailors scurried about loading provisions. "I was both anxious and excited," he related. "My anxiety was mostly about how well I would measure up to the expectations of the crew and the other officers. I knew that the crew was made up of both regular Navy officers and Reserve Navy officers and men. How would these men judge this 'ninety-day wonder?' "[14]

---

*Parche*'s crew spent two hectic days loading supplies, ammunition, and torpedoes before she was finally pronounced ready for sea again on 10 September 1944. Among the new hands making their first patrol would be electrician's mate Hurschel Chambers. Engineering officer Dave Green noticed in his records that Chambers had spent a considerable amount of time on destroyers previously.

"You're not switching to subs because you know what they can do to us with their depth charges, are you?" Green chided.

Chambers shot back, "Actually, sir, I was thinking subs would make a better place for me to hide than on those destroyers because I know what it's like to be torpedoed. I know that if a destroyer can't see us, he can't get us." Chambers was recalling his experience serving on board the USS *Kearney* (DD-432) during 1941. Two months before the Japanese bombed Hawaii, *Kearney* had been nearly cut in two by a submarine torpedo. "We limped into Iceland under our own power and finally made it back Stateside for repairs on December 31, 1941," Chambers said.

During the final training days before *Parche* sailed on her third patrol, Lieutenant Green had held tryouts for new battle stations planesmen to replace two key members he had lost to transfers. Charlie McNutt and Pinky Pannell dropped into the seats as *Parche* made a dive. Green ordered 60 feet and the duo put her dead on with a zero bubble on the inclinometer. They brought the boat back up as ordered and then were told to level at 100 feet. "We put that baby right on," McNutt recalled. Green, impressed with their accuracy, turned to Ramage and said, "Captain, I think we've got our new battle stations planesmen." From that moment on, McNutt would be on the stern planes and Pannell would be on the bow planes during submerged torpedo attacks.

For *Parche*'s third patrol, Red Ramage had consulted with Admiral Lockwood about his potential patrol areas. "My evaluation was that the Japanese weren't going to be able to continue running the convoys through the Convoy College area and they undoubtedly would seek to break out somewhere through the Surigao channel or San Bernadino channel," he recalled. In the face of this thought, he requested that *Parche* be allowed to patrol off the entrance to San Bernadino Channel on his next run.[15]

"This suggestion was met with very little enthusiasm," Ramage related. Admiral Nimitz was preparing his fleet to invade the Palau Islands at this time and an invasion of Leyte in the Philippines was slated to follow. Ramage doggedly stuck to his request and finally received the admiral's blessing to conduct his next patrol in this new area. "We departed with high expectations and a real chance to surprise the Japanese because we had no submarines to my knowledge patrolling off either of these passages before."

For this patrol, *Parche* was officially head of ComTaskForce 17 and her group was designated as 17.2.6. *Parche* was under way from Pearl at 1430 on 10 September with *PC 579* as an escort. En route to Saipan—now designated as a refueling base for submarines—during the next eleven days, *Parche* conducted daily dives, training exercises, and fired all of her guns, including the new 40-mm, at improvised targets. For the first time, *Parche* would be making an independent run, free of the wolf packs she had run with on her first two runs.

While at Pearl Harbor, *Parche* had a new ice cream machine installed in her galley. Baker Bob Hall served the crew the basic flavors that came with the ice cream maker: chocolate, vanilla, and strawberry. Once at sea for a while, he decided "it would be nice to have some different flavors. There were no other flavors for us, though, so I decided to experiment with different colors." To jazz up the morale, Hall would mix up his color variations such as Lizard Green and Saipan Blue. "For some reason, Red Ramage wasn't too gung-ho about my color variations, however," he said. "He said we should stick with the basic three variations and my concoctions were soon crossed off the menu."

*Parche* entered the Saipan safety lane on 17 September and exchanged IFF signals with a PBM patrol plane on 19 September. Two more PBMs were sighted the following day as she approached Saipan. Commander Ramage did not have too much faith in the APR-1 radar detector that had been installed before his second run. At times, it would show a full-scale pip for an aircraft target that was still 20 miles out. "You know, that thing is nothing but an infernal antagonizer," his Chief of the Boat Mark Goding advised. Ramage agreed. "I turned the damn thing off and said the hell with it because a couple of times we had been on the surface at night and planes went right over us. I was convinced that Japanese radar wasn't good enough to pick us up."[16]

*Parche*'s SJ and SD radar sets were an entirely different matter. John Gray ensured that they remained in perfect working order. On 21 September, *Parche* rendezvoused with *Sawfish, Drum,* and her escort ship, USS *Downes,* at 0600. At 0645, the *Icefish* joined up and the group proceeded to Saipan, entering the torpedo nets of Tanapag Harbor at 1120. *Parche* moored alongside *Sealion* on the port side of *Holland* fifteen minutes later. *Parche*'s starboard screw touched *Sealion* upon mooring as Ramage attempted to make a "smart" landing. "We thought the starboard screw had been damaged," Bob Erwin recalled.[17]

Ramage took his boat out the next morning in company with the destroyer *Cassin* to check on her starboard screw outside of the harbor. She made a dive and then ran submerged at all speeds to allow *Cassin*'s soundmen to monitor the sounds being made by her starboard screw. There was no vibration and all sounds were normal so she returned to port for final pre-patrol repairs.

*Parche* received two additional men on 22 September, F1c Charles M. Nutt and another officer, Ens. Ralph Flack from Ohio, bringing the total number on board for the third run to 73 enlisted and 10 officers. An air raid alert caused the crew to go to battle stations that afternoon, but this was secured in a half hour. Tanapag Harbor was now a busy place for the U.S. Navy, although several sunken Japanese ships were still visible. By this time B-29s were flying out of Saipan and Tinian to raid mainland Japan.

*Parche* was under way from Saipan at 0455 on 23 September. "We thought we were going back to the South China Sea and Luzon Strait," Erwin recalled. As *Parche* parted with her escort at 0900, however, a radio message from ComSubPac provided Red Ramage with the patrol orders he had specifically requested. "We were to proceed to the east side of San Bernardino Strait at the south end of Luzon and report anything that came through the strait. To make matters worse we were supposed to only report and not shoot even if we saw something," Erwin recalled.[18]

*Parche* was heading out just as the largest carrier battle in history was shaping up in the Philippines, the Battle of Leyte Gulf. Adm. Bill Halsey had boldly proposed that his Task Force 38 should bypass landings on Palau and Mindanao and instead leap directly to Leyte in the Philippines. Marines were landed on Palau but the Leyte invasion was stepped up by two months.

*Parche*'s gunners performed a mock battle surface that afternoon and the 20-mm and 40-mm guns were fired at a drifting buoy. PBMs and Liberators were sighted on her outbound leg during the next two days, which created several tense moments for the duty officers and their quartermasters. Recognition and IFF signals were used to prevent unnecessary dives but, according to Ramage's patrol report, one pesky Liberator caused him to fire a flare "to get him to go on his way."

Ens. George Tubb had been instructed by Exec Mac McCrory to learn his new boat during his first two weeks. In Tubb's mind, the fleet boat *Parche* "was the equivalent of a Rolls Royce" in comparison to the 1921-era *S-17* training boat that he likened to "an old Model T Ford." He spent every off-duty moment exploring each compartment to learn the function of every valve, gauge, and instrument on board his crowded submarine. At first, "I felt that I always found someone or something in my way. Then the space seemed to double or triple what had been available before. Instead of finding things and people in my way, I found ways to avoid being in their way."[19]

"Gib" Tubb soon found his way in his role as *Parche*'s commissary officer and assistant communications officer. For battle stations, he would assume the role of plotting officer in the conning tower to map the course of his ship against the enemy ships while Bob Erwin manned the TDC. He enjoyed poker, reading books, or watching movies in the torpedo room once he became a little more accustomed to his boat. His bunk in the officer's compartment was adjacent to the pipes controlling the hydraulic bow planes. "Every time the planesman decreased or increased the bow plane angle, a fairly loud intermittent pressure knock would sound," Tubb wrote. In short order, however, he was able to block out these noises and sleep soundly when time permitted.[20]

---

*Parche* entered her patrol area on 26 September as she closed the west coast of Luzon. At 1030 the following morning, Ramage received a ComSubPac dispatch directing him to proceed to an area 200 miles to the eastward of San Bernardino Straits to conduct a search for downed aviators. *Parche* searched the designated area through the next morning but found no signs of the flyboys. A floating mine was spotted that afternoon and the 20-mm gun crew was called topside to sink it. Gunner Joe Nichols calmly stitched the floating "hellpot" with a string of 20-mm shells until the mine sank from view.

Nichols was back in action the following day when another drifting mine was spotted and sunk. Admiral Lockwood sent new directions during the evening of 29 September, directing Ramage to discontinue his search for the flier and to proceed to San Bernardino Straits. *Parche* had covered about 1,500 square miles in the fruitless search for the downed aviators.

Lt. Dave Green (left) on *Parche*'s bridge at sea. Lt. Cdr. Mac McCrory (right) shoots the sun with his sextant. *Courtesy of Bob Erwin.*

The next day passed uneventfully except for one aircraft sighting and a third encounter with a floating mine.

In addition to Nichols on the 20-mm, steward's mate Carl Kimmons was asked to lug one of the .50-caliber machine guns topside to try his hand at blasting mines. This was a welcome chance to go topside for Kimmons, who had trained on the .50-caliber during his previous runs on *Plunger* and had become a good shot. The able steward, often working in his pantry an arm's length from the wardroom, was obviously privy to many conversations between Ramage and his fellow officers that he was trusted not to repeat. Kimmons had become quite close to the skipper and had earned his full respect both with serving the wardroom and in such topside special duties. As with the previous two mines, this one slowly sank from sight without exploding after it had absorbed a direct hit.

*Parche*'s newest officer, Ralph Flack, rotated into the watch schedule on 1 October as a JOD. Hurschel Chambers, one of the new electrician's mates, enjoyed his occasional trip topside to stand lookout watches. "We had what we called health watches for one hour every six days," he recalled. "It gave some of us a chance to go topside on lookout duty for an hour each week just to get some fresh air in our lungs."

It also gave Chambers a break from the wrath of his boss, Snuffy Vukovcan, in the maneuvering room. He found Vukovcan to be particularly tough on his new sailors and he soon felt that he did not have the chief electrician's full confidence. Even the electricians who had been with *Parche* since commissioning had their challenges with Snuffy. Joe Caruso and some of his companions once went to the Exec to complain about

Vukovcan's tobacco spitting. "He would sit back there in the cubicle in the maneuvering room and spit his tobacco into the trash cans," said Caruso. "We made a formal complaint to McCrory that we weren't going to clean any more trash cans that Snuffy had spit in."[21]

*Parche* patrolled San Bernardino Straits during the next week but sighted only a couple of fighter planes and a sampan. "To pass time and to relieve the boredom we would count coconuts floating out in the Strait," recalled Bob Erwin. He found that most of his four-hour daytime watches were spent with his face glued to the periscope. He was often very happy to be relieved from such monotony. "One memory of this time was of John Parks, my diving officer, standing watch in his undershorts, sandals on his feet and no T-shirt. He had an overhanging beer belly and looked very sloppy. It was hot and he was usually bathed in perspiration."[22]

*Parche* was a hot boat during this time. Her air-conditioner was designed for a maximum of 74-degree seawater and the boat was operating in 78-degree water, making the air-conditioning system unable to keep up. Commissary officer Bob Ashe had more than his normal share of complaints during these warm, boring days of patrolling without targets. Fresh fruits and vegetables were not available but there was an ample supply of canned mixed fruit. Eggs were also on short supply after two weeks at sea. Red Ramage preferred them fried during the first week and then scrambled as they became more aged. Baker Bob Hall continued to turn out fresh pies for post-watch snacks and meals. In order to create the necessary room for 17 fresh pies, machinist Nick Casassa built a vertical stainless steel pie rack for the galley. "That's just the kind of innovation our people had aboard ship," Hall recalled.

Hall further related, "I would do 17 loaves of bread, a dessert and cinnamon rolls for breakfast. I had a pie rack which stacked pies 14 or 15 high. It would take 14 pies to feed the crew and usually I made 17 or so for snacking. I'd start my baking around 8:00 PM and finish about 5:00 AM in order to be out of the breakfast cook's way."

Bob Erwin in particular enjoyed baker Bob Hall's cinnamon rolls, the smell of which wafted through the boat when he was baking during the early morning. Hall knew that his former commissary officer enjoyed these rolls, so he often had one sent to the bridge while Erwin was on watch. There was generally no cooking for lunch as there was a need to limit the heat-producing machinery while submerged. Lunches generally included cold meats and cheeses. "The cold meats were mostly large sausages like bologne and salami," recalled Erwin, "so the usual lament at noon from the crew was, 'Oh, no, horse cock again.' "[23]

Chow time in the *Parche* galley. Left–right are Charlie McNutt, Adolph "Pop" Russel, and Ed Mokos (pouring). Just beyond Mokos is Jim Hawkey. Larry Lawrence is in the lower foreground with fork in hand. *Courtesy of Bob Hall.*

Senior cook Lamar Brown, an Alabama native who had acquired the nickname "Rebel," took most of the ribbing from the crew in stride. Ed Mokos recalled sitting at a mess table one day with motormac John "Boston Blackie" Nania, who found the soup du jour not to his liking.

"Hey, Brown," hollered Nania. "What the hell kind of soup is this today?"

"Chicken soup," Brown snapped.

"Well, that chicken must have been wearing rubber boots when you ran him through your grinder, because it tastes that way!" Nania chided.

Charlie McNutt, who stopped by the galley for a bowl of soup and a few slices of bread before going on lookout duty, was equally turned off by Brown's meal. "His soup tasted like bath water, so I threw it out and headed for the control room," McNutt recalled.

The officer on duty, Lieutenant Green, asked him if there were any good snacks in the galley.

"They have a pot of soup on," said McNutt. "You should go try it."

Green tried it and returned in minutes, saying, "McNutt, I could kill you!"

Stewards Robert Nelson and Carl Kimmons served the same meals to the duty officers as they came off watch. Red Ramage's wardroom rarely had time to enjoy meals together except for dinner, when he tried to gather all but the two duty officers. Rough seas experienced when *Parche* ran through storms compelled the officers to use "fiddle boards" to help hold the contents of their plates in recessed areas. "The board was to keep items from sliding across the table as the eater had only to grab and hold the board instead of trying to catch and hold multiple plates and glasses in case of an unexpected roll," Erwin wrote. "The catching was not always successful. I can remember some misses when boards, plate, food, and all were tossed across the table into another person's lap. This was an occasion for a good laugh if you were not the victim."[24]

---

On 11 October, ComSubPac sent new orders directing the pack to proceed to a patrol area south of Formosa and to join another pack by sunset on 13 October. "This was most welcome news for the monotony of this place is almost unbearable," Ramage logged. Further orders from Admiral Lockwood made it clear to Bob Erwin that *Parche* was "to be out of harm's way" before the U.S. Fleet transited this area en route to meet the Japanese fleet.

*Parche* entered her new patrol area off the eastern end of Luzon Strait on 14 October and she transited Balintang Channel during the next day. After patrolling off the northern tip of Luzon for a few days, Ramage received orders to rendezvous his boat with *Sailfish* (SS-192) to help escort her back to Saipan with a radio that was out of commission. Commander Bob Ward's boat had patrolled off Formosa on 12 October on lifeguard duty for Adm. Bull Halsey's Third Fleet. *Sailfish* had performed a number of daring rescues, picking up a dozen U.S. aviators from the water and fighting off a Japanese patrol boat in the process. Ward's radio had conked out the next day, forcing him to retire toward Saipan, more than 1,200 miles to the east in the northern Mariana Islands.[25]

Ens. George Tubb had the watch at 2320 on 17 October when *Parche* rendezvoused with *Sailfish* to exchange orders. *Sailfish* was the former *Squalus*, which had sunk in 1939 due to her main induction not closing during a dive. *Squalus* had been salvaged and recommissioned as *Sailfish*, although some submariners ruefully dubbed her the "Squailfish." Ramage reluctantly broke off his patrol to help escort his fellow submariners back to base. The ensuing week was without incident, save for a convoy of six small ships spotted on 19 October. Due to the close proximity of land, *Parche* was unable to close these ships to a satisfactory distance for attack.

*Sailfish* and *Parche* proceeded on the surface at 17 knots toward Saipan. Two lieutenants, Bob Erwin and Bob Stevenson, had the deck at 0950 on

20 October when one of his lookouts sighted a Japanese aircraft low on the water to starboard at six miles. The bomber had slipped in under the radar and both boats were forced to make crash dives. "We were at about 65 feet when the one bomb he dropped exploded fairly close," recalled Erwin. "Not our first experience like this but the first while I was officer of the deck."[26]

During this time the naval battle of Leyte Gulf was beginning to play out in the vicinity. The Japanese fleet would suffer heavy losses in this major naval conflict. *Parche*'s crew was unaware of this major action but heavy radio dispatches gave some indication that some battle was taking place. "It became quite evident" to Red Ramage why Lockwood had been very hesitant to honor his request to patrol near the San Bernadino Strait. "It was Admiral Nimitz's standard policy that he would not permit any of our submarines to operate in areas where our air and surface forces would be operating."[27]

*Parche* pulled into Saipan on 24 October and moored alongside *Fulton* at 1030. She remained in Saipan for three days to effect voyage repairs from the *Fulton*'s relief crew. There were no bar facilities ashore for the crew to enjoy so shore liberty involved little more than swimming in Tanapag Harbor. Several men picked up cases of foot fungus while swimming alongside the ship.[28]

Junior officer George Tubb "was handed a pistol and scabbard and was instructed to escort a boatload of our crew ashore for sightseeing. The area, just months after our Marines had captured the island, was still a prime example of a big battle scene." Tubb found that destroyed tanks and landing craft still littered the beaches. "We walked by a vacant church and through the town square that housed a ceremony platform with a roof," he recalled. "Underneath the platform was a human skull, probably the remains of one of the Japanese defenders."[29]

Commander Ramage had dutifully performed the necessary escort duty of shepherding *Sailfish* back to port in Saipan. In the process, his *Parche* was absent from the San Bernadino Strait area at a crucial time as the Battle of Leyte Gulf played out. It was a cruel twist of fate that had diverted his boat away from intercepting the enemy's capital warships off Leyte.

"The whole damn Jap fleet came through San Bernadino Strait," Ramage later reflected. "I had asked for it and I was there. To me it was a calculated risk." The Battle for Leyte Gulf erupted in full force on 24 October as *Parche* refueled in Tanapag Harbor. "If we had been there we would have nailed the first damn Japanese ship to come out of there," he mourned.[30]

# CHAPTER TEN

# "The Bendix Log Blew Up"

The fact that ten men had new orders detaching them from the boat in Tanapag Harbor was not unexpected; unfortunately, one of these ten was Chief of the Boat Mark Goding, who had orders to become a sub school instructor. Dave Green's engineers took on 51,000 gallons of fuel and 2,000 gallons of fresh water while Mac McCrory sorted through the paperwork of the other necessary transfers: Chief Yeoman Dingman, Chuck Gooden, Dave Hussey, Bill Hilditch, Morris Gormley, Francis Stammen, Phil Bukowski, Hurschel Chambers, and Levi Pepenger. *Parche* remained moored to the tender *Fulton* for several days in between sister subs *Pomfret* and *Sailfish*.

Chief Torpedoman Don Walters was asked to assume the role of *Parche*'s chief of the boat and thus became the fourth man in less than three patrols to fill this key slot. He would receive eleven new hands while in Saipan. Some, like QM3c Lowell Brodsky, had never made a war patrol. Motor machinist's mate second class Arnold Bashwiner, on the other hand, was a seasoned submariner from New York who had made patrols on *Grouper* and soon proved to be an able replacement auxiliaryman for the departing Phil Bukowski.

Seaman First Class Joe Sheppard, a tall, blond-haired youth from Alabama, joined the forward torpedo room as a torpedoman striker. Firecontrolman Third Class Bobby C. Hall, a new hand from Poteau, Oklahoma, had volunteered for the Navy in April 1943 and was fresh from fire control school and the San Diego submarine school. With Bob Hall the baker already on board, the newer Hall was always known as Bobby to distinguish the two.[1]

Radio Technician Second Class Alden Leroy Lawrence joined Barney Barnett's radio gang at Saipan. His life had started under trying circumstances when he was born prematurely in February 1923 in Danbury, New Hampshire. He required an incubator to stay warm but no such device was

*Parche* enters Tanapag Harbor on Saipan. *Courtesy of Bob Erwin.*

available in his pre-Depression rural home. "So, they placed me in the oven of the wood stove in the kitchen where the family could keep a close eye on me," Lawrence recalled. His mother died within three days of his birth and his father opted not to take on the burden of raising his son. He took his older son and left young Alden to be raised by another poor family in rural Danbury.

He helped in his foster parents' grocery store and took on other odd jobs while in high school. One of them was riding in the back of a highway district truck to spread gravel on the roads by hand. Lawrence earned 15 cents per hour, but it was a brutal job during the New Hampshire winter riding in the exposed air. He excelled in baseball in high school and enrolled in the University of New Hampshire at age 18 during the fall of 1941. When word spread of the attack on Pearl Harbor, Lawrence walked out of college and enlisted in the Navy.

During his Rhode Island boot camp, Lawrence acquired the nickname "Larry," and he thereafter never used his formal name, Alden, signing official paperwork instead as "A. L. Lawrence." A relative non-swimmer, Lawrence managed to pass the Navy's swimming test by mixing in with the throng in the pool and then climbing out and getting checked off the list without ever swimming the required distance in the pool. Lawrence attended radio and sonar schools as well as advanced radar schooling at Texas A&M.

Two of the new men joining *Parche* at Saipan midway through her third patrol were RT2c Alden "Larry" Lawrence (left), who joined the radar gang, and S1c Joe Sheppard (right), who joined the torpedo gangs. *Courtesy of Keith Lawrence and Bob Hall.*

*Parche* lost Warren Dingman, who had pending orders to new construction back Stateside. Red Ramage went on board *Fulton* to secure an able replacement from SubSquad Eight. Chief Yeoman Allan Goodson was on duty in *Fulton*'s office when Ramage came on board. "He told me that his yeoman had been ordered to new construction and asked me if I wanted to volunteer," Goodson recalled. "I was fed up with staff office work, so I told him yes but he would have to ask the squadron commander because I didn't want him to think I wasn't appreciative of his treatment."[2]

So, Goodson left "the easiest job I ever had in the Navy" to join a fighting fleet boat. As he was preparing to go on board *Parche* the next day, Goodson noted another newly reported chief yeoman, Leslie Chambless, who was not qualified in subs. "I arranged with McCrory, the XO, to let me run the office and let Chambless get qualified," Goodson related. "I felt it would be best for Chambless and the sub force. I fully expected him to be transferred off after this run and I would stay with *Parche*." Goodson soon found a familiar face in Chief Don Walters, whom he had served with previously on *Guardfish* and the *O-3* in Philadelphia.

Lonnie Hughes collected addresses and autographs from several of his departing shipmates, including Chuck Gooden, Chief Goding, Phil Bukowski, Francis Stammen, and Torpedoman Bill Hilditch. Several of his shipmates had entered a little betting pool on what date Hughes' new child would be born. All of the dates had already passed. Hughes had picked the latest date in the pool and thus took their money as he still awaited news from home. "You won, except for the date," Mark Goding wrote in Hughes' journal.

Electrician Hurschel Chambers was among those caught up in the transfers although he had only reported weeks before. He had been assigned to
the night shift standing watch in the maneuvering room as the right-hand
man on the controls with Snuffy Vukovcan. "For some reason, Snuffy took
a disliking to me, even though he never told me so directly," Chambers
said. "I guess you could say that I had a lot of personality." Vukovcan
campaigned to Exec Mac McCrory and was successful in having his new
electrician transferred due to their lack of compatibility. Ironically, one of
the ship's cook strikers on his next boat *Blenny* would proclaim before the
crew in the mess room, "You're about the happiest guy I ever met. You're
always cheerful." And so, "Happy" became Chambers' nickname on his
new boat and it would stick with him for life.

In replacement for Chambers, Vukovcan received EM3c Benjamin
Harrison Couture from *Fulton*. Couture hailed from Oregon and had been
living in the Seattle area when America went to war. Although he had
finished sub school in late 1943, his war during the year that followed had
been as a relief crewman aboard the tenders in Australia and Saipan. His
first duties on *Parche* would be those of a junior enlisted man, standing
lookout watches and serving as a mess cook, but he preferred these over
more time on the tenders.

———

*Fulton*'s repairmen overhauled both high-pressure air compressors and
the hydraulic plant, which had been acting up on the patrol. *Parche* was
assigned on 27 October as part of a new wolf pack that included *Sailfish*
and *Pomfret,* with *Parche* serving as the pack's flagship. The crew could
only hope for better results now, as they had spent more than six weeks on
patrol without making a single attack. The new pack was dubbed "Red's
Rowdies," with Ramage in command.[3]

*Parche* was under way from Saipan on 28 October with an escort in
company with *Pomfret* and *Sailfish*. Commander Ramage was proud to be
sailing in company with one of his brothers who was serving on *Pomfret*.
*Sailfish* developed main bearing troubles a half hour out from Saipan and
was forced to turn back for port. *Pomfret* and *Parche* proceeded to station,
holding communication drills on the wolf pack frequency on 29 October.

Al Goodson, one of the two new yeomen aboard, took his seat at the
stern planes for *Parche*'s first dive after leaving Saipan. Red Ramage was
standing by as Dave Green took her deep to test the soundness of the
boat's refit. As *Parche* passed 300 feet, Goodson asked the diving officer

at what depth he should level the boat. Realizing the yeoman's former boat *Guardfish* had been a thin-skinned *Gato*-class sub with only a 300-foot test depth, Green smiled and said, "Six hundred."

"I checked him with a 'Say again, sir,' and Ramage almost split his sides laughing," Goodson recalled. "I hadn't realized *Parche* was a thick-skinned boat, so he had played a joke on me."

*Parche* was packed with fresh food in every possible spot. "The shower stalls on my sub were packed with food for the trip," recalled Officer's Cook Carl Kimmons. "When the food was used up, the shower was just another empty space! Showers were a no-no. . . . Maybe just before arrival back at port there would be enough condensation water for a quickie—but that would be a luxury. When everybody smells the same, you get used to it."[4]

For sanitary purposes, "the cooks and the baker could take showers daily," recalled Bob Hall. "The off-duty cook didn't take a shower on his day off, but who was counting?" Even such "Navy showers" called for limited water use by wetting one's self, soaping and scrubbing without running water and then quickly rinsing off. Hall spent his nights in the galley baking goods from dusk to dawn. The extra touches provided by *Parche*'s cooks did not go unnoticed by the crew. Torpedoman Jim Hawkey appreciated the special cakes Hall made for the crew on each man's birthday and the smell of the cinnamon rolls as he came off his 0400–0800 watch. Fire controlman Bobby Hall enjoyed baked beans the most while Nick Casassa appreciated the fresh bread and baked pies.

Torpedoman Charlie Welton felt that his boat's cooks were "top notch. We had the best food in the service." While waiting for his chow one evening, Welton found irony in a photo he saw while flipping through a recent issue of *Life* magazine. "The photo of the week in this issue was of a dog-faced soldier having his first meal in more than a week while leaning against his vehicle," he recalled. "And here we were preparing to eat a turkey dinner on our sub."

By the third patrol, the senior deck officers were three lieutenants, Dave Green, Bob Erwin, and Jim Campbell. Junior officers Bob Stevenson, John Parks, and George Tubb stood JOD duties with these three senior officers while Ralph Flack and Bob Ashe assisted with maintenance of the deck log during the four-hour watch periods in each full day cycle and did the bulk of the time-consuming decoding work.

Red Ramage conducted a practice battle surface on 30 October in which all guns were test-fired. New hand Larry Lawrence helped pass 4-inch shells up the after battery hatch with steward's mate Robert Nelson, who was also making his first patrol. Both men were standing almost directly under the open hatch. Lawrence was amused when Nelson asked, "Are we surfaced or submerged?" even though the sky could be seen through the open hatch.

Ben Couture, one of the new hands received at Saipan, was eager to take part in this drill. In his zeal, he injured himself while hoisting one of the guns topside. "I grabbed the gun and made a twist that gave me a hernia," he recalled. The young sailor was helped below by Doc Shaw, who put him on bed rest for the remainder of the day.

In the after battery compartment, leading electrician Lonnie Hughes had the bunk above Couture. He was aghast when he saw his young electrician's shape the next day. "My intestine was bulged out and was hanging down by my leg," recalled Couture. Doc Shaw wrapped the sailor in a girdle-like hernia harness to help hold his intestines in the proper position for the remainder of the patrol. "He was afraid of the tendons sealing off and leaving that intestine without any nutritional support," Couture said.

Shaw put him on light duty for the rest of the patrol during which time Couture assisted in the galley and worked on his qualification notebooks. School-of-the-boat classes were held in the forward torpedo room for new hands to become submarine qualified. Chief Walters called this "*Parche* Tech—College of the Pacific."

Contacts were few en route back to station. *Pomfret* reported sighting a possible periscope the following day and *Parche* maneuvered to avoid. On 1 November, Bob Stevenson dived *Parche* to avoid a Mavis patrol plane at 1040. A short time after dodging this aircraft, there was a mishap with one of the machine guns that had been test-fired during the battle surface drills.

Chief Dick Hawn was sitting in the forward torpedo room "shooting the shit" with radio technician John Gray and his best friend Bob Daufenbach, who sat before him on a tool box. Hawn noted leading gunner's mate Jim Plumley enter the compartment with one of the two .50-caliber machine guns that had been fired the day before during the surface drill. "To my left with his back to me and the others was the underwater sound man," Hawn recalled. "He had just taken his position manning the sound gear. This meant he was wearing headphones and he was training the sound gear head around listening for suspicious sounds. Next to him was one end of the 1MC, which was a microphone/loudspeaker system connecting the two torpedo rooms, maneuvering room, control room and conning tower."[5]

One of the duties of a gunner's mate was to inspect and grease the .50-calibers after surface action to remove the threat of saltwater corrosion. Plumley had placed the machine guns on the top of a large box the size of a steamer trunk, which held his tools. "The muzzle of the machine gun the gunner's mate had just placed on the bench was right behind Gray's ass and pointing directly at the Bendix log three feet away," Hawn recalled. "The Bendix log was a glass-enclosed instrument filled with gears and selsyn motors which constantly measured our speed through the water and put that information directly into the fire control computer."[6]

Hawn casually watched as Plumley grasped the .50-caliber's firing handle and curled his finger around the trigger as he prepared to grease the gun. "He had not cleared the chamber and the loudest noise in the world went off," Hawn later wrote. "The flash singed Gray's ass and he leaped off the bench like Superman. The bullet smashed into the glass cover and tore into the Bendix log, coming to rest in a selsyn motor."[7]

Torpedoman Jasper Hill was present for the mishap. "The gun was lying on a bench while the gunner's mate was cleaning it," he recalled. "It wasn't supposed to be loaded." Plumley was unaware that the last man to use it had left a round in the chamber.[8]

Red Ramage was in the conning tower with Lieutenant (jg) Stevenson when he heard "a helluva BANG over the intercom" at 1145.[9]

"What the hell was that?" Ramage shouted into the 1MC.

The sound man in the forward room, Nelson Fournier, turned around to see what had happened and saw only that the Bendix log had been smashed.

"The Bendix log blew up, Captain," Fournier reported.

"That's impossible!" Ramage snapped before racing out of the conning tower. Bob Erwin, seated in the wardroom just one compartment forward of the forward torpedo room, heard the explosion and raced forward with Mac McCrory. "Plumley was holding the still smoking .50-caliber machine gun in his lap," he said. "The Bendix log was a shambles. It looked like a surrealistic painting with wires and gears and springs hanging out of its face."[10]

Commander Ramage was furious with the "weak response" he had gotten about the explosion by the time he reached the forward room. Dick Hawn admittedly "had been struck by the incongruity of the soundman's response and broke out into a fit of laughter."[11]

Hawn was still howling with laughter when Ramage charged into Don Walters' forward room. "What's so goddamned funny, Hawn?" he snapped.

Hawn composed himself as the skipper and a gathering crowd inspected the wrecked Bendix log. The .50-caliber round had lodged in the transmitter motor after piercing the speed dial and wrecking several small gears. Fortunately, the bullet had not killed anyone and the Bendix log had perhaps saved the shell from tearing through the pressure hull. But *Parche* was in a fix as she prepared to transit Balintang Channel. The Bendix was used to measure *Parche*'s speed and distance through the water, thus effectively immobilizing the boat's torpedo control system.

Nick Casassa and instrument tech Sam Roberts set to work trying to repair the Bendix with the parts they had available. The only part they did not have as a backup was a six-inch-diameter gear with dozens of gear teeth. Jim Campbell traced out a pattern from the remnants of the ruined gear and Casassa set about filing out a new one by hand with the lathe. "I had some lathe experience because my father had been a machinist," recalled Campbell. "We took gear segments and hand-worked the lathe to make the gears and then knocked them in by hand." Casassa admitted that "it was making the gearing that was a little bit touchy," but his work would pay off after many hours of labor.

---

*Parche* entered her patrol area that afternoon and her machinists converted the No. 4 fuel ballast tank to a main ballast tank. Auxiliaryman Ed Mokos joined Ray Van Eperen's crew to go into the superstructure to convert the tank. "It was a potentially dangerous duty in the event an airplane caught us on the surface," he recalled, "but as a 19-year-old kid, you just don't worry too much about such dangers."

By 2300 that night, the Bendix log was back in commission registering distance but no speed input for the TDC as yet. *Parche* passed within 15 miles of Bataan Island on 2 November and proceeded to transit Balintang Channel. At 2220, *Pomfret* radioed that she had located a convoy and was attacking. Several explosions were heard during the next hour. By 2320, John Parks reported that *Parche* had picked up the convoy at 25,000 yards on radar. The crew went to battle stations and commenced tracking.

The moon was full and the sky was clear as *Parche* raced to intercept these ships during the late hours of 2 November. Ramage was unable to complete an end around to gain position before these ships reached their anchorage. He commenced closing the shore in hopes that the convoy would come south before entering the harbor. By 0033, the convoy was north of Sartang Island and "definitely heading for anchorage."

Morale took a dip on *Parche*'s third patrol as such contacts failed to develop into torpedo attacks. "Ramage did not seem to be his old aggressive self," fourth officer Bob Erwin recalled. Several of the junior officers, including Mac McCrory and Dave Green, discussed the skipper's lack of aggression in the control room but quietly kept their concerns to themselves.[12]

Ramage would later relate that the missed targets were "terribly disappointing. The remaining ten days that we were with the group were equally frustrating."[13]

At least some of his officers—unaware that their skipper had selected his own patrol area—would later wonder if Ramage had been sent to a low-action area because of the fact that he had been slated to receive the Medal of Honor. The first two submarine officers to receive the Medal of Honor had been awarded this posthumously, leaving some speculation that the brass wanted Ramage to survive to get his.

During this pursuit, Ramage received word that *Sailfish* was heading for a position southeast of Sartang Island. *Parche*'s men heard several distant explosions at 0450 as *Sailfish* scored on 3 November, blowing the stern off the destroyer *Harukase*. This warship was towed to shore but was never again operational. *Pomfret* also managed to sink a ship on 2 November but *Parche* was unable to get in on the action.

Distant pinging from patrol boats near the island was heard during the morning and aircraft were seen through the periscope. Two patrol boats swept the area during the morning, pinging consistently. That night, *Sailfish* reported four freighters still at anchor in Sartang Channel. The ships remained at anchor as the pack hung around offshore, dodging pinging patrol boats into the next day.

During the early morning hours of 4 November, *Parche*'s radar had three patrol boats at ranges from 8,500 yards to 15,000 yards. They made efforts to close on *Parche* but Ramage opted to open up speed and run from these patrol craft. He dived and remained submerged, patrolling without a shipping contact through the next day.

Such running dives sometimes provided humor below decks. Ship's baker Bob Hall had just put a cake into the oven when *Parche* made a quick dive. Due to the change in pressure, Hall found that the cake "came up three or four inches high on the down side and one or two inches high on the up side. I called it my 'angle-food' cake."

Upon diving, the helm switched from the conning tower to the control room where Doc Shaw had the helm duty. Commander Ramage remained in the conning tower, continuing to monitor the radar blips of the Japanese patrol craft. Radioman Glenn Meise, on duty in the radio shack, recalled another humorous moment of this early morning dive. "Submerged, it was standard practice for the Skipper in the conning tower to occasionally give the helmsman the word 'Stand by,' followed shortly by the word, 'Mark,'

Al Rick types up messages in
*Parche*'s radio shack. *Courtesy of
Bob Erwin.*

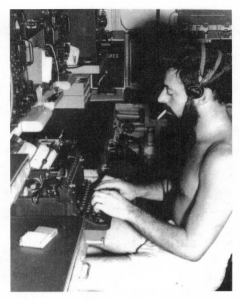

at which time the helmsman would give the compass direction we were headed." Shortly after submerging to get away from the Japanese picket boats, Ramage called, "Stand by," and quickly followed with, "Mark."[14]

Doc Shaw gave his heading per procedure. "The Skipper was flabbergasted at the reading and said on the intercom, 'What the hell are you doing way over there?' " recalled Meise. "It turned out that Doc, although we were submerged, was still steering a zigzag course. He never lived it down."

That evening, the SJ radar picked up another patrol vessel at 15,000 yards and Ramage maneuvered to avoid it. The TDC showed the PC to have speeded up and turned toward *Parche*. Ramage put two engines on the line and changed course to avoid. "We usually had two to three knots advantage on the surface," recalled Bob Erwin. "This activity was becoming very frustrating. We were seeing plenty of enemy ships but nothing to shoot at. Most of them were chasing us."[15]

By 0015 on 7 November, *Parche* finally shook off the patrol boat that had made radar contact on her. At 1000, *Parche* suffered another major fire control failure. The follow-up system of the master gyro failed, thus offering no directional signal to the TDC or to the torpedo gyros. Fire control technician Sam Roberts was diligent this day working many hours to repair the gyro. "The apparent fault was in the main output cable that consisted of twenty to thirty separate circuits," torpedo officer Erwin recalled. "When the cable was removed and was laying on the deck, all the circuits checked

*Parche* baker Bob Hall at work in the tiny galley. *Courtesy of Bob Hall.*

okay. When reinstalled, it did not work. After doing this at least twice, Roberts went to look for a replacement and one was available." By 1700, Roberts had properly installed the new wiring and the gyro was reported to be back in operation along with the repaired Bendix log.

The wind and seas increased in intensity on 9 November. "Weather has all appearances of a small typhoon," Ramage logged at 1900. "Wind force 8 with long heavy swells from northwest." The typhoon continued to blow through the next day and the seas did not begin to moderate until the evening of 11 November. The three wolf pack boats rendezvoused on 12 November to exchange new orders from the pack commander.

In the midst of these rough seas, new radar technician Larry Lawrence was tasked with climbing the mast atop the periscope shears to work on the radar. The pitching and rolling of the boat was greatly amplified at this height and the young sailor realized he was becoming seasick. Lawrence looked down and noted that the captain was on deck below him. Thinking fast, he used his cap to catch the effects of his queasy stomach before sailing it over the side to land in the ocean.

Red Ramage, watching the cap drop, gazed up toward the mast and hollered, "Looks like you'll need a new hat, Lawrence!"

"Yes, sir," came the weak reply.

The rough seas even made life challenging for the galley crew. Bob Hall's role as *Parche*'s baker entailed slaving in the tiny kitchen area from 2100 each night until about 0600. "The cooks usually worked 24 hours on and 24 hours off, but as the baker I had to work all night every night," he recalled. Armed with Navy cookbooks and some of his mother's recipes, Hall prepared fresh bread, pies, cookies, biscuits, cinnamon rolls, and other treats.

For lemon meringue, he had to triple the Navy cookbook recipe by separating 72 eggs to whip up the necessary quantity. "When it came to pies, I had to make 14 to feed the whole crew," Hall recalled. "But I usually made three extra in case there were people who missed their meal or who wanted a snack as they came off watch." His more common flavors were apple, lemon, creme, pumpkin, and chocolate.

The typhoon conditions experienced during *Parche*'s third run added an extra level of challenges for Hall, Brown, and Johnson. Most of the galley's large pots and pans were square so that they could be wedged into place without sliding around during rough seas. "One night I thought I'd be smart and brace the square pot with a large can of unopened mushrooms to keep it from sliding," he related. "The mushroom can promptly exploded and I had to learn that lesson the hard way."

Diving officer Dave Green found keeping the ship in trim ready to dive challenging in the angry seas. Senior electrician Lonnie Hughes often passed time in the forward torpedo room smoking cigarettes with his best friend Bob Daufenbach, who enjoyed cigars in his forward bunk when *Parche* was surfaced at night. Hughes recalled one night when Lieutenant Green was unable to keep the boat properly level on the surface during this typhoon. "Green called out to send Duffy aft, being that Duffy was so big," Hughes related. "We then started calling him the walking regulator."[16]

A contact report of enemy vessels to the southwest was received on the evening of 14 November. The pack commander assigned each boat new stations to search. *Parche* made radar contact on two small ships at 12,000 yards at 0048 on 15 November. Ramage stationed his tracking team and commenced closing. Two small escorts were found and *Parche* avoided these while continuing to look for whatever they might be guarding. Radar interference was noted during the morning hours but all contacts developed into small patrol boats or sea trucks. *Parche*, *Pomfret*, and *Sailfish*, plus another neighboring wolf pack, were all frustrated by the lack of worthwhile torpedo targets.

Ships worthy of attack were nowhere to be seen during the next few days on station. A duty less garnered than mess cooking on a wartime submarine was the maintenance of the heads, which often fell to the auxiliarymen. This seemingly routine job was not simple. "The tank was emptied by opening the outlet to the sea, closing the inlet and blowing compressed air into the tank until it was empty," Bob Erwin explained. "Then the outlet valve was closed, the inlet valve was opened, and the tank was vented."

During the third patrol, skipper Red Ramage fell victim to a sanitary tank that had not been fully vented. The contents of the head blasted the skipper and compelled him to take an unplanned shower. "There were a few choice words exchanged, and I am sure Ramage's words would have been very colorful as he had been colored by the experience," recalled Erwin. Upon surfacing that night, a diver was sent overboard to check on the faulty valve to the sanitary tank. A pair of boxers marked with "R. Ashe" was found clogging the valve. The junior officer who had flushed the undershorts into the system to be blown into the sea was not in Ramage's favor from that point.[17]

Heavy seas and winds plagued the search efforts again on 17 and 18 November. It was standard Navy practice to send messages of major family incidents to sailors over the regular radio channel. Chief Lonnie Hughes finally received the important news from home that he had been waiting for. Glenn Meise, who normally stood watch in the radio shack from midnight to 0800, was on duty when he copied the Fox schedule announcing that Hughes' wife Nancy had given birth to a baby girl they named Lonni after her father's own nickname.

"In Latitude 18, Longitude 116 on Nov. 17, 1944, as message came to me," Hughes wrote in his diary. "It was sent on the Fox sched. all coded up with the Japs trying to jam it out. Meise, RM3c, copied it. It said Nancy had a baby girl and both were fine. That's all good news. In fact, the best news in the world."[18]

A properly illuminated hospital ship was sighted on 20 November but attack-worthy targets continued to be elusive. Rough weather on 21 November prevented *Parche* from making anything better than one engine speed on the surface. The wind had reached gale force again and waves periodically crashed over the bridge and dumped water down the conning tower hatch.

During this period of rough seas, Rebel Brown served fried oysters for dinner and many of the officers and crew became sick. The heavy rolling of the boat caused many to lose their meal. "During this stretch of weather, I remember being thrown out of a bunk while sound asleep when the ship snapped back quickly from a bad roll," Erwin wrote.[19]

Heavy seas made the deck watches dangerous on 22 November. *Parche* was driven under while trying to surface this day. Fireman Jim Denman was entering the control room when a sudden roll of the ship caused a hatch to slam shut on his right index finger and right middle finger. Both

*Parche* enters Midway's lagoon following her third war patrol. *U.S. Navy photo, courtesy of Ray Karr.*

fingers were fractured and one had been partially severed. Doc Shaw had to apply nine stitches in Denman's index finger and three more above the fingernail to control the bleeding. Denman went right back to duty.

*Parche* passed through the eye of the typhoon this day. "It was like passing through a wall of wind and rain into a foggy, misty calm," Erwin wrote. "It was an eerie feeling. It did not take long to move back into the storm."[20]

*Parche* passed through Bashi Channel on 22 November and she departed the patrol area for base the following day. On 24 November, the welcome word was received to proceed toward Midway for refit. En route, she was directed to search for a downed B-29 crew that had been returning from a Tokyo raid. Lookouts had spotted four red flares, a distress signal. *Parche* reversed course and *Bang* helped join in the search for several hours. Ramage swept the area until 2200, firing Very stars every 15 minutes. Finally, at 2330, the word was passed to the subs to break off this search and proceed, as no known American crew had been lost in their area.

*Parche* arrived at Midway at 0827 on 2 December and ended her luckless third war patrol moored to Pier No. 7 at the sub base. The local band was on hand to greet *Parche* but the celebration was much more subdued than that of her previous returns to base. *Pomfret* and *Sailfish* had each scored but *Parche* turned in her first zero run.

Electrician Lonnie Hughes was deeply troubled by the rumors he heard that the submarine *Escolar* was "overdue and presumed lost." She had been lost with all hands during October in the vicinity of Tsushima Strait,

Another view of *Parche* entering Midway with Red Ramage (left side of photo) and Mac McCrory on the bridge following her third patrol. Note the Japanese flags flying from the periscope to represent the nine ships she claimed as kills during her first patrols. Forward of her weathered conning tower are the 4-inch deck gun and the new 40-mm gun on the platform. Spare 20-mm gun barrels (circled) are mounted on either side of the conning tower. *U.S. Navy photo, courtesy of Jim Ramage.*

---

**USS *Parche* Third War Patrol Summary**

| | |
|---|---|
| Departure From: | Pearl Harbor |
| Patrol Area: | San Bernardino Straits/Formosa |
| Time Period: | 10 September–2 December 1944 |
| Number of Men On Board: | 83: 73 enlisted and 10 officers |
| Total Days on Patrol: | 89 |
| Miles Steamed: | 16,629 |
| Number of Torpedoes Fired: | 0 |
| Ships Credited as Sunk: | 0/00 tons |
| JANAC Postwar Credit: | 0 |
| Shipping Damage Claimed: | 0/0 tons |
| Return To: | Midway |

---

likely to an encounter with a Japanese mine. Hughes had gone through sub school in New London with one of *Escolar*'s crewmen, RM1c Ken Campbell, and had spent some time on liberty with Campbell again in August at Honolulu before *Escolar* departed on her maiden patrol. Upset by the loss of his friend, Hughes wrote in his diary soon after reaching Midway, "I can't understand why it is necessary for things like that to happen. I'm not going to write any more this time."[21]

Spending 86 days on patrol, 49 in her areas in the San Bernadino Strait and south of Formosa, the boat made only one contact worthy of torpedoes, but this could not be developed. This had been one of the longest war patrols in the duration of the war. Most disappointing for the new hands was the fact that, for the first time, the coveted Submarine Combat Insignia pin was not authorized for this patrol.

# CHAPTER ELEVEN

# Tragedy at Sea

P*arche*'s second refit period at Gooneyville commenced on 2 December as the crew turned their boat over to the capable hands of the Submarine Division 241 relief crew. Most were eager to hear from home, as no messages had been sent or received in three months of patrolling. Some relatives back home had become concerned due to the long stretch between hearing from their loved ones on *Parche*.

Among the welcome letters, and much to the surprise of all, were numerous newspaper clippings from hometown papers. *Parche*'s romp through convoy MI-11 during the night of 31 July had been released to the press as one of the rare instances when a U.S. submarine was named publicly for its successes in the Pacific. "I recall being totally surprised at all the publicity *Parche* got," Bob Hall said. "There was a definite lid on the release of wartime submarine activity. Perhaps *Parche*'s actions motivated the powers that were to release information."

*Parche* maneuvered into USS *ARD-8,* a floating Navy dry dock, on 4 December and was positioned on keel blocks before the dry dock was pumped empty. The major items of work accomplished were the removal of two main engine mufflers, an overhaul of the two main engines and installation of a new Bendix log master unit. Sam Roberts worked with the tender to repair a timing light motor that had gone out on his TDC and managed to remove the necessary parts from another boat that had returned from patrol.

During the second day in dry dock, Vice Admiral Lockwood and his staff came aboard *Parche* on 5 December to make an inspection. Two days later, on the third anniversary of the Japanese attack on Pearl Harbor, the dry dock was flooded and *Parche* returned to the Sail-7 pier.

During the rest period at Midway, yeomen Allan Goodson and Les Chambless typed up the transfer paperwork for 14 enlisted men who had orders to other duties. Among the commissioning crew leaving before the fourth patrol were Cory Maupin, Claude Lutz, Henry Bougetz, Snuffy Vukovcan, Mo Taylor, Zach Vogedes, Don Green, Jasper Hill, Al Rick, and Carl Kimmons.

Also among the transferees was Chief Goodson. "I had a large abscess on my neck which had to be surgically removed," he recalled. *Parche* would sail before he could get back and Chambless, the other chief who had gotten on board at Saipan as his assistant, ended up staying with *Parche* as she prepared for her fourth patrol. Ben Couture, the young electrician who had suffered a hernia during gun drills, was also sent ashore for a proper operation.[1]

Steward's mate Kimmons, who had become quite close to skipper Red Ramage, had learned that his captain would not be in command of *Parche* when she sailed on her next patrol. "When Commander Ramage, who was a great skipper and a great guy, was transferred after the third patrol, I decided it was time to get off, too," Kimmons related. "I thought that McCrory would be an over-anxious fighter since he was on the patrol on which Ramage had been so aggressive. So, during our two-week stay at Midway, I looked for someone to take my place. I did not want to take any chances." He found a willing volunteer in Leroy Braxton, a mess attendant on the relief crew who hailed from Philadelphia and had no prior sub runs.[2]

*Parche*'s crew enjoyed beer busts and spent time writing letters back home while off duty on Midway, but there was only so much entertainment to be found on Gooneyville. Motormac Joe Leiching tried swimming in the ocean "but the damn water was cold. At Midway there was nothing else but gooney birds and beer." Liberty for him was a welcome change from the life in the engine rooms where he went without seeing sunlight for weeks. "I don't even remember taking showers aboard," Leiching related. "Everything smelled so much of fuel oil, it just didn't make a difference."

Chief of the Boat Don Walters and his R&R companion Lonnie Hughes sorted out many incidents involving their crew without reporting things to their Exec or skipper. One afternoon they noticed Torpedoman Cory Maupin involved in a fight on the beach with another of their sailors. Walters found that Hughes did not shy away from any confrontation. "Hughes just stepped up and knocked the aggressor to the sand," he recalled. "That ended that fight right there and we didn't bother to report it."

The beer busts, ball games, and bird watching soon became tiresome. "It was said that once you learned to talk to the gooney birds it was time to leave," recalled Bob Erwin. Boredom and liquor often combined to produce trouble for submarine sailors. Torpedoman Ray Karr later admitted that "three unnamed *Parche* sailors burglarized the Admiral's liquor cache on Midway. During the celebration that night, they caught a number of gooney birds, put them in the crew quarters of the *Hammerhead* and wired the doors shut. The wildly upset birds defecated, screamed and bit anyone near them. This was because the *Hammerhead* beat us in a softball game. The *Parche* crew was restricted to the boat after that but the burglars were never officially identified."[3]

Erwin and others hitched rides with the Marines on their daily reconnaissance flights. Once airborne, the pilots claimed that their aircraft were condemned and should not be flying. They then put their planes through turns and flips to spook the submariners. "We got even," Erwin recalled. "We invited a group of them on a training run to get a good meal they couldn't get on base. We told them we were going to run an especially dangerous exercise and they would all have to stay in the forward torpedo room."[4]

The bulkhead door was closed and then the *Parche* men put their boat into a steep dive. At the same time, one of the torpedomen dumped a full torpedo tube of water into the compartment. "Without having had the experience, a 15-degree down angle is scary enough without the water," wrote Erwin.

---

As expected, Red Ramage had new orders. Admiral Lockwood's policy was to rotate skippers with five command patrols to keep his skippers fresh and to promote new fleet boat commanders. Ramage had already made four war patrols in command of *Trout* plus his three on *Parche*. His new assignment following a 30-day-leave Stateside was to be personnel officer for ComSubPac back at Pearl Harbor.

On 11 December 1944, the crew was mustered back on board ship for a change of command ceremony. Commander Ramage read his orders, followed by Lt. Cdr. Woodrow McCrory, who announced to the *Parche* crew that he was officially taking command of their ship. "Most of us were sad to see Ramage leave, but it was not unexpected," Bob Erwin recalled.[5]

Ramage returned to the East Coast for a welcome reunion with his wife and family, including Christmas in New London. His new assignment as Lockwood's submarine force personnel officer would be briefly delayed by a much-anticipated visit to the White House. Ramage had been notified that his Congressional Medal of Honor for *Parche*'s second patrol had been approved.

Upon returning to Midway after *Parche*'s third patrol, he received a letter from Capt. Frank T. Watkins of the Office of the Chief of Naval Operations in Washington. In a letter dated 10 November 1944, Watkins had expressed his congratulations:[6]

When I first read your account of the "Ramage Rampage" of July 31st I knew it had all the earmarks of the most outstanding submarine action of the war. Your modest diary had to be interlined, however, to dig out the elements of personal heroism "above and beyond the call of duty." Fortunately everyone up the line from Christie to Nimitz were able to do it. The recommendation for the Medal of Honor arrived here early this week and the Navy Department Board of Medals and Awards acted favorably upon it yesterday. This Board is always skeptical of the grandioise write-ups which habitually accompany the recommendations for high awards.

Knowing this, I decided to let the recommendation rest not upon Admiral Christie's write-up but upon your own words. For this purpose, the famous *Parche* Second Patrol Report was introduced and the pertinent extracts were read into the Board's Record. Following this, a vote did not have to be called because every member was on his feet with his thumb up. It received a unanimous Aye.

I have told you the above so you will know that it was not a borderline case. When the decoration is pinned on you, you will know that there was not a single dissenting vote and it was your own modest account of the action and not somebody's vocabulary of twenty-dollar words that won the award.

My heartiest congratulations to you. This is the first Medal of Honor awarded to a living submariner. Thank Heaven we did not have to pad the record to get at least one submariner so decorated.

Red Ramage thus reported to the White House on 12 January 1945 to be presented with the Congressional Medal of Honor by President Franklin Roosevelt. He was accompanied into the Oval Office by his wife Barbara, his father, stepmother Marion, and Barbara's uncle and aunt, Admiral and Mrs. Hustvedt. Barbara Ramage was so nervous she "spent the whole night before in sleeplessness." She waited anxiously with the family outside the Oval Office along with Gen. George Marshall and Admiral King, noting that her husband seemed perfectly calm. Inside FDR's inner office, a room full of photographers snapped photos as the president read aloud the citation for Ramage's Medal of Honor. All Barbara could think as she listened solemnly to these words was, "And you're here and I am here with you."[7]

Ramage found the ailing president to be thin and weak. "He was just terribly emaciated. His face was so narrow it almost looked like a knife blade. His legs had withered away and it didn't look as if he had any legs in his pants," he related. "He looked like he was just kind of set up in the chair."[8]

Commander Ramage receives the Congressional Medal of Honor from President Roosevelt in January 1945 for *Parche*'s second war patrol. *Courtesy of Jim Ramage.*

Ramage sent copies of the photo with the president to his shipmates. "He told us he was holding the Medal of Honor for each of us, meaning that every man of his crew deserved it," recalled Carl Kimmons. Ramage, in fact, made up certificates for each man who had served under him on *Parche*'s second run. Each certificate included a photo of his Medal of Honor and his signature. His notes said, "The Captain wishes to emphasize the fact that the Medal of Honor was accepted from the President of the United States as the Nation's tribute to a fighting ship and her courageous crew. He feels that every officer and man whose loyal cooperation and able assistance contributed to the success of the '*Parche*' has an equal share in this award which he holds in trust for you."

New skipper Mac McCrory's *Parche* crew was also honored for the results of their first patrol while in Pearl Harbor. The commander of Submarine Division 24 came on board on 17 December as the crew lined up topside. Silver Stars were pinned on McCrory and Chief John Gray for their work

*Parche*'s crew receives awards on 17 December 1944 at Midway for their actions on the first war patrol. Signalman Chet Stanton (left) and Fire Controlman Sam Roberts (center) were pinned with the Bronze Star. CRT John Gray (right) received the Silver Star. *Submarine Force Museum, New London, Connecticut.*

in directing *Parche*'s torpedoes on the first patrol. In addition, Bronze Stars went to Lt. (jg) John Parks, FC2c Sam Roberts, CTM Don Walters, and QM2c Chet Stanton.

*Parche* went through an intensive training period from 17 to 27 December to help break in her new officers and crewmen. During this period, Jim Campbell learned that his old *S-48* skipper, Lt. Cdr. John Walling, had taken command of the submarine *Snook*. Although his old skipper offered to take him, Campbell found his move blocked. "Lieutenant McCrory wouldn't sign my papers," he recalled. Sometimes fate worked well in submarines, for Walling and *Snook* were lost with all hands months later.

*Parche* received 19 new enlisted men and four new officers while at Midway. New skipper McCrory was assigned a new executive officer, Lt. Richard Morgan Wright, a Californian who had graduated from the Academy class of 1941. "I chose the Naval Academy because that put me in line with my ambitions from childhood," Wright later related. He had been inspired to join the Navy since visiting the fleet at Long Beach with his father at age ten. His older brother had received an appointment to West Point but Dick Wright was fascinated with the sea. His first assignment was on board the battleship *Tennessee*, on which he rode out the Japanese attack at Pearl Harbor in 1941. He helped direct his ship's antiaircraft fire that morning as he watched the nearby battleship *Arizona* explode, the *Oklahoma* capsize, and the *West Virginia* sink. *Tennessee* survived the surprise attack but required Stateside repairs before beginning wartime cruises between the States and Hawaii.[9]

Wright eventually applied for a transfer to submarines because "it looked like the war was going on and I wasn't going to be in it." Following submarine school, Wright made five patrols on *Pogy* and helped in the destruction of eight ships. When he reported to Mac McCrory in December 1944, Wright was found to be an ideal candidate to help his new skipper run a tight ship. *Parche*'s enlisted men and some of the junior officers, however, would come to resent the strict disciplinary tactics employed by Lieutenant Wright.

McCrory and Wright's wardroom went through some shuffling of assignments due to the transfer of engineering officer Dave Green and junior officers Bob Ashe and John Parks. Preparing to leave his beloved *Parche*, Lieutenant Green noted in Chief Lonnie Hughes' maneuvering room autograph book on 11 December, "This is a bad day for Green of Navy because today I leave the best bunch of lads I ever had the privilege of serving with." Jim Campbell stepped into the third officer role as engineering and diving officer, while Bob Erwin maintained his billet as torpedo and gunnery officer. Three additional new officers were received: Lt. John Hennessy Jr., Lt. (jg) Max Morton, and Ens. John Michael Holleran.

Jack Holleran, a Reservist from Pittsburgh who had attended Carnegie Tech before joining the Silent Service, would be making his first run as *Parche*'s assistant engineering officer. Denver native Max Morton, also making his first war patrol, assumed the duties of assistant first lieutenant. John Hennessy had gotten to know the *Parche* wardroom as a participant on board her for one day of training at Pearl Harbor. He was fresh from *Skipjack*'s tenth war patrol and Lieutenant Commander McCrory welcomed Hennessy as *Parche*'s first lieutenant on 26 December following the transfer of John Parks. Chief Lonnie Hughes recalled that Hennessy's "family wanted him to go to West Point because the family was all Army. He went the Navy way." Lt. Bob Stevenson would handle communications for the upcoming run, while Ralph Flack tackled commissary and George Tubb became the assistant gunnery officer.[10]

Jim Campbell found "Spike" Hennessy to be a "strictly regulation Navy man." When the new lieutenant moved into officers' quarters, Hennessy selected a middle bunk and moved Campbell's personal gear to a top bunk. "He figured he outranked me and would take his pick of bunks," Campbell recalled, "but we got that sorted out real quick."

Fourth officer Bob Erwin found that things "were very much the same" with McCrory as the new skipper. He had been with the ship since commissioning so the crew was not subjected to the stress of learning the ways of a completely new senior officer. They had already come to understand the nature of McCrory. Husky, blond-haired "Steve" Stevenson became Erwin's JOD and the two became close friends.

*Parche*'s various departments received new hands to fill in the vacancies created by the necessary transfers. One of the key positions in the auxiliary gang was filled by MoMM2c Hollis Larsen, who came from the farmlands of Canistota, South Dakota, where he was the oldest of three boys. He had put *Pogy* (SS-266) into commission and on her fifth run he drew a sketch of a torpedo riding a wave with a raised periscope. His skipper took the sketch back Stateside and had Disney artists create a proper logo for *Pogy*. Ray Van Eperen soon found Larsen to be an old pro on the manifold during torpedo attacks.

In the torpedo rooms, Ray Karr had taken charge of the after room with Mo Taylor's departure. The forward room lost Jasper Hill and in return received TM3c Wayne Davis, striker Bob Swanson, and veteran Torpedoman Bob DeMonge. Torpedoman's Mate First Class DeMonge had enlisted in the Navy in 1940 from Cincinnati, Ohio. After sub school, he was assigned to the *Sculpin* and made her first eight war patrols. Shortly before her fatal ninth run, he was assigned to new construction on board the submarine *Plaice*. He made one run on her before being transferred to the relief crew at Midway, where he caught *Parche*. His companions would soon learn that his experience with torpedoes was equally matched by his experience with running stills.[11]

Percy Barnett, promoted to chief radioman, lost one of his top radiomen in Al Rick in the transfers. He received RM3 Henry Gay, a young man from Georgia fresh out of radio and sub schooling, as a replacement. Myron Grover had become handy with tuning the transmitter, learning much from John Gray in the way of repairs, making himself more valuable.

In addition to Barnett, newly promoted CMoMM Dana Jensen joined the CPO watch schedule under the direction of Chief of the Boat Don Walters. Bob Hall found Walters to be "a gentleman and a likeable cuss who did his job just like everybody else." As chief of the boat, Walters' time was tasked with completing new watch schedules and ensuring that the new hands were properly indoctrinated into the ways of the boat.

Fortunately for him, *Parche*'s new recruits for the fourth patrol were high-quality men. Motor Machinist's Mate Second Class David Forbes, who had been on relief crews at Midway and Australia thus far in the war, was happy to join the engine rooms as a new throttleman. Electrician's Mate Third Class Dick Frank, a 20-year-old Colorado native, had worked for the Western Electric Company and the Air Force Modification Center in Pueblo after graduating high school. Enlisting in the Navy in 1943, he attended electrical school at the University of Minnesota and sub school in New London before being shipped to Midway. Frank drew a bunk in

Motormac Bob Silvis, seen at left in his engine room, and RM3c Henry Gay (above) were among the new hands joining *Parche* before her fourth war patrol. *Courtesy of Bob Hall.*

the after torpedo room and became the starboard controllerman in the maneuvering room.[12]

Fireman First Class Bob Silvis, who had spent seven months on the relief crews at Midway after finishing his New London sub schooling, was also excited to be on board a combat sub. While working on *Parche* during her refit, one of the leading motormacs on the relief crew told him, "Bob, this boat has a damn good crew and a damn good group of officers." The next day, the base yeoman told Silvis that there was an opening on the *Parche* for the engine rooms. Silvis looked the yeoman in the eye and announced that he would go on board.[13]

"Don't you want to think about it?" the yeoman asked.

"I already have," Silvis replied confidently.

Late that night on 17 December, Bob Silvis reported to the new Exec, Dick Wright. He was assigned to sleep in the after battery compartment and quickly joined the routine of submarine life. Silvis found that there were simply not enough bunks for the 80-plus men and hot bunking was the prescribed routine. "There were times we came off watch and climbed into a hot bunk that was wet with sweat," he recalled.[14]

*Parche* was at sea each day during late December for extensive training and underway exercises. The crew was at sea for Christmas day, but they had already enjoyed Christmas ashore. In the long barracks where the crew stayed at Midway while on leave, they celebrated their Christmas by unwrapping all of the gifts mailed to them, saved to open together. "Red Cross packages were delivered to us, containing cigarettes and candies," recalled George Tubb. "For Christmas dinner we were served turkey and all the trimmings with baked-Alaska cake for dessert." Bob Hall reflected,

Ens. George Tubb (above, left) stands before the Gooneyville Lodge on Midway on Christmas 1944. *Courtesy of George Tubb. Parche's* torpedomen supervise the loading of torpedoes down the skids into the forward room. *Courtesy of Glenn Meise.*

"That place was probably a foot deep with wrapping paper and cookie crumbs by the time we finished opening our Christmas gifts."[15]

The routine of loading stores and ammunition was conducted on 28 and 29 December in final readiness for sea. Bob DeMonge and Ray Karr's torpedo gangs loaded eight Mark 14-3A torpedoes and eight Mark 23 steam torpedoes forward and another eight Mark 18-1 electric torpedoes aft.

Chief Johnny Johnson awoke to use the head during the final night of provision loading. As he glanced from the after battery into the crew's mess, he noticed "a young sailor loading a cargo bag from our food lockers in the mess hall." Johnson ordered the Midway relief crewman to put the goods down and escorted him topside. To his chagrin, Johnson spotted "another guy going over the gangway with a big bag full of canned food from our mess hall" as the Midway gangway watch stood by to see what their companions could liberate from the *Parche* crew. Johnson "jumped all over the deck watch and reported it to McCrory when daylight came but we both just forgot it because we were getting under way right then."

*Parche* got under way from Midway at 1400 on 30 December with an escort plane overhead for a patrol in the Nansei Shoto area. She crossed the international date line on New Year's Eve. Foul weather of cyclonic proportions again dogged the boat as she drove toward her patrol station during the early days of January 1945. On 3 January, speed had to be reduced to 4.5 knots. "Still shipping water down conning tower hatch and main induction," logged Mac McCrory. "Reduction gears taking a beating" when the screws came out of the water.

By 5 January, *Parche* was back to two-engine speed, but one day behind schedule. The attack periscope became frozen in train at 1300 and could not be lowered three feet from the raised position. After six hours of work, a loose pigtail was found in the panel and it was lowered but still caused problems with freezing. Ray Van Eperen's repairmen worked through the next day to flush out the scope's lower bearings several times and repack it with grease and new seals.

*Parche* continued to battle the storm during the ensuing days. When she surfaced at 1127 on 9 January only 150 miles from Chichi Jima, the barometer was again falling with force 4 wind and seas. She passed through the dead center of the cyclone at 1540. Within two minutes she had gone through "a breath-taking calm with no rain and improved visibility," per McCrory's log.

Shortly thereafter, McCrory logged at 1557, "Wonders never cease." The SJ radar picked up a plane moving fast across the bow from starboard to port at 10,500 yards. He remained on the surface in the driving storm and there was no evidence the plane had spotted them. Van Eperen's auxiliary gang had more problems to battle on 10 January when the auxiliary generator grounded out due to improper work done during the most recent refit. *Parche* entered her assigned patrol area the next morning just south of Tokuna Shima in the Ryukyu Islands.

Eight small ships were sighted through the periscope at 1559, range 21,000 yards, apparently heading for Amani-O-Shima. Closing the distance, McCrory noted that the ships were strung out in column with one maru of about 400 tons patrolling ahead from side to side. He also spotted another similar size maru, one lugger, and five smaller vessels. "Individually they were not targets worthy of expending our valuable torpedoes," thought George Tubb. "We needed to save those for the big ships. It was possible that we could have picked off the ships one by one with our 4-inch gun. We thought they had no big artillery."[16]

*Parche* went to battle stations surface at 1610, manning only the rapid-fire guns. Bob Erwin served as senior gunnery officer with Bob Stevenson as his JOD while George Tubb helped direct the fire of the 20-mms. *Parche* raced in to hit the last small ship in the column. As soon as *Parche* was sighted, however, the smaller ships were seen to be escorts. One vessel hoisted signals and challenged *Parche* with his searchlight. The other escorts, the lugger and two small marus fled. McCrory opted to open fire with his 20-mms and 40-mm in the direction of the escorts.

Motormac Joe Leiching, an engineman making his second run on *Parche*, hauled one of the .50-caliber machine guns topside to the bridge hoping for his first chance to shoot at the enemy. The Japanese put up a hail of fire ranging from .25-caliber to something approaching 37-mm. "It was evident this was no task for one submarine," Lieutenant Commander McCrory wrote. *Parche* turned away at full speed at 1646 as the escorts pursued her. They continued firing wildly out to 6,500 yards. One 37-mm hit was registered in *Parche*'s starboard afterdeck over the maneuvering room. Ensign Tubb recalled that this shell hit "very close to our 36"-diameter engine air-induction tube which, if ruptured, would make us unable to dive. It was a 'discretion is better than valor' situation and we broke off the attack."[17]

At the moment when the shell struck, Chief Lonnie Hughes was on duty in the maneuvering room with Dick Frank on the starboard controls and Dixie Howell on the port controls. "I was running the engines wide open and cold from the maneuvering room," he recalled. Senior motormac Dick Hawn had made his way aft to see why Hughes was running his engines so hard. Hawn started to light a cigarette as he entered the compartment to confront Hughes.

"The air from the main induction made it so that you had to strike the match and while the sulphur burned use it for a light," recalled Hughes. "As soon as Dickie struck his match we took a shell in the superstructure right over his head. Dickie became very quiet, as it is most difficult to talk with your heart in your mouth."[18]

In his diary, Hughes added, "My boys really put on the emergency speed when the Capt. asked for it. Hawn didn't squawk about overloading the engines, either." McCrory opted to depart the area in favor of finding larger, torpedo-worthy shipping in his assigned area. "We gave this one to the enemy," wrote Bob Erwin.[19]

---

*Parche* patrolled submerged on 13 January 12 miles off the west coast of Tokuno Shima but not even a sampan was in sight for two days. McCrory patrolled off Okinawa Jima and then across the traffic route west of Tori Shima the next two days without sightings. By 15 January, an alarming knock had developed in the superstructure that sounded something like a distant bombing. "Its frequency had become so great that something had to be done about it, or we could never escape if detected submerged," wrote McCrory.

*Parche* patrolled on the surface 40 miles west of Tori Shima through the night as the source of the knocking sound was tracked. It was determined to be near the forward loading hatch. In spite of heavy seas, an inspection was conducted at 0630 on 16 January. The knocking was found to be the solid athwartships bulkhead forward of the forward loading hatch, which, partly torn, had broken loose from its weld to the hull, allowing it to buckle in and out.

Preparations were made at 1000 to cut it loose with the oxygen-acetylene torch. The oxygen and acetylene bottles were secured in the forward escape hatch. The lower hatch was closed and volunteers crawled into the escape trunk. The upper hatch was opened and the torch lines were led out. *Parche* put the heavy seas astern and went ahead at standard speed as the repair work commenced. Even with this maneuver, the decks were pooped by waves continually and a bucket brigade was formed at the escape trunk drain in the forward torpedo room to keep the trunk dry.

The ship's first lieutenant, John Hennessy, and the leading auxilia-ryman, Ray Van Eperen, cut the plate out in about one hour, working underwater half the time. In the event of diving, they had orders to jump down the escape trunk and shut the hatch if the order was given from the bridge. "I was happy not to be first lieutenant on this occasion," recalled Bob Erwin.[20]

Fortunately, the radar remained quiet and Van Eperen and Hennessy completed the job at 1217. Just as they were securing their gear, the APR radar detector picked up interference. A Tess plane came over less than 30 minutes later but there was no indication *Parche* had been sighted. With the repair work complete, McCrory followed new orders from ComSubPac to change her patrol area by heading north into the force 5 wind and seas. *Parche* was to cover the north-south routes to Naha, 60 miles west of Yokoate Shima, a tiny volcanic island 150 miles northeast of Okinawa.

*Parche* conducted a periscope depth reconnaissance of Takara Jima on 18 January, noting a lookout station with barracks on the island's peak. No shipping was present, however, and nothing of military significance was sighted. With improved weather on 19 January, McCrory opted to take a look inside the harbor at Naze Ko on Amami-o-Shima. *Parche* dived ten miles northwest of the harbor at 0548 and started closing to the east. Dick Wright took control of the watch for the remainder of this day, staying in the conning tower through midnight. Torpedo officer Bob Erwin found that his new Exec, Wright, was "diligent and professional in his work" of plotting *Parche*'s course throughout the entire transit into and out of the tight Japanese harbor.

"An artillery site was on one side of the entrance to the harbor and a Japanese airfield was just six miles away," recalled George Tubb. As communications officer, he had special responsibilities in the course of such a bold attack. If *Parche* was lost in such shallow waters, he was directed to make sure that her coding equipment, TDC, code books, and secret communication materials were completely destroyed to prevent divers from recovering them. "I put a large hammer adjacent to our coding machine," Tubb wrote. "If we were in imminent danger of being sunk, I was going to smash our coding wheels and decoding machines into small pieces and throw them overboard. I also would have cut up our code books and thrown them overboard as well."[21]

The boat was rigged for silent running as she slipped into the enemy harbor. Bob Erwin found that this additional bit of caution "increased the crew's apprehension." There was already the worry of encountering a mine on the surface. By 0850, two tall masts and the stack of a ship had been sighted at the entrance to Naze Ko. The tracking party plotted the anchored maru as McCrory kept running east to get a good look down the channel between two tall peaks on the island. The weather was much improved this day and the seas were glassy calm.[22]

*Parche* closed the 100 fathom curve at 1111 and found nothing in sight down Naze Ko from seven miles out except for the anchored freighter. The anchored merchant ship was inside the 10-fathom curve but made a tempting target. By 1400, *Parche* had crept to 1000 yards off the 100 fathom curve to take a better look into the anchorage. McCrory soon made out a large tanker outlined against the land to the east of the channel. McCrory found that the tanker "had all the appearances of a new ship, but the paint on the side of his middle deck house had sloughed off, giving a nice point of aim."

This big, fat, sleeping beauty presented a fair share of problems. To get within decent firing range, *Parche* would have to go about one mile inside the 100-fathom curve into dangerously shallow water during daylight. Coastal guns and an airfield in the vicinity further complicated the options. McCrory hoped to ease up and wait for a twilight shot. Nerves were rattled in early afternoon when the JP sonar picked up two sets of fast screws approaching. *Parche* went to battle stations and began closing the tanker, fearing that escorts might be approaching.

Not everyone on board was thrilled with creeping into an enemy harbor. Lonnie Hughes felt that his new skipper was taking undue risk by making such a daylight entrance. "We went all the way into the harbor," said Dick

(Left) Lt. Bob Stevenson was Bob Erwin's junior officer of the deck (JOD) on the fourth patrol. *Courtesy of Bob Erwin.* (Right) Lt. Cdr. Woodrow Wilson "Mac" McCrory, *Parche*'s original executive officer, had taken over as skipper for the fourth run. On 19 January 1945, he boldly maneuvered his boat into a Japanese harbor to make a torpedo attack. *U.S. Navy photo, courtesy of Gene Payne.*

Wright, who maintained the ship's log throughout the 20 hours of action in the Naze Ko harbor. He felt that the daylight reconnaissance "was a little special" in terms of boldness.[23]

At 1605, a sigh of relief was breathed by many as the ships heard on sonar were identified as two large trawlers. McCrory secured from battle stations and headed south to allow the trawlers to pass through his intended line of approach to the tanker. A heavy fog rolled in and obscured the two ships from view for 30 minutes, during which time another large trawler returned to port at Naze. Bob Erwin was on the TDC while George Tubb and Lieutenant Wright carefully plotted the course of this trawler. "We thought we would be safe from mines if we followed their tracks," Erwin explained. "The water depth was adequate so we could stay submerged."[24]

*Parche*'s crowded conning tower made for tight quarters due to the number of men who comprised her fire control team. Mac McCrory directed the efforts as skipper with Wright as his assistant approach officer. Quartermaster Thornton Hamlin, a California native who had just joined the boat for his first war patrol, was assigned as the new battle stations recorder, keeping the log book in the conning tower. "I was the recording quartermaster, logging the action and the various orders given by the skipper during our attacks," he explained. Two other members of his quartermaster gang, Chet Stanton as the battle helmsman and Bob Daufenbach as the battle talker, worked near Hamlin.

Senior sonar operators Barney Barnett and Desmond Christy carefully tracked the harbor traffic on their gear throughout the long approach.

*Parche*'s electronics experts also monitored their gear carefully throughout this perilous entry. John Gray made periodic sweeps with the radar to keep tabs on aerial dangers while Glenn Meise manned the sonar gear in the forward torpedo room. Myron Grover and his newest assistant, RM3c Henry Gay, stood watch in the radio shack throughout the approach.

In the control room, diving officer Jim Campbell monitored the work of Charlie McNutt and Pinky Pannell on the stern and bow planes each time *Parche* eased up for a radar or periscope sweep. By 1700, their boat was well within the 100-fathom curve. The next hour was tense as *Parche* slowly worked her way between the two mountain peaks behind the trawlers' course at a 60-foot depth.

McCrory decided that he would have to take his shots around 1815, just before sundown, while visibility was still in his favor. Senior electrician Lonnie Hughes wrote in his diary that he and his maneuvering room companions had been "sweating it out all day" while at silent running. More than 12 hours had passed since *Parche* had commenced her submerged entry into the Japanese harbor. Hughes felt it was "probably the longest approach ever made by a submarine at that point."[25]

Right on schedule, McCrory had slipped *Parche* into firing position and lined up his bow tubes on the big tanker. The point of aim on the middle deck house of the tanker was clearly visible.

At 1821, he ordered, "Fire one!"

*Parche* shuddered as the first of three Mark 23 steam torpedoes belched from the forward nest. The range to the tanker was 5,500 yards with a torpedo depth setting of five feet. McCrory then fired the other three forward tubes, which were loaded with Mark 14s. He then slowly swung *Parche* about to bring the after tubes to bear on the smaller anchored freighter. During this process, five distinct explosions were heard through the hull and by the sonarmen.

At 1827, *Parche* commenced firing her after tubes from 4,000 yards at the freighter. All four were slower running electric Mark 18s set at only two feet. One minute later, McCrory observed through the periscope and the men heard the explosion of another hit in the tanker, two minutes after the first five explosions. An investigation later showed that the forward torpedo gang had mistakenly reset tubes 2 and 4 back to high power, accounting for the five early explosions. The regularity of the first five explosions indicated that they may have exploded at a 6,300-yard distance.

McCrory only counted one of the six fish as hits. "We were not sure if they hit a dock, a reef, or the ship," admitted Bob Erwin. "The larger ship was at a dock while the smaller one was anchored away from the dock."

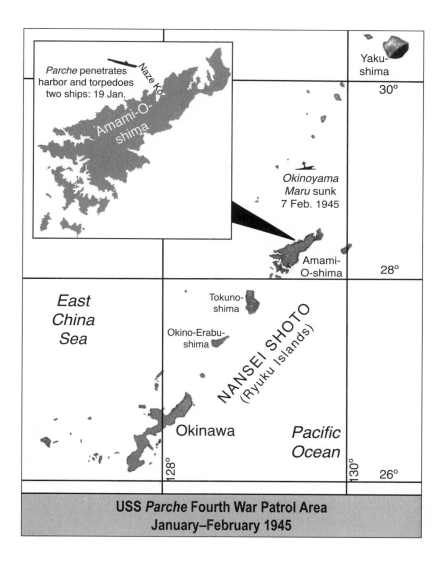

USS *Parche* Fourth War Patrol Area
January–February 1945

The skipper ordered Jim Campbell to blow 1,200 pounds of air into the tanks and *Parche* leaped to the surface at 1831. Battle lookouts Ray Karr, Joe Nichols, and Glenn Meise raced to the bridge as *Parche* went all ahead emergency speed to clear the stirred-up Japanese harbor. From the bridge, both targets were seen to be enveloped in smoke. As *Parche* was pulling away, the last after torpedo was seen to explode just short of the freighter, perhaps having struck a reef.

In the noise of surfacing, no explosions were heard from the other three stern tubes. "It was considered more important to surface than wait to observe results," McCrory explained. Smoke was seen to be billowing from the freighter, however, both through the periscope and by the bridge personnel. It was believed that the first or second torpedo had hit the target and the other two exploded on the beach. Postwar analysis did not bear out any sinkings for this foray into Naze Ko but *Parche* had certainly inflicted heavy damage upon two Japanese marus.

*Parche* raced at full speed out of the harbor at 18 knots, expecting to take gunfire at any moment. Fortunately, none came and nothing showed on Chief Gray's SD radar. A half moon was getting very bright when a fortuitous cloud moved in and covered it to help mask *Parche*'s escape. The sub hauled clear of the harbor at full speed and the crew felt relieved that these Japanese were poorly organized. Lookout Ray Karr recalled that "Cap'n Mac" had a good laugh as *Parche* successfully cleared the Japanese harbor unscathed, one of the very few times he recalled his normally serious skipper to enjoy a lighter moment.[26]

*Parche* dived ten miles west of Akuseki Jima on 20 January and spent the morning circling six miles to the west and north of the island. Only three trawlers were sighted coming out of Akuseki during the morning but sound picked up screws and pinging between Akuseki and Suwanose at 1448. Two minutes later, two Petes were seen circling to the east at ten miles.

Suspecting a convoy, McCrory increased speed to get between the islands. The tops of four ships were sighted at 1530 at about 20,000 yards. *Parche* could not close for a submerged attack so she went to 300 feet and set speed at 6 knots to round Akuseki and trail the convoy. These ships were moving fast at 12 knots in the calm sea as sound continued to track them. *Parche* surfaced at 1805 when 11 miles south of Akuseki. There was a half hour of daylight left and a half moon was coming out. McCrory went to full speed, patrolling the probable route of the convoy while hoping that if he was on the wrong bearing at least nearby subs *Blueback* or *Sea Fox* could intercept.

The Japanese made radio transmission between the subs more than the usual challenge. "It is evident that Jap convoys listen on the wolf pack frequency in use," McCrory reported. "Where practical it is strategic to send contact reports immediately after a shift in frequency." Radio operator Bill Gilcher recalled that "while on radio duty the jamming of transmissions was a real bitch."

A seemingly routine task turned tragic for *Parche* on 10 February en route to Midway. Ens. Jack Holleran—Jim Campbell's assistant engineering officer—and two enlisted men were sent topside to convert the No. 3 and No. 5 fuel ballast tanks to main ballast. This conversion allowed the fuel tanks to become operational ballast tanks and helped with diving and surface speeds. The converted tanks also allowed *Parche* to ride higher in the water while surfaced and save fuel. The only problem was the bolts on the tops of the tanks had to be manually removed to convert them.

The weather was not ideal this day for such a conversion but the task was one that was performed as needed on patrol. No problems were foreseen as Holleran led his auxiliary gang topside. Ray Van Eperen added Motormac Harris "Lefty" Leffler as a last-minute replacement to this detail. New auxiliaryman Louis Jarco recalled, "I was on watch in the engine room. I was supposed to go but he wanted his buddy."[33]

Leffler, who was eager to learn more about his ship, followed the procession topside. As they passed through the control room, auxiliaryman Ed Mokos also assumed he would be joining the topside group until he found that Ensign Holleran had given his okay to the switch. "He was an inquisitive young fellow who was very anxious to learn all aspects of the boat," Mokos recalled of Leffler. "As I recall, he had been an All-State swimmer before the war in his hometown." Mokos ducked down into the pump room to gather up extra tools that might be needed for the conversion.

Dick Frank was on duty in the control room as the conversion team headed topside. As they passed by, Leffler tapped him on the shoulder and kidded, "Well, Frank, it's been good knowing you." The statement, although made in jest, would later trouble the young electrician.

Lt. (jg) Max Morton had the deck watch along with JOD George Tubb on the starboard side of the bridge and three lookouts above. The wind and seas were at force 3, so Holleran's conversion gang donned foul weather gear to endure the moderate seas topside. As Van Eperen and Leffler entered the deck lockers at 1300, Ensign Holleran went down on the main deck aft of the superstructure to check on the No. 4 vent. He would order the men topside in case a ship or plane was spotted. A quick wave suddenly pooped the afterdecks, briefly dropping the fantail below the surface. Holleran, not holding onto a lifeline, was washed overboard to starboard at 1307 by the force of the swell. "Man overboard!" shouted one of the alert lookouts.

Max Morton quickly swung *Parche* to port to recover the lost officer. Below decks, the call of man overboard was a sobering cry heard through all compartments. Extra men were ordered to the bridge as lookouts to help spot Holleran. Charlie McNutt, Ray Karr, Glenn Meise, and John Barnes scrambled up on the shears from the control room as the boat crashed through the heavy waves. "We all held on the best we could," McNutt said. "There must have been ten extra eyes on the man in the water. All the while the Captain, having taken over, was turning the boat around to enable us to pick up this man."

Lefty Leffler came out of the superstructure as *Parche* was heading back for Holleran. McCrory waved at him and called him to come to the bridge.

"Stop the conversion and get back inside the boat!" he ordered.

Leffler hurried aft and shouted to Van Eperen to cease tightening the bolts. He came out from below the deck and was informed that they were to get below. As the pair stood on deck aft of the conning tower, another larger than normal wave swamped *Parche*'s fantail. As the deck was engulfed with the seas, Leffler and Van Eperen were swept away.

"There they go!" shouted one of the lookouts at 1309.

To Mac McCrory's horror, the man overboard emergency had now increased from one lost man to three. "Our bad luck continued," recalled Ensign Tubb. "They were about to be caught up in our boat's wake. We threw out life buoys in the hope that they could get to them."[34]

Charlie McNutt caught a brief glimpse of Leffler and Van Eperen as they struggled in the heavy swells "trying to reach out for each other." The auxiliarymen were last seen about 25 yards astern close together, with Leffler swimming toward Van Eperen. Lieutenant Commander McCrory decided to go ahead and recover Jack Holleran as the boat was up sea from him and he had been in the water longer. Several lookouts and both periscopes were put on the other two men. It was cloudy and growing darker as if rain were imminent.

*Parche* bobbed in the direction of Holleran's last sighting as Leffler and Van Eperen disappeared astern. Minutes later, one of the lookouts noted a circling seagull. When he looked down below the bird, he spotted a man swimming. McNutt also spotted the seabird, which he found "hard to believe that he would be this far from land." *Parche* maneuvered alongside Ensign Holleran and he was helped back on board at 1319. During his twelve minutes in the ocean, the alert officer had removed all of his foul weather gear and heavy boots. His excellent swimming abilities had no doubt helped save him.

As Holleran was helped below to the shower, McCrory ordered his boat back around to search along the bearing on which the other two men were last seen. In the interim, the periscope watch and the lookouts had both lost them. Neither man was sighted again although they were not more than 1,500 yards from Ensign Holleran.

Heavy seas washed three *Parche* men overboard on 10 February 1945. Ens. John Michael Holleran (left) was recovered. *Courtesy of Dave Hall.* Two men—MoMM1c Raymond John Van Eperan (center) and MoMM2c Harris Palmer Leffler (right) were not recovered. *Courtesy www.oneternalpatrol.com website.*

Exec Dick Wright took over the deck and directed the rescue and search efforts during the next five hours as McCrory continued to search the ocean to no avail. At 1800 the search was abandoned due to the sheer darkness. "This tragic loss is deeply regretted," McCrory logged. The names of the lost were transmitted to ComSubPac three hours later. "The crew was really down about it," said McNutt. Torpedoman Charlie Welton found these losses to be "pretty sobering."

Motormac Ed Schiefer had been pouring himself a cup of coffee in the galley when the man overboard commotion commenced. He noted that Ensign Holleran was pulled back aboard "half frozen." As for the two enlisted men, Schiefer felt that "between their heavy clothes and the cold water they didn't have much of a chance. It was a sad incident."[35]

Bob Hall, asleep at the time of this incident, awoke to find that "it was a somber ship." Lonnie Hughes felt that it was "a tough loss for everyone." Leffler had the bunk below Hughes and the two had often lain awake at night talking. He had gotten to know Van Eperen well. "Van was a young man with a lot of good humor and a whiz on the air and trim manifolds," Hughes related. "Both of these young men were sorely missed." Dick Frank recalled McCrory ordering a moment of silence for their lost comrades. "We did a lot of crying," he would later admit. At least one crewman also recalled the skipper retiring to his stateroom to sob over his losses.

During the return trip to Midway, the officers made a chance discovery of the crew's gilley still hidden in a locker in the after torpedo room. "It was a beautiful piece of work and since we had never had any alcohol-related problem while we were on patrol we left it for the relief crew to find," recalled Bob Erwin. This lack of discipline for such an offense was likely the result of the personnel losses just days before.[36]

*Parche* continued en route to Midway without further event and rendezvoused with *Threadfin* prior to entering Midway. John Hennessy had the deck watch as *Parche* moored at berth S-7 at 1156 on 20 February, ending her fourth patrol. Although the stay at Midway was brief, Chief Hughes encountered Henry Bougetz, who had been transferred off before *Parche*'s fourth run. "Bougetz gave me a picture of Nancy and Lonni he found in a paper there. We also heard that Capt. Ramage got the Congressional Medal of Honor," he noted in his diary.[37]

After refueling, *Parche* departed Midway at 1522, en route to Pearl Harbor. She rendezvoused with USS *PC-580* off Oahu on the morning of 20 February and moored at berth S-7, U.S. Submarine Base, Pearl Harbor at 1156.

Lieutenant Commander McCrory credited two lieutenants, Jim Campbell and Bob Erwin, for the work they had done in training the crew in the areas of engineering and ordnance. *Parche*'s fourth patrol had been made with a crew whose average age was 21 years, nine months. Three officers and 27 men who had placed the boat in commission remained on board at this time.

*Parche*'s fourth patrol was deemed successful and Lieutenant Commander McCrory would be approved for the Bronze Star for sinking at least one ship and heavily damaging two others. In his endorsements to the patrol report, Commander Grenfell commended Mac McCrory and his crew on an "aggressive and successful war patrol" and expressed "his deep regret and condolences for the two men lost overboard."

---

### USS *Parche* Fourth War Patrol Summary

| | |
|---|---|
| Departure From: | Midway |
| Patrol Area: | Nansei Shoto area |
| Time Period: | 30 December 1944–20 February 1945 |
| Number of Men On Board: | 87: 77 enlisted and 10 officers |
| Total Days on Patrol: | 53 |
| Miles Steamed: | 11,765 |
| Number of Torpedoes Fired: | 14 |
| Ships Credited as Sunk: | 1/2,000 tons |
| JANAC Postwar Credit: | 1/984 tons |
| Shipping Damage Claimed: | 2/23,014 tons |
| Return To: | Pearl Harbor via Midway |

# CHAPTER TWELVE

# "That Ship Was Gone"

Junior officer George Tubb found shore leave in Honolulu far more enjoyable than what he had experienced at Midway. "The crew could test their legs on safe, solid ground, go to new movies in real theaters, eat at real restaurants, whistle at real girls, and drink beer at real taverns," he related. Downtown Honolulu was a place where "Silent Service" sailors often bragged about their exploits to other sailors, aviators, and Marines. "Submariners took great pride in their chosen service," Tubb stated. "One of our mottoes was, 'The difficult we do immediately; the impossible takes a little longer.' On my first patrol with the USS *Parche* I learned the truth of that motto."[1]

Submarine Division 45's relief crew took over at the Pearl Harbor Submarine Base on 21 February and *Parche*'s crew was free to unwind at the Royal Hawaiian for two full weeks. The gilley juice gang once again smuggled their little still into the Pink Palace to brew more batches of their secret concoction. In spite of a small fire started by the still, its benefactors managed to escape the attention of the hotel sentries and their senior officers.

Submarine sailors by nature bent the rules while on liberty and often got away with it. Baker Bob Hall, alerted to how strictly meat was being rationed for civilians during the war, opted to share a little of *Parche*'s stores with two aunts he had living in Honolulu. "I got the bright idea of swiping a case of beef from the ship," he admitted. "We were literally climbing over all these boxes of meat to get to something in our walk-in freezer." Figuring the Navy could do without one more 55-pound box of beef, Hall smuggled one ashore to his aunts. "If they would have caught me, I'd probably still be in the brig," he related. "I got away with it but it was a stupid stunt."

The crew returned to the ship on 7 March. Lieutenant Commander McCrory felt that "the refit was the most extensive and best the ship has had." Thirty-eight alterations were made, the most important of which

Lt. Bob Erwin (above, left) receives the Bronze Star following *Parche*'s fourth patrol. *Courtesy of Bob Erwin*. Shipmates on liberty (left–right): QM3c Thornton Hamlin, GM2c Max Geier, MoMM2c Dave Forbes, and TM3c Wayne Davis. Also seen on liberty after the fourth patrol (right) are, clockwise from top left: QM2c John O'Brien, Thornton Hamlin, SM3c Harry Slajer, and TME2c Ray Karr. *Courtesy of Ray Karr.*

was the installation of a 5-inch gun aft, the installation of an ST radar periscope, and modification of the bow planes to permit rigging out on a 15-degree dive. Two main engine mufflers were replaced and a thorough job of cleaning and repainting all main ballast tanks was done.

Gunner Plumley's deck crew received the welcome addition of a larger, more powerful 5"/25 gun installed aft of the conning tower and their old 4-inch gun was removed. With the 40-mm antiaircraft gun forward, the 20-mm mounted aft, and a spare 20-mm that could be carried topside to mount on the forward deck, *Parche* would go to sea with some impressive firepower as compared to her first runs. Plumley's new 5"/25 deck gun was a rifled cannon that fired a 5"-diameter shell from a 125-inch barrel. Each 65-pound shell had an effective range of 8,000 yards, or more than 4.5 miles.

*Parche*'s new radar-equipped periscope featured an ultra high frequency (UHF) radar that would allow the conning tower attack team to obtain target ranges while submerged to improve fire control accuracy. Chief John Gray would spend many hours trying to keep this new instrument in commission.

McCrory's wardroom was revamped at the end of the two-week leave as Lieutenant Wright, Lieutenant (jg) Flack, and Ensign Tubb received orders to new assignments. Dick Wright was ordered to Guam where *Spadefish*

(Above) Shipmates Joe Caruso and Charlie McNutt (right) pose near the volleyball courts at Waikiki's Royal Hawaiian Hotel after the fourth patrol. *Courtesy of Bob Hall.* (Right) RM3c Paul Kuter joined *Parche* before her fifth patrol to serve as one of her new radar operators. *Courtesy of Susan Reed.*

(Above) Chet Stanton, Chief Dick Hawn, and Bob Daufenbach after the fourth run. *Courtesy of Bob Hall.* (Left) *Parche* electrician's mates, clockwise from top left: Howard Ernest, Paul Vetter, Dick Frank, and Charlie McNutt. *Courtesy of Bob Hall.*

(Left) Bob Erwin and fellow officer Bob Stevenson (to right) on leave in Honolulu.

(Right) MoMM2c Ed Frye (left) in Hawaii with EM1c Joe Caruso. *Courtesy of Bob Erwin and Bob Hall.*

Another group of *Parche* sailors on liberty in front of the Royal Hawaiian Hotel. Kneeling (left–right) are Jim Hawkey, Howard Ernest, and Ed Mokos. Standing (left–right) are Joe Nichols, Paul Vetter, Dale Mielke, and Charlie McNutt. *Courtesy of Bob Hall.*

was in need of a new Exec. Few on board *Parche* were sad to see him go. Red Williams, for one, felt that the "crew was down" with Wright's hard-nosed inspections and attitude.[2]

Noting that some sailors were relieved to see their strict XO depart, George Tubb discovered that he would be missed by some of his shipmates. He had been assigned as the squadron communications officer on board the tender *Fulton*, which would soon be departing for Guam. "Some members of the crew presented to me two gold dolphin-insignia bookends that I treasure to this day," Tubb wrote. "They came from the best crew that any ship could ever hope for."[3]

Lt. Jim Campbell, one of the remaining commissioning officers, became *Parche*'s new executive officer. He was well prepared to handle the administrative duties that were required. In addition to submarine school, Campbell had completed extensive postgraduate training in mechanical design, navigation, and electrical engineering before joining *Parche*. "McCrory seemed most interested in using me to make sure that all departments aboard ship were running efficiently," he related. "He handled all the rest." *Parche*'s skipper and his new Exec had plenty of history together, having commissioned their boat and having served together on *S-48* early in the war. Campbell found that McCrory was a perfectionist in every way. He was even involved in the selection of new personnel for his ship. "He would drive me crazy going over the records and education of every prospective crew replacement before the patrol," Campbell recalled.

In order to keep his new Exec focused on all departments, McCrory made the unique move of naming Lt. Bob Erwin as the ship's navigator for the fifth patrol. Although this role generally fell to the sub's executive officer, Erwin was tapped to navigate to keep Campbell free to keep up with all the personnel issues.

Erwin had gone to the Sub Base sick bay with a sore neck but was kept hospitalized due to a scare of meningitis that was prevalent in Honolulu.

Wounded Marines were coming back from Iwo Jima and were being treated at the Pearl Harbor hospital. Erwin thus found it impossible to be discharged due to all the activity. After three days, a worried Lieutenant Commander McCrory called to find out if Erwin would be discharged in time to make the boat's mandatory training period. "The next day I signed myself out of the hospital and never saw a doctor after my admission," he recalled. "I was on the ship for the second day of training."[4]

Two ensigns, Lloyd Cornell and Dean Axene, reported on board to help fill the vacancies in the wardroom. Twenty-one-year-old Axene was a June 1944 Naval Academy graduate fresh from the Submarine School at New London. "I was young and patriotic—not yet 22—but I was anxious to help win the war," he recalled. "My first assignment was to a relief crew at Pearl Harbor where I became involved in the refitting of the submarine USS *Parche*. At the end of the refit, I was ordered aboard as the assistant gunnery officer." For Axene, he felt that things could not be much better. "Here I was a junior officer in a modern fleet type submarine—carrying the war to the very doorstep of the enemy. I was very young—and very naïve."[5]

Cdr. Donald F. Weiss came on board on 9 March for a one-week underway training period. The new replacements "were excellent and very definitely showed the effect of the training schools being maintained by Comsubtrainpac," wrote McCrory. "A great number of the regular crew and officers also attended these schools during the training period and the results were quite beneficial." During the training period, *Parche* fired four practice torpedoes and lifeguard exercises were held with planes.

Chief Dana Jensen, now *Parche*'s senior engineman, spent the training days wisely easing the new hands into their new assignments. The forward engine room was now under the charge of MoMM1c Orvail Buckner while MoMM1c Freddy Frederick supervised the after room. One of Frederick's new men was MoMM2c August "Gus" Kulick from Pennsylvania. Fresh from sub school, Kulick had worked for Westinghouse Electric Co. during the first year of war before joining the Navy in October 1942.[6]

Hollis Larsen had become head of *Parche*'s auxiliary gang with the tragic loss of Ray Van Eperen and Lefty Leffler on the previous patrol. His small group of Ed Mokos and Louis Jarco added F1c Charles Keenan as their fourth hand to fill the vacancy. Hailing from New Orleans, Keenan had recently completed motor machinist's mate and submarine school on board the *S-34* in San Diego.[7]

Charlie Keenan soon found companionship in two other new hands who hailed from Louisiana, F1c Bill Hollinger and S1c Joe DeSola. Shipmate

Fred Richards recalled, "Keenan, DeSola, and Hollinger were best buddies because they all came from the swamp area. We called them swampies." Life had been tough on 28-year-old Joe DeSola. Following his mother's death on Christmas Day 1925, Joe and his three older siblings lived meagerly as their father moved them from Houston to New Orleans and thereafter struggled to hold a job. There were days when the DeSola kids ate only apples stolen from a market stand or half-eaten food left out back by sympathetic restaurant workers. Joe and his brother Ben eventually hopped freight trains and hitchhiked to find occasional work in Detroit factories and other industrial northern cities as they grew older.

The brothers returned to New Orleans where Joe married his sweetheart in 1939. He returned to Houston with his wife and older brother Charlie and worked until patriotism tugged at his heart to join the war effort. The three DeSolas joined the Navy, and Ben was an electrician's mate on *Archerfish* in November 1944 when she sank Japan's largest aircraft carrier, the 59,000-ton behemoth *Shinano*.

*Parche* also added two new radar operators, RT2c Pete Klapach and RM3c Paul Kuter, for Chief Gray's watch schedule. Kuter, a married man with a young son, had enlisted in the Navy out of Chicago in May 1944. He had since gone through sub school at New London and extensive radar training. As a top radar operator, Kuter had the option of drawing service on board an aircraft carrier or a submarine. He elected to volunteer for the Silent Service, figuring that everyone on board a sub had an equal chance of coming home in one piece versus a carrier that was frequently the target of kamikazes.

Kuter had been assigned to *Sea Dog* on 1 March, but after a week's practice run on board her, he was reassigned to *Parche* on 8 March. Kuter found conditions crowded in *Parche*'s after battery compartment. There were more men than there were bunks, so a hot-bunking system had been instated. Those coming off watches simply dropped into a bunk that had been vacated by another going onto watch.

Submariners were, by nature, a superstitious lot and the recent loss of Leffler and Van Eperen still weighed heavily on the hearts of many *Parche* men. Kuter was assigned the empty bunk of Leffler, which in spite of hot bunking, he had all to himself.

Chief Yeoman Chambless gained Y3c Carl Joseph Meyer from Philadelphia to assist new Exec Jim Campbell with the administrative paperwork. Meyer joined the Navy out of high school in 1943 at age 17 and completed yeoman school on the East Coast. He volunteered for sub school because he was dating a girl in Massachusetts and figured he could continue seeing her by going through sub school at New London. Upon completion, however, he was shipped out to Pearl Harbor and soon was assigned to *Parche*. Meyer found companionship in mess attendant Leroy Braxton, who also hailed from Philadelphia.

Another new man joining *Parche* prior to her fifth patrol was 16-year-old RM3c Fred Richards, the youngest man ever to serve on the boat. He had falsified his birth records and actually enlisted in the Navy on his 15th birthday in May 1943. Richards had seen the movie *Destination Tokyo* and from that moment he knew that he wanted to serve. Richards' father had died before he was born, leaving his mother to raise three boys. His older brothers had already joined the Navy and Richards was admittedly "pretty rebellious. I think my mother thought it was just as well that I joined the Navy."

Richards joined Chief Barnett's radio gang, his true age remaining unknown to his skipper for the time being. "The survival rate was the lowest of all the Navy but kids don't think about that," he later admitted of the Silent Service. "They want to be a hero and have the girls smile at them. Most of the men were 18 or 19 when I was aboard. Many of the chiefs and officers were in their early 20s. That was really old."

An awards ceremony was held on 10 March as Adm. John Brown presented awards for the second patrol. Mac McCrory and Jim Campbell were each pinned with the Silver Star for their actions. Bob Erwin, CRT John Gray, and CTM Carroll Kinkel each received the Bronze Star for their work during the rampage of 31 July. Letters of Commendation were also awarded to Dana Jensen, Courtland Stanton, and Hollis Larsen, the latter for his service on board his previous boat. Ironically, former *Parche* officer Ed Rauscher—now a member of Babe Brown's staff—was the one who had written the commendations for these *Parche* officers and crewmen. Although Rauscher had been present on the bridge with Red Ramage for much of the action that night, he had been passed over for an award due to his standing with his former skipper. Rauscher stood by on deck as Captain Brown took each medal from him and pinned it on the various *Parche* men. As he handed one of the awards to his boss, Rauscher recalled Brown turning toward him and whispering under his breath, "You should be getting one of these."

The training period continued during the ensuing days with only one significant mishap. *Parche* lost her power steering due to some faulty yard work leaving the harbor on 15 March and almost hit a ferry. Bob Erwin, who had the deck, gave a danger signal to a twin-engine ferry barge, which narrowly cleared *Parche*'s bow. "We were able to back down and just narrowly missed," Erwin recalled. "I am not sure the ferry driver ever knew how close he came to being cut in half." Erwin quickly had the crew switch to emergency steering in order to proceed through the torpedo nets. Steering was restored and *Parche* proceeded with firing test torpedoes that day.

The following day, Lieutenant Commander McCrory and his crew trained in lifeguard exercises. The potential rescue of downed aviators while on patrol had become a normal routine for submarines operating near Japan, as the bombing raids against the Empire had increased late in the war. The Navy dropped an aviator and his rubber raft in the ocean off Oahu while *Parche* lay submerged. McCrory watched as the pilot, Ens. W. F. Smith, parachuted down and scrambled into his life raft. *Parche* had a tow line attached to one of her periscopes and towed it to the pilot. Erwin recalled that Smith grabbed the line and was towed "for a few hundred yards as if we were clearing a harbor." Erwin found that the pilot was very shaken when he was hauled on board because he had seen no sign of a submarine when he had landed in the ocean.[8]

*Parche* received another officer that day in Lt. Cdr. Bricker McDonald Ganyard, who would make the next run as a Prospecting Commanding Officer (PCO). Such PCO cruises were fairly routine in the submarine service in order to fully qualify a new skipper for his own command. With an extra hand on board, Mac McCrory took the opportunity to transfer Ensign Cornell, who had only been on board for two weeks.

Fourth officer Bob Erwin found Lieutenant Commander Ganyard and *Parche*'s remaining new officer, Ens. Dean Axene, to be worthy additions to the wardroom. "Both Axene and Ganyard had Ohio connections," recalled Erwin. "I had met Axene's father in Columbus, as he was branch manager for IHC there and had been in the Agricultural Engineering Department at the university a number of times. Ganyard's family owned the Meyers Pump Company in Zanesville and the department had done some work with them."[9]

By the start of the fifth patrol, *Parche* had lost many of her commissioning crew. Only three of the eight original officers remained—McCrory, Erwin, and Campbell. Of 70 enlisted men who put *Parche* into commission, only 20 now remained: Orvail Buckner, Nick Casassa, Bob Daufenbach, Walt Ekelund, Howard Ernest, Nelson Fournier, Freddy Frederick, John Gray, Myron Grover, Bob Hall, Jim Hawkey, Dixie Howell, Dana Jensen, Carroll Kinkel, Phil Mackey, Blackie Nania, Joe Nichols, Sam Roberts, Chet Stanton, and Don Walters.

Mac McCrory felt deep remorse for the loss of his two sailors on the previous run. Three of his men being transferred back Stateside to new construction were able to visit the Van Eperen family—Johnny Barnes, Ray Karr, and Charles Miller. Red Ramage, serving as personnel officer on Admiral Lockwood's staff at Pearl Harbor as the three prepared for their leave, requested that the three *Parche* sailors visit the Van Eperen family.

Karr recalled of his meeting with Commander Ramage that "he had some special jobs for the three of us." First, they were to check in at the Mare Island Naval Hospital to participate in a psychological study about combat fear. Barnes, Miller, and Karr were assigned as gunners on the troop transport *General Stewart* with a four-man stateroom to themselves en route to California. "We got to practice every morning with shotguns and clay pigeons followed by real shooting with the 20-mm at flying drones, which we shot at till we brought 'em down," said Karr.

Upon arrival at Mare Island, the trio spent two weeks being interviewed by dozens of Navy doctors with questions that did not make a bit of sense to the submariners. In April, the *Parche* veterans flew by military air service to Chicago and boarded a train for Green Bay to visit the Van Eperen family. "It was a really tough visit," Karr admitted. "They were most hospitable but really hurting" over their loss. After offering their sympathies to the Van Eperens, each man had a 30-day leave before reporting to his new construction boat. Karr reported to the Boston Navy Yard for the new boat *Amberjack*.[10]

During *Parche*'s final loading period on 17–19 March at Pearl, Mark 14-3 steam torpedoes were loaded forward and Mark 18-2 electric torpedoes were loaded aft. In addition, the after room had a new weapon, a small, sound-homing torpedo nicknamed "the Cutie." It was designed to be fired from 200 to 300 feet below the surface and, in theory, would swim up to hit an attacking destroyer. Because of its slow speed, McCrory opted to save the Cutie for a true emergency.

For this run, *Parche* would again be part of a wolf pack in company with *Trutta* and *Lionfish*, with *Trutta*'s skipper, Cdr. Arthur Chester Smith, serving as group commander. The pack departed Pearl Harbor at 1357 on 19 March, escorted out by *PC-580*. Smith's wolf pack would lay over at Saipan for refueling before heading for the east coast of Honshu, one of the main Japanese home islands. Key Japanese shipping, decimated by continual submarine and air attacks, was becoming increasingly difficult to find by this point in the war. Admiral Lockwood had duly opened up all types of enemy shipping as fair game. Many boats thus increased their battle surface gun actions against smaller targets of opportunity in late 1945 to help break the Japanese supply and communications lines.

Quartermaster Third Class Dale Milo Mielke came on board *Parche* prior to her third patrol. He kept a secret diary aboard ship during *Parche*'s final two Pacific war patrols. *Courtesy of Dave Hall.*

*Parche*'s departure once again brought a nervous excitement to many of her crewmen as they struck out into the Pacific again. Among them feeling this rush of adrenaline was QM3c Dale Milo Mielke, a 22-year-old originally from Omaha. Just over one year prior, he had married his sweetheart, Mildred Chadwell, in San Diego and the couple now had a new son, Ron. Mielke had joined *Parche* as a seaman second class prior to her third run. With two runs under his belt, he had worked his way into the signalman/quartermaster gang and stood regular watches as such while *Parche* was at sea.

"Realizing my great responsibilities to those I love, my wife, my son, and family, I am looking forward to this adventure while I am still young enough to be inspired by the danger," he wrote as *Parche* departed Pearl Harbor on her fifth patrol. Mielke had picked up a little diary in the Hawaiian Islands in which he planned to write his thoughts regularly—although keeping such a journal was strictly forbidden. "If it is God's will that I come through this with all my faculties and my health, in later years it will be interesting to reread and relive this greatest adventure of my life," he wrote.[11]

While en route to Saipan for nearly two weeks, *Parche* maintained visual contact with *Trutta* on her port quarter while making 15 knots. The usual training dives and wolf pack exercises were conducted as well as special search doctrines. All guns were test fired on 20 March as the subs proceeded under good weather.

Chief Lonnie Hughes wrote in his diary that "this started as a bad run from the beginning. On the way to Saipan from Pearl we had lots of trouble making good trim dives. We had to blow out of a lot of them because of a bad hatch in the tower." During one of these practice sessions, Hughes was breaking in new CPO Carroll Kinkel on the hydraulic manifold.[12]

## USS *Parche* Officers and CPOs
## Fifth War Patrol

| Officers On Board | Prior War Patrols | Position |
|---|---|---|
| Lt. Cdr. Woodrow McCrory, USN | 4 | Commanding Officer |
| Lt. Cdr. Bricker M. Ganyard (PCO), USN | 0 | Prospective CO |
| Lt. Churchill J. Campbell, USNR | 4 | Executive Officer |
| Lt. Robert L. Erwin, USNR | 4 | Navigator |
| Lt. John H. Hennessy Jr., USN | 5 | Engineering Officer |
| Lt. Robert T. Stevenson, USNR | 3 | Torpedo/Gunnery |
| Lt. (jg) Max T. Morton, USNR | 1 | First Lieutenant |
| Lt. (jg) Francis O. Gadd, USNR | 1 | Communications |
| Ens. John M. Holleran, USNR | 1 | Assistant Engineering |
| Ens. Dean L. Axene, USN | 0 | Assistant Gunnery |

| Chief Petty Officers On Board | Prior War Patrols | |
|---|---|---|
| Barnett, CRM Percy E., USN | 4 | |
| Dingman, CY Warren E., USN | 5 | |
| Gray, CRT John C., Jr., USNR | 4 | |
| Hughes, CEM William, USNR | 4 | |
| Jensen, CMoMM Dana C., USN | 10 | |
| Kinkel, CTM Carroll E., USN | 11 | |
| Plumley, CGM James L., USN | 8 | |
| Walters, CTM Donald E., USN | 7 | Chief of the Boat |

"We had three watch sections aboard the *Parche*," recalled Chief of the Boat Don Walters. "I normally stood the evening watch and Lonnie took the next watch. In order for us to have three qualified chiefs on the manifold, it was a normal process for him to be qualifying another man to rotate with us."

*Parche* had just come up from a dive when Lieutenant Commander McCrory ordered the duty diving officer, Frank Gadd, to take her down again. To Hughes' horror, "we went down with the main induction open. Kinkel thought the induction was open so he tried to close it but what he really did was open it." *Squalus* had been lost in 1939 to just such an accident involving the flooding of her main induction. Lieutenant Gadd quickly avoided tragedy for *Parche* by immediately blowing the safety tank and then all ballast to bring her back up. Hughes dismissed the near tragedy in his diary with, "Kinkel is a good kid and I never worried afterwards when he was on watch. Accidents happen to everyone."

Dale Mielke found the days en route to Saipan to be uneventful aside from the usual drills and routines. "We have a movie projector aboard and have a picture twice a day which is really something," he noted in his diary. "My bunk in the forward torpedo room is very cool and I need a blanket over me below the surface. I am completely surrounded by torpedoes, two alongside and two under me, but they are only potentially dangerous and cause me no concern at all. It is remarkable how many men and torpedoes share the same confined space."[13]

Submarine life had its challenges, however. Mielke often felt "dirty" from his inability to shower. "We are allowed one shower in six days because of small water production capacity of the ship," he noted. "So, it is a case of grin and bear the poor situation." The temperature aboard ship increased as *Parche* made for Saipan. By 26 March, Mielke wrote that "most of the officers and crew are running around in skivvies because of the heat."

Dale Mielke stood the 0000–0400 quartermaster watch each morning, followed by eight hours off and then another rotation for the 1200–1600 shift. "During my on-duty hours, I stand two hours on the bridge, standing after starboard lookout and handling signals if any," he wrote. "The other two hours I spend in the conning tower, keeping the rough log and the Quartermaster Notebook. Nobody works hard, but one has to be more than alert in cases of emergency as split seconds count then." Such was the case during his watch on 22 March when one of *Parche*'s pack mates, either *Trutta* or *Lionfish*, made an appearance. He had "the good fortune to see a periscope of one of the other subs in time for us to prevent her making a successful approach on us. It only appeared for a couple of seconds, and I happened to be looking at the exact spot with the binoculars." Mielke was praised by skipper Mac McCrory for spotting this periscope at such a great distance.

Baker Bob Hall continued to invent special treats for his shipmates, often calling upon some of his mother's recipes. "I tried to make the food appealing," he related. "The fact that it was a small galley with only one guy in there, everyone knew darned well who cooked the food that day. So we tried our best to make a good meal because there was nobody else to blame that day if the food was bad. It wasn't like a battleship where you had 13 cooks and you could blame it on somebody else if the food was bad one day."

Hall respected *Parche*'s officers but did not live in fear of them. He refused to make them any special treats and did not allow special cuts of meat to get past his fellow enlisted men. "We had 55-pound boxes of steaks," he explained. "There was always about a hunk, maybe six pounds of tenderloin in each. I couldn't get enough to feed the entire crew and I'd be darned if I was going to send it all to the officers showing favoritism, so it never got out of the galley. I remember making tenderloin sandwiches." Hall also treated the enlisted men to special cakes baked on their birthdays. Such was the case en route to Saipan on 25 March when Chief Hughes celebrated his 27th birthday.[14]

Heavy winds and seas set in on 26 March and delayed the wolf pack's arrival in Saipan until 30 March. Lieutenant Erwin, now serving as *Parche*'s navigator to free up new Exec Jim Campbell, made morning and evening star sights with Quartermaster Bob Daufenbach when the weather was clear to fix the boat's position. As the pack neared Saipan, Erwin found that their tracking did not always agree with the navigational fixes made by *Trutta*'s more senior navigator. "The *Lionfish* navigator and I tended to agree on our position," he recalled. "I had plenty of training as both Ramage and McCrory had made sure all officers could navigate."[15]

*Parche* finally moored alongside the tender *Fulton* in Tanapag Harbor with sister subs *Sunfish, Trutta,* and *Lionfish.* Dale Mielke recorded the rough weather in his diary as his boat approached Saipan.[16]

Our last night at sea was a nightmare of hellish weather. The wind was about 50 miles an hour and drove the rain into my face like hail. Even with all our main gear on, we were soaked through and water sloshed in our shoes. Clinging to the shears, quite frequently a tremendous wave would completely engulf me, leaving me gulping and gasping for breath. It was sheer hell and the glamour of sea duty was certainly not in evidence. We found out later that one of the other boats with us had three men badly injured in this same storm. They are now in the hospital at Saipan with broken bones.

Provisions, ammunition, and fuel were stowed to capacity while the skippers attended a conference with the wolf pack commander. Yeoman Carl Meyer, new to submarines, was pleased when his skipper allowed the off-duty enlisted men to make liberty on Saipan during their overnight stay. "We had a big beer party on the beach," he recalled, "which seemed a bit ironic to me at the time since it happened to be Good Friday." Dale Mielke noted that he and his shipmates were taken ashore from the tender in a launch to a beach where the first landings had been made by the Marines months before. "We had about three cans of beer each, which was a treat after about ten days at sea," he recorded.[17]

*Parche* transferred three men while in Saipan and in turn took on board three replacement sailors from Submarine Division 81. One of them was a familiar face, Chief Yeoman Warren Dingman, who had been transferred off at Saipan after *Parche*'s third run. Chief Chambless, slated to only make a short run on *Parche* to gain experience, happily went back aboard *Fulton* after serving five months on his "temporary" assignment. Dingman, whose orders to new construction had never come through, was pleased to be back on board the submarine he had helped commission, particularly with young Carl Meyer to assist him with the boat's paperwork.

Motor Machinist's Mate Third Class Roland Burker, who had joined the Navy in 1944 from Maryland, also came on board at Saipan from the tender *Fulton*. "I came aboard specifically to join the gun crew because I was a six foot tall big guy," he related. "My job as third loader was to grab the shells as they came up through the hatch from down below." Burker became friends with Red Williams, another member of the 5-inch gun crew who also served with him in Orvail Buckner's forward engine room.

The third new man taken on board was S1c Carl Zeller, who had been through submarine school and sonar training at Point Loma in San Diego. Zeller was technically a radioman striker but he would spend most of his first patrol mess cooking in *Parche*'s galley. He and another new hand, S1c Travis Bush, helped fill the shoes of new SC2c Caleb Harris, whom skipper McCrory transferred at Saipan.

Junior officer Dean Axene handled the commissary duties and oversaw the loading of additional stores at Saipan with head cook Rebel Brown. "We were topside loading the stores and some of the cases we were stowing contained mutton," recalled Carl Zeller. When Brown spotted the contents of these boxes, he had words with Ensign Axene that no mutton was going to be cooked on board his ship. "We got those traded out for cases of steak right away," Zeller said.

---

Commander Smith's wolf pack was slated to include his own *Trutta* plus *Parche*, *Lionfish,* and *Sunfish.* A second conference was held on 31 March at 1400 with Cdr. Norvell "Bub" Ward of the ComSubPac staff present to brief the four skippers. He reviewed the operation orders and pack procedures before sending the four skippers back to their boats to get under way.

The patrol's departure was challenging: *Lionfish* was unable to depart Saipan due to a broken window in her ST periscope and *Parche* was delayed due to repairs on her SJ transmitter. Mac McCrory finally had his boat under way at 1747, following *Trutta* and *Sunfish* outside Tanapag Harbor to set course for Japan. *Trutta* radioed the next day that she was returning to port because of excessive shaft vibrations from an encounter with a submerged cable, leaving *Parche* and *Sunfish* to proceed to an area east of Honshu, north of Tokyo. Without *Trutta*, McCrory became the senior skipper, but with only two boats this patrol would now be conducted less as a wolf pack and more as two boats staying in close contact. Friendly submarine traffic was heavy as *Puffer* and *Peto* were both passed on opposite courses this day.

The PCO aboard *Parche*, Lieutenant Commander Ganyard, assisted with the watches and generally tried to fit in with the crew. "He should have bunked with the officers, but he volunteered to come back and join us," recalled Chief Walters. Ganyard thus took a bunk in the CPO quarters to avoid displacing one of *Parche*'s officers.

Nasty weather caught up with *Parche* again on 2 April. McCrory continued at three-engine speed in the evening but started taking water in her engine rooms. The wind shifted during the night and increased to 40 knots, forcing *Parche* to slow to two-engine speed as the barometer continued to plummet. McCrory sent all lookouts below and kept the conning tower hatch closed half the time as the engineers pumped the engine room bilges.

Quartermaster Mielke, standing vigil on the after shears during the early hours of 2 April, recorded, "The third boat [*Sunfish*] could not stand the pace because she has dropped behind. So it seems the *Parche* is all alone now, the most fit survivor of the four." He found the storm rough for those topside as solid waves broke over the periscopes and the boat rolled 30 degrees from side to side. "Visibility was absolutely zero and you could not see the lookout standing alongside," Mielke wrote. "I had never seen the like of it before."[18]

She passed west of Iwo Jima on 3 April, suffering from the effects of the storm. The armatures of both the Kleinschmidt freshwater compressors and the feed pump grounded out. Upon making a trim dive, a leak was suspected in the forward trim manhole because the gauge readings had increased considerably since the last dive. *Parche* was approached by three planes this day and identified herself with her IFF gear. The third came as close as 1,500 yards before turning on his running lights.

Port lookout Carl Zeller heard the after lookout announce the third plane as it zoomed in from astern below the radar. "We challenged him with the IFF and finally got a response but that SOB nearly attacked us," he recalled. "He had his bomb bay doors open and all." Zeller could not help but think that "we never had any friends out there but God on our side." McCrory boldly remained surfaced although he admittedly was allowing "probably too much faith in our zoomies."

New hands such as 16-year-old Fred Richards were quickly broken into the life or death speed in clearing the bridge that was required of such crash dives. As soon as he heard the OOD's shout of "Dive! Dive!" he leaped from the periscope shears and jumped through the open conning tower hatch. In the process, he landed squarely on the shoulders of the after lookout and rode him down the ladder.

When *Parche* surfaced a short time later, Richards was met by skipper McCrory as he returned to his lookout post. "Were you scared?" McCrory asked. Richards was uncertain what his skipper meant until another officer asked him, "What he meant was, were you scared when you went down the hatch on that guy's shoulders?" In sheer honesty, Richards could only mutter in reply, "No, sir, I just wanted to get down!"

John Hennessy's engineers finished rinsing and baking out the dampened armatures the following day as the duty officers kept close tabs on approaching flights of friendly planes. The winds increased to force 6 again that night as *Parche* made for a position off the east coast of Honshu. "We are heading for the heart of Japan, and as I write this I have the feeling that, not too far away are all those nice yellow people who started this mess," Mielke logged. *Parche*'s first radar interference from the enemy was picked up at 1244 on 5 April at a position 100 miles off the big island.[19]

The weather grew colder as *Parche* neared Honshu. Navigator Bob Erwin and assistant Bob Daufenbach found their work easy going up the coast of Japan because radar contact could generally be made with islands or the mainland. The worsening weather now meant "we had to use dead reckoning using radar ranges and bearings as we had no star fixes for two days due to bad weather," Erwin recalled.[20]

Three shore radar stations were detected near Shioya Saki on 6 April. Dale Mielke recorded that the weather this day was about 35° and "it was bitter cold in the torpedo room." He found sleeping difficult as "the hull acts like a big refrigeration plant for the cold water around it." For lookout duty at night, Mielke and his companions on the bridge dressed in layers of heavy clothing. "One hour on the bridge is an age, and you pray for your relief to come up just one minute sooner than required," he wrote in his secret diary. "To add to the discomfort, we have to keep those cold binoculars to our eyes to keep a sharp lookout. Each star seems to be a plane, each whitecap the feather of a periscope, and each wave or cloud on the horizon a small or large enemy ship. It takes self-control not to shout out what you imagine you see and wait patiently until you see the real thing."[21]

The previously rough weather had improved but the sonarmen were plagued with several bogeys during the night due to what was likely large fish returning their echoes. Carl Meyer was victim of this while on sonar duty. He became groggy and was only semiconscious when strange sounds suddenly filled his headset.

As he was nearing the point of dozing off, his elbow bumped the amplifying switch. "Suddenly, the ocean sounds were magnified about twenty times more than normal and it made me think of what a torpedo might sound like if it was fired at us," he recalled. Meyer shouted to the duty officer to take evasive action. There was a flurry of excitement in the conning tower until the sailor's mistake was quickly realized. The ribbing Meyer received from his shipmates would take longer to live down.

Meyer recalled another humorous event that occurred while he was standing lookout duty topside before dawn close to the coast of Japan. "We were so close I felt like I could spit on Japan," he said. It was around 0500 just before dawn as he swept the horizon with his 7x50s. Meyer suddenly spotted a faint red glow on the horizon and hollered to the JOD, Frank Gadd, that something was burning on the horizon.

One of the other lookouts, Joe Leiching, heard Meyer call, "Ship on fire! Ship on fire on the horizon!"

Lieutenant (jg) Gadd took a look and then replied, "Put down your glasses and look again!"

Meyer did as ordered and then sheepishly noted that his "burning ship" was actually the first fiery red rays of the sun beginning to rise over the horizon. He would take quite a bit of ribbing about his ship.

Quartermaster Mielke found the frigid temperatures a little more bearable when Chief Kinkel allowed his men to break out some new blankets for sleeping. "Finding our bearing is no problem at all, as we have definite landmarks ashore, mountains and lights and towns, to guide us," Mielke wrote. "Evidently the Japs don't give a damn, because we saw a town last night that had all its lights on."[22]

At 0650 on 7 April, *Parche* was submerged just off Todo Saki when Lieutenant (jg) Gadd and those on watch heard a series of about fifteen long, rumbling sounds. "At about the same time there was a scraping sound on the starboard side that started forward and passed down the complete length of the ship," Erwin recalled. The crew immediately feared this to be a mine cable and tense seconds ensued as the scraping worked its way along the length of the boat. "I happened to be lying in my bunk reading when this happened and I was truly scared for a few seconds," Erwin recalled. If the cable was to snag on something on *Parche*, it could pull the mine down and set it off. Fortunately, the scraping sound ended and *Parche* emerged unscathed. Radioman Glenn Meise, who listened in fear to the "scrapings of metal against metal on our hull," felt that "luck was with us again" as his boat escaped without damage.[23]

Four U.S. submarines were lost in this area off the north Honshu coast in 1943 and 1944, possibly to mines. The Japanese reported that *Albacore* was destroyed on 7 April close to the shore of Hokkaido and *Scamp* was lost a week later off Tokyo Bay. *Parche*'s first ship sighting was a large steam trawler observed hugging the coast on the morning of 7 April shortly after the mine encounter. McCrory conducted a submerged patrol south along the 100-fathom curve off Honshu. "On direct orders from the captain, we avoided sweeping over enemy land more than was considered absolutely necessary," wrote SJ operator Paul Kuter. His radar sweeps were thus "usually one quick sweep each five minutes."[24]

Two patrol boats and three trawlers were sighted by Bob Stevenson and John Hennessy during the day in shallow waters. *Parche* and *Sunfish* rendezvoused that night and agreed to patrol along the 100-fathom curve. They would exchange shipping information on a routine basis and exchange their patrol stations every third day. McCrory found that the absence of radar stations and the few patrol planes sighted thus far would make it easy to approach Honshu's coastline for attacks. Most of the shipping was small and known to be hugging the coast for safety. Lookout Carl Zeller, for one, was not impressed with how close *Parche* moved along the Japanese coastline in search of shipping departing the harbors. "On one occasion, we were so close in to shore that there were flocks of birds circling about," he related. "It would have been almost impossible to pick out a Japanese plane from these birds."

Zeller was soon startled by another sight through his 7x50 binoculars. "We were close enough to land that I could see a farmer tilling the soil with his tractor through my binoculars," he related. When Zeller pointed this out to his skipper, McCrory decided it was time to pull the plug and ease out from the coast to avoid being spotted.

Rebel Brown and Travis Bush served up tuna fish salad for lunch, which was followed by chocolate pie prepared by steward Robert Nelson. Dale Mielke noted in his diary that baker Bob Hall also helped to ease the frigid weather with fresh "bread and some kind of pie or cake for us each day. Every other day we have ice cream, so we do eat well in spite of the unusual conditions."[25]

A PC boat was observed departing a harbor on 8 April and a small oiler clinging to the coastline was also considered not worthy of the chances involved in chasing it close to shore in the daylight. At 1225, however, OOD John Hennessy's lookouts sighted a small freighter headed south along Sangan Shima that looked more promising. *Parche* went to battle stations at 1245, but before McCrory could fire the ship zigged 90 degrees right toward a harbor. Welcome orders were received during the early hours of 9 April from ComSubPac, directing *Parche* and *Sunfish* to extend their patrol area north to Hokkaido.

Max Morton sent word to the captain at 0403 that the SJ radar made contact with a ship at 35,000 yards. McCrory went to battle stations and started closing on the surface. Day was breaking but the horizon was clear beyond the target and an obscured horizon beyond *Parche* helped mask her approach. The SJ picked up another small target but McCrory continued toward his first contact until visual sighting was made at 0440 at 10,000 yards. *Parche* dived in the growing light to escape detection as the skipper started his approach. The vessel was a small power-driven barge stacked high with rough lumber. He was cutting across the 100-fathom curve, forcing McCrory to break off the attack in order to not run down his battery with a fast submerged pursuit.

Numerous fishing vessels were avoided through the morning until OOD John Hennessy reported two sizable ships at 1215, both headed up the coast about 4,000 yards offshore, zigzagging. *Parche* went to battle stations seven minutes later at a point 6,000 yards off Kobe Zaki. The leading ship was identified as a medium transport about 400 feet long and the more eastward vessel was seen to be a 1,200-ton destroyer making smoke. The transport was zigging as much as 70 degrees on three- to six-minute legs, making about 13 knots. The destroyer was zigging 20 degrees and headed directly for *Parche*.

McCrory continued his approach on the transport, gaining firing position for his bow tubes at 1,500 yards even as the destroyer was heading directly for him, blissfully unaware of the impending danger. McCrory considered the tin can to be "the sorriest escort imaginable, as he did not detect us, beam on, under perfect sound conditions."

McCrory took a last peek through the scope at 1222 and found the transport to be in perfect condition for firing. A quick check on the destroyer showed that he would pass away on a zig that would take him 800 yards astern. McCrory shifted his setup for the Mark 18s aft, hoping to get both ships in a multiple attack.

Jim Campbell, as assistant approach officer, spent much of his time for submerged attacks in the control room. "We had the best people at their best positions for torpedo attacks," he recalled. "My job was to ensure that the routine was followed to the letter."

Fortunately for Campbell, the conning tower approach team was seasoned. With the skipper on the scope, John Gray on the radar, Bob Stevenson on plot, Barney Barnett on sound, and Bob Erwin with Sam Roberts at the TDC, he had little to worry about. Larry Lawrence backed up Barnett on sound to monitor the other convoy ships and give updates on the various vessels to his skipper several times per minute.

Don Walters, standing vigil by the Christmas tree in the control room, was pleased that his skipper planned to take out the convoy's destroyer first. "I completely agreed with McCrory on that attack," said Walters. "If he would have concentrated on the merchant ships first, that destroyer would have raced in and worked us over."

*Parche* commenced firing three torpedoes at 1303 at the destroyer from a range of 1,000 yards. McCrory shifted his setup to the forward Mark 14s. In Chief Kinkel's forward room, Yeoman Carl Meyer had been assigned to man the battle phones during torpedo attacks. He relayed the word from talker Bob Daufenbach and stood by the manual firing plunger just in case the electrical firing from the conning tower didn't work. Kinkel's senior members of the forward gang included plank owner Jim Hawkey and Ralph Giordano, a new hand who had come on board with two patrols on *Sterlet* under his belt.

At 1305, *Parche* also fired four forward torpedoes at the transport ship. He had zigged and was now crossing *Parche*'s bow very fast. Just as the third torpedo was launched forward a terrific explosion rocked the boat. McCrory saw the transport swinging left just after the explosion. "A quick check on the destroyer showed a column of smoke and steam 1,000 feet high, with his bow standing vertically 100 feet in the air. The torpedo had hit a fire room." This torpedo victim was later identified as the 702-ton minesweeper *W3*. McCrory stepped away from the scope and motioned Jim Campbell and some of the other attack officers to take a confirming peek. "Mac allowed me a quick look through the periscope before we turned back to the AP and I saw my second torpedo sinking," TDC operator Bob Erwin recalled. "A skipper liked to have someone besides himself see a sinking."[26]

McCrory swung back to the transport to fire two more torpedoes but this ship was now fishtailing wildly away from the submarine, having likely sighted her periscope. "Decided it would be a waste of torpedoes." He took *Parche* deep and took advantage of a half-knot southerly current to evade. At 300 feet, the forward trim was flooding steadily from the sea at about 10,000 pounds per hour. "We could control it easily with the trim pump but there was a loud hissing noise from the leak, which could be heard clearly in the forward room and all around the dials on all sound gear," McCrory noted. The leak was believed to be in the manhole cover on top of the tank, so pressure could not be used in the tank to stop the flooding. This leak had been suspected en route to the area from Saipan but had not previously appeared on deep submergence. *Parche* eased back up to 150 feet to reduce the leakage.

The only counterattack was six aerial bombs dropped at 1450 at a distance of three to five miles. The last bomb was a dud. "We heard them plainly in the boat, but nobody seemed worried, so I didn't mind," recorded Mielke.

This first successful shipping attack of the fifth patrol was written up by Lt. (jg) Max Morton, who had been appointed the ship's reporter in response to a recent ComSubPac report that all boats should instate one. His write-ups included news of the world captured by the radio gang. Morton's first news bulletin, the *Parche Prattler*, was preceded by this tongue-in-check prologue, "While the world's radio and press facilities are screaming of great triumphs in the Pacific, this modest memorandum is being issued to give you all a few of the details of the *Parche*'s best, although humble, efforts to help our allies the zoomies in this war."

Morton's memo for Monday, 9 April, described the sinking of the Japanese destroyer. He noted that *Parche* slipped away unscathed from the attack while "some time after distant aerial bombs began to pulverize the place where the *Parche* used to be. Summary: One more precious Jap man-of-war scratched from the roster."

Junior officer Dean Axene recalled his first run on *Parche*, "Life in *Parche* under Captain McCrory was pretty austere. Life and death submarining against the Japanese was serious business, and the captain took it seriously all the time."[27]

*Parche*'s SJ radar picked up two targets during the evening hours of 9 April at ranges up to 46,000 yards. McCrory ran on the surface 22 miles east of Kuro Saki as these ships were tracked. His repair crews were preparing to correct *Parche*'s forward trim so he continued toward the eastern part of his patrol area outside the probable range of air search. Planning to remove the manhole cover on the forward trim the following day, McCrory had Frank Gadd send word on the pack frequency for *Sunfish* to patrol this area and exchange stations on 22 April.

Dale Mielke's detailed diary entries give a clear indication of how life on a World War II submarine could change from routine to hair-raising in an instant. His entry for the morning of 10 April:[28]

Today we were awakened by the boat heading for hell with a 16°
down angle. They dived at dawn, but someone had things figured
wrong and someone else did the wrong thing so we practically
stood on our heads in our bunks. They reversed the engines and
blew the forward tanks and finally got the angle off her. Never a dull
moment, and I can see why such young fellows look so old before
they are able to vote.

*Parche* patrolled submerged on 10 April, surfacing at 1548 to effect
repairs on the forward trim manhole cover and to surface her guns. *Parche*'s
engineering officer John Hennessy and first lieutenant Max Morton were
kept busy on this run with such repairs. "This was a dangerous time," Bob
Erwin related. "With men on deck we could not dive without losing them
and we would have control problems with an open trim tank." A new gasket
was put on the manhole cover in an hour and *Parche* conducted air pressure
and deep submergence tests, finding the work satisfactory. Hollis Larsen's
repair gang found that the manhole cover had been reinstalled during the
last refit with the dish up instead of down so that it did not seat properly.

McCrory surfaced and ran west toward Kinkasan at one-engine speed
while charging the batteries. The radio gang had difficulty with Japanese
jamming as they sent off a full report to ComSubPac. At 0035 on 11
April, while 30 miles northeast of Kinkasan, Paul Kuter on the SJ radar
announced, "Contact, 11,000 yards." *Parche* continued to close the coastline as she approached this ship, which was making six knots as the barometer dropped and the weather worsened.

Kuter continued to monitor the SJ as the ship was picked up sporadically
during the early morning hours. McCrory sent his crew to battle stations
surface at 0433 and headed in for the small target. New hand Carl Zeller
was directed to go topside to stand battle lookout on the periscope shears
for the action. He was less than thrilled with the prospects, protesting that
he had joined the Silent Service to shoot at the enemy, not to be shot at. "I
was sent down below to pass shells and was not asked to go topside for gun
actions ever again," Zeller recalled.

The weather was still bitterly cold topside. After starboard lookout Dale
Mielke reached the bridge after rolling out of his bunk and racing topside
with shoes he had not even laced. Only after arriving topside did he wish he
had taken a few more seconds to don foul weather clothing. "I was bitterly
cold and could not keep from shaking and shivering all the while trying to
see through the very heavy fog," he wrote. Exec Jim Campbell noticed the

*Parche*'s forward 40-mm crew prepares to fire on a Japanese ship. Ens. Dean Axene is standing behind the 40-mm gunner, MoMM2c John "Blackie" Nania. Standing aft on the bridge with binoculars looking toward the target ship is Mac McCrory. Farther aft, the barrels from one of *Parche*'s 20-mm guns and her 5-inch deck gun can be seen. One of Nania's shots caused a small ship to disintegrate in a violent explosion. *U.S. Navy photo, courtesy of Jim Campbell.*

shaking young quartermaster and handed Mielke his gloves so he wouldn't drop his binoculars.[29]

With the range at 4,000 yards, another contact was detected beyond the first target at 9,500 yards and closing. McCrory hoped that both ships, suspected to be patrol boats, could be destroyed. The second target, however, disappeared from the radar screen at 7,000 yards and was never seen again. The first target could not be seen until *Parche* had closed to 1,400 yards and Mielke was the first to spot it—"a ship of about 500 tons, and it broke out of the fog about 700 yards away without even being aware of our presence."[30]

Gunnery officer Bob Stevenson had his gunners standing by as McCrory conned his boat in to open fire. The new assistant gunnery officer, Ensign Axene, was assisted on the bridge by former gunnery officer Bob Erwin. *Parche* fairly bristled with firepower—the newer 40-mm gun forward, a 20-mm mounted aft, and another 20-mm that could be mounted on the forward deck. Torpedomen Jim Hawkey and Dave Manns took their stations as gunners on the 20-mms with Pinky Pannell and John O'Brien as their loaders.

Motormac Blackie Nania, a former 20-mm gunner, had taken over as the gunner on the new 40-mm mount. Jim Plumley, recently promoted to chief gunner's mate "for meritorious conduct in action," directed the 5-inch deck gun team. Fire controlman Bobby Hall stood ready to set the fuses on the 65-pound shells as they were hustled toward the big gun by handlers Shaky Jake Slajer, Bob Silvis, and Roland Burker.

Such actions presented certain hazards due to the large number of men topside to load and fire all of these guns. Additional crewmen volunteered to handle the smaller caliber weapons in case close-in action was required. Motormac Gus Kulick, one of *Parche*'s new hands, lugged the .50-caliber machine gun up onto the bridge and stood ready to fire with gunner's mate Harry Reed as his loader. "Can you imagine that a machinist's mate was a gunner and the loader was a gunner's mate?" he thought later. "I was just a better shot than him."

Lieutenant Commander McCrory had his JOD, Max Morton, maneuver to put his target on the port beam at a range of 1,000 yards. During the approach, McCrory suspected that his target was a small, diesel-driven Japanese freighter. Postwar analysis would show this to be the 133-ton picket boat, or guardboat, *Kosho Maru No. 2*.[31]

"Commence firing!" McCrory ordered at 0513.

Hawkey, Manns, and Nania began pounding away at the little maru with their 20s and 40-mm. *Kosho Maru*'s sailors returned fire with a small caliber machine gun in their bow. "Our 20 and 40-mms were hitting but started no fires and the 5-inch would not shoot so opened the range to 2,000 yards to get the 5-inch firing," wrote McCrory.

Radioman striker Carl Zeller, sent below to help pass the shells up from the galley through the hatch above, worked with a shipmate to safely lift each heavy 5-inch shell. Submarine sailors found ways to inject humor into any situation. "My buddy reached down in the galley locker and grabbed a potato," Zeller related. "He shoved that onto the nose of the big shell, saying, 'Let's see them throw this at 'em!' And so, we passed that shell, potato and all, up through the hatches."

"We were struggling with our gun," admitted 5-inch trainer Red Williams. "We had the wrong grease in our gun and couldn't get it to fire," said loader Burker. Once *Parche* cleared the hot zone, Plumley's crew removed the heavy grease behind the firing pin and the gun was successfully test-fired. Satisfied, McCrory started in for a second run. *Parche* opened fire at 900 yards as the target turned toward *Parche*.

The 20-mms and the 40-mm began landing hits on *Kosho Maru*, primarily along the waterline, as *Parche* and the Japanese ship converged on each other. "He finally opened up on us and I saw three shots from a gun of about 3" caliber," wrote lookout Dale Mielke. "Then I saw tracers cross our bow at the height of my eyes about 100 yards ahead, and I did some very fast praying that they didn't move aft. It was the first time I had been under fire and frankly I was too cold and excited to realize how close the end really is."[32]

The sea was heavy with fog as the bridge gunners claimed a 75-percent hit ratio during this second exchange. Plumley's 5-inch deck gun only managed to kick off one round from a distance of 600 yards when the gun battle suddenly ended with a violent explosion.

The 40-mm gunner, Blackie Nania, landed a direct hit on the ship. "The ship came out of a fog bank and John cut loose on it," recalled electrician Lonnie Hughes. "It must have been a gasoline tanker because it exploded with a horrible blast. The heat and the pressure could be felt down in the boat." Bob Erwin, helping to direct the fire for Nania's 40-mm, believed that one of the projectiles hit some fuel drums on deck. Erwin and several others topside suffered bleeding ears from the force of the blast. Skipper McCrory wrote that *Kosho Maru* "blew up in our faces in a tremendous red ball of fire, probably a gasoline explosion." Red Williams on the deck gun recalled, "Everybody below thought that we were hit because of how close the explosion was. There was nothing left of the ship."[33]

The PPI scope for the SJ radar in the conning tower showed the target ship disappearing, then a large pip, and then it completely disappeared at 1,100 yards. "Observed target explode and indication on SJ quickly disappeared," radar operator Paul Kuter noted in his journal. Seated at the sonar gear close to Kuter in the conning tower, Larry Lawrence felt the heat from the explosion through the open hatch.[34]

The tremendous blast was felt throughout *Parche*. Carl Zeller, passing up shells from the galley, felt his boat shudder heavily. Ed Mokos, standing near the open hatch in the control room, even felt the force of the blast down in the control room.

As the pall of smoke cleared, nothing could be seen from the bridge. Gunner Gus Kulick, standing by on the .50-caliber gun, was disappointed. "There was a ball of fire, a wave of heat and then that ship was gone," he said. "I didn't even get to fire my .50-caliber that time."

*Parche* had expended 84 rounds of 40-mm, 120 rounds of 20-mm, and only four rounds of 5-inch, the latter including two thrown overboard from droppage on deck due to turns in the swell. Ship's reporter Max Morton wrote in his daily memo, the *Parche Prattler*, that the Japanese ship exploded violently due to her cargo of "what has variously been suggested to be (a) gasoline, (b) ammunition, or (c) sake." Gunner John Nania would later be recommended for the Bronze Star for landing the deadly hit on this Japanese vessel.

———————

*Parche* had been fortunate in finding targets in the shipping-depleted lanes off Japan. "Japan's maritime forces had been pretty heavily mauled by mid-1945 and targets were scarce," said Dean Axene. "We had to scratch for targets, and we did—with considerable success."[35]

The weather was bitterly cold topside at 36° with a heavy swell developing from the south. *Parche* remained off the 100-fathom curve of Ksennuma on 12 April, sighting an 800-ton patrol boat. She could not close the distance in time for an attack but Frank Gadd sighted a small freighter that afternoon at 10,000 yards. *Parche* went to battle stations but could only close to 7,000 yards before the small merchantman, zigging wildly, disappeared into the surface haze. McCrory surfaced at 1729 and headed north to cut off this ship from the coast. Paul Kuter soon had the little ship on radar at long range. McCrory reached attack position less than an hour later at 1,400 yards off the ship's port beam. The little ship suddenly increased speed, smoking heavily. *Parche* had evidently been sighted.

McCrory pulled out ahead to wait for more darkness. "It was going to be no easy job roping and tying this Jap," he logged. "He steered every course on the card, changing speed from 6 to 10 knots, but finally decided to head west." Lieutenant (jg) Morton noted in the ship's daily memo, "After two hours of uninterrupted tracking, the rather unsatisfactory solution was reached that we certainly didn't know where the Jap was headed, and the odds were long that he didn't either."

*Parche* reached attack position on his port beam at 1,650 yards at 2013 and commenced firing three Mark 14s forward. The track to the freighter was lighted from the phosphorescence set up by the torpedoes. "He should have sighted them but did not," thought McCrory. Radar operator Kuter noted in his journal, "The wake of the torpedoes was seen on the A scope and PPI." The first two fish barely missed astern but 80 seconds after firing, the third torpedo caught the 3,200-ton merchant ship amidships. The

Chief Electrician's Mate William "Lonnie" Hughes kept a diary on board *Parche*. These pages describe some of the fifth war patrol. *Courtesy of his daughter, Lonni Hughes.*

hit was accompanied by a violent explosion that spread the length of the ship and blew it to bits. The freighter disappeared from sight and the radar screen in 90 seconds—although Japanese records postwar gave no indication as to this ship's identity.[36]

Battle lookout Dale Mielke, tracking this ship with his binoculars, "had a grandstand seat for the entire show." He had watched all three torpedoes streak toward the Japanese ship, "which was clearly silhouetted in my glasses." It was pitch dark, but the phosphorescent wake of the torpedoes made a white path as they ran forward. He watched *Parche*'s first fish barely miss and then felt the second one had passed under the ship before the third torpedo struck home. "There was a big flash of fire and a black pall of smoke, and the Jap ship sank from sight," Mielke wrote. "I will never understand why they didn't open fire on us as we were about 1,700 yards away when we fired."[37]

Chief Lonnie Hughes noted that *Parche*'s attack on this ship had been troubled by a noise in the attack periscope's hoist motor. "I started to work on the brake and it took 56 hours to get it back in working order," he wrote. *Parche* retired to the east for an hour after her latest attack, then made a sweep north and south just outside the 100-fathom curve. "While we had the attack scope out of commission we used the radar scope," Hughes logged. "It's real big by comparison."[38]

The next day, Friday the 13th, to the north the ship sighted what appeared to be the foremast of a destroyer or patrol craft. It turned out to be a lighted, marked fishing net. A trawler was soon sighted hauling in its nets. For over an hour, McCrory thought that *Parche* had been caught in one of the nets. He could not lose the nearest floating marker and there was a strange tugging sound in the superstructure and the marker continually lay in the water as if *Parche* was tugging it. "As a last resort, we dropped down to about 90 feet and went ahead 2/3 speed," Hughes wrote in his diary.[39]

McCrory believed that the trawler was hauling in his nets as both stakes eventually disappeared from sight. Unable to free his boat from the fishing net, the skipper decided he would battle surface and shoot up the vessel to get free. Bob Stevenson's gunners were already standing by as McCrory passed the word, "Battle stations, surface." Fred Richards, standing duty on the battle phones in the after torpedo room, was surprised to hear the call, "Three hands needed to go topside with knives." The skipper was only wanting volunteers to help slice away any fishing nets that remained tangled around the periscope shears but Richards at first assumed the captain wanted a boarding party to board the trawler.

*Parche* battle surfaced at 1051 at 3,500 yards from the vessel's starboard quarter. Whatever had been fouled on *Parche* somehow worked free at this moment. "Fate let the net off the scope and we manned the guns," Hughes wrote. From the bridge, McCrory noted the appearance of his gunners' new target. "He was a clean-cut wooden steam trawler of 200 tons, 150 feet long, clipper bow, high bridge amidships, two tall masts, and mounted two machine guns." The trawler maneuvered fast, continually presenting a small angle.[40]

"My job as the trainer was to crank the gun up and down to get it on target," related Red Williams. "My sight setter, Joe Nichols, would tap me on the back and yell, 'Sight set!'" Williams then kicked off each round by depressing the firing pedal with his right foot. "When we were dead on, I could see the shells slam into the target," he said.

*Parche* opened fire at 2,000 yards and shortly got enough 5-inch hits in this ship to stop its engines and start it sinking by the stern. Two men abandoned ship in a lifeboat and others were seen scurrying back and forth on deck. The Japanese ship opened up twice on *Parche* with his forward machine gun but the fire was ineffective. Battle lookout Dale Mielke wrote in his diary of this day's first attack.[41]

He fired a machine gun at us and I pressed myself close to the shears as possible, but I never did see where they hit. He was a

*Parche*'s 5-inch gun crew in action during 1945. Bill Coleman (foreground) holds a ready shell as Jake Slajer prepares to load the next one. Just forward of Slajer looking back toward the cameraman is gun captain Jim Plumley. To Plumley's left, wearing the headset, is Joe Nichols. Red Williams is seated on the left side of the gun. *Courtesy of Bob Hall.*

trawler of about 150 tons, 150 feet long and had a Rising Sun painted on his bridge as well as some Jap characters. I watched the destruction, as chunks of him flew in the air and pieces were torn out of his sides. We were about 600 yards away and could see the Japs running around on deck [and] also see the bodies flying through the air. He began to sink by the stern and was level with the water when we left.

At 1057, another trawler was sighted closing from the northeast at about five miles. *Parche* closed to 500 yards of the sinking trawler to inspect it. There was a brief scare at 1104 when Bob Stevenson and one of the lookouts reported periscope shears at 4,000 yards to the north. McCrory, however, quickly decided this was actually just another fishing net and proceeded to attack the new ship. At 500 yards, *Parche*'s 40-mm and 20-mms started several fires on the trawler but each new hit from the 5-inch gun blew out the fires. "We closed on him and began cutting him apart," wrote Mielke. "Masts fell and pieces flew all over, and the tenement-shaped pagoda amidships took a tumble."[42]

Joe Leiching, standing by waiting for his chance to fire his .50-caliber machine gun, noted, "When we got through with these little ships, they wouldn't have a square foot that didn't have a hole through them. But they would remain afloat because they were made of wood."

With the trawler's stern under water, the gunners concentrated on his bow and got a good fire started. "His masts were down and the superstructure a shambles," wrote McCrory. "Started to circle to come in closer but noted a large net astern." The gunners had by this time expended 41 rounds of 5-inch shells for 23 hits, 125 rounds of 40-mm for about 60 hits, and two magazines of 20-mm. *Parche's* latest victim was the 265-ton auxiliary minesweeper *Misago Maru No. 1*.[43]

At 1115, McCrory opted to save his remaining ammunition and break off the attack to the west. *Misago Maru* was left sinking by the stern with a good fire raging forward. As the gun crews went below, Red Williams was suffering from the powerful blasts of the 5-incher. "My eardrums were sliced from the explosions," he said. "Some of us never wore cotton when we battle surfaced. I guess we were just ignorant." When Doc Shaw examined Williams below decks, he found the motormac had blood seeping from his ears.

Radar soon picked up another contact 32,000 yards to the south and tracking was commenced. During this time, Lonnie Hughes and Dixie Howell had been laboring with repairing the noisy hoist motors of the attack periscope. Once they were satisfied with their work, Hughes "ran her up to test it and took a peek. I swear there was a mast."[44]

Lieutenant John Hennessy took a quick look through the attack scope at 1245 and confirmed that there was indeed a small ship resembling a sea truck at 12,000 yards. *Parche* went back to battle stations surface at 1313 and closed on this small ship's starboard quarter. The ship was sailing blissfully unaware of trouble with its canvas up as *Parche* raced in. Paul Kuter noted that the SJ had tracked the small vessel in "to 27,500 yards and lost it. Continued closing on it and came within sight of it—another sampan—and still could not pick it up on SJ. Finally picked it up at 6,000 yards."

*Parche* remained undetected until she opened fire and then a few men showed themselves on deck of the Japanese vessel. This ship had a steel hull with an after bridge, high forecastle, two masts, and two machine guns mounted. She flew a Japanese triangular pennant along with the name in Japanese characters on the hull.

*Parche* commenced firing at 1333 from a range of 1,200 yards. The gunners completely wrecked this ship's sails and superstructures. Blackie

Nania's 40-mm started a fire in the bow and the 5-inch gun was holing the vessel repeatedly, although it was difficult in the increasing swell to get good hits in the waterline. McCrory closed to 600 yards and soon had the ship raging with fire from stem to stern. Total expenditures for this engagement were 32 rounds of 5-inch for 21 hits, 97 rounds of 40-mm for about 55 hits, and three magazines of 20-mm.

This second gun action victim of 13 April was later identified as the 302-ton auxiliary minesweeper *Togo Maru*, which lost three crewmen in her sinking. Japanese sources reported that both *Misago Maru* and *Togo Maru* departed Yamada Bay and that both were torpedoed and sunk at the mouth of the bay. As *Parche* completed her handiwork on these naval auxiliaries at 1350, two Japanese aircraft were suddenly spotted on the approach.[45]

Lonnie Hughes noted in his diary that these incoming planes were spotted by chance. "While shooting at the ship a young fellow got his hand caught in the 5" [gun]. He jerked so hard to get free that he turned around when he pulled his hand out. That saved every one of us for he saw planes coming in on us."[46]

"Clear the decks!" shouted Lieutenant Hennessy. All guns were left loose with much ammunition exposed on deck as the crew raced for cover below decks. The planes circled in toward the submarine, low on the water from four miles out. Red Williams was sitting in the trainer's chair on the 5-inch gun across from pointer Max Geier. "I was waiting on Joe Nichols to hit me on the back and say, 'Sight set!' When I looked around, there was nobody on the deck but me." Williams scrambled for the bridge, where Quartermaster Bob Daufenbach was urging him to hurry. He slid down the ladder without touching a rung and Daufenbach spun the dogs shut on the hatch as *Parche* was knifing under the waves.

Machine-gunner Gus Kulick fumbled around momentarily on the bridge with his .50-caliber gun. His loader, Harry Reed, finally shouted, "What the hell are you going to do, carry the goddamned thing down?"

Kulick abandoned his machine gun and leaped down the hatch, smashing his nose on one of the rungs of the ladder in the process. He reached the control room and took his seat at the bow planes, "bleeding like a son of a gun." In the confusion of the moment, he did not notice his busted nose until Doc Shaw came around to check him out. Dale Mielke noted that "there was a mad scramble to get below" from the bridge. "We got to the hatch and jumped, often landing on the fellow ahead, but nobody minded."[47]

"I reconstructed the scene afterward and counted 23 people on deck, three hatches open, guns loose, and one ammunition locker open," wrote Lieutenant Erwin. "In spite of this we got down quickly."[48]

Within a minute, *Parche* was nosing under the waves, heading for depth with rudder full right to reverse course and pass under the blazing ship. Chief Hughes noted that skipper McCrory rang up full speed ahead as he cleared the bridge and then hollered down to diving officer Spike Hennessy, "Take me as deep as you can as fast as you can!"[49]

*Parche* nosed down at a hard angle, clawing for depth as the Japanese bombers zeroed in on her. "This was the best dive I have ever made on a boat and it was made with the worst conditions," wrote Hughes. "Full right rudder and the conning [tower] hatch [showed on the Christmas tree board as] red right to the last second. I forget the time but he took us to 350 feet with a 10° angle without a bubble."[50]

At 1400, she was just reaching 300 feet when a very close explosion shook her directly overhead and sent cork insulation raining down. "Hard on the light bulbs," logged McCrory. "Hoped it was not our 5-inch ready locker, which had not been tightly shut." Quartermaster Mielke felt this was "a terrific explosion nearby which shook us badly." The skipper went to deep submergence and pulled clear of the area, content not to press his luck any farther. "Would defy Friday the 13th no further," he wrote.[51]

Ship's reporter Max Morton made light of the air patrol that forced *Parche* under in his daily memo. "The guns were still smoking when the *Parche* slipped beneath the waves, retiring to 450 feet, rigged for depth charge and silent running. One lollapalooza exploded right between the tables in the crew's mess, and all was quiet." Two more bombs exploded at 1645 but at farther distances.

When *Parche* resurfaced at 2124 to head east, the gun crews went topside and threw overboard a lot of water-soaked ammunition, including nine rounds of 5-inch shells. "We have used up practically all the ammunition for our guns," wrote Mielke in his diary. "Maybe we will not make any more of these damn battle surfaces."[52]

Two members of the 5-inch gun crew, shell handler Roland Burker and trainer Red Williams, were suffering temporary deafness. Williams' ears, already ruptured in the earlier morning gun battle, were further damaged while Burker's ears had been ruptured after the cotton he had used became dislodged during the extended gun action. Doc Shaw believed that their hearing damage was not permanent and he felt that it steadily improved during the course of the patrol. Burker found that the ear drops applied by Shaw "hurt worse than the explosions that had deafened me." They would be given a thorough medical exam upon completion of the patrol. "I couldn't hear anything for two and a half months," said Burker. "It didn't matter too much working in the engine rooms where you couldn't hear anything anyway."

During the early hours of 14 April, *Parche*'s radiomen sent out a full report of the patrol's results to date and the patrol stations for *Parche* and *Sunfish*. Paul Kuter, who had previously served as a radar instructor for new recruits before joining *Parche*, was amazed by some of the readings his unit produced off Japan. "One of the points of interest is the appearance of targets on radar at over 30,000 yards and then disappearing when in closer," he wrote. "Possibly abnormal atmospheric conditions." Another distinct possibility for at least some of these disappearing targets was a Japanese submarine.[53]

During this time, *Parche* was apparently being tracked by a Japanese I-boat. Her radarmen had picked up a pip during the gun action on the 11th but it had quickly disappeared. On 14 April, the sonar operators felt sure that they had detected a submarine again and for the next day and a half *Parche* made intermittent sound and radar contact with this phantom. "Lieutenant Commander Ganyard and I maintained almost constant tracking watch but we were never very close," Bob Erwin recalled. "I don't think we ever got closer than 15,000 yards. We were quite sure the other sub was doing the same and we were afraid of each other." Ganyard, who assumed command of *Lionfish* for his next patrol, would later be credited with sinking two Japanese I-class submarines with his own boat. Lieutenant Erwin, exhausted after nearly two days of tracking the phantom submarine, had to be physically awakened for duty even after the battle stations klaxons had sounded.[54]

The following day, McCrory patrolled south along the 100-fathom curve north of Shioya Saki. *Parche* remained on the surface more than usual this day thanks to a heavy fog that prevailed during the morning hours. "We saw lots of mallards and seals, which we often mistook for planes and periscopes," noted lookout Dale Mielke. "We even saw a whale and, while interesting, kept our nerves on edge."[55]

Increasing air patrols forced two dives to avoid planes this day. Max Morton and Frank Gadd had the deck at 1606 when a Betty bomber approached the ship within three miles. "He was close enough that I could see the fire burning from his exhausts through my binoculars," recalled port lookout Carl Zeller.

Mielke was standing nearby when he heard Zeller exclaim, "Jesus Christ, look at that!" *Parche* was in clear sight and the Japanese bomber had obviously moved in low using radar to inspect this surface blip. "When I looked up at it, he was so close that I had no trouble identifying him from my recognition training," wrote Mielke. Lieutenant (jg) Morton hit the diving alarm immediately and hollered, "Clear the bridge!"

According to Mielke, "I never hit a rung in the ladder, just dived through the hole in a heap. We dove deep and waited for aerial bombs, but nothing happened. I was terrified and was shaken for hours by the experience, as the plane had come in on us without being seen and had us like a duck in a shooting gallery. As long as I live, I'll never understand it." He could only think that perhaps this Betty was not carrying bombs or that the pilot did not make proper recognition until it was too late. "Eight hours after it I am still nervous as a cat," Mielke wrote in his forward torpedo room diary that afternoon.[56]

This crash dive had been even more interesting for some in the control room. Two of the new hands on board had plopped into the diving planes seats, Radioman Fred Richards on the bow planes and Yeoman Carl Meyer on the stern planes. Following orders, Richards had rigged out the bow planes and pushed hard dive. *Parche*'s bow nosed down into a steep dive with a sharp down angle. "We took a steep drop and started down fast for the depths," Meyer recalled. An alert auxiliaryman blew air into the tanks to check the sharp descent as Richards quickly took the bow planes off hard dive. "I think I gave Meyer religion on that dive before we got her straightened out," he recalled.

Chief Barnett's radio gang picked up a message from Admiral Nimitz and Uncle Charlie Lockwood that night that congratulated *Parche* on her recent sinkings in the Japanese homeland waters. *Parche* continued to patrol close to shore again through the early morning hours and avoided another trawler due to her greatly reduced ammunition levels.

Fred Richards had another interesting event before dawn on 16 April. He was standing on the port side sweeping the ocean at 0252 with his 7x50s when a chill ran up his spine. There, racing toward the *Parche*'s bow was a phosphorescent mass of light moving at a good clip.

"Incoming torpedo on the port bow!" Richards shouted.

John Hennessy, the OOD, immediately shouted evasive orders to the helmsman without thinking to question the youngest sailor on his boat. In the case of a potential emergency it was far better to react quickly and second-guess later.

Fortunately for *Parche* and her crew, the incoming "torpedo" was a false alarm on this occasion. "It turned out to be a large blackfish crossing our bow," Richards admitted. "There were two kinds of fish that scared the hell out of us on the bridge at night. One was a porpoise that would zigzag about while chasing us and even leap in front of the bow for fun. The other fish that would sometimes startle us were these long blackfish. At night you could see the incoming phosphorescent glow from their long bodies and they just swam straight as an arrow like a torpedo would run."

The sonar operator confirmed that no propellers had been heard and the incoming warhead was eventually chalked up to being just a fish sighting. Those aware of the sighting at the time, however, were not sure for a while. Lieutenant Hennessy recorded in the deck log, "sighted torpedo wake, maneuver to avoid." Radarman Paul Kuter made a casual entry in his little notebook: "avoided torpedo." Dale Mielke also noted the fish event in his diary. "They crossed our bow and, when they got on the other side, jumped playfully a few times and disappeared. The water around here is alive with good-sized fish and seals."[57]

Fellow officer Bob Erwin reflected on the fear such fish sightings could have on the topside watch. "On a dark clear night in this water you could see our wake forever and you could see any place the water was disturbed by a big fish and wave tops. It was common for dolphins to seemingly play around the boat. What was not good was when one came straight at the boat from far away and on a straight line. I held my breath more than once until it stopped or turned away. Hennessy did take a little ribbing over this report, though."

---

*Parche* avoided a trawler and two patrol craft on 16 April and was unable to complete an attack approach on a small freighter inside the bay at Yoshihama on 17 April due to heavy fog. McCrory patrolled west back toward Kobe Zaki the next day. At 0935 on 18 April, *Parche* began an approach on a 1200-ton freighter that Bob Stevenson had spotted heading north along the 100-fathom curve. As the range decreased to 1,200 yards, McCrory passed the word to the after room, "Fire one!"

Bob Swanson, on the interlock between the torpedoes, quickly set the data that was coming down from Bob Erwin's TDC in the conning tower. Fire controlman Sam Roberts hit the firing keys to launch the first of three Mark 18s at 1020 while senior Torpedoman Bob DeMonge in the after room hit the plunger to fire the war fish manually. By the time the third one was on its way, Mac McCrory noted with disgust that the electric torpedoes were going to miss.

The attack data was later determined to have been faulty as the ST scope was out of tune and could not be used. End-of-run explosions were heard seven minutes after firing these shots. Erwin found this to be "very disappointing to me as TDC operator. We had fired electric torpedoes and we were beginning to think they ran slower than the setting we had been given. The cold water reduced their voltage and their speed. If they were not running as fast as we thought, they would all miss astern of the target as these did."[58]

This ship escaped and McCrory retired to the northeast to continue patrolling at periscope depth. *Sunfish* radioed on the evening of 19 April that she was out of torpedoes and was departing the patrol area. "That explained a lot of bombs and depth charges we had heard the last few days," McCrory noted. *Sunfish's* skipper, Lt. Cdr. John Ward Reed, was lucky enough to find and sink four ships for 5,461 tons between 16 and 19 April off the east coast of Honshu. Only 27 out of 87 war patrols mounted from Pearl Harbor and Guam from January to March 1945 recorded any sinkings. *Parche* was fortunate also to have been productive during this time.[59]

Lieutenant Commander McCrory tried to add to his score by pursuing a medium-sized tanker and its destroyer escort on 20 April, but could not obtain a successful firing position. "We could clearly see a Jap lighthouse, and its inhabitants through our periscope, also snow-covered mountains in the distance," Dale Mielke logged in his diary. "Meanwhile we continue to suffer from extreme cold and dampness of the boat." He spent his off-duty hours trying to read, shooting the bull with shipmates or drinking lots of hot tea. "Getting in bed serves two purposes," Mielke wrote, "one of which is obvious, and the other is to warm up and get your feet off the cold, damp deck."[60]

*Parche* spent part of the morning of 21 April "playing hide-and-seek" with two small picket boats. Worthwhile targets did not present themselves this day but *Parche* remained near Kone Saki on 22 April, as this area seemed to be productive. The two patrol boats remained in the area that morning but better targets soon appeared.

At 0835, the smoke from the first of three small tankers in column was sighted by lookout Dave Manns, who later received a Letter of Commendation for his alert watchstanding. This little convoy was proceeding north along the coast just south of Okama Saki. Lieutenant Hennessy called for the skipper and *Parche* went to battle stations and started closing for an attack. One of the little patrol boats was moving along about 3,000 yards north of *Parche* but caused no trouble.

Lonnie Hughes noted in his diary of this attack, "We came in straight on them and dropped to 90 feet to let the escort with the saddest soundman in the Jap Navy pass right over the top of us. Boy, he stunk."[61]

McCrory fired three Mark 14s at the second tanker in column from 2,200 yards. He shifted his setup to the third tanker and 30 seconds later fired three more Mark 14s from the same range. He had fired with one foot of scope out of the water and was thus unable to see due to a change in trim forward during the first of two muffled explosions that were heard. Immediately after the last explosion, he could see the third tanker in column covered by a cloud of smoke and down by the stern.

Sweeping right, McCrory could see only one of the leading tankers. The firing intervals, as taken by both Quartermaster Thornton Hamlin and plotting officer Bob Stevenson, checked for torpedo runs of 2,400 yards and the explosions were "characteristic for empty tankers. Only three explosions were heard." After the explosions, sound could only identify one set of screws from the original three. Two of the three ships had evidently been at least stopped. Postwar Japanese records failed to clearly show which ship was attacked by *Parche*. The mostly likely victim was the 875-ton freighter *Irako Maru*, which was due to reach Ofunato on 27 April with her load of cement. Records show that she ran aground and sank off Okamaishu Cape in this area; her destruction may well have been due to *Parche* torpedoes.[62]

*Parche* turned right and went deep to 250 feet to avoid any counterattacks while opening up to the southeast. Although his boat was armed with the new Mark 27 acoustic torpedoes for this run, Mac McCrory opted not to try a shot this time. "The PC turned on the pinger but never did come close enough to let us use our new sonic fish," wrote Chief Hughes. "I was glad, too." Only one random depth charge astern was heard more than two hours later.[63]

Dale Mielke believed that *Parche* had sunk both of these ships, "but it remains for the higher ups to decide whether we get credit for both or not." His entry for 22 April's attack continued:[64]

These two make a total of seven ships to our credit, but more important, we have three torpedoes left, which we must get rid of before getting out of this miserable place. Everything is dripping water; our beds are wet and everything in our lockers soaked from condensation water. We keep our spirits up by counting or enumerating the three fish we still have to go. Any minute we can see them fired, then we can get from hence.

*Parche* was on the surface that night, patrolling south toward Kinkasan when Paul Kuter on the SJ announced to Bob Stevenson that he had picked up a pip just a little south of her last distant contact with the morning's torpedo victims. By 2312 radar had this ship at the extreme range of 43,000 yards (24.4 miles). The pip tracked nicely during the next few hours and Mac McCrory hoped to make another surface attack to expend his remaining torpedoes.

By 0230 on 23 April, the range had decreased to 10,000 yards. The target "started steering crazy courses and varying speed," wrote McCrory. "Decided he was lost, trying to make a daylight landfall on Kinkasan, so got west of him for a daylight submerged attack." Several radio transmissions were overheard from this ship during the next hour as he either was calling for help in directions or had spotted the submarine's phosphorescence. Max Morton sighted a small ship to the east at 0402 in the growing light and dived on his track. Pinging was picked up right away on sonar and the target was soon identified as a fast PC boat. "This was a trap, pure and simple, and not knowing the extent of the plot, evaded to north and east," McCrory logged. "The PC was not aggressive, but continued his sweep to the west." Paul Kuter, upon finding the target had turned out to be an antisubmarine vessel, noted in his journal, "We submerged and [the] attack reversed."[65]

One small bomb exploded at 0521. *Parche*'s diving officer, John Hennessy, found an unexpected 5-degree temperature gradient and got beneath it at 450 feet to spoil any chance the PC had of making contact. The stern tubes leaked excessively at this depth, with packing taken up to the danger point, and Chief Hughes' electricians could not get suction on the maneuvering room bilges. *Parche* had a 12-degree up-angle and her crew resorted to a bucket brigade to keep the water down until the boat could ease back up above the thermocline. These made for "a few anxious moments," Bob Erwin recalled.[66]

Silent running always took a mental toll on the crew as they worked to keep silent as the Japanese stalked them. Carl Meyer, the new junior yeoman, was on diving planes duty as the depth charges rocked the boat. The experience of life or death while remaining quiet as a church mouse was still new to him. He was more than a little shocked when one of the officers passed through the control room and tripped, making a large racket as he hit the deck.

"Get quiet, you stupid son of a bitch!" snapped another sailor before he had time to notice the source of the clamor.

"To my surprise, nothing was made of his outburst," recalled Meyer. He soon realized the lack of formality that was the way of life in a combat situation. In this situation, silence equaled survival.

Another string of depth charges exploded at 1017. *Parche* eased away submerged and only one more string of ash cans was heard at 1551. Dale Mielke did his best to catch some sleep after his duty shift ended, although his napping was periodically interrupted by the depth charge explosions. He wrote that the living conditions were "hellish; no heat because it uses up electricity, no light for same reason, no hot meals for same reason. It is phenomenal to realize the amount of abuse you can take and still retain a certain sense of humor and civility."

At age 22 and making his third war patrol, Mielke found himself already something of a seasoned "old man" in comparison to some of his "young" shipmates. "The really young kids eighteen, nineteen, and twenty are, in some cases, sullen and irritable," he wrote, "while the older fellows seem to realize the situation and for the most part hold their tongues and patience."[67]

*Parche* surfaced after dark and patrolled south toward Osaki. Mielke's diary entry for 24 April summarizes *Parche*'s efforts to dispose of her last three torpedoes. "This morning found us submerged right at the entrance of a Jap harbor, about ¾ of a mile from the beach," he wrote. "We waited and watched and listened as the small ships and boats passed close by. We had plenty of targets, but we waited for a big one. Finally we picked up a nice size freighter with a small escort."[68]

John Hennessy had the watch at 1230 when the small freighter and its little escort vessel were sighted, range 8,000 yards, proceeding north hugging the coast. The escort was 1,500 yards to seaward of the freighter and not pinging. *Parche* went to battle stations and started closing the track of the freighter. At 1245, she ducked down to 90 feet and the escort ship passed by overhead moments later. "We did not need sonar gear to hear his screws," wrote Erwin.[69]

*Parche* was back at 65 feet at 1303 and commenced firing her last three Mark 14s from forward at the freighter from 1,550 yards. All three went out in a perfect spread but one torpedo was seen to broach before settling into its run. Just before the torpedoes should have hit, McCrory raised his periscope just in time to see the target ship turn away 90 degrees. All torpedoes missed and *Parche* turned right while heading down to 200 feet. The escort showed no interest in attacking, opting instead to turn away and run. McCrory eased his boat down to 300 feet and cleared the area to the southeast. Several sets of screws and two pingers were heard in the afternoon, but none attacked aggressively.

With torpedoes expended, McCrory surfaced at 1955 that evening and headed south. Radio messages were exchanged with *Cero*, which had been ordered to this area to replace *Parche* upon her exit. *Parche* rendezvoused with *Cero* at 0935 on 25 April. McCrory gave her a copy of *Parche*'s track chart in the area and a list of all ship contacts by firing over the info with his ship's line throwing gun. He found that *Cero* had taken two Japanese prisoners. One had already died of his wounds and *Cero* hoped to send over the other but the seas were too rough.

*Parche* received orders that afternoon to proceed to Midway for her refit. Dale Mielke happily relaxed in the forward torpedo room on 26 April and summarized his thoughts for the ending of another successful patrol with thoughts of liberty.[70]

> I never really expected we would go home this time, so do not feel badly. I am completely tired and want to relax the tension of the past 1½ months. My toes ache and feel slightly frost bitten, and walking is a painful effort. I hope it is nothing, and that a few warm baths will fix them up. I expect we will get to Midway in another four days and I am anxiously waiting to read all the letters that have accumulated for me.

The return trip was relatively uneventful. Ship's cooks Rebel Brown and Travis Bush made sure to use up all of the extra steaks during the return leg. "We had so much steak that I was sick of eating it," recalled mess cook Carl Zeller. "During the return run, we had steak for breakfast, lunch, and dinner."

Navigator Bob Erwin found the six-day return trip to be stressful due to the inability to take a good star fix. "It was all dead reckoning with some sun lines and a few moon shots," he recalled. "I was worried the whole way. Midway was a small spot in the vast Pacific." About 0300 on 30 April, Bob Daufenbach woke Erwin to announce that they should be near

New *Parche* crewmen after receiving their first combat pins following fifth patrol. Front row, left–right: F1c Tom Hayes, F1c Bob Dillon, S1c Joe DeSola, Ens. Dean Axene, Lt. Cdr. Bricker Ganyard, MoMM3c Roland Burker, and QM3c Milton Cantor. Standing, left–right: RM3c Fred Richards, TM3c Dave Manns, MoMM3c Gus Kulick, Y3c Carl Meyer, RT2c Pete Klapach, S1c Carl Zeller, F1c Charles Keenan, S1c Melvin Terry, F1c Bill Hollinger, and MoMM3c Tony Herman. Note: RM3c Paul Kuter had already been transferred from *Parche* when this photo was taken. *Courtesy of Joe DeSola Jr.*

Midway and to say that the night sky had cleared. Daufenbach thought it might be possible to get a good star fix. "We were able to get a pretty good fix with the sextant even with a blurry horizon," said Erwin. He recalled that *Parche* "missed our rendezvous point by only a few miles. We found our escort or he found us."[71]

*Parche* entered the channel at Midway on 30 April and by 1035 was moored to Pier S-9 at the Submarine Base. Mac McCrory had the quartermaster gang break out the ship's battle flag to fly from the No. 2 periscope. Fourteen Japanese flags were stretched from the periscope to the forward 20-mm gun to show *Parche*'s torpedo sinkings. "A launch came out in the channel to meet us and brought us our mail, ice cream, oranges and apples," wrote Dale Mielke. "When we reached the dock, the band started playing, and the gold braid reception committee came aboard. I was pretty engrossed in my very important mail to pay much attention to all the fuss."[72]

Frank Gadd and a few crewmen remained to supervise the relief crew while the remainder of the *Parche* men went ashore at 1535. It had been the most action-filled patrol of *Parche*'s five in terms of the number of different shipping contacts. She had made 26 shipping contacts although most of them had been disappointingly small. Mac McCrory's crew had been efficient in their efforts to disrupt Japanese shipping with the use of torpedoes and gun attacks. Two minesweepers had been destroyed during battle surface actions and the picket boat *Kosho Maru* had exploded violently from a 40-mm shell hit. Two other ships, including another minesweeper, had been sunk with *Parche*'s torpedoes and the small freighter attacked on 22 April was also likely destroyed.

| USS *Parche* Fifth War Patrol Summary | |
|---|---|
| Departure From: | Pearl Harbor |
| Patrol Area: | East of Honshu, Japan |
| Time Period: | 19 March–30 April 1945 |
| Number of Men On Board: | 87: 77 enlisted and 10 officers |
| Total Days on Patrol: | 43 |
| Miles Steamed: | 10,643 |
| Number of Torpedoes Fired: | 24 |
| Ships Credited Sunk (wartime): | 3/5,200 tons |
| Alden Postwar Credit: | 6/5,646 tons (3 to gun action) |
| JANAC Postwar Credit: | 1/615 tons |
| Shipping Damage Claimed: | 4/6,800 tons |
| Return To: | Midway |

For turning in one of the few productive war patrols during the spring of 1945, McCrory was awarded the Navy Cross for *Parche*'s fifth run. The new hands on board, including PCO Bricker Ganyard, were pinned with the combat insignia pin while at Midway.

*Parche*'s officers stand topside to supervise the deck crews taking in the lines as the boat returns from patrol. Officer on main deck to far left (head turned) is Ens. Dean Axene. Moving right are TM2c Ralph Giordano and QM3c Milton Cantor. Handling the line are two unknown sailors and MoMM3c Roland Burker (rightmost of the three). Standing with his back to the conning tower is F1c William Hollinger. Skipper Mac McCrory is leaning on the bridge railing below the periscope shears. The lookout standing on the shears above McCrory is S1c Melvin Terry. *Courtesy of Fred Richards.*

# CHAPTER THIRTEEN

# Lifeguard League

The *Parche* crew turned their boat over to the relief crew on 1 May and hauled their gear ashore for two weeks of R&R on Gooneyville. Bob Erwin, making his third leave on Midway, had become tired of the place. He and his fellow crew went ashore "where we could become better acquainted with the gooney birds and learn more of their language." Carl Zeller, making his first liberty on Midway, found it to be "a beautiful place but there just wasn't much to do there. The only thing female on Midway was the gooney birds and you weren't allowed to touch them by law."

Six crewmen who had made all five war patrols were notified early in their liberty period that they would be among those transferring on to other duties: Nick Casassa, Phil Mackey, Chet Stanton, and three chiefs, Kinkel, Hughes, and Barnett. By the time *Parche* was ready for her next patrol, only 17 plank owners would remain on board. With the departure of Barney Barnett, RM1c Myron Grover became the senior petty officer in charge of the radio gang.

Lonnie Hughes, who had long held the duty of senior chief of the maneuvering room watch, was transferred by Mac McCrory so that he could have Stateside leave to meet his new daughter Lonni before she reached her first birthday. Dixie Howell thus became the senior electrician's mate and took over as senior watchman in the maneuvering room.

Grover admitted, "I was pretty ornery when I got ashore. I really liked to live it up." Shipmate Hollis Larsen was equally rambunctious ashore. "When he got some beers in him, he liked to fight and found his way into trouble," said Grover. On the night of 5 May, Larsen was walking back toward *Parche* after enjoying a beer bust on the beach with some of his shipmates. "He spotted this jeep coming along that was being driven by an officer and a couple of other guys," Ed Mokos recalled. "Larsen, who was a powerful guy for his size, flagged the jeep down and then decked the officer and took his jeep."

The joyride was short-lived on an island the size of Midway. Larsen was soon subdued and hauled off to the base brig to sober up. Although very serious, the event was humorous to many of his shipmates. "Now, where in the hell are you going to go in a stolen jeep on an island that's only one and a half miles long?" thought Carl Zeller.

Duty officer Max Morton was notified at 0830 by the Submarine Base executive officer that Larsen had been detained in the brig for unauthorized use of a vehicle. Larsen asked to see fellow auxiliaryman Greek Mokos. "I visited Larsen in the brig," Mokos recalled. "He was expecting that he would be transferred from the *Parche* and he asked me to help pack his clothes. He told me he had a .32-caliber tucked in his skivvies in his locker in the pump room and asked that I hide it for him. Unfortunately, when I got back to the boat, two other guys had already sorted through his belongings. When they picked up his skivvies, the gun fell out, hit the deck and one of our officers confiscated it."

On 11 May, a Captain's Mast was held, during which Larsen was charged with drunkenness and unauthorized use of a vehicle. He was released from the brig and sent back to *Parche* under restrictions and under supervision of his skipper. A Summary court was ordered. On 14 May, Erwin served as the senior member of the three-officer court, which included Max Morton and Bob Stevenson. They adjourned waiting on orders of the convening authority. Larsen was given a dishonorable discharge with a recommendation for leniency. As the convening authority, Mac McCrory opted to change this to a 90-day probation with a fine of $50.40 per month for two and a half months because Larsen had hit the base officer when he took his jeep. His 90-day probation period was set to end on 12 August, "the estimated date the *Parche* would be back in San Diego for overhaul." Exec Jim Campbell felt McCrory had decided to stick with Larsen "because he was good. He was worth his weight in gold when he was on the manifold during torpedo attacks."[1]

During the refit, word was received by radio that Germany had surrendered to the Allied forces in Europe. The United States and Great Britain simultaneously broadcast the unconditional surrender of Germany at 0900 on 8 May and the *Parche* crew found one more reason to celebrate the approach of the war's end.

Most of the crew enjoyed their time ashore with fewer brushes with authorities. Motormac Gus Kulick found that he simply did not have the taste for the gilley juice enjoyed by some of his shipmates. He preferred sipping beer and playing craps at Midway. Beer was rationed and enlisted men each received a couple of coupons per day that entitled them to draw

Five of *Parche*'s six war patrols were declared eligible for the Submarine Combat Insignia pin. (Above) Bob Erwin's combat pin denotes one successful patrol. The three stars indicate three more successful patrols. *Author's photo.* (Right) Dixie Howell's card, received after *Parche*'s fifth patrol, shows that he had completed four successful runs. *Courtesy of Jack Howell.*

beer ashore. "We played craps for beer coupons and I really had a hot hand," he admitted. Kulick was doing so well that he was up some 300 coupons at one point. Not willing to lose his seat, he had buddy Bob Dillon take coupons to fetch two beers for both of them. Kulick declined selling off his extra tickets but became quite popular with shipmates as he shared his "winnings" from the craps table.

Radioman Paul Kuter, one of the radar operators, received orders for more advanced schooling while at Midway. He boarded a C-47 plane for a flight back to Pearl Harbor, where he enjoyed additional liberty at the Royal Hawaiian before his training commenced.

*Parche*'s crew was back on board by 15 May. Per Lieutenant Commander McCrory, the refit work had been excellent with "only minor deficiencies appearing during the training period." Repair work had included the renewal of one engine muffler and a port strut bearing plus sound isolation of the I.C. motor generators. The wardroom received two new officers, Lt. (jg) Robert Louis Mottner and Ens. Harry Lloyd Milhan, the latter a recently married 1944 Academy graduate who would be making his first war patrol.

The usual allotment of replacement sailors was received at the conclusion of the refit period. Exec Jim Campbell was quick to help analyze the new men for positions where they would best serve the boat. Among the men reporting on board from the relief crew was Torpedoman Cory Maupin, who had made *Parche*'s first three runs. As *Parche* was preparing

*Parche*'s crewmen around a campfire during liberty. Kneeling (left–right) are: Roland Burker, Harry Slajer, Walter Ekelund, and Chet Stanton. Standing in rear are (left–right): Ron Williams and two unknown shipmates. *Courtesy of Bob Hall.*

for her sixth patrol, Campbell happened to spot a couple of sailors horsing around on deck. "I saw this one husky sailor holding one of his buddies by the ankles, dangling him above the water," Campbell recalled.

He promptly walked over and tapped the sailor on the shoulder. "Come see me in the wardroom," he ordered.

This sailor, MoMM3c Bill Coleman, had just reported on board. As he shuffled down the ladders below decks for the wardroom, he could only imagine how his first encounter with his new Exec would turn out. Coleman was much relieved, however, when he found that Campbell had other plans for him.

"Coleman, you're just the man I need," he said. "We've got this new 5-inch deck gun and I need a strong man as second loader to haul those heavy shells from the hatch to the first loader."

"Yes, sir," Coleman answered with great relief. From that point on, he would serve as one of the key hands for *Parche*'s deck gun actions.

Campbell and Chief of the Boat Don Walters had their crew organized on deck for an awards ceremony with the local brass on 18 May. Skipper Mac McCrory was presented with a Bronze Star by Cdr. Gail Morgan and Letters of Commendation were awarded to Lt. Bob Stevenson, CY Warren Dingman, MoMM1 Orvail Buckner, and EM2c Howie Ernest.

Mac McCrory and Jim Campbell's challenges with crew-related escapades did not end with the Larsen incident. The beer busts ashore allowed the submariners to let off some steam, but this luxury created opportunities for trouble. "Some of the guys didn't drink, so you could collect extra coupons," recalled Cory Maupin. "We saved a lot of these up for the last night of our liberty." A group of about nine *Parche* sailors put their extra coupons to use on the evening of 20 May and had a beach party with their excess beer.

After a few too many beers, the inebriated sailors began scheming ways to obtain extra booze once their supply ran out. The officers could, of course, buy hard liquor at the little bar at the Pan American hotel on Midway where they stayed. One of the sailors decided they should break into the supply building where they believed the extra liquor was stored. "We argued around and two of us finally decided that we would go get a bottle of booze," admitted Maupin.

Maupin and S1c Harry Reed, a gunner's mate striker, slipped off into the dark to pinch a bottle of liquor. Reed's fellow .50-caliber gunner, Gus Kulick, tried to convince them to give up the idea. "We kept telling them the guards were too close and not to go, but they went anyway," said Kulick. Reed broke into a building while Maupin stood guard. The plan failed when a Marine guard approached him in the dark.

"What are you doing out here?" the guard asked.

"I'm just out taking a walk," Maupin slurred.

About that time, Reed emerged from the building and the Marine shouted for him to halt. Maupin and Reed immediately took off running in the dark. The Marine guard again ordered Reed to stop and then fired several shots at the shadowy figure who had emerged from the building. Maupin made it back to *Parche* unharmed but his companion was less fortunate. Reed was winged in the left arm by one of the Marine's shots.

Jack Holleran was the duty officer at the time when Reed returned to the boat shortly before midnight on 20 May with a gunshot wound to the left arm. "He came back to the boat, crossed the gangplank—Lord knows how—and fell down on deck," recalled Charlie McNutt. "I was sitting there on deck when Reed came aboard," Fred Richards recalled. "I could see that he was bleeding and was in trouble."

The duty guard tried to help Reed to his feet but found that he was bleeding heavily. Doc Shaw offered emergency treatment but the wound needed more attention. An ambulance arrived from the naval dispensary and picked up Reed for further treatment. "Of course, he told on me while he was in the hospital," said Maupin.

Two hours later, guards returned to *Parche* and escorted Cory Maupin from the boat to the base brig for questioning in regards to the Reed shooting. This was by request of the base commanding officer, who was none too pleased with the actions of the *Parche* crew thus far. By the time *Parche* was ready to sail on patrol again, both Reed and Maupin had been transferred from the boat.

---

*Parche*'s pre-patrol training period, including underway exercises and the firing of five practice torpedoes to break in Bob Stevenson as the new TDC operator, had commenced on 19 May. Lieutenant Commander McCrory, eager to put Midway in his wake, found a new challenge to overcome. During the final loading period, *Parche* docked twice for a squeal that had developed in the port shaft and the port propeller was renewed. Several of the crewmen were sent down in the lower extremes of *Parche* to help trace the source of the squeal. "I went through six towels in one day just soaking up the sweat while we traced the source of that squeal," recalled Carl Zeller.

*Parche* entered the ARD-8 floating dry dock on 22 May to inspect the propellers. She left the dock the next day, conducted sound tests in Midway's lagoon and was dry-docked again that afternoon so that the errant shafts could be examined again. By 24 May the sound tests were satisfactory and *Parche* was released to prepare for her next war patrol. The new hands

(Opposite) *Parche* crew at Midway about 18 May 1945 prior to the sixth patrol.

First row (left–right): CTM Don Walters, CRT John Gray, Lt. (jg) John Holleran, Ens. Harry Milhan, Lt. (jg) Robert Mottner (head down), Lt. (jg) Frank Gadd, Lt. Cdr. Mac McCrory, Lt. Bob Erwin, Lt. Max Morton, Lt. Jim Campbell, Ens. Dean Axene, CGM Jim Plumley, CY Warren Dingman, and CMoMM Dana Jensen.

Second row (left–right): Charles Lee, Carl Meyer, Joe Sheppard, Orvail Buckner, LB Frederick, Robert Flanagan, Louis Jarco, Bobby C. Hall, Harry Reed, Charlie McNutt, Jim Hawkey, and Harry Slajer.

Third row (left–right): Larry Lawrence, Carl Zeller, Bob Hall, Dick Frank, Paul Vetter, Dale Mielke, Walter Ekelund, Glenn Meise, Lamar Brown, Henry Gay, Bob DeMonge, Howard Ernest, Dixie Howell, and Murray Johnston.

Fourth row (left–right): Milton Cantor, Rex Shaw, Hollis Larsen, Sam Roberts, Gus Kulick, Bob Swanson, Wayne Davis, John Nania, Ralph Giordano, Fred Richards, Travis Bush, Arnold Bashwiner, Jack Kimball, and Robert Dillon.

Fifth row (standing, left–right): Charles Keenan, Joe DeSola, Adolph Russell, Ed Mokos, Dave Manns, Roland Burker, Red Williams, William Hollinger, Max Geier, Leroy Braxton, and Thomas Hayes.

received on board showed the benefit of the training classes maintained at Midway, which had been attended by some of the older hands as well.

The wardroom had a new mess attendant, 22-year-old L. C. Fisher to replace Robert Nelson. Lillie and Charles Fisher had given their son only initials for a name but some of his closer service friends, such as *Parche*'s former steward Carl Kimmons, would call him Leo. Fisher, orphaned at a young age, had moved from Florida to New York where he was raised by a Jewish family. A personable and religious man, Fisher quickly became favored in McCrory's wardroom.[2]

The most interesting new face among the crew was that of Navy photographer Harry Lee Heaton, who had seen considerable action in the Pacific documenting the island campaigns. By the latter days of the Pacific War, Admiral Lockwood was routinely placing photographers aboard many of his submarines to document the little-publicized exploits of the Silent Service. For the common sailors not in the know, scuttlebutt was rampant with the arrival of Heaton concerning how important *Parche*'s next mission must be.

Senior torpedomen Bob DeMonge and Tom Worley's gangs spent nine hours loading five Mark 18-1 and nine Mark 18-2 electric torpedoes forward and eight Mark 14-3 steam torpedoes aft. Engineering officer John Hennessy and his chief motormacs Dana Jensen and Corlet Madison supervised the fueling process, in which 30,267 gallons of fuel oil and 1,920 gallons of lube oil were received to bring *Parche* to her 116,000-gallon capacity. Following lunch on 25 May, the maneuvering watch was stationed and Max Morton had the deck as skipper McCrory maneuvered *Parche* out from Midway at 1532.

Lt. Bob Erwin, a *Parche* plank owner, was among those with new orders. "I had mixed feelings as I watched *Parche* depart for Guam and her sixth patrol," Erwin recalled. "I was happy to be headed home and to a new ship but I was sad to be leaving a ship with a crew that was really a family. There was also a doubt that any of us would ever see each other again. At this point in the war about five submarines were coming back out of six that went out."[3]

QM3c Dale Mielke was happy to have a familiar face join the quartermaster/signalman gang prior to the sixth patrol in the form of SM1c Eugene Mettee. He noted in his diary that Mettee "was my instructor in New London. Small world! I spoke for him at Midway, and they took him aboard for this run." Mielke resumed his diary entries as *Parche* departed from Midway as something of a celebrity with a band playing, command staff at the dock, and movie cameras rolling.[4]

### USS *Parche* Officers and CPOs
### Sixth War Patrol

| Officers On Board | Prior War Patrols | Position |
|---|---|---|
| Lt. Cdr. Woodrow McCrory, USN | 5 | Commanding Officer |
| Lt. Churchill J. Campbell, USNR | 5 | Executive Officer |
| Lt. John H. Hennessy Jr., USN | 6 | Engineering Officer |
| Lt. Robert T. Stevenson, USNR | 4 | Torpedo/Gunnery |
| Lt. Max T. Morton, USNR | 2 | Communications |
| Lt. (jg) Francis O. Gadd, USNR | 2 | First Lieutenant |
| Lt. (jg) Robert L. Mottner, USNR | 0 | |
| Ens. John M. Holleran, USNR | 2 | Assistant Engineering |
| Ens. Dean L. Axene, USN | 1 | Assistant Gunnery |
| Ens. Harry L. Milhan, USN | 0 | Commissary |

| Chief Petty Officers On Board | Prior War Patrols | |
|---|---|---|
| Dingman, CY Warren E., USN | 6 | |
| Gray, CRT John C., Jr., USNR | 5 | |
| Jensen, CMoMM Dana C., USN | 11 | |
| Madison, CMoMM Corlet R., USN | 3 | |
| Plumley, CGM James L., USN | 10 | |
| Walters, CTM Donald E., USN | 8 | Chief of the Boat |

Our departure was rather auspicious, as we had a photographer aboard taking pictures and a plane flying close overhead taking more of them from the air. We passed a tug which followed us for a while, also taking movies. We looked pretty good with our battle flag flying and our Jap victory flags strung out. Most of these shots of us will be in a movie called the "Silent Service" which the Navy is making. I will be in most of the shots as I was the QM on the bridge, which is the most prominent spot on the ship.

My feelings at the start of this patrol are much different from those last time. I am very anxious to go in and get it over with because this time I know we are going back to the States after the patrol. Then, too, I know exactly what to expect and have a good deal more confidence.

En route to Guam heavy vibrations started in the starboard shaft, believed to be in the strut bearing. McCrory made exhaustive tests in changing speeds and rudder but the vibrations persisted. *Parche* proceeded on the port shaft and made preparations for braking the starboard shaft as vibration continued with the shaft idling.

A message was sent on this condition on 29 May, and McCrory felt he might have to return to Midway. At daylight, engineering officer John Hennessy went overboard with a diving mask at 0600 to conduct an inspection of the port shaft, strut bearings, and screw. Hennessy found a small dent in one blade of the starboard propeller but the condition of the strut bearing was normal. As tests continued over the next hour, the vibration finally disappeared completely. *Parche* radioed her improved condition and was directed to proceed to Guam.

Carl Zeller, happy to have been relieved of his mess-cooking detail by other new hands on board for the sixth run, spent most of his time standing watches in the radio shack transmitting messages. "One night while trying to raise Guam to relay our message to Pearl Harbor, I actually picked up the Brooklyn Navy Yard," he recalled. "They said they would relay my message to Pearl, but I said not to worry about it. I would get it to Guam like I was supposed to." For Zeller, such freak atmospheric conditions "would do some amazing things occasionally with our reception."

Radioman Fred Richards, who falsified his papers to enter the Navy at age 15, had felt compelled during his liberty after the fifth patrol to admit his true age to a clergyman. The truth of his current age, now 16, made it to Lieutenant Commander McCrory, who apparently decided that war was war and Richards was mature enough to continue serving. "The skipper found out about my true age," said Richards, "but he did not let it be known who it was. I recall standing watch on the sixth patrol and hearing some whispering amongst the crew about there being a youngster on board who had already made one patrol. Some of my shipmates incorrectly assumed it had to be Mel Terry because he also came aboard before the fifth run and he looked very young. I just decided to keep quiet and let them assume it was Terry."

*Parche* entered the eastern end of the safety lane to the Marianas the following day. The occasional squeak in the starboard shaft and cavitation far ahead of the port shaft persisted. During a practice dive conducted by OOD Jack Holleran on 31 May, lookout EM3 Arne Hansen took a nasty fall while clearing the bridge. It took five stitches from Doc Shaw to sew up Hansen's injured right shin.

*Parche* rendezvoused with USS *Doherty* (DE-14) at 0530 on 3 June and proceeded into Guam's Apra Harbor. Two sub tenders, *Proteus* and *Holland*, were at Guam to handle administrative details and voyage repairs, as well as a floating dry dock. *Parche* would remain at Guam for four days alongside *Holland* as repairs were made on her screw. McCrory allowed navigator Jim Campbell to handle the tricky maneuvering into the dry dock. "I had Bob Daufenbach on the helm because he was the one I trusted the most to maneuver the boat in such tight quarters," Campbell recalled. Once inside the floating dry dock, Guam's relief workers began pumping the water from the dock and a gangway was put aboard for the crew to be relieved.

Lieutenant Campbell was worn down from the previous war patrol and the incessant work on tracking the squeal in the shaft. "After docking the boat, I started to walk across the gangplank and I just passed out stone cold," he said. Muscular Bob Stevenson alertly caught his Exec before he could plunge into the dry dock and hauled him across the gangplank.

"I guess I was suffering from exhaustion," Campbell recalled. "I weighed 240 pounds when I started the war and stood six feet tall. Toward war's end, I was down to 199 pounds in full uniform. This was probably due to the stress, the lack of sleep and a lack of good eating. I never had much of an appetite with all of the foul air in the boat."

The repairmen found that one blade of *Parche*'s starboard propeller was turned and slightly bent, indicating that the boat had likely struck something on the morning of 29 May. Bits of welding slag were also found in the outer stern tube bearing, scoring both the shaft journal and bearing. This bearing was cleaned and the starboard propeller was renewed while in dry dock. While these repairs proceeded, the crew enjoyed the facilities at Camp Dealey.

Dale Mielke enjoyed a sightseeing bus trip around the island. "I saw the places that had been destroyed in the fighting as well as the new buildings we are setting up all over the place," he wrote. "It is really a beautiful island, lush and fertile, but the heat for us was unbearable and spoiled things for us. I did see some women ashore; I guess they were Chomoros, and each of them was washing clothes. I suppose they were doing laundry for the G.I.s for a living."[5]

Some of the men enjoyed a few too many at the beer hall on Guam and came back on board ship in a boisterous mood. "In the evening, most of the crew were topside yelling, singing and carrying on," recalled Charlie McNutt. It was getting dark and the noise of the drunken sailors became irritating to the Guam dry dock workers. The lieutenant in command of the dry dock got on his ship's speaker system and ordered all of the *Parche* submariners to go below decks and quiet themselves.[6]

"As the crew was going down the hatches, somebody made a remark to the lieutenant that he should have sex with himself," McNutt related.

When word of the insult was relayed to skipper McCrory on the base, he was not pleased. At the next morning's roll call, he put all enlisted men on restriction to the boat. The boredom of confinement in the dry dock and the excessive tropical heat served to sober up more than a few sailors. "You could not pump enough air-conditioning into our boat to keep it cool," thought McNutt.

Testing on 5 June showed both shafts to be functioning normally. *Parche* finally got under way from Guam at 1500 on 7 June en route to the Lifeguard League south of Honshu. Lieutenant Commander McCrory had orders to join other submarines in the area to fish downed aviators from the sea during planned air strikes against the Japanese mainland. Lookouts spotted a large plane making a water landing in the distance that night but *Parche* was unable to locate its crew. *Parche* stood by during the night as a destroyer moved in to search the waters.

Another destroyer arrived around 2300 and several planes were flying about the area in search. McCrory finally opted to depart the scene "knowing that the presence of a submarine would complicate the rescue." *Parche* entered her assigned patrol area off Honshu on the morning of 11 June and commenced patrolling the seas while expecting to be called to lifeguard duty.

A wave of Mustangs was sighted en route to make a fighter sweep on Tokyo during the morning. Lookout Carl Zeller watched the departing aircraft in amazement, marvelling at how close his boat was to Japan. One report was received during the day of a ditched plane and McCrory headed for the position to join the search. She was soon called off of this hunt and set course for her assigned lifeguard station for a fighter strike on Nagoya scheduled for the following day.

Radio traffic was steady during the next three days as *Parche* awaited orders to pick up any downed aviators. One pilot with a bad engine was monitored during the strikes on 15 June, but he was able to nurse his crippled aircraft past Iwo Jima for home. The 20-mm gunners, Joe DeSola and Pinky Pannell, were called to the bridge to shoot up a floating mine spotted at 1835. An hour later, a second mine was spotted at 800 yards. Jack Holleran maneuvered *Parche* in to 200 yards before the gunners cut loose and blew this one up. "The explosion was spectacular, throwing shrapnel and smoke high in the air and breaking several lights in the boat," McCrory logged.

One of the lookouts, Joe Leiching, recalled that Navy photographer Harry Heaton had come topside to document this action. "We maneuvered close so he could get a picture of the guys shooting up this mine," Leiching

Mess attendant "LC" Fisher serving skipper Mac McCroy and the *Parche* wardroom. In left foreground is Lt. (jg) Robert Mottner. To the right of photo is Lt. Max Morton. *Courtesy of Jim Campbell.*

said. "That one blew up and threw shrapnel all over the place." Fortunately no one was hurt.

Another lookout, Dale Mielke, found the mine destruction to be a welcome bit of excitement after a week of dull lifeguard cruising. He recorded in his diary:[7]

> We sank the first one with the 20-mm, but the second one exploded about 100 yards from the ship and scared the daylights out of us. The explosion was upward and certainly gave us something to think about for a day or so. They were rusty and had barnacles on the underside of them and were ugly things with horns sticking out all over it. I was on deck at the time of the explosion and ducked behind the conning tower when it unexpectedly exploded.

The lifeguard duty meant days of cruising with little action. By this point in 1945, lifeguard duty around the main Japanese islands was commonplace for U.S. subs. Carl Vozniak, an electrician's mate from

Philadelphia who had joined *Parche* at Midway after the fifth patrol, was used to lifeguard duty. Vozniak had three previous runs on *Finback* and during the sub's tenth patrol she had picked five aviators from the ocean. Two of these rescues had been particularly noteworthy.

On 2 September 1944, Lt. Cdr. Robert R. Williams Jr. moved *Finback* in close to the beach off Megame Island near Haha Jima in the Bonins to rescue Hellcat pilot Ens. James W. Beckham from the carrier *Enterprise*. "We came under heavy shell fire while approaching the island and our skipper said, 'the hell with that,' " Vozniak recalled. So, *Finback* submerged and pulled Beckham out five miles to safety with a line tied around the periscope. "We lost that flier three times before we got him safely out. I guess he wasn't too good at surf-boarding."[8]

The other noteworthy rescue had occurred during the same morning off Chichi Jima when *Finback* had moved in to rescue *San Jacinto* Avenger pilot and future U.S. president Lt. (jg) George Herbert Walker Bush from his life raft. Carl Vozniak didn't mind such rescue work because his older brother, who did not survive the war, had been an Army Air Corps flyboy.[9]

A fighter sweep planned against Nagoya was postponed due to heavy weather on 16 June, leaving *Parche* with little to do but submerged reconnaissance. Heavy wind and seas, combined with low visibility, again cancelled the air strikes the following day.

Ens. Dean Axene later reflected upon his duties as an officer aboard *Parche*. "The wardroom was very quiet. Seldom was there a poker game, a game of acey-deucy, or even a cribbage hand. We had a very high-quality, multi-band radio, but playing it was frowned upon. Basically, Captain Mac felt that if an officer was not on watch or doing ship's work, he ought to be sleeping to ensure that he would be physically ready for the next combat encounter." Axene felt it somewhat difficult to adjust to this prescribed routine. He enjoyed background music while engaged in other activities and "felt lost" without being able to check the news broadcasts periodically to find out what was happening in the world around him.[10]

Finally, the raid went off on 18 June in spite of less than desirable weather. The radiomen monitored the lifeguard circuit and listened to reports of a downed pilot a considerable distance from *Parche*'s position. Unable to assist with the day's downed pilot, *Parche* was finally released that night to proceed on war patrol against shipping targets. As she moved toward her station, *Parche* was put through tests to prepare the crew for action. Diving officer John Hennessy made a deep dive to check for leaks and noise. McCrory ordered a practice battle surface at 1732 to test-fire all the guns. He then set course for the 100-fathom curve off Kinkasan to patrol there overnight.

Lookout Dale Mielke noted that the temperature became colder each day as *Parche* approached Honshu. "I broke out my heavy shoes and sweaters and socks, as I expect to be pretty cold before long," he wrote. "The water is shark-infested, and almost anytime you can see a fin sticking out of the water. I sure loathe the damn things, and I can't help but think of how long you would last in the water."[11]

*Parche* rendezvoused with *Piranha* at 1820 on 20 June and was given valuable information by the line-throwing gun on her track charts and contacts. *Piranha* passed along patrol instructions for *Parche* and *Devilfish*, also operating near Honshu. *Parche* proceeded to the area of Tsugaru Strait. The next morning, McCrory took his boat in close to the coast of Honshu while hoping to spot shipping traffic. *Parche* remained about two miles offshore, close enough to view houses, a lighthouse, and signal towers through the periscope.

Mielke had the quartermaster watch during the early hours of 21 June. "I was on the periscope and made the first contact of this patrol," he noted. "It was a PC boat coming out of the harbor." McCrory opted to let this and several other small boats pass by that were viewed heading east from Shiriya Saki. This area proved to be busy right away.

At 0908, Max Morton sighted a convoy consisting of a medium freighter and a small freighter with a destroyer escort headed north for Shiriya and hugging the coast. McCrory was unable to close them submerged, but he moved his boat to within 5,000 yards of shore to catch the next shipping.

At 1245, a gunboat was sighted rounding Shiriya Saki headed south. McCrory went to battle stations and commenced tracking. "Ship was changing course and speed, acting peculiarly," he noted. Lt. Jim Campbell took over the deck watch for the attack. At 1310, with the tubes ready and prepared to shoot, *Parche*'s target suddenly stopped. At that time an SC type escort joined the gunboat from the south. A quick sweep around with the scope showed a small freighter rounding Shiriya Saki to the south, explaining the gathering of these escort ships.

McCrory's team made two ST setups on the freighter and at 1322 *Parche* commenced firing four Mark 18s from the forward nest. The range was 1,300 yards and the depth setting was five feet. In less than a minute and a half one of the torpedoes hit the freighter, properly timed for the first torpedo. Breaking up noises were heard on the sonar. John Hennessy had lost depth control at the time of the hit but this was regained in less than a minute. Nothing could be seen on the surface except for a veil of dense white smoke. One or two torpedoes had broached several times in the state 2 seas but were not seen by the Japanese.

The sub chaser had passed between *Parche* and the freighter immediately before firing. Expecting countermeasures, McCrory took his boat to 200 feet but no depth charges came down. He eased back to periscope depth within the hour and a periscope sweep showed the sub chaser and gunboat still moving around the scene of the sinking. Six other small patrols had joined the scene, apparently searching for survivors. The 947-ton cargo ship *Hizen Maru* was *Parche*'s first victim on her sixth war patrol but far from the last.[12]

Quartermaster Mielke, while resting during his off-duty time in the forward torpedo room, pondered in his diary why the Japanese escort ships had not attacked *Parche*.[13]

We thought he went for help, but all day long we waited and nothing happened. About 1600 a "Rufe" came circling around, but we saw him first and went to 150 feet. We surfaced at night and ran north till the area cooled off a bit. The explosion must surely have been heard and seen on the beach. We were submerged 16 hours and felt light-headed from the pressure we were under all day. I still can't figure those damn Japs out; they never do as you would expect them to do.

# CHAPTER FOURTEEN

# "One Hell of a Beating"

**P**arche continued on her patrol east and north of the entrance to Tsugaru Strait on the surface through the night after sinking her first ship of the patrol. Max Morton and Chief Dingman's *Parche Prattler* for the sixth run continued its tongue-in-cheek recording of the boat's actions on 22 June: "Visibility was next to nothing, and the first few hours of periscope watching produced nothing but a grave doubt as to just where in the hell we were and the sighting of a few more Jap small fry hugging the beach."

By 0954, the fog had begun to lift and a small coastal freighter was spotted 3,600 yards away as it headed down the coast. The merchant vessel soon reversed course to the south and another freighter appeared in the opposite direction. A heavy fog momentarily foiled an approach attempt but Mac McCrory headed north to exit the fog.

A small, flat craft was spotted 5,000 yards to the east at 1130. This vessel was apparently escorting three luggers who were astern of him. *Parche* worked to the east in hopes of making a battle surface as they passed. Nothing else came into sight during the next two hours, so at 1340 *Parche* battle surfaced five miles astern of the lugger group. "As we drew up to starboard the luggers remained in perfect column, apparently intent on shooting it out with their machine guns, each lugger mounting two," Lieutenant Commander McCrory logged.

The call for "battle stations, surface" resulted in two dozen men taking position on the main deck as lookouts, duty officers, or bridge gunners. Exec Jim Campbell took control of the bridge with skipper McCrory conning *Parche* into the attack. Gunnery officer Bob Stevenson and Dean Axene helped spot for and direct their gun crews. On the main deck aft, Chief Jim Plumley served as the 5-inch gun captain with Red Williams seated on the left side of the gun as pointer, GM2c Max Geier on the right as the setter, and fire controlman Bobby Hall standing by as their spotter.

*Parche* gunners in action on the sixth patrol. In the foreground, Dave Manns is handling the after 20-mm cannon while fire controlman Bobby Hall as loader faces forward. Directly behind Hall wearing the cap and headset is Lt. Bob Stevenson. On the main deck below them, Bill Coleman and Shaky Jake Slajer (farthest right) sit on the rails as the 5-inch gunners prepare to fire. At the 5-inch gun, sight setter Joe Nichols is wearing the talker's headset. Farthest forward beyond the deck gun is gun captain Jim Plumley. *Courtesy of Bob Hall.*

As the heavy shells were passed up from below, MoMM3c Bill Coleman—who had just joined *Parche* at Midway—was the second loader on the 5-inch behind Shaky Jake Slajer. "Japan had lost so many freighters that she had to start using sampans for coastal trade," explained Jim Campbell. "Practically all of the small vessels were equipped with radio gear and were acting as picket boats reporting all submarine sightings. That and a 5-inch deck gun gave us a lot more incentive for battle surfaces."

At 1410, *Parche* started raking the last lugger in the column from 1,800 yards. About eight 5-inch hits left this vessel in shambles. Motormac Bob Silvis and shipmate Gus Kulick answered the call when Lieutenant Stevenson asked for volunteers to man the .50-caliber machine guns. "By the time we got the .50-caliber from the forward torpedo room to the control room and wrestled it up through the conning tower and onto the bridge the 5-inch gun crew had already sunk the first trawler," Silvis recalled.[1]

The gunners then shifted to the next lugger that immediately turned toward *Parche* and opened up with his machine guns. About ten 5-inch hits from 1,200 yards stopped this ship and left him sinking and on fire

Parche's forward 40-mm crew prepares to fire. Ens. Dean Axene is standing behind gunner Blackie Nania. Lt. Cdr. Mac McCrory looks on from the side of the periscope shears. Bobby C. Hall is visible in the lower foreground beside the forward deck-mounted 20-mm gun. *Courtesy of Bob Hall.*

in the bow. Engineman Gus Kulick had been denied the chance to fire on the first vessel and he was eager to do his share of damage now. "The Old Man wanted to see what they had, so he told me to hold on until he gave the word," he recalled. Once the deck gun had crippled the lugger, McCrory moved *Parche* in closer and gave the nod to his .50-caliber gunners. "I opened up and it only took a minute to sweep her decks," said Kulick.

The third brave little lugger had also turned toward *Parche* and opened up with her machine guns. Two 5-inch shells slammed into her bow and she was set on fire. Several strings from their machine guns had peppered *Parche*'s bridge, 40-mm gun platform, and the periscope shears, but fortunately none of the men topside had been hit. "I could hear the machine-gun bullets hitting our hull," recalled Bill Coleman, "but we kept fighting the dog."

Bob Silvis, now manning the .50-caliber, enjoyed his share of the action as the third trawler's bullets whistled overhead. "The Japanese were knocking paint off the periscope shears which was unfortunate as we had just gotten a new paint job," he related. Glancing up at the periscope shears, Silvis saw the lookouts were taking cover behind the periscopes "but still in position to see if any aircraft were coming in."[2]

Silvis then noted the aviation photographer, Harry Heaton, higher up "sitting in between the two periscopes with his legs wrapped around one of the periscopes. He had his camera in hand and he was taking pictures with a grin on his face from ear to ear. He was in seventh heaven because he could see the action and take pictures." All Silvis could think was that the foolhardy photographer should get down before he caught one of the bullets.

Dale Mielke, another of the battle lookouts high atop the shears, was less thrilled than Heaton about the shooting. "I had the narrowest escape of anyone else in that two bullets hit the periscope 6" from my back and several more traced a pattern directly over my head," he wrote in his diary. "I was sure lucky to have my skin intact after that, as it was the closest I've been yet."[3]

The escort ship had turned back once to join the fight but she reconsidered and headed on toward Chikyu. The third lugger had had enough and she headed off toward the west, licking her wounds. McCrory did not feel that the situation warranted chasing her in toward the coast. His second lugger victim was slowly sinking so he turned *Parche* to allow his gunners to polish off the first victim. Four more 5-inch hits were landed, one in the lugger's stern, which left her sinking with two men having abandoned ship in a small boat. McCrory broke off the gun action at 1445 and headed west. *Parche* had fired 38 rounds of 5-inch, 52 rounds of 40-mm, six magazines of 20-mm, and four belts of .50-caliber.

Electrician Dick Frank was called on to help haul the .50-caliber machine guns down from the bridge. Donning gloves, he took the hot barrels as they were passed down from the bridge. One of the new junior officers, not expecting to see him there, asked, "Dick, what are you doing up here?" Without thinking, Frank turned and passed him one of the hot gun barrels in explanation. "He never asked me about anything again," Frank laughed.

The next morning, 23 June, more trawlers were sighted about eight miles to the northeast. *Parche* went to battle stations and closed the small craft. The three closest trawlers were roughly in line offering a good opportunity to shoot up all of them. The gunners took the deck once again and opened fire at 0927 from a range of 2,000 yards. Plumley's crew landed six direct 5-inch hits, which sank the first trawler.

*Parche* shifted to the second trawler and scored with eight 5-inch shells. This vessel was also left sinking and four men were seen to abandon ship. This vessel was under the waves before *Parche* pulled clear. At 0937, McCrory opened fire on the third trawler, which had turned his tail toward the American submarine. Seven 5-inch hits at 1,200 yards left him flooded to the gunwales with no target left for the gunners. Only the second trawler had been armed but she had not fired on *Parche*.

At 0940, McCrory called for a cease-fire and cleared the area to the south. His gunners had been busy, shooting up six small vessels in two days and claiming five of them as sunk. The gunners on 23 June had expended 30 rounds of 5-inch shells, 52 rounds of 40-mm, and five magazines of 20-mm.

"Our crew is almost perfect in that they lay most of their shells right on even with our ship rolling and pitching as a sub will," recorded battle lookout Mielke. "In three days on this station, we have sunk one tanker, two trawlers and two spit-kits. Also destroyed, because we did not see them actually sink, one trawler and one more spit-kit."[4]

---

*Parche* surfaced and patrolled toward Shiriya Saki during the night. After daylight, she closed to within eight miles of the coast but could not see land due to fog again. Ship's recorder Max Morton wrote that *Parche* was this day "groping once more through the pea soup." Passing back through the scene of the previous gun actions, *Parche* spotted the wreckage of her third trawler victim from the previous day. The trawler was a wreck, fully flooded. "Curiously, its anchor was still down and it was awash and a complete, hopeless wreck," Mielke noted from the periscope shears. "I will say it is sunk although it will probably float around for years." Another trawler spotted the submarine and headed in, so McCrory eased away from the scene.[5]

At 1406, Larry Lawrence on the SJ radar announced that he had picked up a ship contact at 12,000 yards. Bob Stevenson called the skipper to the bridge as his lookouts strained to spot the distant enemy vessel. The fog made visual sighting difficult and McCrory was wary that this might be an alerted destroyer escort. "We couldn't make out the ship very well," lookout Bill Coleman stated. "She wasn't following a straight course."

By 1543, the ship could barely be made out in the fog at 6,000 yards. Quartermaster Mielke finally exclaimed, "I see it! It's a big one . . . three or four decks."

Mac McCrory studied the ship with his binoculars and decided that it looked like a transport ship. "It was running with no lights and zig-zagging," Lawrence recalled. With all indications that this was a worthy target, McCrory cleared the bridge and dived *Parche* to make a submerged attack approach.

"Open the forward tubes," Daufenbach called over the 1MC as the Bells of St. Mary's bonged for battle stations. *Parche* closed the range to 2,200 yards with her forward tubes flooded and ready to fire. As the ship became more visible through the fog, the skipper suddenly caught a good glimpse of it through the ST attack scope. A large white flag was flying astern, showing "all the markings of a hospital ship, probably the *Takasago Maru*," Lieutenant Commander McCrory logged dejectedly.

"Oh, my God, it's a hospital ship," McCrory exclaimed. He immediately broke off the attack. Larry Lawrence heard his skipper mutter, "I sure would have been in trouble if we'd sunk it."

The neutral ship, not following the prescribed procedure for maintaining a straight course with running lights, had come within moments of catching torpedoes. "That guy will never know just how close he came," wrote Lieutenant Morton in the *Parche Prattler.*

Dale Mielke assisted McCrory with identifying the ship by flipping through the recognition books as the skipper had called out the features. "I identified him as the *Tatasugo Maru*, 9,367 tons, 463 feet, and [it] is in reality a Jap hospital ship although we will never know what he was carrying or why he was so far north," he wrote. "After it was all over, the captain sent a message to all other subs in the neighborhood to guarantee safe passage for the Jap. That ship was just a press of a button from being sunk, and he was lucky to be identified in time."[6]

*Parche* moved toward Todo Saki on 25 June, bucking heavy wind and seas from the south as the fog cleared. She sighted nothing but small fishing and patrol craft all day, however. Lookouts such as Mielke found the weather cold enough "to warrant wearing heavy clothing" while on the bridge. "The sea is teeming with seals, porpoise, and other fish including whales. I saw one spout twice the other morning and got a kick out of it." In between watches, many of the crewmen attended *Parche*'s school of the boat to continue their qualification process. Mielke enjoyed his submerged watch time with his former New London instructor, Eugene Mettee, "a swell guy" who helped him pass the long hours on duty in the conning tower.[7]

While patrolling on the surface at 0130 on 26 June, Bob Stevenson, Frank Gadd, and their bridge watch had the rare opportunity to witness an eclipse of the moon. McCrory closed the coast at 0445 to patrol off Kone Saki again. At 0902, smoke was spotted from one ship about 20,000 yards down the coast headed north. Subsequent periscope observations showed three large ships and six escorts—prime targets. The large ships were roughly in column, zigzagging one mile off the shore with *Chidori*-type escort vessels about 5,000 yards to seaward. Two sub chasers patrolled ahead of the convoy and two were ahead and to starboard. All escorts were alertly pinging "and working as if they had been briefed by the Emperor himself," thought McCrory.

*Parche* went to battle stations at 0913 and closed for an attack position 4,000 yards off Okama Saki. A Rufe patrol plane was spotted over the convoy as *Parche* moved in.

Diving officer John Hennessy did his best to battle a moderate swell and a 6-degree negative gradient at periscope depth but it made scope observations difficult on McCrory. TDC operator Bob Stevenson and plotting officer Dean Axene soon arrived at a target speed of eight knots, avoiding using the ST primarily in favor of their navigational plot. *Parche* swung right to shoot at 1025 as the two leading sub chasers passed 500 yards to starboard.

One deck below in the control room, Radioman striker Carl Zeller took in the scene around him. Chief of the Boat Don Walters had his normal station at the Christmas tree to monitor the hull opening indicators' status. Zeller admired leading auxiliaryman Hollis Larsen's work on the manifold during torpedo attacks. "He had a sixth sense about him when it came to the manifold." Anticipating the diving officer's orders, "he would start adjusting the balance before the torpedoes were even fired to keep our boat in trim."

The leading freighter got by but McCrory, sweeping the waves with his attack periscope, settled on the second ship in column. "Make ready the forward tubes," he ordered and battle talker Bob Daufenbach repeated the command to the forward room.

Thomas Worley, the new senior torpedoman heading up the forward room, had already anticipated the order. Ralph Giordano, Wayne Davis, Joe Sheppard, and the rest of Worley's crew took their positions as the outer hydraulic tube doors opened. The order to fire came at 1027 and three Mark 18s belched out from *Parche*'s bow and sped toward the Japanese convoy. The range was 1,700 yards for these electric torpedoes, whose depth had been set at seven feet.

McCrory decided that his first target ship was possibly a Japanese naval auxiliary because of the flag he was flying. The skipper quickly swung his scope and settled on the third ship in column. Stevenson quickly announced that everything was set on the TDC and *Parche* proceeded to empty the other three tubes of her forward nest from a like 1,700-yard distance.

At 1029, Quartermaster Thornton Hamlin logged two torpedo explosions heard on the first ship. Sonarman Larry Lawrence reported that the explosions were accompanied by loud breaking up noises as the ship went through its death throes. Two more explosions followed in thirty seconds, these timed to be in the second target. "Heard no breaking up noises on this bearing although two sets of screws were stopped, sound only having one set of heavy screws," McCrory recorded. No hits were observed because John Hennessy had again temporarily lost depth control due to the added difficulty of excess water forward.

Postwar analysis would later show that *Parche*'s torpedoes had been quite effective in this attack on Convoy No. 1624, which had departed

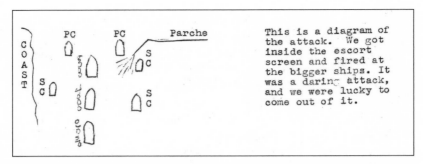

QM3c Dale Mielke placed this sketch in his diary for the attacks made on the convoy on 26 June 1945. "I added this bit a few days later, and it is the dope put out by the captain," he recorded. *Mielke diary courtesy of USS* Bowfin *Museum.*

Yokosuka on 24 June for Hakodate. The 2,721-ton auxiliary gunboat *Kamitsu Maru* was hit by two torpedoes at 1030 and sank instantly with 192 lives lost. The 6,903-ton freighter *Eikan Maru* was also hit in the No. 2 hold and badly damaged. The Japanese sailors managed to run her ashore at Iwate Ken. After some cargo was salvaged, *Eikan Maru* broke in two on 10 July in a gale. Allied aircraft later strafed the battered, beached freighter and she was abandoned as a total loss.[8]

McCrory was trying to ease back up to periscope depth for an observation when at 1031 two "token" depth charges exploded at a comfortable distance. He quickly ordered 200 feet and started swinging to the left. Two minutes later, sound reported an escort coming in sharp on the port bow.

The swishing of the angry escort vessel's screws could be heard clearly as *Parche* eased down to 200 feet. Instead of taking his boat on down to safer depth, Lieutenant Commander McCrory opted to take advantage now of the Mark 27 homing torpedoes he had not used on his previous patrol.

"Prepare the Cutie," he ordered the after torpedo room.

Radioman Fred Richards, standing duty in Bob DeMonge's after room as the battle talker, quickly relayed the orders. Nicknamed a "Cutie," the Mark 27 acoustic torpedo was the Navy's first such weapon to leave a torpedo tube under its own power. The 720-pound missile literally swam out of the boat under its own propulsion toward the target at about ten knots.

Bob Swanson, standing by his interlock station between the tubes, found their senior torpedoman DeMonge to be cool and efficient under pressure, even as a Japanese escort ship was bearing down on *Parche* at her relatively shallow depth. In order to protect the submarine, the Mark 27's warhead would not activate below 100 feet, thus requiring *Parche* to be below 150 feet before releasing one of these classified weapons.

It had been designed to attack enemy submarines by homing in on their propellers after being dropped by aircraft. The Mark 24 aerial torpedo was modified late in the war to become a Mark 27 Cutie. The Cutie had seen its first use in U.S. submarines in late 1944, and by war's end about 100 of them had been fired with an efficiency of about 33 percent. This fish had a diameter of about 19 inches, was 90 inches in length, had a weight of about 720 pounds and was built by Western Electric.

Turning to Joe Nichols, DeMonge ordered the hydraulic door to be opened on the tube in which the Cutie was inserted. The approaching escort's screws could be heard through the hull even without the aid of sonar as DeMonge started the Mark 27's motor. The Cutie gained speed and departed *Parche*'s after nest without the aid of the normal blast of compressed air. Jim Campbell, standing by with the skipper in the conning tower, recalled, "With this homing torpedo, our goal was to simply send it toward the loudest sound. With the escorts bearing down on us, this process was quite simple."

The after torpedo gang waited silently as their special torpedo headed toward the Japanese attacker on the surface. Shortly after releasing the small, stubby Mark 27, *Parche* was rocked by a heavy explosion. "We thought at first that damned thing had come back and gotten us," recalled Swanson, "but it was either the torpedo hitting its target or a close depth charge." Mac McCrory and his crew felt that their Mark 27 had disabled one of the onrushing Japanese antisubmarine vessels. Analysis of Japanese records would later show that sub chaser *CH-51* had narrowly managed to dodge the Cutie.[9]

McCrory did not wait around to find out the source of this heavy blast that rocked his boat. "Take her to 400 feet," he ordered Lieutenant Hennessy as soon as the Cutie had been fired. Four more depth charges exploded at 1035 as *Parche* eased down at 70 turns of her screws per minute. Throughout the boat, all unnecessary machinery had long since been shut down in order to achieve true silent running.

The minutes ticked by and soon the screws from the Japanese attackers above seemed to fade away. After the escort activity had been calm for a short while, McCrory opted to have Hennessy plane the boat back up toward periscope depth so that he could get a peek at the results of his handiwork. "This was a mistake since the escorts were only listening prior to a concerted depth charge attack," the skipper wrote.

Two of the Japanese convoy's escorts, *Shisaki* and sub chaser *CH-51*, had been lying in wait for just such a move from the American submarine. Their sonar operators quickly picked up *Parche* as she rose to shallower depths and they moved in with a vengeance. By the time their counterattack efforts ceased this day, at least 67 depth charges had been expended against the submarine. It was the most prolonged depth charge attack *Parche* had suffered to date and many aboard her felt it was nearly their last.[10]

———————

Larry Lawrence remained hunched over his sonar gear, his headset pressed tight to his head as *Parche* eased back to periscope depth at 1106.

"Two escorts, *Chidori* types, coming in fast on each quarter!" Lawrence whispered to his skipper.

He quickly flipped on the speaker to his sonar gear for the officers in the conning tower to hear. The angry swishing of screws was accompanied by the deliberate pinging of their sonar. As *CH-51* and *Shisaki* approached, they immediately shifted to short scale pinging and locked in solidly on *Parche*. Sonar conditions this day were in the favor of the escorts.

"Take her to 400 feet!" McCrory called down. "Stand by for depth charge attack."

The old hands needed no warning. They clearly knew what they could expect next. Each compartment was manned by a sailor wearing a battle headset to hear instructions from the skipper. Those who had no specific instruments to maintain could only look at the hull above them and sweat silently as they awaited the inevitable hell from above.

In the control room, Jack Holleran stood ready to take over the diving duties in case Lieutenant Hennessy's services should be needed in the engine rooms during the action. Charlie McNutt and Pinky Pannell, stripped to their shorts as they silently labored with the stern and bow planes without hydraulic power, worked to level their boat at the prescribed depth. Nearby in the radio shack, Myron Grover and Henry Gay sat at their gear listening to the incoming screws above.

As the men quietly awaited the next string of depth charges, Ens. Dean Axene took in the scene playing out around him. "Under these conditions, the ship always took on an eerie aspect. Most of the lights were out; no ventilation was running; people spoke in whispers, if at all, and every sound seemed to reverberate through the ship, seemingly loud enough to be heard in Tokyo." He felt that some of the first depth charges experienced "were close indeed."[11]

Mac McCrory took the opportunity to spread his officers out in each major compartment throughout the boat to supervise the on-scene corrective action for whatever mishaps might occur. Ensign Axene, as assistant gunnery officer, took up station in the after torpedo room. "We could hear the screws of the attacking destroyers through the hull as they approached for an attack and then receded to prepare for another," he recalled. "We could roughly judge the proximity of the attack by the loudness of the screw noises and ensuing explosions, which usually came two at a time. The experience was harrowing."

Senior auxiliaryman Hollis Larsen stood ready at the trim manifold while Ed Mokos stood sentry over the air manifold as the two Japanese warships roared overhead. "He had made enough patrols that he knew when the depth charges were coming," Mokos recalled. The sonar gang could certainly hear the splashes as ash cans were rolled into the ocean but Larsen listened carefully to the sound of the destroyers' propellers racing by overhead.

"Hey, Greek, hang on," he whispered to his buddy. "They're making their drops now."

Mokos braced himself against the air manifold and silently counted the seconds as the depth charges sank toward his boat's depth. *Click—WHAM! Click—WHAM!* The clicks of the detonators were followed almost instantly by violent explosions that shook *Parche* and granulated light bulbs in the control room. "I remember seeing blue flashes during the explosions," Mokos said.

Sixteen very close depth charges began exploding at 1110 around *Parche*. McCrory felt that these were "definitely set beneath us from the shaking up we got." Radioman Glenn Meise related, "The inner hull was lined with painted-over cork. With all of the depth charging we took, a lot of cork was coming loose."[12]

In the maneuvering room, senior electrician Dixie Howell grabbed hold of Dick Frank, who was seated at the starboard controls, to steady himself as the boat lurched from each blast. Carl Vozniak on the port side recalled, "When you see that cork flying like it's snowing, you know damn well they're close. I said plenty of Hail Marys that day, believe me. We took one hell of a beating."

Dale Mielke lay in his bunk in Tom Worley's forward torpedo room as this string of depth charges exploded. "I was terrified and gave myself up for lost, but our hull took the pounding like a major," he recorded. "Light bulbs popped all around us, lockers flew open [and] my bed collapsed with me in it. It was sheer hell, and I never want to go through it again."[13]

Lt. Max Morton's entry in *Parche*'s unofficial history for this day included: "The avalanche descended. Cork flew off the bulkheads, light bulbs were bursting, Brown thought he had a gusher in the galley sink."

Thornton "Ham" Hamlin was the duty quartermaster keeping the log in the conning tower during this shellacking. He managed to count one close string of eleven consecutive depth charges. One of his buddies, Carl Zeller, later quizzed Hamlin, "How the hell did you count eleven different explosions? All I heard was *Wham! Wham! Wham!* right on top of each other all at once!"

Lieutenant Commander McCrory remained vigilant in the conning tower, allowing his officers to report in from their various compartments as to any damage incurred. "If someone was hesitant in their reports, the skipper sent me down to check things out and report back," Jim Campbell recalled.

In the control room, stern planesman Charlie McNutt watched one of the chief motormacs, Corlet Madison, who was trying to control some of the leaking valves by hammering plugs into them. "The plan was to hit the plug when a depth charge went off," wrote McNutt. "His timing was not good; the depth charge would go off and then you would hear him hammer the plug. He finally got the plugs installed and we lived another day."[14]

McNutt had been impressed with the Navy photographer, Harry Heaton, who had come on board for this patrol. "He had a world of experience and had been with the U.S. Marines and Army going from island to island in the South Pacific," he later wrote. "He was really into his work, climbing up with the lookouts and going topside to take pictures of our sinking sampans off the coast of Japan." As *Parche* had commenced her attack on this convoy, Heaton had set up in the control room to take photos of the action. McNutt noted that when the first close depth charges rocked the boat, Heaton "closed up his camera and left the control room."[15]

The damage from this first extended series of blasts was mainly superficial but it created quite a mess in the after battery compartment. The No. 2 sanitary tank flooded completely through the outboard vent, partially running over into the galley before the outboard valve was reshut and the drain line was closed. Motormac Joe Leiching had been lying in his bunk following the attack. As the escorts raced in to attack *Parche*, he had heard the *swish, swish, swish* of their screws and knew what could be expected next. The force of the explosions driving *Parche* down deep was enough to bring Leiching to his feet. The smell of the sanitary tank's contents flooding into his compartment was unpleasant. "We were a mess," Leiching admitted.

Carl Zeller was another sailor who had no set battle station and was in the after battery compartment. "I was assigned to plug all the holes in the john to prevent flooding," he recalled. When the sanitary pipe burst, Zeller found "we had a lot of leaking from the high pressure water and the effect of the depth charges going off."

Photographer Harry Heaton, having abandoned the control room in favor of the after battery, found this mess to be no picnic. Even worse, he was quickly assigned the "important" duty of holding this sanitary valve flapper shut throughout the remainder of the depth charge attack. Lieutenant Campbell, passing through on one of his compartment inspections, was amused to see the photographer "just sitting there on the pot holding that flapper closed."

The Japanese escort ships were persistent, turning to make more runs to lay down depth charges against the American submarine. The flooding in the after battery area made *Parche* more negatively buoyant and created some tense moments for diving officer John Hennessy and the entire crew. *Parche* managed to keep a good down-angle on but while passing 500 feet she was quite heavy with the sanitary flooding. The sonar operators on both the conning tower's JP gear and the JK set in the after room reported abnormal shaft noises at 70 turns. McCrory slowed to 60 turns and by increasing occasionally to 70 turns, he was able to run between 500 and 550 feet with an 8-degree up-angle.

The next close string of depth charges exploded above the ship and the concussions from these blasts forced the boat far deeper than skipper McCrory cared to take her. "I read 625 feet on the after torpedo room depth gauge," recalled Dean Axene. "The ship was designed and built to operate down to a maximum depth of 412 feet."[16]

Fred Richards wore the battle phones throughout this attack in the after torpedo room. He noted that Tony Herman and others were stretched out in their bunks because the word had been passed that those not doing anything should help conserve oxygen. "The rudder angle indicator went out at some point during the attack," he recalled. "We decided I was the skinniest guy in the room and since I was already wearing the phones, they sent me to crawl back there between the tubes and monitor the dial that showed the rudder's direction for the control room. I stayed back there about two hours and it was a little unnerving because of the single hull we had aft. When the ships came over to drop their depth charges, you could hear their screws going *chug, chug, chug.* When the attacks finally ended, Tony grabbed hold of my ankles and pulled me out of there."

At 1148, another string of seven close depth charges rocked the boat. McCrory believed that these were not as bad as the previous explosions, since his boat was now so deep. The sonar operators reported that their Japanese opponents appeared to have one listener on *Parche*'s port beam and three "pingers" astern making sonar-guided attack runs. The escorts alternated their runs, always shifting to short scale, but not dropping on every run. McCrory felt that it was "apparent that they could hear us and the gradient at 60 feet did not give much protection." He thus ordered the last I.C. motor generator secured to reduce the high noise level aft.

Red Williams was sweating it out in Chief Dana Jensen's after engine room. "My job was to control the leaks that came in around the shaft back by the stern tubes," he recalled. "The leakage was not too bad for me; it was controllable." One of Williams' after room companions, Gus Kulick, was assigned to crawl down in the bilges during the depth charge attack. He carefully inspected the various fittings and valves for leaks as the boat rocked from the explosions. Kulick was young enough and busy enough crawling through the confined spaces that he simply "didn't have time to be scared," although he already considered this to be his worst depth charging experience.

In Orvail Buckner's forward engine room, Roland Burker was also down in the bilge flats keeping watch for leaks. "That was about the hottest place in the ship during silent running," Burker recalled. The escort vessel continued to comb the seas for *Parche* for four and a half hours, making periodic runs. Ensign Axene found this day's anti-submarine attacks to be "a very close call indeed."[17]

Mac McCrory finally managed to work his boat away to a safer distance to the southeast by the afternoon, taking advantage of a current to the south. Many sailors were shaken up by the heavy pounding they received. Electrician Dick Frank, on duty in the maneuvering room throughout it all, later joked that he could only wonder "when was I going to get my pants cleaned?"

During the long interval of depth charging, the crew had time to ponder their chances of coming up to fight it out. In the forward engine room, motormac Bill Coleman felt, "They were just waiting for us to come up, but we didn't. We just worked on eluding them and we finally managed to slip away."

Motormac Bob Silvis noted that photographer Harry Heaton, "who was so happy taking pictures during our battle surface, developed a severe case of diarrhea during our four and a half hours of depth charging. I will admit I didn't think I would ever have to worry about getting another sunburn."[18]

By 1500 *Parche* had safely cleared the area of the escorts and McCrory eased his boat back to periscope depth at 1645. Although random depth charging was noted astern during the remainder of the afternoon, *Parche* had survived her close brush. She finally surfaced again at 2023, 30 miles southeast of Todo Saki and commenced a patrol to the east.

Motor Machinist's Mate Third Class Tony Herman, the oldest man on the boat, contributed a little poem to the *Parche Prattler* after this long depth charge attack:

'Twas in silent running
After firing some fish.
Hoping no Japs would find us,
Was our fondest wish.

The sound gear was manned,
All hands were alert;
"Keep quiet!" You bastards,
Or someone will get hurt.

"400 feet, sir," a J-P contact
"Make ready the Cutie" in case of attack.
"First contact fading,"
Another strong one comes in.
If you ain't prayed before
Now's a good time to begin.
All hands not on duty
Are doing sack time,
According to Depth Charge Rule 29.

Pearly Gate? Or Golden Gate?
Is the big question now.
"All clear on the J-P,"
Answers that one, and how!

So up from below
Comes the *Parche* once more
To chalk up more runs
For our side of the score.

---

Those tasked with cleaning up the human waste in the after battery from the ruptured septic tank were less than pleased. "We had to use some mattresses to soak up the waste and the smell was just terrible," recalled Carl Meyer. "We ended up weighting those mattresses down and tossing them overboard at night so they would sink."

*Parche*'s galley had four tables that could hold six men each. Seated in first row on left of photo are (left–right) unknown, Larry Lawrence, Orvail Buckner, unknown, and Myron Grover. Seated on the middle row are John "Blackie" Nania (nearest to the bulletin board), Charlie McNutt, and Carl Zeller at the far right. *Courtesy of Bob Hall.*

The torpedo gang reloaded their tubes during the morning of 27 June. Dale Mielke, exhausted from the previous day's action, kept his journal entry brief this day. "We ran out a ways and submerged and repaired the damage. As a relaxation, we had a movie which sure was a treat." A prolonged random depth charging was heard in the direction of Todo Saki about sunset. *Piranha* was scheduled to depart the area the following day, so McCrory sent word to *Devilfish* to continue her patrol in Tsugaru Strait until her scheduled departure four days later. *Parche*'s lookouts sighted a small picket boat during the night but this was avoided due to her close proximity to shore.[19]

A small, 800-ton freighter was spotted on 29 June but *Parche* was unable to close to within suitable firing range. She proceeded to patrol 15 miles off the 100-fathom curve en route to Tsugaru Strait that night. The following day at 0500, lookouts sighted the body of a Japanese soldier in the water. "He was quite dead and bloated, and from this evidence we gathered that other boats were operating successfully in the neighborhood,"

Mielke recorded. While turning to investigate, a heavy vibration was noted in the boat's port shaft similar to the vibration experienced in the starboard shaft en route to Guam. Heavy fog dampened observations throughout the rest of the afternoon.[20]

On 1 July, recurring noises and vibrations continued in the port shaft. At times the vibrations were felt through the hull in the after torpedo room. Recurring noises were identified as scraping, but McCrory hoped that they might work themselves out.

At 1311, two trawlers were spotted at 8,000 yards by Bob Stevenson and Frank Gadd's lookouts, some four miles off the coast. *Parche* battle surfaced at 1355 and closed the trawlers. Several other trawlers appeared out of the fog as she closed to attack. At 1408, the 5-inch gun opened fire on the first trawler to starboard at a range of 1,850 yards. At the same time, the second trawler on the port bow was fired upon from 1,400 yards by Blackie Nania on the forward 40-mm gun. Five hits from the 5-inch gun left the first trawler sinking by the stern with two survivors in the water. "Our photographer got some good shots of the action, and I saw the Japs dive overboard as the shells started over," wrote lookout Mielke. "We were about 5 miles from the beach, and through the binoculars I saw a town and streets."[21]

The 40-mm scored several hits in the second trawler but did no real damage. *Parche* swung left at 1411 and put the 5-inch gun on this vessel, closing the range to 600 yards. Four 5-inch hits "completely wrecked him and left him fully flooded." McCrory then cleared the scene to the west and contacted another trawler on the way out.

At 1421, *Parche* opened fire on the third trawler of the afternoon with the 5-inch gun from 1,800 yards. She closed to 1,400 yards. The trawler was still under way, attempting to close the coast to the north, and, showing *Parche* his stern, was difficult to hit. Finally, five solid 5-inch hits left this target flooded. Ammunition expended was 26 rounds of 5-inch and 40 rounds of 40-mm.

McCrory called off his gunners and dived ship at 1500 to take a break from the action before air cover was called in. Heavy fog set in during the night and visibility the following day was only 300 yards on average. One floating mine was sighted during the day but, due to fog, contact could not be regained to sink it. McCrory slowed the boat during the day long enough to allow his deck crew to retrieve a Japanese fishing ball as a souvenir. The following day, Quartermaster Mielke wrote that "the fog is so dense that we are not going in too close because we know these waters are heavily mined. This fog is so thick you cannot see the bow of the ship."[22]

After three days of struggling through this fog, the weather improved by midday on 4 July. An SJ contact was made at 16,500 yards at 2225, and it proved to be two ships close together. Max Morton commenced tracking and called for the captain. One of the ships was sweeping with radar. *Parche* let them go by at 11,000 yards to the east and then trailed them to the north, suspecting an antisubmarine sweep prior to a convoy coming out of Hachinohe.

McCrory's instincts paid off for at 0417 on 5 July, visual and radar contact was made on two large ships at 20,000 yards. "I was on lookout at the time and got a look at the largest one," wrote Mielke. "It looked very big, about the size of a Victory ship." *Parche* started an end-around to starboard at flank speed, finding that this convoy was heading for Shiriya Saki. An hour later, two small escorts and a patrol craft were sighted between *Parche* and the merchant ships. *Parche* was running through heavy fog patches and only had a short time to see them. Although the radio gang picked up repeated transmissions from the larger ships, they were lost after they changed course somewhere in the fog. The smoke of a frigate was spotted at 0630 at long range and this ship was seen to be headed for Shiriya at full speed. The tops of the larger ships were soon spotted again and *Parche* headed north to close the coast before diving.[23]

McCrory took her down at 0705 and closed toward attack position. He began an approach on the leading freighter, which had one *Chidori*-class escort circling ahead. The other ships and escorts were seen to be patrolling northeast of Shiriya. *Parche* closed on these vessels with her screws making 80 turns per minute. The JP sonar operator, however, soon reported abnormal shaft noise and high reduction gear whine. The engineers confirmed it and McCrory was forced to break off the attack due to the noise. Heading east, he found that *Parche* had the same recurrent scraping in the port shaft plus a light squeal.

After the leading escort had taken his freighter around Shiriya, he turned and headed in for *Parche*, apparently alert to the noisy submarine. When he closed to 7,000 yards, *Parche* went to 250 feet, where a sound gradient was found. There McCrory ordered the port shaft to be stopped, running at only 75 turns on the starboard screw. One bomb was dropped astern before the escort's screws were heard to draw away to the south.

*Parche* surfaced that evening and headed for the eastern part of her area. Silent running tests on 6 July confirmed that the squealing and scraping sounds in the port shaft persisted. "We got a four day extension so we have to stay on station for another ten days or until 16 July," wrote Mielke. "It is tough, but bitching will not make it easier." *Parche* continued to patrol on the surface in the area south and east of Hokkaido during the next few days. She hoped to at least find some picket boats to attack but even these were scarce.[24]

"We still have eight more days to go and each one is an eternity," Mielke wrote in his diary on 8 July. He passed some of his time chatting with a shipmate about homes back in New York. "It sure makes you miss a home of your own, living like this in an enlarged section of sewer pipe." Mielke's time on lookout duty was made at least a little more entertaining by the large number of whales, "which seem to own this part of the ocean." One such playful whale "breached 20 feet from the ship and scared us silly till we realized what it was. I was so close to it I saw his vertebraed backbone and his dorsal fin and his tail flip when he dived."[25]

The 20-mm gunners destroyed an encrusted floating mine on 8 July but the ensuing days were void of contacts. *Trepang* sent a contact report early on 12 July of a Japanese submarine that had been seen diving in her vicinity. *Trepang* was en route to an assigned lifeguard duty so *Parche* moved into her area to investigate the Japanese sub. McCrory had his boat in the reported area by 2200 and he proceeded to scour the area in heavy seas. No contact was made and no interference from the submarine was detected before he was forced to give up the hunt and proceed to *Parche*'s next assigned lifeguard duty.

*Parche* took up position 20 miles south of the Erimo Saki lighthouse to man the lifeguard frequencies for a planned carrier strike on 13 July against northern Honshu and Hokkaido. The weather was heavy during the day, however, and this strike was scrubbed. McCrory took up the same position the following day and at 0415 the first flight of carrier planes were seen heading west over the lighthouse, apparently heading for the Tsugaru Strait area.

McCrory felt admiration for the flyboys who carried out their mission this day in weather that left a low ceiling until noon. The radiomen picked up numerous transmissions through the morning of pilots calling to other submarines and making attacks on Japanese shipping. At 0825, they monitored the chatter of a downed pilot on the lifeguard frequency. *Parche* was overflown by a fighter at 1030 that attempted to help direct her toward the last known position of a downed aircrew. Relief fighters arrived in the afternoon and joined the search for the downed aviators.

*Parche*'s lookouts were not able to spot any downed aviators during the night and by early morning on 15 July she discontinued this search in order to reach her next assigned lifeguard station for duty in that day's additional air strikes. Two flights of about 40 planes each passed over *Parche* at 0735, heading north for the coast of Hokkaido. From then on, flight after flight of carrier planes were seen heading in to Japan. During the afternoon, visible results of the American bombing and gunfire were seen on the coast to the northeast.

Reports were heard this day on the lifeguard frequency of three downed pilots, one in *Cero*'s station area. The planes returned to their carriers in the afternoon and nothing was reported in *Parche*'s area. McCrory thus departed his lifeguard station at 1730 to patrol to the northeast to keep clear of friendly surface forces. At 0230 on 16 July—the same day that the first atomic bomb test was exploded in Los Alamos, New Mexico— ComSubPac orders were for *Parche* to make one day's further search for survivors of a plane reported down on the 14th, south of Erimo Saki lighthouse, and upon conclusion to rendezvous with *Cero* to take off her recovered aviators.

*Parche*'s search results were negative again this day. In two days, she had covered an area approximately 40 square miles. *Cero* radioed that night, requesting the rendezvous for aviator transfer. *Parche* and *Cero* rendezvoused at 0430 on 17 July and she took aboard three fliers via a rubber boat transfer. They were Ens. Burton W. Noah, ARM3c Harry A. Leake, and AOM3c Charles W. Hester, an Avenger crew from the carrier *Randolph*'s VT-16. *Cero* and *Parche* also exchanged movies during this shuttling of passengers. With the aviators on board, *Parche* left her patrol area and headed for Midway.

Dale Mielke noted the arrival of the American aviators in his diary that night. "They had been three miles from the beach when forced down, and instead of rowing for it and capture, they headed out for sea. The Japs came after them but our planes strafed them, and our pilots got away at night. They paddled for 21 hours when the sub picked them up."[26]

The return run for Midway was uneventful during the next week. The aviators found submarine life difficult to adjust to. "They didn't complain about submarine food," recalled Don Walters, "but they called our officers 'inveterate coffee drinkers.' They couldn't believe how much coffee we consumed per day." One night in the forward torpedo room, they were watching a movie. During the course of the movie, *Parche* had a rough surfacing as junior auxiliaryman Charles Keenan inadvertently blew only the port tanks. *Parche* quickly heeled over sharply to starboard due to the heavy weight of the excess water that had not been blown from the starboard tanks. In the forward room, personnel were tossed against the bunks or bulkheads until the starboard tanks were blown.

Auxiliaryman Ed Mokos raced from the torpedo room to the control room. He quickly took over the manifold and helped bring the boat back to its level trim. Fred Richards, helping to run the movie projector, saw that at least one of the aviators was more than a little shaken. "How much longer before we reach Midway?" he snapped.

In reassurance to their passengers, Richards recalled that "we told them we didn't surface sideways very often."

Two ensigns, Harry Milhan and Dean Axene, and Lt. (jg) Bob Mottner took over some of the deck watch duties during the return run. Don Walters also received notice during the sixth patrol of his promotion to warrant torpedoman. Upon joining the mustang club, Walters began standing junior officer of the deck watches to gain experience in his new billet while his buddy Dana Jensen stepped up to assume the duties of chief of the boat.

*Parche* rendezvoused with patrol aircraft outside Midway on 23 July and moored near the tender *Bushnell*. She took on fuel, unloaded her remaining torpedoes, and the fliers were left at the air station. A draft of twelve men came aboard for passage back to Pearl Harbor. *Parche* also received her mail and enjoyed a night's stay at Midway due to heavy seas that would have slowed her progress.

*Parche* was under way from Midway on 24 July and made a fast run into Pearl Harbor, arriving at the submarine base at 1015 on 28 July to end her sixth war patrol. The standard patrol report submitted made no mention whatsoever of the classified use of the Cutie acoustic torpedo. The administrative division commander, Capt. Lowell T. Stone, recommended that *Parche* be sent back to the West Coast for overhaul to correct her

### USS *Parche* Sixth War Patrol Summary

| | |
|---|---|
| Departure From: | Midway |
| Patrol Area: | East of Honshu, Japan |
| Time Period: | 25 May–28 July 1945 |
| Number of Men On Board: | 88: 78 enlisted and 10 officers |
| Total Days on Patrol: | 65 |
| Miles Steamed: | 14,890 |
| Number of Torpedoes Fired: | 12 |
| Wartime Credit: | 2/7,200 tons |
| JANAC Postwar Credit: | 2/3,669 tons |
| Alden Postwar Credit: | 11/11,021 tons (including eight from gun actions) |
| Shipping Damage Claimed: | 2/7,700 tons |
| Return To: | Pearl Harbor via Midway |

noisy shafts and he commended the *Parche* crew for their "aggressive and efficient patrol during which the enemy merchant and fishing fleets were further reduced by their efforts."

Lieutenant Commander McCrory was later awarded the Legion of Merit for this patrol. Postwar analysis by JANAC only credited *Parche* with two ships sunk for 3,669 tons, as vessels smaller than 500 tons were not included in sinking tallies. More recent analysis of Japanese records by submarine veteran John Alden credits *Parche* with three ships sunk by torpedoes. In addition, *Parche*'s busy gunners had shot up nine smaller vessels, sinking at least eight of them.

# CHAPTER FIFTEEN

# Epilogue

A fter reaching Pearl Harbor, the *Parche* crew enjoyed some R&R at the Royal Hawaiian. Carl Meyer noticed that some of the relief crew who came on board were bothered by the smell of human waste that still lingered in the after battery from the septic line that had been ruptured by the depth charging. "The stench was horrible to them, I guess, but we had gotten used to it after a few weeks," Meyer related. "When you live in a shithouse long enough, you get used to the smell of it."

*Parche* remained in Pearl Harbor only three nights. Capt. Lowell Stone, Commander SubDiv 104, came on board on 30 July to present combat insignia for the successful sixth patrol. Lt. John Hennessy was detached to SubDiv 282 for duty this day.

Sailors were allowed ashore while at Pearl Harbor. When senior Radioman Myron Grover returned some 14 hours late to the boat from liberty, he found Exec Jim Campbell was "madder than hell at me. He wanted my liberty card." Grover sheepishly fished in his pockets for the card. As he did so, he made eye contact with his buddy Blackie Nania, who was lying in his bunk nearby. Nania casually shook his head to indicate "no" while pointing toward the grating in the deck. Picking up on Nania's suggestion, Grover slowly extended his liberty card toward Lieutenant Campbell's outstretched hand. He then let the card drop and slip through the deck plates where it could not be retrieved.

"Campbell was roaring mad because he had to take heat from the skipper, who told him, 'I don't think you know how many hours you're giving your men!'" recalled Grover. He avoided Captain's Mast for being AWOL but was not in his Exec's good graces for the next few days.

Admiral Lockwood ordered *Parche* back to the West Coast for a full overhaul because the boat had not returned Stateside since going to war in early 1944. Lt. (jg) Harry Milhan had the deck as Mac McCrory conned his boat out of Pearl Harbor for the welcome transit to California.

*Parche*'s crew receives the Presidential Unit Citation for the boat's first two patrols while at Hunter's Point, California, on 7 August 1945. Jim Campbell is handing an award to ship's cook Lamar Brown. *Courtesy of Bob Hall.*

En route to San Francisco, the 20-kiloton atomic bomb nicknamed "Little Boy" was dropped over Hiroshima, Japan, on 6 August. The effects were devastating and 80,000 people were killed. Ens. Dean Axene was alone in the wardroom working on a report. "I donned headphones and tuned to a short wave, English language broadcast," he related. "Almost the first thing I heard was that the United States had dropped a super bomb on Japan—a bomb that was reputed to be atomic in nature."[1]

Axene was the first aboard *Parche* to learn of the atomic bombing of Hiroshima. "I quickly shared my knowledge with others who were up and about, and almost instantly a majority of the crew and officers, including Captain Mac, were monitoring that radio broadcast." Carl Meyer, like many, could not make sense of the news. "What the hell is an atomic bomb and where the hell is Hiroshima?" he asked a buddy in bewilderment.

Approaching San Francisco on 7 August was a treat for those on board *Parche* who had been gone from the mainland for a long time. Carl Vozniak had a fellow electrician cover for him in the maneuvering room so he could go topside. "I wanted to see the Golden Gate Bridge because I had been out in the Pacific for two and a half years," he recalled.

Lieutenant Commander McCrory maneuvered his boat into the dry docks at Hunter's Point and the ship's first complete overhaul commenced.

*Parche* officers and men at a ship's party after returning to the West Coast. Standing (left–right): Lt. Bob Stevenson, Jack Kimball, and Lt. Jim Campbell. Front row (left–right): Francis Gabik, Charlie McNutt, Bob Dillon, and Dixie Howell. *Courtesy of Bob Hall.*

At 1130 that day, an awards ceremony was held to present the ship with the Presidential Unit Citation. Capt. Warren D. Wilkins and his staff came on board for the presentations.

The boat was stripped in preparation for overhaul as all torpedoes were off-loaded at Hunter's Point. A Navy Yard pilot helped conn *Parche* alongside the ammunition pier at Mare Island and all ordnance was also removed. During these first days in port, eight of her old hands—Jim Plumley, Bob DeMonge, Howard Ernest, Pop Russel, Glenn Meise, Dana Jensen, John Gray, and Blackie Nania—were transferred to other duties. Radar operator Paul Kuter (transferred after *Parche*'s fifth run) similarly soon found that he had new orders to be a radar instructor at the Naval Submarine Base in Groton. Lieutenant Campbell advised him that he could pretend that he hadn't received the orders if he wanted to come back on board. Kuter declined and Campbell admitted, "If I were in your shoes, I would make the same decision."

The *Parche* crew found 9 August to be memorable for two reasons. The first was that half of the crew was detached from the ship on 30 days leave Stateside. Bob Stevenson, Robert Mottner, Frank Gadd, Don Walters, and 35 enlisted men happily departed for homes they had not seen in many months.

The second major event of the day was the dropping of the 22-kiloton atomic bomb named "Fat Man" on Nagasaki. More than 70,000 Japanese were killed in an instant, forcing Emperor Hirohito to seek an immediate peace with the Allies. On 14 August, the Japanese accepted unconditional surrender, and Gen. Douglas MacArthur was appointed to head the occupation forces in Japan. This day was officially declared Victory in Japan Day, or V-J Day, by the U.S. government. News of Japan's surrender swept the country and the sailors on the *Parche*. "We savored the moment," recalled Ensign Axene. "It was, without question, a real turning point in my life and the lives of the entire *Parche* crew."[2]

Bill Coleman recalled hearing of V-J Day. "We had one engine that we couldn't fix. They had marked our deck and were going to take torches to cut a big hole in the deck to remove that engine. They had the torches ready to cut the hole in our deck but just before they did it was V-J Day."

Ed Mokos was on liberty in San Francisco when the news came. "People were all boozed up and crazy," he recalled. "You'd be walking down the street and people would take a swing at you." Fred Richards and Myron Grover took a bus from San Francisco to Peta Luma to check out a bar they had heard about. Unfortunately for them, there were more soldiers than girls and a bar fight ensued. They ended up in jail for the night with little ready cash to make bail the next morning. "Fortunately for us, the bail was just exactly what we had on us," said Richards.

V-J Day had special meaning for Yeoman Carl Meyer. While home on liberty, he was reunited with his long-lost brother, who had been shot down over Germany and had survived the war in a POW camp.

---

*Parche*'s popular second skipper, Woodrow Wilson McCrory received new orders and was officially relieved of command of his beloved boat on 25 August 1945 at the Mare Island Navy Yard. In a brief ceremony, Lt. Cdr. Henry Grady Reaves Jr.—an Academy graduate from the class of 1939— read his new orders, which gave him command of *Parche*.

During his leave, McCrory took it upon himself to seek out the families of Ray Van Eperen and Harris Leffler. While *Parche* was in Mare Island, McCrory went on leave and took a train to Appleton, Wisconsin, to meet with Van Eperen's folks for an hour and a half before catching the next train back to Chicago. "It exemplifies the kind of skipper we had," recalled Bob Silvis. He felt obligated to explain to the families how their sons had been lost in action during the fourth patrol. They had previously only been visited by three *Parche* sailors and a Navy officer, who brought a box of their belongings and explained that their sons had been lost in action. The *Parche* crew felt that McCrory had gone above and beyond in visiting the families. "He felt very bad about the loss and felt responsible," Bob Erwin recalled.[3]

*Parche* Exec Jim Campbell was also detached on 25 August from the submarine he had put into commission with McCrory. In the shuffle of wardroom duties, Bob Stevenson took over as *Parche*'s Exec. Frank Gadd became the engineering officer, Dean Axene the torpedo and gunnery officer, and Don Walters handled commissary and the assistant gunnery duties. Various other officers were temporarily assigned to *Parche* during her California refit.

The crew continued its shuffle to and from Stateside leave during September as the refit progressed. Captain Wilkins came on board for another awards presentation on 5 October in which Max Morton received the Letter of Commendation with ribbon and Ron Williams received a Bronze Star for their fifth patrol achievements. Awards for the sixth patrol caught up with *Parche* on 16 October for those hands still on board. Capt. Frank W. Fenno pinned Bronze Stars on Max Morton and Dean Axene that day.

*Parche* finally moved from the Mare Island yards to Tiburon Bay on 7 December 1945 in preparation for returning to active duty in the Hawaiian Islands. "We had been undergoing preparations to be decommissioned in California and we had gotten rid of our spare parts and tools," Red Williams related. "When word came that we would be going back out to the Pacific again, we had to scramble to get the boat ready again." *Parche* was ordered to duty in the Hawaiian Islands in December 1945. She departed Tiburon Bay, California on 2 January 1946, in company with *Puffer*, other submarines, and USS *Florikan* (ASR-9). She arrived at Pearl Harbor 9 January.

Hank Reaves lost veteran officers Stevenson, Morton, and Gadd to transfers before departing California. The wartime wardroom continued to thin with Don Walters' transfer in February and Jack Holleran's orders to *Skipjack* in March. By April 1946, only Dean Axene and Harry Milhan remained of the officers who had been on board *Parche* for at least one war patrol. The enlisted men similarly completed their service periods or were moved on to new assignments, leaving only a dozen crewmen on board by late May 1946 who had made at least one war patrol: Roland Burker, Bob Flanagan, Nelson Fournier, Jim Hawkey, Dixie Howell, Doc Shaw, Bob Silvis, Harry Slajer, Mel Terry, Carl Vozniak, Red Williams, and Tom Worley.

The boat operated with a skeleton crew of 45 men as warships gathered in Hawaii for an historic weapons test known as Operation Crossroads. *Parche* shifted to Hilo shortly before departing for Bikini. Seaman First Class Gene Haba, an 18-year-old who hailed from Bridgeport, Connecticut, would never forget his unplanned swim in the waters off Hilo. "We couldn't tie to the dock right away because an inter-island tanker was unloading fuel," he related. "When we finally docked, some of our lines had gotten fouled in the screws, so we had to don diving gear to go over the side and clear the screws." Haba was unnerved when the locals on the shore warned the divers about the ever-present sharks near the pier. He found the experience of groping under the dark hull of his warship with a knife to saw at the lines more daunting with the added threat of sharks in the water.

*Parche*'s crew was afforded liberty time in Hilo—including a beer bust atop the volcanic mountain. Harry Slajer dashed off a quick note home to his mother on 21 May describing the last-minute loading of supplies on *Parche* and the fact that he had sent a Japanese rifle back home as a war souvenir. Slajer added, "I guess it will be a couple of weeks before I will be able to write so don't worry."

At Pearl Harbor, Slajer had asked his skipper if he could bring on board a small terrier as the ship's mascot. Reaves agreed and the little dog, Seaweed, headed to Bikini for the tests. "The crew loved him but Slajer was his mom," the skipper recalled.[4]

---

When *Parche* finally departed Pearl Harbor on 22 May 1946, she had been assigned to Operation Crossroads as a target ship for atomic bomb test-

A little terrier named Seaweed—seen with a cast on his front paw—came on board as *Parche*'s mascot in early 1946. (Above) Carl Vozniak passes Seaweed down the hatch to Joe Nichols. *Courtesy of Glenn Meise.*

ing in Bikini Atoll. She reached Bikini Atoll in the Marshall Islands on 31 May and moored alongside the tender *Fulton* in a nest with *Dentuda* and *Pilotfish*. Some 93 warships had gathered at Bikini and preparations began for the test.

The battleship *Nevada* was designated as the main target ship and every other vessel was assigned a point on a map in relation to *Nevada*'s position. Dress rehearsals ensued during June as the crews prepared for the real atomic blast. A test drop was made in late June by a plane dropping a flash bomb on *Nevada* to simulate the real test. The crew spent their idle time fishing and swimming off the island.

"It seemed like we were on vacation," Gene Haba thought. He spent idle days fishing and playing cards but found the lack of refrigeration to be a nuisance. "We got to drink beer on the atoll, but it was hot as hell," said Haba. Shipmate Harry Slajer wrote home about the water's incredible visibility but he found swimming alongside *Parche* to be a concern because "there are quite a few sharks around here."[5]

Ship's mascot Seaweed had the run of the boat during the preparation time at Bikini. "Jim Hawkey took care of Seaweed and kept him in the after torpedo room," recalled Carl Vozniak. "But that dog got around the ship and they even taught him how to climb the ladders."

The only trouble with this came when Seaweed attempted to descend a ladder and fell down the forward torpedo room hatch at Bikini, breaking his two front paws. "Slajer took him over to the transport that had the vets aboard and brought Seaweed back with splints," recalled Lieutenant Commander Reaves. "He got along fine but he was very wary of hatches after that."[6]

Test Able went off as planned on 1 July 1946 as a B-29 named "Dave's Dream" flew over the atoll and released history's fourth atomic bomb—a 23-kiloton MK-3A fission bomb. *Parche* was anchored 2,000 yards off the aft starboard quarter of the battleship *Nevada*. *Parche*'s crew—and all others—were evacuated to transport ships to observe from the "safe" distance of about ten miles from the point of impact. "I was one of the last people to leave *Parche* before we boarded the transport," Gene Haba recalled. "I wanted to test the force of the blast so I created my own little test by hanging a water pitcher on a valve in the crew's mess."

Some 42,000 sailors present for Test Able were told to sit facing away from ground zero with their heads between their knees. "All hands were warned not to watch the blast but when the plane came in to drop the A-bomb, I think most of the crew were gambling the loss of one eye," recalled Bob Silvis. "What a beautiful sight it was; the colors and the cloud formations were really something to see. Nobody really knew how bright it would be and it was a safety precaution not to watch."[7]

The shock wave rolled over the distant transport ships and a towering mushroom cloud rose into a pure white cap with dirty clouds of smoke and flame underneath it. In the early afternoon, some of the crew sailed back into the lagoon as the mushroom cloud began dispersing to the west. They found the carrier *Saratoga* burning fiercely. The USS *Gilliam* was sunk, and four other vessels were either sunk or severely damaged. The atomic bomb had fallen 980 feet short of *Nevada* and exploded just abeam of the submarine *Skate*, whose periscope shears were bent completely over to port.

When the men found *Parche*, she was riding at anchor just as when they left her as if nothing had occurred. *Parche* had suffered only very minor damage—mostly some optical equipment that had been placed topside and gotten blown away. However, the entire port side was completely blackened as if someone had gone over it with a blowtorch. The next day most of the crew was back on board to more closely inspect their ship. Gene Haba was surprised to find that the pitcher he had hung on a valve in the crew's mess was still in its place.

Shaky Jake Slajer was among those who went on board *Parche* with a canteen of fresh water and K-rations for food. He found that "all of the paint on the port side was burned off. It sure did make a mess of the ships near where it went off though."[8]

The second atomic bomb test, known as Test Baker, was scheduled for 23 July. The submarines anchored in Bikini were to be submerged by blowing two of their ballast tanks to a properly trimmed depth and weighting them down with anchors. Hoses were run to their ballast tanks to refloat the ships once the weight was removed following the bomb test. "After everyone debarked, the ASR vented the two ballast tanks and the boat submerged," Reaves related.[9]

Test Baker involved another 23-kiloton Mark 3A fission bomb detonated from a steel cassion suspended directly beneath the landing ship *LSM-60*. Seaman Gene Haba recalled that *Parche* was the only sub present—the others being *Apogon, Dentuda, Pilotfish, Skate, Skipjack,* and *Tuna*—to endure both atomic tests on the surface. Skipper Hank Reaves related the change of plans for *Parche*: "Originally, the plan was to submerge for the underwater test, but at the last minute they wanted me on the surface. All the other subs were submerged for the test and *Parche* being on the surface got the engulfing fog bath that was very radioactive."[10]

The ensuing blast destroyed or capsized eight ships, including the *LSM-60*, the carrier *Saratoga*, the battleship *Arkansas,* and the submarines

In June 1946, *Parche* was among the U.S. Navy vessels anchored in Bikini Atoll for Operation Crossroads. Two atomic bombs were detonated to test their effects on shipping. The 23-kiloton bomb for Test Able was dropped from an aircraft, while the fission bomb used for Test Baker (left photo) was detonated underwater. *Courtesy of Bob Hall.*

*Apogon* and *Pilotfish*. Eight other ships were severely damaged by Test Baker. Red Williams felt that the underwater blast "was the most spectacular of the two atomic tests. We wondered when the billowing cloud was going to stop going up." To Haba, "the whole lagoon came up with the blast and then all the water came down and bathed every ship that was there."

Radio technician Walt Brown actually recorded the blast of Test Baker with *Parche*'s hydrophones. "The news media wanted to hear the gurgling sounds before the blast," he related. "I remounted the hydrophones down in the waterline in the superstructure on the *Parche*. I hooked the audio signal into the transmitter and it was transmitting at the time the blast went off."

Following this test, several days passed before the first boarding party was allowed to inspect *Parche*. "That made for a lot of poker time aboard the evacuation transports," Hank Reaves related.

The six-man group was issued GI clothes and shoes ruefully dubbed "Oklahoma oxfords" to wear for their first trip back. "We then went aboard

This view of *Parche* was taken following the Bikini atomic blasts. *Courtesy of Bob Hall.*

another landing craft that took us to the *Parche*," wrote Bob Silvis. "An officer went aboard with a Geiger counter to check the radioactivity. He then checked his chart and determined that we could stay aboard for twenty minutes."[11]

The small group of sailors who volunteered to go back on board was headed by Red Williams as the senior enlisted man. "I went down below and started the engines to ventilate the boat," Williams recalled. Roland Burker, another of the volunteers, spent his short time with a mop and a bucket of strong lye and water solution. The group scrubbed *Parche*'s exterior until relieved by the next group twenty minutes later. "Then we went back on the LST, removed our clothes and were scrubbed to remove any possible contamination," Williams related. "Then we were checked with Geiger counters because they had no idea what if any radiation we took on."

As one of the senior electricians assigned to *Parche*, Carl Vozniak was sent on board to start a pump to supply water to help wash down the boat. "The big joke of it was that they had us pumping up water from the very lagoon where the atomic bomb had been detonated to wash the radiation from the *Parche*," Vozniak related.

"They were giving us C rations to eat when we went over on the boat to work all day," said Walt Brown. "At that time, at the end of the war they were terrible. The only thing good was the orange juice so we used to throw the rest of the C rations over the side. On the way back and forth to the boat, we'd see all these fish floating around belly up from the bomb blast. We'd joke, 'Oh, God, they ate those C rations!' "

This process continued for about a week as volunteer groups made short visits to scrub their submarine. Each time they returned to the troop ship to scrub and be examined with Geiger counters. "It was not uncommon to have to take two or even three showers to get decontaminated," Silvis

*Parche* is seen at Mare Island in Pacific Fleet Reserve on 17 October 1946, shortly before decommissioning. *Courtesy of Bob Hall.*

recalled. "Due to all of the exposure to radioactivity we were told that we might be sterile but after ten beautiful children my wife and I shot the hell out of that theory."[12]

A short time later, "we sailed from Bikini to Kwajalein to continue decontaminating the boat before we returned to Pearl Harbor," said Williams. During this return voyage, Hank Reaves found that he and his topside watchstanders were "limited to two hours a day" for safety precautions. *Parche* was put into the shipyard at Pearl long enough for civilian workers to further decontaminate the ship. "These workers were given extra hazard pay for having to work on a contaminated vessel," Gene Haba recalled. "We had been scrubbing our boat for weeks drawing only standard Navy pay. I felt we certainly weren't paid enough for the risks we had to take."[13]

*Parche* proceeded from Hawaii to the Mare Island Naval Shipyard in late November 1946 and was there assigned to Naval Reserve training duty in Oakland. She was then removed from service on 10 December 1946. Hank Reaves recalled, "I received a letter from the shipyard commander, quote, 'I hereby accept physical custody of the USS *Parche*.' Neither he nor his people came aboard."[14]

Only Dixie Howell and Jim Hawkey were still on board for the decommissioning from the crew that had originally placed *Parche* into commission in 1943. Their boat was moved to Alameda, California, in March 1947 and on 1 December 1962, *Parche*'s classification was changed to Auxiliary Submarine, AGSS-384. In late 1969, *Parche* was replaced as Naval Reserve Training Submarine by *Charr* (AGSS-328).

*Parche* was decommissioned in March 1969 and was struck from the Navy list on 8 November 1969 and sold on 18 June 1970. With that, another chapter of the U.S. Submarine Force ended. Her original conning tower barrel was removed before the ship was towed off the coast and sunk, where she remains as an artificial coral reef. A section of her original conning tower barrel and two working periscopes are located at the USS *Bowfin* Submarine Museum and Park in Honolulu, Hawaii.

Red Williams, one of *Parche*'s World War II veterans, was serving as the administrative officer for the Pearl Harbor Submarine Base at the time the conning tower was selected in 1970 and he could not have been more pleased. Williams completed 30 years in the Navy before retiring as a lieutenant commander, 27 of which had been on board subs. After leaving *Parche*, Williams had served on *Pomfret, Trumpetfish, Argonaut,* and *Seadragon* before being advanced to New London as director of the Submarine School Engineering Department. He concluded his Navy career as a test director for the Triton Missile firing at Cape Kennedy and later served 15 years as a chief planner for the Electric Boat Company in Mystic, Connecticut.

"I was told by Frank Allcorn that Admiral Ramage had a lot to do with *Parche*'s conning tower and superstructure being sent to the Sub Base and museum in Hawaii," Bob Erwin recalled. The periscopes are mounted next to the conning tower so visitors can look through them. The bridge structure, shears, and upper deck gun from the *Parche* are on display at the Submarine Base, Pearl Harbor, Hawaii.

At the time *Parche* was stricken from the Navy's list 26 years after her commissioning, she was one of the very last surviving World War II–era submarines remaining in service.

--------

### Postwar Careers

Among the obvious pieces of evidence as to the quality of the men who served on board the famous *Parche* during World War II is the fact that three of them rose to flag rank. Some 25 percent of the wartime Silent Service skippers were given the retirement rank of rear admiral but only 12 of 465 wartime submarine skippers would rise to the rank of vice admiral.[15]

Lawson Paterson "Red" Ramage, the first U.S. submariner to have been awarded the Congressional Medal of Honor without having died while earning it, was among these prestigious dozen vice admirals. During his commands of *Trout* and *Parche*, Ramage had sunk at least eight ships with torpedoes, another five smaller vessels with his deck guns and had inflicted damage on at least 69,000 tons of Japanese shipping, including the aircraft carrier *Taiyo*.

Following his stint as personnel officer for Admiral Lockwood, Ramage commanded Submarine Division Two and later served in the office of the Chief of Naval Operations for the Navy's guided missiles program. He commanded the attack transport ship *Rankin* (AKA-103) and made rear admiral in 1956. During the Vietnam War, Admiral Ramage commanded the First Fleet and flew his flag on the cruiser *St. Paul*. In 1966 he became deputy commander in chief of the Pacific Fleet and retired in 1970. Ramage remained close to his former *Parche* shipmates, hosting many of them in his home and answering their letters in earnest. Ramage succumbed to cancer in his home at Bethesda, Maryland, in 1990 and is buried in Arlington National Cemetery. Ramage Hall, the administrative building of Norfolk's Submarine Training Facility, is named in his honor.

*Parche*'s second wartime skipper, Woodrow Wilson "Mac" McCrory would also rise to the rank of vice admiral before his retirement. At the age of 31 after the war, McCrory commanded the first snorkel-equipped U.S. submarine, *Halfbeak*, and later a radar submarine picket division. His last submarine duty was that of officer-in-charge of the New London Submarine School. In addition, he also commanded the destroyer *Taussig*, the attack transport *Bayfield,* and the cruiser *St. Paul*, all flagships with the latter being his former skipper Ramage's flagship. McCrory climbed the ranks with a number of key staff positions, including commander, Naval Forces, Korea, from 1956–66. He continued in the Navy until two heart attacks forced him into retirement. Red Ramage recalled that McCrory moved to New Orleans for a short time, where he and his wife paid them a visit. McCrory then settled in San Antonio, Texas, and later suffered a third and fatal heart attack in 1977. Admiral McCrory was also buried in Arlington National Cemetery in Virginia. He had been decorated with the Navy Cross, two Silver Stars, the Bronze Star, and the Legion of Merit while on board *Parche*.

The third *Parche* officer to reach flag rank was Dean Lane Axene, who served 33 years in the submarine service and became a rear admiral. He served as executive officer of the world's first nuclear-powered submarine, USS *Nautilus* (SSN-571), when it was placed in commission in 1954. He also served as the skipper of two other nuclear boats, *Croaker* and *Thresher*, and on the staff of the Supreme Allied Commander Atlantic. He retired from the Navy in 1974 and spent eleven years working for the

Former *Parche* officer Bob Erwin in 2010 with the Silver Star and Bronze Star medals he earned during his five war patrols. *Author's photo.*

Westinghouse Electric Corporation on international nuclear power plants. Axene retired to Florida, where he passed away in late 2008.

Former *Parche* executive officer Jim Campbell returned to the oil fields as an engineer after the war. He and his wife Mary, now retired in California, have been instrumental in honoring the *Parche* crew with a memorial plaque that was dedicated at Pearl Harbor. Another former *Parche* Exec, Dick Wright, was horribly burned in 1949 following a hydrogren explosion aboard the submarine *Cochino*, one of the first boats to be equipped to charge its batteries without surfacing. Wright helped extinguish the fires and was awarded the Navy and Marine Corps Medal of Valor for his actions.

Dave Green stayed with submarines for a while but decided against joining the nuclear boats. "I asked to be excused from the submarine desk so I could get command of 'the next biggest size' ship," he recalled. He was given command of a destroyer and later a tanker. "The submarine detail officer thought I was crazy," Green admitted. "I thought then and still think so that being skipper of anything is better than being ComSubDiv or later ComSubRon."[16]

Frank Allcorn completed seven war patrols in the Pacific, his final as Exec of *Lapon* during the closing weeks of the Pacific War. He received two Silver Stars and a Bronze Star, continued to serve in the Naval Reserve, and retired with the rank of captain. Allcorn became a certified life underwriter with Northwestern Mutual in Atlanta and later a banking business development executive. Allcorn Theater in Ramage Hall on the Norfolk Submarine Training Facility was named in honor of Allcorn and his torpedo

The first *Parche* crew reunion was in 1973 at the Coronado Hotel in San Diego at the Submarine Veterans of WWII Convention. Front row (left–right): Max Morton, Doc Shaw, Fred Richards. Second row (left–right): Frank Gadd, Harold Staggs, Ron Williams, Phil Mackey, Thornton Hamlin, Bob Swanson, and Harry Slajer. Third row (left–right): Quentin Brown, Montgomery Oliver, Dana Jensen, Dan Hayes, Jim Campbell, Les Chambless, Alfred Rick, Lonnie Hughes, Tony Herman, Don Walters, and Bill Coleman. *Courtesy of Jim Campbell.*

handiwork during *Parche*'s most famous patrol. He and his wife Dee competed in sailing events and lived for a period of time on board their 42-foot Grand Banks Trawler until 1997, touring the Bahamas, south Florida, and Chesapeake Bay for months at a time.

Bob Erwin had leave in the States after *Parche*'s fifth run and then helped commission *Remora* (SS-487) in Portsmouth. He was discharged from active duty in March 1946 but stayed in the Reserves, earning a promotion to lieutenant commander. He returned to Ohio where he worked in agricultural engineering research before going to work for Ford for the next 32 years as a design engineer. Erwin's group designed tractors and other farm equipment both in the United States and during the four years he spent as an engineering manager for Ford in London. He also spent five and a half years in France in charge of the design of excavators and tower cranes. He is now retired in south Florida where he enjoys playing golf.

Harry Milhan served as skipper of *Carbonero* (SS-337), a diesel boat converted to a snorkel boat, from 1955 to 1957 and retired in 1965. George Tubb, transferred to the tender *Fulton* after *Parche*'s fourth run, spent the last months of the war anchored at Guam. Following his discharge in 1946, Tubb completed graduate schooling in Texas and then worked as a geologist for the oil and gas industry.

Proudly displaying their *Parche* battle flag at a boat reunion are (left–right): Jim Campbell, Harold Staggs, Paul Vetter, and Ed Mokos. *Courtesy of Bob Hall.*

Chief of the Boat Don Walters, promoted to officer during the war, was graded back to chief petty officer postwar. After being discharged from the Navy he went to work for the police department in Wichita, Kansas. Walters also put in 25 years working for a suburb near San Diego before he and his wife retired back to their home state of Kansas.

Carl Kimmons became the first black submariner to make officer who had started in the submarine service as an officers' cook. After retiring from the Navy, Kimmons attended Connecticut College and received his bachelor's degree, magna cum laude. Then he got his master's from the University of Connecticut and a Sixth Year Certificate from Southern Connecticut State University. Starting in 1973, he taught social studies at a Connecticut junior high for ten years. He became a private airplane pilot in 1965 and flew his own small aircraft for 26 years. He is now retired in Connecticut with his wife of more than 60 years, Thelma Jean.[17]

Kimmons was lifelong friends with another *Parche* steward, LC Fisher, who did stints postwar as a chauffeur for movie stars Katharine Hepburn and Robert Goulet in Connecticut. Fisher attended theology seminary in New York, serving as a pastor in New London and also founder of a Pentecostal rescue mission until his death in 1993.[18]

Torpedoman Jim Hawkey was one of only two *Parche* veterans to remain with *Parche* from its commissioning through its decommissioning in 1946. Postwar he served on a number of submarines, namely *Pomfret* (SS-391), *Plaice* (SS-390), *Tiru* (SS-416), *Tilefish* (SS-307), *Diodon* (SS-349), and *Carbonero* (SS-337). He was commissioned an ensign and was later assigned as weapons officer on the staff of Commander Submarine Squadron Four. Hawkey retired as a lieutenant commander after 30 years of active military service and took on military contracting positions in the Washington state area.[19]

USS *Parche* veterans at the Billings convention are (left–right): Jim Campbell, Bob Silvis, Bob Erwin, Ben (Couture) Harrison, Bob Hall, Ray Karr, Fred Richards, Gus Kulick, and Harold Staggs. *Courtesy of Bob Hall.*

Many of *Parche*'s enlisted men put in enough years with the Navy to draw retirement pay before they returned home to begin civilian careers. Zach Vogedes put in 22 years of service before returning to civilian work in the Baltimore area. Signalman Claude Lutz completed 20 years of Navy service, including time as a warrant officer and deep sea diver, before retiring to civilian life in Connecticut. He opened a formal wear business that his son still runs. Johnny Barnes put *Pomodon* (SS-486) into commission at war's end and served five years on that boat. He remained in the Navy for 20 years, including service on two other submarines, before retiring to civilian life in New Jersey.[20]

Torpedoman Bob DeMonge was assigned to the *Sablefish* in New London at the end of the war and remained in the Navy through 1959. He worked for Morton-Thiokol, Inc., building solid rocket motors until his retirement in 1987 in Sunset, Utah. Chief Percy Barnett continued to serve in submarines after the war but his life was cut short by cancer. After more than 18 years in the Navy, he died in 1958 at age 36 while stationed at Pearl Harbor on board the submarine *Bluefish*.[21]

Motormac Dana Jensen served postwar on the submarines *Pomfret, Tuna, Blackfin,* and *Queenfish*, and his final submarine duty was assisting the Turkish Submarine Force for three years. He completed 30 years of Navy service in 1970 and then went on to earn a degree from San Diego State and became a stockbroker. Roland Burker put in ten years in the Navy including two years on *Parche*. He did another ten years in the Reserves after retiring from the Navy in 1954. He returned to Baltimore and worked in air-conditioning and refrigeration.[22]

Gus Kulick returned to civilian life briefly in 1946 to work for Westinghouse again but he returned to the Navy and submarines in short order. He served on seven other boats before retiring in 1966 after 24 years

USS *Parche* veterans at the 1970s Nashville convention are (front row, left–right): Lonnie Hughes, Rear Adm. Mac McCrory, Doc Shaw, Bobby C. Hall, and Phil Mackey. (Rear, left–right): Bill Hollinger, Arnold Bashwiner, Dan Hayes, Fred Richards, Harold Staggs, and Charlie McNutt. *Courtesy of Fred Richards.*

combined naval service and going to work for Westinghouse in Baltimore for the third time. His time included a tour on a nuclear boat and on the Navy's first snorkel boat, *Greenback*. He is now retired in California.[23]

Some of *Parche*'s crewmen who were transferred after the early patrols made interesting patrols on other submarines. Electrician "Happy" Chambers finished out the war on the *Blenny*, on board which he helped destroy a record number of small ships on her last run off Japan. Cook Dan Hayes went from *Parche* to *Pampanito* in 1944, where he helped the boat earn a Presidential Unit Citation for rescuing Australian and British POWs.[24]

Harold Staggs made *Sea Raven*'s thirteenth and final war patrol after leaving *Parche*, remained in the Reserves, and was recalled to active duty in 1950 to serve on *Cusk* (SS-348). He joined the City of Arcadia Fire Department in 1957 and had become a captain before retiring in 1979. He completed his career as a painter for the city of Los Angeles water and power department and is now retired in Azusa, California.[25]

Ben Couture, whose time on *Parche* was cut short due to the hernia he suffered on patrol, recovered and served on the *Piranha* until the war ended. Couture was showing a movie aboard *Piranha* at Pearl Harbor when word of Japan's surrender was received and the harbor erupted into celebratory gunfire. He also served on the submarine *Menhaden* (SS-377) during the Korean War before heading to the University of Washington for a degree in forestry. After the war, he legally changed his name to Benjamin Harrison, dropping the last name Couture.

Radio technician Desmond Christy finished out the war on *Salmon* before being discharged in November 1945. He went to work as a master carpenter and spent many years traveling the world to work on big government contracts for large corporations before retiring to Florida in the late 1970s.

Many of *Parche*'s enlisted men opted to return to civilian life as soon as their service periods ended after the war. Glenn Meise went to work for the post office after the war and remained with it until 1980. After that he did volunteer work at a local hospital for the next seven years. Ed Mokos returned to his hometown of Chicago to work various jobs until his retirement. Carl Zeller, transferred from *Parche* before the Bikini bomb tests, worked as a manufacturer's rep for Gray Publications and later became a plant manager. Joe Leiching worked on tugboats for a while with his brother before getting on with IBM for 35 years. When they began turning out computers in 1955, Joe went into management and became a systems analyst.

Engineman Dave Hussey, who was key in designing the original *Parche* battle flag, attended the Museum School of Fine Arts in Boston after the war and became a commercial prepress artist in the printing industry. Cory Maupin, the torpedoman who was thrown into the brig at Midway following the post–fifth patrol shooting incident, became a successful businessman in civilian life. He worked 33 years for the Warner- Lambert pharmaceutical company before starting a wholesale business that remains in his family today. Motormac Arnold Bashwiner formed his own air-conditioning company. Charles Keenan was discharged from the Navy in 1946 and attended Louisiana State University, becoming a marine and real estate broker in New Orleans.[26]

Torpedoman Ralph Giordano was a tool and die equipment designer. Bob Swanson taught high school and doubled as a basketball and football coach. Radioman Myron Grover returned to Des Moines in 1946 for two years of business school. He worked for a produce company, then with the state tax division, before getting on with Goodyear Tire and Rubber Company.

Charlie McNutt helped decommission *Bream* and then went to *Sea Dog* before getting out of the service. He got into electrical contracting doing estimation and project management in Chicago. He and his wife eventually retired to the Little Rock area to be near his wife's family.

Howard Ernest helped decommission *Muskalunge* after the war and was discharged from service in 1948. He later graduated from Northeastern University in Boston with an electrical engineering degree at the same time as his son Howard and worked for Boston Edison. Charlie Welton, having seen what the young officers could accomplish during his patrols on *Kingfish* and *Parche*, decided that he should finish his education. Following his return to civilian life in 1946, he completed his high school education and then earned an engineering degree from Northeastern.[27]

Signalman Chet Stanton later served as an instructor at the U.S. Submarine Quartermaster Signal School. After his Navy service he returned to work at his prewar employer, Ingersoll-Rand, and later filed eight patents while working with Corning Glass Works before retiring in 1983. Stanton also designed the radiation windows for the atomic submarines, tested them at the GE facilities, and installed them on the submarines.[28]

Electrician Dick Frank was married on V-J Day, August 15, 1945. He moved to Boulder, Colorado, graduated in Architectural Engineering from the University of Colorado in 1950, and worked throughout the United States, Canada, Mexico, and South America, in addition to earning his pilot's license. He and fellow Denver-area *Parche* veteran Max Morton teamed up to work on several construction projects where Morton was chief of construction and Frank was the lead designer.[29]

Chief Lonnie Hughes went to work at the Boulder Dam powerhouse near Las Vegas in 1948 and was still on this project when it was renamed the Hoover Dam. An accomplished baseball player, he also coached a boy's team that won the Nevada state championship for their age bracket. Chief Charlie Johnson served on *Sarda* from 1945 to 1946, followed by *Sabalo* and finally *Tilefish* in 1951. He retired from the Navy in 1956 after 20 years' service.[30]

The youngest man to ever serve on *Parche*, Fred Richards, sold life insurance after the war, dabbled in the greenhouse business, and is now retired in southern Florida. Radioman Henry Gay returned to Georgia and went to work for the railroads. Fire controlman Bobby Hall returned to his hometown of Poteau, Oklahoma, where he operated an auto parts store for many years.[31]

*Parche II* (SSN-683) under way off Bremerton, Washington. *Courtesy of Jim Campbell.*

Fourteen members of the *Parche* crew attended the *Ramage* christening at Pasca-goula on 23 April 1994. Left–right: Charlie McNutt, Dean Axene, Bernice McNutt, Pat Richards, Dave Hussey, Mrs. Barbara Ramage, Fred Richards, Mary Anders, Jim Campbell, Dee Allcorn, Frank Allcorn, Al Casassa, Nick Casassa, Norma Manns, Dave Manns, Al Goodson, Sam Roberts, Dana Jensen, Phil Mackey, Judy Hall, Bob Hall. Present but absent from the photo were Jane Mackey, Dick and Emme Hawn. *Courtesy of Bob Hall.*

The other Bob Hall, the baker, returned to the University of Maine after the war. He and his wife Judy have two sons and are retired in New Hampshire, where he is currently the *Parche*'s official historian. For decades, he has tirelessly kept his former shipmates updated with regular *Parche* newsletters.[32]

---

***Parche* in Memorial**

Less than four years after *Parche*'s name was stricken from the Navy's rolls, the World War II boat was honored by giving its name to a new nuclear submarine USS *Parche* (SSN-683), commissioned on 17 August 1974. Elements of the original *Parche* battle flag, including the phrase "Par Excellence," were incorporated into the nuclear *Parche*'s flag, and a copy of the original diesel boat's flag was donated to the new sub as well.

*Parche II*, as she was known to the former diesel boat sailors, became the most decorated boat in U.S. Navy history, receiving a total of nine Presidential Unit Citations, 10 Navy Unit Citations, and 13 Navy Expeditionary Medals during 30 years of service. *Parche* completed a number of classified spy missions, including successfully tapping into Soviet underwater military communication cables in the Barents Sea in 1979 as part of Operation Ivy Bells. Most of *Parche*'s operations have been

USS *Ramage* (DDG-61) was named in honor of Adm. Red Ramage. *Official U.S. Navy photo, courtesy of Bob Hall.*

kept tightly under wraps—as is fitting with the Silent Service—although this submarine was named in some newspaper articles as "one of the world's most prolific spy submarines" during the Cold War. *Parche* was also reportedly involved in recovering Soviet missile fragments from the seabed following test launches.

Red Ramage was honored by having a destroyer (DDG-61) named for him, the USS *Ramage.* The admiral's widow Barbara Ramage christened the new warship by shattering the traditional bottle of champagne on its bow on 23 April 1994. Thirty-three former members of the diesel boat *Parche* were in attendance as guests of the Navy when *Ramage* was commissioned on 22 July 1995.

Preceding this ceremony, the skipper and crew of the new *Ramage* honored the former *Parche* crew members with a ceremony, brunch, and tour of the ship on 21 July. A crowd of more than 10,000 was on hand to witness the commissioning. "It was a tremendous thrill to be present for such a special event," recalled Bob Silvis. A copy of the original World War II *Parche* battle flag was flown from the turbine-engine ship's yardarm in Boston that day. "There likely wasn't a dry eye in the *Parche* seating section," Bob Hall wrote. "Counting wives, widows and families, *Parche* seated some 70 people for the ceremony."[33]

On 21 July 1997, six *Parche* veterans met *Ramage* at a Boston pier to board and ride her to rendezvous with the USS *Constitution* at Marblehead, Massachusetts, to escort the historic sailing ship once known as "Old Ironsides" back to Boston. The group included Frank and Dee Allcorn, Bob Erwin, Ron and Jewel Williams, Bob and Mary Dillon, Bob and Judy Hall, Dave Hussey and his brother Larry, and Jim and Carolyn Ramage (a son and daughter-in-law of Admiral Ramage). She was escorted to her

Visitors to the USS *Bowfin* Submarine Museum and Park at Pearl Harbor can view the *Parche*'s conning tower. (Left) Mary Campbell and veterans of the World War II *Parche* crew dedicate a plaque at Pearl Harbor that contains the names of the wartime *Parche* sailors. *Courtesy of Bob Hall.*

new berth by the nuclear *Parche* and a frigate. "As *Constitution* was sailing again after 116 years with only the breeze to propel her, honored guests were invited to at least lay a hand on the ship's wheel as a token 'hand on the helm' for that historic moment," recalled Bob Hall.[34]

In July 2000, the retired crew of the SSN-683 had a reunion in Bremerton, Washington, and four crew members from the diesel SS-384 were in attendance. Four *Parche* veterans and several members of the Ramage family attended the decommissioning of *Parche II* on 19 October 2004. The World War II *Parche* crew has been holding annual reunions

Veterans of the World War II *Parche* and the second, nuclear-powered *Parche* gathered in late August 2010 at Fort Mitchell, Kentucky, for a reunion. Standing, left–right: Bob Lewis *(Parche II)*, Fred Richards, Jim Ramage (son of Admiral Ramage), and Robert Bissonette *(Parche II)*. Seated, left–right: Bob Hall, Cory Maupin, Hal Staggs, and Carl Vozniak. Also present were *Parche* veterans Bob Erwin and Ron Williams.

since 1973. Former Radioman Fred Richards was instrumental in tirelessly researching contact information for all of the former *Parche* crew to begin the proud boat's annual reunions. These gatherings have continued for more than 35 years with the most recent *Parche* reunion occurring during the Submarine Veterans Convention in August 2010 in the Cincinnati area.

Those attending the Fort Mitchell, Kentucky, reunion in 2010 were veterans Bob Hall, Fred Richards, Bob Erwin, Hal Staggs, Ron Williams, Carl Vozniak, and Cory Maupin. Other veterans were represented in the form of Norma Manns (wife of the late Dave Manns), Jim Ramage (son of the first skipper), Joe DeSola Jr. (son of a *Parche* veteran), his son Doug DeSola, children and family members of Glenn Meise, and two veterans of *Parche II*, Bob Lewis and Robert Bissonette. Those present were able to review an early draft of this book and help answer questions in a lively round-table discussion.

Admiral Ramage was recently honored by having the Headquarters Building at Submarine Base New London renamed Ramage Hall. His

Four veterans who served under Red Ramage during World War II were present on 20 August 2010 when the Headquarters Building was renamed Ramage Hall at the New London, Connecticut, base. Left–right are Bob Hall, Carl Kimmons, Deen Brown (USS *Trout*), and Ron "Red" Williams.

*Parche* veteran Fred Richards (left) organized the first boat reunion in 1973. He is seen with the author (center) and Jim Ramage at the 2010 *Parche* reunion.

children—Alfred Ramage, Virginia Ann Ramage-Ross, Dr. Joan Ramage-Mitchell, and James L. Ramage—were present for the grand unveiling of Ramage Hall on 20 August 2010, as were four of Ramage's wartime submarine comrades: Carl Kimmons, Bob Hall, and Ron Williams from *Parche,* and Deen Brown from *Trout.*

Mary Campbell, wife of former *Parche* Exec Jim Campbell, thought that all of those who brought *Parche* home safely should be remembered. She dedicated a plaque in their honor at the *Bowfin* Submarine Museum in Pearl Harbor. Many of the former crewmen were on hand as Mrs. Campbell unveiled it next to the *Parche* conning tower. It contains the ranks and rates of those who served on board *Parche* during the war.

In fitting tribute to World War II's Silent Service, the U.S. House of Representatives on 6 October 2009 commemorated these veterans in House Resolution 773 for the important roles they played in the Allied victory. In short, this recent bill resolved that the Pacific War could not have been won "without the brave and selfless efforts" of these pioneers of the World War II Submarine Force. The House therefore resolved that it:

1) is committed to promoting and sustaining the spirit of unity shared by members of the United States Submarine Force;

2) is committed to paying tribute once again to the seven submariners who were awarded the Medal of Honor, including two who were awarded the medal posthumously;

3) wishes to keep alive the memory of the Submarine Force veterans and honor their service just as their fellow shipmates do at their gatherings by performing the ceremony known as the "Tolling of the Boats"; and

4) is committed to keeping alive their memory so that the American people never forget their courage and sacrifice.

# USS *Parche* World War II Roster
### *First through Sixth Patrols*

Note: First rank or rate for officers and crew indicates highest held while on *Parche* during the war. Previous ranks and rates held are also shown.

   \*   Served on *Parche* prior to first patrol.
 \*\*   Served on *Parche* between war patrols.
\*\*\*   Lost at sea during fourth patrol.
3.1   On board first half of third patrol; left *Parche* in Saipan in October 1944.
3.2   Joined *Parche* in October 1944 at Saipan for second half of third patrol.
(n)   No middle name

| | | | |
|---|---|---|---|
| 1c | First Class | MoMM | Motor Machinist's Mate |
| 2c | Second Class | MM | Machinist's Mate |
| 3c | Third Class | OS | Officers' Steward |
| Bkr | Baker | PhM | Pharmacist's Mate |
| BM | Boatswain's Mate | PhoM | Photographer's Mate |
| C | Chief Petty Officer (CPO) | QM | Quartermaster |
| Capt. | Captain | RM | Radioman |
| CCK | Chief Cook | RT | Radio Technician |
| CCS | Chief Commissary Steward | S | Seaman |
| Cdr. | Commander | SC | Ship's Cook |
| EM | Electrician's Mate | SM | Signalman |
| Ens. | Ensign | ST | Steward |
| F | Fireman | StM | Steward's Mate |
| FC(S) | Fire Controlman, Surface | TM | Torpedoman's Mate |
| GM | Gunner's Mate | WT | Warrant Torpedoman |
| Lt. | Lieutenant | Y | Yeoman |
| Lt. (jg) | Lieutenant (junior grade) | | |

### OFFICERS

| Name | Rank | Patrols |
|---|---|---|
| Peterson, George Edmund | Capt. | 1 |
| Ramage, Lawson Paterson | Cdr./Lt. Cdr. | 1–3 |
| Parks, Lewis Smith | Cdr. | 2 |
| McCrory, Woodrow Wilson | Lt. Cdr. | 1–6 |
| Ganyard, Bricker McDonald | Lt. Cdr. | 5 |
| Allcorn, Frank Walter, III | Lt. | 1–2 |
| Campbell, Churchill James | Lt./Lt. (jg) | 1–6 |

| | | |
|---|---|---|
| Erwin, Robert Lee | Lt./Lt. (jg) | 1–5 |
| Green, David Hepburn | Lt. | 1–3 |
| Hennessy, John Harold, Jr. | Lt. | 4–6 |
| Morton, Max Thomas | Lt./Lt. (jg) | 4–6 |
| Stevenson, Robert Thompson | Lt./Lt. (jg) | 2–6 |
| Wright, Richard Morgan | Lt. | 4 |
| Flack, Ralph Francis | Lt. (jg)/Ens. | 3–4 |
| Gadd, Francis Oliver | Lt. (jg) | 5–6 |
| Mottner, Robert Louis | Lt. (jg) | 6 |
| Parks, John Henry | Lt. (jg) | 1, 3 |
| Rauscher, Edward Askew | Lt. (jg) | 2 |
| Ashe, Robert W. | Ens. | 2–3 |
| Axene, Dean Lane | Lt. (jg)/Ens. | 5–6 |
| Bergren, William Joseph | Ens. | 1 |
| Cornell, Lloyd W., Jr. | Ens. | ** |
| Holleran, John Michael | Lt. (jg)/Ens. | 4–6 |
| Milhan, Harry Lloyd | Ens. | 6 |
| Tubb, George Gilbert | Ens. | 3–4 |

## ENLISTED MEN

| Name | Rating | Patrols |
|---|---|---|
| Allard, Clarence Joseph | CMoMM/MoMM1 | 1–2 |
| Balfe, Robert Bird | TM1 | ** |
| Barnes, John Balderson | TM3/S1/S2 | 1–4 |
| Barnett, Percy Edward | CRM/RM1 | 1–5 |
| Bashwiner, Arnold Franklin | MoMM1/2 | 3–6 |
| Bougetz, Henry Francis | MoMM3/F1 | 1–3 |
| Braxton, Lee Roy | StM1 | 4–6 |
| Breckenridge, Charles George | QM3/S1 | 2–4 |
| Brewer, Percy Edward | RM2 | * |
| Brodsky, Lowell Burton | QM3/S1 | 3.2 |
| Brown, Lamar William | SC1 | 2–6 |
| Brown, Quentin Lowry | PhM1/2 | 1–2 |
| Buckner, Orvail Albert | MoMM1/2 | 1–6 |
| Bukowski, Philip George | MoMM1/2 | 1–3.1 |
| Bulceco, Rufino (n) | CCK | * |
| Burker, Roland Ernest | MoMM3 | 5–6 |
| Bush, Travis Clyde | S1 | 4–6 |

| | | |
|---|---|---|
| Cantor, Milton (n) | QM3 | 5–6 |
| Caruso, Joseph Richard | EM1/2 | 1–4 |
| Casassa, Nicholas Mario | MoMM1/2/3/F1 | 1–5 |
| Chambers, Hurschel Monroe, Jr. | EM3 | 3.1 |
| Chambless, Leslie Warren | CY | 3–4 |
| Chmolack, Mitchell Joseph | F1/S1/S2 | 1–2 |
| Christy, Desmond Albert | RT1/2 | 1–4 |
| Cierebiei, Boleslaw Thomas | MoMM1 | 1 |
| Coleman, William Frederick | MoMM3 | 6 |
| Couture, Benjamin Harrison | EM3 | 3.2 |
| Daufenbach, Robert Louis | QM1/2/3 | 1–6 |
| Davis, Wayne Kemp | TM3 | 4–6 |
| Delaney, John Lewis | S1 | * |
| DeMonge, Robert Louis | TM1 | 4–6 |
| Denman, James Allen | F1 | 3 |
| DeSola, Joseph Seigle | S1 | 5–6 |
| Dilley, Carl Thomas | TM1/2 | 1–2 |
| Dillon, Robert Emmett | F1 | 5–6 |
| Dingman, Warren Earl | CY/1 | 1–3, 5–6 |
| Doyle, Norman Henry | MoMM3 | ** |
| Ekelund, Walter Allen | EM1/2/3 | 1–6 |
| Elliott, Alvin Earl, Jr. | S1/S2 | * |
| Ernest, Howard Edward | EM2/3 | 1–6 |
| Faehnrich, John (n) | EM1 | 6 |
| Felder, Leonard Shider | MoMM3/F1 | * |
| Fisher, "LC" | StM3 | 6 |
| Fisk, William Arthur | MoMM1/2 | 1 |
| Flanagan, Robert Edward | MoMM1 | 5–6 |
| Folse, John Stephen | RM3 | 1 |
| Forbes, David Allen | MoMM2 | 4 |
| Fournier, Nelson Carl | RM2 | 1–6 |
| Frank, David (n) | S1/S2 | * |
| Frank, Richard John | EM3 | 4–6 |
| Frederick, "LB" | MoMM1/2/3 | 1–6 |
| Frye, Edward Seely | MoMM2/3 | 3–4 |
| Gay, Henry Grady, Jr. | RM3 | 4–6 |
| Geier, Max (n) | GM2 | 4–6 |

| | | |
|---|---|---|
| George, Ray Hiram | CEM | * |
| Gilcher, Paul William | RM3/S1/2 | 2–4 |
| Giordano, Ralph (n) | TM1/2 | 5–6 |
| Glimpse, Arthur Lew | EM2 | * |
| Goding, Mark Alden | CMoMM | 1–3.1 |
| Gooden, Charles William | TM2 | 1–3.1 |
| Goodson, Allan Douglas, Jr. | CY | 3.2 |
| Gormley, Morris William | MoMM2 | 1–3.1 |
| Gray, Clyde (n), Jr. | MoMM3 | 4 |
| Gray, John Campbell, Jr. | CRT/RT1 | 1–6 |
| Green, Donald Nelson | EM2 | 1–3 |
| Grover, Myron Woodard | RM1/2/3 | 1–6 |
| Gubaney, Robert Edward | S1/S2 | 1 |
| | | |
| Hall, Bobby Coy | FC3 | 3.2–6 |
| Hall, Robert Ames | Bkr2/3/S1 | 1–6 |
| Hamlin, Thornton Huntington, Jr. | QM2/3 | 4–6 |
| Hansen, Arne Christopher | EM2 | 6 |
| Harmon, James Walton | EM2 | 1 |
| Harris, Caleb Seymore, Jr. | SC2 | ** |
| Hawkey, Robert James | TM2/3/S1 | 1–6 |
| Hawn, Richard Gatling | CMoMM/1 | 1–4 |
| Hayes, C. M. | CRM | * |
| Hayes, Daniel Edward | SC2 | 1 |
| Hayes, Thomas Wallace | EM3/F1 | 5–6 |
| Heaton, Harry Lee, Jr. | PhoM1 | 6 |
| Hemperly, Claude Herr, Jr. | EM2/3 | ** |
| Herman, Anthony Baldwin | MoMM3 | 5–6 |
| Hervey, James Robert | S2 | * |
| Hilditch, William Patrick | TM3/S1/S2 | 1–3.1 |
| Hill, Jasper Gaines | TM2/3 | 1–3 |
| Hollinger, William Warren | F1 | 5–6 |
| Howell, Joseph Ray | EM1/2 | 1–6 |
| Hughes, William Alonzo | CEM/EM1 | 1–5 |
| Hussey, David Franklin | F1/F2 | 1–3.1 |
| | | |
| Jarco, Louis Joseph | MoMM3 | 4–6 |
| Jefferies, James Robert | F1 | 3 |
| Jensen, Dana Clayton | CMoMM/1 | 1–6 |
| Johnson, Charles Franklin | CCS/SC1 | 1–4 |
| Johnston, Murray Wayne | EM3 | 4–6 |

| | | |
|---|---|---|
| Karr, Raymond Walter | TME2/3 | 1–4 |
| Keenan, Charles Gerard, Jr. | F1 | 5–6 |
| Kimball, Jack Reily | TM3/S1 | 3–6 |
| Kimmons, Carl Eugene | StM1/StM2 | 1–3 |
| Kinkel, Carroll Edward | CTM/1 | 1–5 |
| Klapach, Peter (n) | RT2 | 5–6 |
| Kulick, August Leo | MoMM2/3 | 5–6 |
| Kuter, Paul Everette | RM3 | 5 |
| | | |
| Larsen, Hollis Ray | MoMM2 | 4–6 |
| Lashley, William Danford | F1/2 | 1 |
| Lawrence, Alden Leroy | RT1/2 | 3.2–6 |
| Lee, Charles Wayne | TM3 | 4–6 |
| Leffler, Harris Palmer *** | MoMM2 | 3–4 |
| Leiching, Joseph Daniel | MoMM2/3 | 3–6 |
| Lippincott, Wayne C. | S1 | 4 |
| Loveless, Chester (n) | EM1/EM2 | 1 |
| Lucas, Norman Robert | GM2 | 6 |
| Lutz, Claude Anthony | SM1 | 1–3 |
| Lyman, Jack Neilsen | FC(S)3 | * |
| Lynn, Hugh (n) | EM3 | 2 |
| | | |
| Mackey, Phillip Earl | MoMM1/2 | 1–5 |
| Madison, Corlet Rodgers | CMoMM | 6 |
| Maloney, Harold Joseph | EM2 | 5 |
| Manns, David Joseph | TM3 | 5–6 |
| Mason, Allyn Leroy | F1/2/3 | * |
| Mathews, Kenneth Jesse | CMoMM/MoMM1 | 1–3 |
| Maupin, Corwin Moyle | TME3/S1/2 | 1–3 |
| McGuire, James Thomas | Ck2 | 1–2 |
| McLaughlin, Edward Joseph | MoMM1 | 2 |
| McMahon, Howard Grant | SC3/S1/2 | 1–2 |
| McMahon, Raymond Joseph | TM2 | 2 |
| McNally, William John | GM3 | 3.2 |
| McNutt, Charles Cecil | EM3/F1/2 | 2–6 |
| McQuellen, Phillip Holt | F1 | 6 |
| Meise, Glenn William | RM2/3 | 2–6 |
| Mettee, Eugene Blake | SM1 | 6 |
| Meyer, Carl Joseph | Y3 | 5–6 |
| Mielke, Dale Milo | QM3/S1/2 | 3–6 |
| Miller, Charles Edward | EM3/S1/2 | 1–4 |
| Mokos, Edward Charles | F1 | 2–6 |

| | | |
|---|---|---|
| Moore, Charles E. | F1 | 4 |
| Mullins, George Raymond | TM3 | * |
| | | |
| Nania, John Joseph | MoMM1/2/3/F1 | 1–6 |
| Nelson, Robert Earl | StM1/2 | 3–5 |
| Nichols, Joseph Edward | TM2/3 | 1–6 |
| Nutt, Charles Melvin | F1 | 3 |
| | | |
| O'Brien, Donald Joseph | S1/S2 | 1 |
| O'Brien, John James | QM2/3/S1/2 | 1–5 |
| Oliver, Montgomery (n) | CMoMM | * |
| | | |
| Pannell, Harold Eugene | TM3 | 3–6 |
| Parker, Luke Godfrey | CTM | 1 |
| Peppenger, Levi Oliver | S1 | 3.1 |
| Petersen, Verlin Trumen | CEM | 1–2 |
| Peterson, Austin Leroy | EM2 | 3.2–5 |
| Plume, George Gustave, Jr. | SM1 | 2 |
| Plumley, James Levell | CGM/1 | 2–6 |
| | | |
| Rauch, George William | QM3 | 6 |
| Reed, Harry James, Jr. | S1 | 3.2–6 |
| Reedus, Otis Wilson | S1/S2 | 1 |
| Richards, Frederick Alexander | RM3 | 5–6 |
| Rick, Alfred Joseph | RM1/2 | 1–3 |
| Roberts, George Henry | F1 | 1 |
| Roberts, Samuel Raymond | FC(S)1/2/3 | 1–6 |
| Russel, Adolph Raymond | EM2/3 | 2–6 |
| | | |
| Sanchez, Chiriaco | CCK | 2 |
| Satterfield, Charles Eldon | MoMM1 | 1–2 |
| Schiefer, Edward Feodor | MoMM2 | 4–6 |
| Shaw, Rex "D" | CPhM/1 | 3–6 |
| Sheppard, Joe Allen | TM3/S1 | 3.2–6 |
| Short, Marion (n) | StM1/StM2 | * |
| Silvis, Robert Thomas | MoMM3/F1 | 4–6 |
| Slajer, Harry Lee | SM2/SM3 | 4–6 |
| Sprague, Wilbur Gordon | CQM | 1 |
| Staggs, Harold Earl | TM2 | 1 |
| Stammen, Francis John | EM2 | 1–3.1 |
| Stanton, Courtland Chester | SM1/2/3 | 1–5 |
| St. Denny, Ralph Bryan | TM3 | 2–4 |

| Swanson, Robert Harvey | TM3/S1 | 4–6 |
| Swettenam, Leroy Kenneth | GM2 | 1 |
| | | |
| Taylor, Marion Dewitt | TM1/2 | 1–3 |
| Terry, Melvin "D" | S1 | 5–6 |
| | | |
| Ussin, Reno (n) | GM2 | 1–2 |
| | | |
| Van Eperen, Raymond John *** | MoMM1/2 | 1–4 |
| Vetter, Paul Joseph | EM3 | 4–6 |
| Vogedes, Frederick Zacharias | MoMM1/2 | 1–3 |
| Vozniak, Carl Walter | EM2 | 6 |
| Vukovcan, William Nicholas | CEM/EM1 | 1–3 |
| | | |
| Walters, Donald Eugene | WT/CTM/TM1 | 1–6 |
| Welton, Charles Errol | S1 | 2–4 |
| Williams, Ronald Edward | MoMM1/2/3 | 2–6 |
| Worley, Thomas Alfred | TM1 | 6 |
| | | |
| Zeller, Carl Joseph | S1 | 5–6 |

## PASSENGERS

| Name | Rating | Patrols |
| --- | --- | --- |
| Ayres, Ronald Wren | BM1 | post 6th |
| Bailey, James Stuart | CMoMM | post 6th |
| Brown, Kenneth Nelson | SF1 | post 6th |
| Edwards, Zane Fred | MoMM2 | post 6th |
| Graham, Lee Eugene | MoMM1 | post 6th |
| Hester, Charles W. | AOM3 | 6 |
| Kiick, Grover Anthony | MoMM1 | post 6th |
| Leake, Harry A. | ARM3 | 6 |
| Mitchell, Joseph Sigler | CTM | post 6th |
| Noah, Burton W. | Ens. | 6 |
| O'Connor, Francis Bernard | SC2 | post 6th |
| Osuna, Rudolph (n) | TM1 | post 6th |
| Perkins, Roger Eugene | SC1 | post 6th |
| Seymour, Harrison Wright | EM2 | post 6th |
| Whisman, David Chadwick | CQM | post 6th |

# USS *Parche* Postwar Roster
*July 1945—November 1946*

Note: The first rank or rate for officers and crew indicates highest held while aboard *Parche*. Previous ranks and rates held are also shown.

OFFICERS

| Name: | Rank: |
|---|---|
| Keating, Robert | Cdr. |
| Kehl, George W. | Cdr. |
| Atkinson, George Oliver, Jr. | Lt. Cdr. |
| Bennett, George S. | Lt. Cdr. |
| Hack, John A. | Lt. Cdr. |
| Reaves, Henry Grady, Jr. | Lt. Cdr. |
| Campbell, Churchill James | Lt. |
| Cousins, Romalo (n) | Lt. |
| Gadd, Francis Oliver | Lt./Lt. (jg) |
| Lowell, Henry T., Jr. | Lt. |
| McDonald, Robert Renwick | Lt./Lt. (jg) |
| Morton, Max Thomas | Lt. |
| Mottner, Robert Louis | Lt./Lt. (jg) |
| Stevenson, Robert Thompson | Lt. |
| Axene, Dean Lane | Lt. (jg)/Ens. |
| Dickson, Thomas A. | Lt. (jg) |
| Guyton, William J. | Lt. (jg) |
| Heltz, Eugene R. | Lt. (jg) |
| Hockfield, R. | Lt. (jg) |
| Holleran, John Michael | Lt. (jg) |
| Mersereau, Charles Robert | Lt. (jg) |
| Milhan, Harry Lloyd | Lt. (jg)/Ens. |
| Picker, William (n) | Lt. (jg) |
| Zwilling, Daniel (n) | Lt. (jg) |
| Billington, Harry H. | Ens. |
| Childers, Russell E. | Lt. (jg)/Ens. |
| Gregg | Ens. |
| Martin, Ralph A. | Ens. |
| Calkins, Don B. | Mach. |
| Hoffman, Beverly H. | Mach. |
| Souza, Edwin Enos | Lt. (jg)/Torp. |
| Walters, Donald Eugene | Torp. |

ENLISTED MEN

| Name: | Rating: |
|---|---|
| Aiken, William S. | S1/2 |
| Alexander, Robert E. | CPhM |
| Alls, James Garnett | MoMM3 |
| Anastos, George (n) | SC2 |
| Ashemore, Franklin (n) | StM1 |
| Asman, Kenneth Luis | ETM3 |
| Ayres, Ronald W. | BM1 |
| Bacon, Jack Loren | EM3/F1 |
| Bailey, James Stuart | CMoMM |
| Barr, George (n) | MoMM3 |
| Bashwiner, Arnold | MoMM1 |
| Billington, Harry N. | EM2 |
| Bing, W. D. | TM1 |
| Borden, John M. | CEM |
| Braan, Richard E. | StM1 |
| Braxton, Lee Roy | StM1 |
| Brown, Kenneth Nelson | SF1 |
| Brown, Lamar William | SC1 |
| Brown, Walter E., Jr. | RT1 |
| Buckner, Orvail Albert | MoMM1 |
| Burker, Roland Edward | MoMM2/3 |
| Butler, Lester G. | MoMM1 |
| Bzullak, Edward A. | CY |
| Canton, Milton (n) | QM3 |
| Cavanaugh, John J. | EM1 |
| Chadburn, Robert B. | S1 |
| Cobb, Oscar T. | StM1 |
| Coleman, William Frederick | MoMM2/3 |
| Collingwood, V. S. | EM3 |
| Comfort, Kenneth E. | TM2 |
| Crumbling, Eugene (n) | SC1/2 |
| Cunningham, Edwin W. | MoMM2 |
| Daufenbach, Robert Louis | QM1 |
| Dauphin, M. H., Jr. | F1 |
| Davis, Jobie Dee | EM1 |
| Davis, Wayne Kemp | TM3 |
| DeMonge, Robert Louis | CTM |
| DeSola, Joseph Seigle | S1 |

| | | | |
|---|---|---|---|
| Dillon, Robert Emmett | EM3 | Hawkey, Robert James | TM1/2 |
| Dingman, Warren Earl | CY | Hawn, Richard Gatling | CMoMM |
| Eccher, Aldo M. | GM2 | Hayes, Thomas Wallace | EM3 |
| Edwards, Zane Fred | MoMM2 | Heath, Murray D. | EM3 |
| Ekelund, Walter Allen | EM1 | Hendrickson, John S. | S1 |
| Emerson, Raymond G. | CQM | Herman, Anthony Baldwin | MoMM3 |
| Ernest, Howard Edward | EM1 | Herrington, Robert C. | S1 |
| Estes, Howard Eugene | Y1 | Hill, Howard J., Jr. | S1 |
| Eurell, Thomas Joseph | S1 | Hinton, James R. | Y1 |
| Fambrough, David G. | MoMM1 | Hollin, Charles Herbert | GM3 |
| Ferrebee, Paul Rex | CRM/1/2 | Hollinger, William Warren | F1 |
| Fisher, "LC" | StM3 | Hoover, Bernard J. | MoMM1 |
| Flanagan, Robert Edward | CMoMM/1 | Hopkins, Robert D. | EM1 |
| Foster, Ken G., Jr. | TM1 | Howell, Joseph Ray | EM1 |
| Fournier, Nelson Carl | RM1/2 | Hudson, Irving Lynn | EM1 |
| Frank, Richard John | EM2/3 | Hudson, Richard M. | Y2 |
| Frederick, "LB" | MoMM1 | Jacobsen, Carl O. | MoMM2 |
| Fritz, Edgar D. | CMoMM | Jarco, Louis Joseph | MoMM2 |
| Frye, Edward Seely | MoMM2 | Jensen, Dana Clayton | CMoMM |
| Gabik, Francis Norman | MoMM1 | Jensen, Lester P. | MoMM2 |
| Gagneaux, Paul Reves | ETM3 | Johnston, Murray Wayne | EM3 |
| Gallagher, Edward J. | QM3 | Kadlic, Keith M. | F1 |
| Gatten, Robert Ross | EM3 | Kelly, Edward E. | ETM3/S1 |
| Gay, Henry Grady, Jr. | RM3 | Kiick, Grover Anthony | MoMM1 |
| Geier, Max (n) | GM1 | Kimball, Jack Reily | TM3 |
| Gilliland, Robert M. | F1 | King, John Henry | RM2 |
| Giordano, Ralph (n) | TM2 | Klapach, Peter (n) | RT1/2 |
| Glass, Richard B. | Y2 | Klein, Julius Daniel | GM3 |
| Glinski, Henry Paul | MoMM1/2/3 | Kulick, August Leo | MoMM2/3 |
| Gordon, William O. | MoMM1 | Larsen, Hollis Ray | MoMM2 |
| Graham, Lee Eugene | MoMM1 | Lauthern, Claude F. | EM3/F1 |
| Gray, John Campbell, Jr. | CRT | Lawrence, Alden Leroy | RT1 |
| Gregory, John (n) | S1 | Lee, Charles Wayne | TM3 |
| Greiner, William R. | CEM | Leiching, Joseph Daniel | MoMM2 |
| Gribkoff, Leo (n) | RM1 | Lennon, William Michael | CEM |
| Grosdidier, Harry, Jr. | MoMM2 | Lindmark, Algot C. | S1/2 |
| Grover, Myron Woodard | RM1 | Little, Charles W. | MoMM1 |
| Gustafson, John P. | ETM3 | Long, Leslie (n) | QM1 |
| Haba, Eugene Edward | S1/2 | Lougheed, Howard (n) | RM3 |
| Hall, Bobby Coy | FCS2 | Lovell, Douglas R. | TME3 |
| Hall, Robert Ames | Bkr2 | Lucas, Norman Robert | GM2 |
| Hamlin, Thorton | | Lyons, Roy Damon | CTM |
|     Huntington, Jr. | QM3 | Maasch, Marvin F. | MoMM2 |
| Hammer, Howard Walter | FCS2 | MacGregor, Norman (n) | GM3/S1 |
| Hansen, Arne Christopher | EM3 | Mackey, Phillip Earl | MoMM1 |
| Harris, H. E. | MoMM2 | Madison, Corlet Rodgers | CMoMM |
| Harris, James Irwin | S1 | Manns, David Joseph | TM3 |
| Hartley, Robert W. | S1 | Maurer, Lester L. | CMoMM |
| Hatt, David Dennis | S1 | Maviglia, Frank A. | EM1 |
| Haugan, Leonard G. | S1 | May, Albert Elden | F1 |

| | | | |
|---|---|---|---|
| May, Felix L. | StM2 | Roberts, William M. | S2 |
| Mazurkiewicz, R. S. | MoMM3 | Rosenfelder, William F., Jr. | SM1 |
| McElroy, Robert W. | CY | Rothe, Charles R. | GM3 |
| McFayden, Peter J. | QM1 | Rothlein, Moe Henry | F1 |
| McKisson, James L. | TM3 | Russel, Adolph Raymond | EM2 |
| McNutt, Charles Cecil | EM2 | Schiller, R. G. S. | SC2 |
| McQuellen, Philip Holt | F2 | Schmelzer, Carl Thomas | CEM |
| Meise, Glenn William | RM2 | Seymour, Harrison Wright | EM2 |
| Mettee, Eugene Blake | S1 | Shaw, Rex "D" | CPhM/1 |
| Meyer, Carl Joseph | Y2/3 | Sheppard, Joe Allen | TM3 |
| Mielke, Dale Milo | GM2 | Shook, Lester C. | TM3 |
| Mitchell, Joseph S. | CTM | Silvis, Robert Thomas | MoMM2/3 |
| Mokos, Edward Charles | MoMM2 | Simmons, William Alfred | TM2 |
| Murch, Russell L. | MoMM3 | Slajer, Harry Lee | SM2 |
| Murray, Arthur E. | S1 | Smail, Everett R. | S1 |
| Myers, Grady Lee | MoMM1 | Smith, Robert E. | EM3 |
| Nania, John Joseph | MoMM2 | Spencer, George T. | QM3 |
| Nelson, Ralph Warren | FCS2 | Standlee, Floyd C. | MoMM1 |
| Nichols, Joseph Edward | TM1/2 | Stewart, John H., Jr. | CCS |
| O'Conner, Francis B. | SC2 | Summers, C. T. | S1 |
| Osuna, Rudolph (n) | TM1 | Swanson, Robert Harvey | TM3 |
| Ott, John H. | EM1 | Sweeney, Edward L. | TM2 |
| Pannell, Harold Eugene | TM2 | Terry, Melvin "D" | TM3/S1 |
| Patton, Paul Lamar | S1 | Terry, S. J. | EM1 |
| Payne, Ozro Ulric, Jr. | S1 | Thompson, Roy V. | EM2 |
| Perkins, Roger Eugene | SC1 | Thompson, William Ray | TME2/3 |
| Peterson, Robert C. | FCS3 | Tisdale, John Francis | S1/2 |
| Plouffe, Patrick E. | F1 | Tuggle, James H. | MoMM1c |
| Plumley, James Levell | CGM | Vetter, Paul Joseph | EM2/3 |
| Predham, Norman J. | MoMM1 | Vozniak, Carl Walter | EM2 |
| Probert, Raymond (n) | EM3 | Wagner, Richard D. | EM3 |
| Prosko, Edmond R. | RM3 | Whisman, David Chadwick | CQM |
| Rahles, Harris Earl | MoMM1 | Williams, Gordon B. | F1 |
| Rauch, George William | QM3 | Williams, Ronald Edward | MoMM1 |
| Rice, Robert F. | MoMM3 | Worley, Thomas Alfred | CTM/1 |
| Richards, Frederick Alexander | RM3 | Yost, Richard W. | F1 |
| Roberts, Herman Ray | SC1 | Zeller, Carl Joseph | RM3 |
| Roberts, Samuel Raymond | FCS1/2 | | |

# Summary of USS *Parche* Ship Sinkings

## SINKINGS AS CREDITED BY JOHN D. ALDEN RESEARCH

| Patrol / Date | Ship Name / Action | Type | Japanese Gross Tonnage |
|---|---|---|---|
| *First War Patrol: Lt. Cdr. Ramage* | | | |
| 4 May 1944 | *Kinrei Maru* | AK | 5,949* |
| 4 May 1944 | *Taibu Maru* | AK | 6,440* |
| | | **Patrol total:** | 2/12,389 tons |
| | | | |
| *Second War Patrol: Cdr. Ramage* | | | |
| 24 June 1944 | Gun action | Patrol Craft | 300 |
| 31 July 1944 | *Koei Maru* | Tanker | 10,238 (shared) |
| 31 July 1944 | *Ogura (Kokura) Maru 1* | Freighter | 7,270 |
| 31 July 1944 | *Dakar Maru* | A-AP | 7,169 |
| 31 July 1944 | *Yoshino Maru* | A-AP | 8,990* (shared) |
| (half tonnage counted for shared kills) | | **Patrol total:** | 5/24,353 tons |
| | | | |
| *Third War Patrol: Cdr. Ramage* | | | |
| September / October 1944 | | **Patrol total:** | no sinkings |
| | | | |
| *Fourth War Patrol: Lt. Cdr. McCrory* | | | |
| 7 February 1945 | *Okinoyama Maru* | Freighter | 984* |
| | | **Patrol total:** | 1/984 tons |
| | | | |
| *Fifth War Patrol: Lt. Cdr. McCrory* | | | |
| 9 April 1945 | *W-3* | Minesweeper | 702* |
| 11 April 1945 | *Kosho Maru No. 2* | XPkt | 302 (guns) |
| 12 April 1945 | Unidentified | Freighter | 3,200 |
| 13 April 1945 | *Misago Maru No. 1* | XAM | 265 (guns) |
| 13 April 1945 | *Togo Maru* | XAM | 302 (guns) |
| 22 April 1945 | *Irako Maru* | Tanker | 875 |
| | | **Patrol total:** | 6/5,646 tons |

*Sixth War Patrol: Cdr. McCrory*

| | | | |
|---|---|---|---|
| 21 June 1945 | *Hizen Maru* | Freighter | 947* |
| 22 June 1945 | unknown | Fishing boat | 100 guns |
| 22 June 1945 | unknown | Lugger | 100 guns |
| 23 April 1945 | Gun action | Trawler | 200 |
| 23 April 1945 | Gun action | Trawler | 200 |
| 23 April 1945 | Gun action | Trawler | 200 |
| 26 June 1945 | *Kamitsu Maru* | XPG | 2,721* |
| 26 June 1945 | *Eikan Maru* | Freighter | 6,903 |
| | | **Patrol total:** | 8/11,371 sunk |

## DAMAGE INFLICTED

| Patrol / Date | Ship Name / Action | Type | Est. Japanese Gross Tonnage |
|---|---|---|---|
| *First War Patrol: Lt. Cdr. Ramage* | | | |
| 30 April 1944 | unknown | Freighter | 6,500 |
| 19 May 1944 | Gun action | Trawler | 50 |
| | | **Patrol total:** | 2/6,550 tons |
| *Second War Patrol: Cdr. Ramage* | | | |
| 31 July 1944 | unknown | Freighter | 4,000 |
| | | **Patrol total:** | 1/4,000 tons |
| *Fourth War Patrol: Lt. Cdr. McCrory* | | | |
| 19 January 1945 | unknown | Tanker | 8,500 |
| 19 Janaury 1945 | unknown | Freighter | 2,000 |
| | | **Patrol total:** | 2/10,500 tons |
| *Fifth War Patrol: Cdr. McCrory* | | | |
| 12 April 1945 | unknown | Freighter | 3,200 |
| 22 April 1945 | unknown | Tanker | 3,200 |
| | | **Patrol total:** | 2/6,400 tons |
| *Sixth War Patrol: Cdr. McCrory* | | | |
| 22 April 1945 | Gun action | Sea Truck | 200 |
| | | **Patrol total:** | 1/200 tons |

USS *Parche* total per John Alden's research was 22 ships of all types sunk with torpedoes and guns for 54,743 total tons; eight more ships claimed as damaged for additional 27,700 tons. Official Joint Army-Navy Assessment Committee postwar totals: 8 vessels sunk for 31,696. Ships smaller than 500 tons were not counted in JANAC assessments.

# Awards Given to USS *Parche* and Crew

## BATTLE STARS

*Parche* sailors earned battle stars for five of the boat's six patrols in the following operations:

1 star: First War Patrol      29 March–23 May 1944
1 star: Second War Patrol      17 June–16 August 1944
1 star: Fourth War Patrol      30 December 1944–20 February 1945
1 star: Assault and Occupation of Okinawa Gunto
        (Fifth War Patrol)      3 April–21 June 1945
1 star: Third Fleet Operations Against Japan
        (Sixth War Patrol)      13–16 July 1945

## PRESIDENTIAL UNIT CITATION

The President of the United States takes pleasure in presenting the PRESIDENTIAL UNIT CITATION to the

UNITED STATES SHIP PARCHE

for service as set forth in the following:

CITATION:

For extraordinary heroism in action during the First and Second War Patrols against heavily escorted enemy Japanese convoys in restricted waters of the Pacific. Boldly penetrating the strong hostile screen at pre-dawn, the U.S.S. PARCHE launched a perilous surface attack with a crippling stern shot into an enemy freighter and followed up with a series of bow and stern torpedoes to sink the lead tanker and damage a second one. Exposed by the light of bursting flares, she defied the terrific shellfire passing close overhead to strike again and sink a transport by two forward reloads, braving the mounting fury of fire from the damaged and sinking tanker to fight it out with a completely disorganized and confused enemy. Maneuvering swiftly to avoid destruction as a fast transport closed in to ram, the PARCHE cleared the bow of the onrushing ship by less than fifty feet but placed herself in the punishing crossfire from escorts on all sides with the transport dead ahead. Undaunted, she sent three smashing 'down-the-throat' bow shots to stop the target, then scored a killing hit as a climax to forty-six minutes of violent action, retiring unscathed with a record of four Japanese ships sunk and another severely damaged. Fighting superbly against all odds, the PARCHE, by her stout-hearted service, has implemented the valor and gallantry of her skilled officers and men.

For the President,<br>(signed) James Forrestal<br>Secretary of the Navy

## INDIVIDUAL COMMENDATIONS

The following awards were also received by officers and enlisted men for service aboard *Parche* in World War II.

**CONGRESSIONAL MEDAL OF HONOR:**
Ramage, Cdr. Lawson Paterson          2nd Patrol
His citation reads:

For conspicuous gallantry and intrepidity at the risk of his life above and beyond the call of duty as Commanding Officer of the USS PARCHE in a pre-dawn attack on a Japanese convoy, 31 July 1944. Boldly penetrating the screen of a heavily escorted convoy, Commander Ramage launched a perilous surface attack by delivering a crippling stern shot into a freighter and quickly following up with a series of bow and stern torpedoes to sink the leading tanker and damage the second one. Exposed by the light of bursting flares and bravely defiant of terrific shellfire passing close overhead, he struck again, sinking a transport by two forward reloads. In the mounting fury of fire from the damaged and sinking tanker, he calmly ordered his men below, remaining on the bridge to fight it out with an enemy now disorganized and confused. Swift to act as a fast transport closed into ram, he daringly swung the stern of the speeding PARCHE as she crossed the bow of the onrushing ship, clearing by less than fifty feet but placing his submarine in a deadly crossfire from escorts on all sides and with the transport dead ahead. Undaunted, he sent three smashing 'down-the-throat' shots to stop the target, then scored a killing hit as a climax to forty-six minutes of violent action with the PARCHE and her valiant fighting company retiring victorious and unscathed.

**NAVY CROSS:**

| | |
|---|---|
| McCrory, Lt. Cdr. Woodrow Wilson | 5th Patrol |

**GOLD STAR** (in lieu of additional Navy Cross):

| | |
|---|---|
| Ramage, Cdr. Lawson Paterson | 1st Patrol |
| Parks, Capt. Lewis Smith | 2nd Patrol |

**LEGION OF MERIT:**

| | |
|---|---|
| McCrory, Lt. Woodrow Wilson | 6th Patrol |

**SILVER STAR:**

| | |
|---|---|
| Allcorn, Lt. Frank Walter, III | 2nd Patrol |
| Campbell, Lt. Churchill James | 2nd Patrol |
| Erwin, Lt. Robert Lee | 4th Patrol |
| Gray, CRT John Campbell, Jr. | 1st Patrol |
| McCrory, Lt. Woodrow Wilson | 1st Patrol |
| Plume, SM1c George Gustave, Jr. | 2nd Patrol |
| Plumley, CGM James Levell | 6th Patrol |

**GOLD STAR** (in lieu of additional Silver Star):

| | |
|---|---|
| Campbell, Lt. Churchill James | 5th Patrol |
| McCrory, Lt. Woodrow Wilson | 2nd Patrol |

**BRONZE STAR:**

| | |
|---|---|
| Axene, Ens. Dean Lane | 6th Patrol |
| Erwin, Lt. Robert Lee | 2nd Patrol |
| Gray, CRT John Campbell, Jr. | 2nd Patrol |
| Hennessy, Lt. John Harold, Jr. 5th Patrol | |
| Kinkel, CTM Carroll Edward | 2nd Patrol |
| McCrory, Lt. Woodrow Wilson | 4th Patrol |
| Morton, Lt. Max Thomas | 6th Patrol |
| Nania, MoMM2c John Joseph | 5th Patrol |
| Parks, Lt. (jg) John Henry | 1st Patrol |
| Roberts, FCS1c Samuel Raymond | 1st Patrol |
| Stanton, SM2c Courtland Chester | 1st Patrol |
| Stevenson, Lt. Robert Thompson | 4th Patrol |
| Van Eperen, MoMM1c Raymond John | 4th Patrol |
| Walters, TM1c Donald Eugene | 1st Patrol |

| | |
|---|---|
| Walters, TM1c Donald Eugene | 2nd Patrol |
| Williams, MoMM1c Ronald Edward | 6th Patrol |

**NAVY LETTER OF COMMENDATION WITH MEDAL (29):**

| | |
|---|---|
| Barnett, CRM Percy Edward | 2nd Patrol |
| Braxton, StM1c Lee Roy | 6th Patrol |
| Dingman, CY Warren Earl | 5th Patrol |
| Ernest, EM2 Howard Edward | 4th Patrol |
| Fisher, St3c "LC" | 6th Patrol |
| Howell, EM1c Joseph Ray | 2nd Patrol |
| Jensen, MoMM1c Dana Clayton | 2nd Patrol |
| Johnson, CCS Charles Franklin | 4th Patrol |
| Kimmons, StM1c Carl Eugene | 3rd Patrol |
| Manns, TM3c David Joseph | 5th Patrol |
| Morton, Lt. Max Thomas | 6th Patrol |
| Stanton, SM2c Courtland Chester | 2nd Patrol |
| Ussin, GM2c Reno | 1st Patrol |

Complete List Unavailable

# Notes

**CHAPTER 1: RED RAMAGE'S RETURN**
Primary sources for this chapter are interviews with Churchill J. Campbell, Nicholas M. Casassa, Robert L. Erwin, Raymond W. Karr, Carl E. Kimmons, Samuel R. Roberts, and Harold E. Staggs.

1. Knoblock, Glenn A. *Black Submariners in the United States Navy, 1940–1975.* Jefferson, N.C.: McFarland & Company, 2005, 308–9.
2. Ibid., 67.
3. Erwin, Lt. Robert L., USNR. *My Navy Story.* Privately published, December 2001, 26.
4. Knoblock, *Black Submariners*, 138.
5. Ramage, Lawson P. "Reminiscences of Vice Admiral Lawson P. Ramage, U. S. Navy (Retired)." Interview by John T. Mason Jr. for the Oral History Project of the U.S. Naval Institute. Annapolis: U.S. Naval Institute, June 1975, 1–2. Hereafter referred to as Ramage Oral History.
6. Ibid., 4.
7. Ibid., 5–8.
8. Ibid., 9–11.
9. Ibid., 15–16.
10. Ibid., 17–18.
11. Ibid., 28–31.
12. Ibid., 29–38.
13. Ibid., 39–43.
14. Ibid., 43.
15. Ibid., 44–45.
16. Ibid., 69–70.
17. Blair, Clay, Jr. *Silent Victory. The U.S. Submarine War Against Japan.* Reprint. Philadelphia: J.B. Lippincott Company, 1975, I: 287.
18. Ibid., I: 287; Ramage Oral History, 79.
19. Blair, *Silent Victory*, I: 317–18.
20. Ibid., I: 328; Ramage Oral History, 96.
21. Blair, *Silent Victory*, I: 328.
22. Ibid., I: 328–29.
23. Ramage Oral History, 103; Blair, *Silent Victory*, I: 329.
24. War Diary, USS *Trout*'s seventh war patrol; Ramage Oral History, 105.

25. Blair, *Silent Victory*, I: 329.

26. Newpower, Anthony. *Iron Men and Tin Fish. The Race to Build a Better Torpedo During World War II.* Westport, Conn.: Praeger Security International, 2006, 27, 158.

27. Ramage Oral History, 107.

28. Ibid., 107.

29. Ramage Oral History, 108; Blair, *Silent Victory*, I: 364.

30. Blair, *Silent Victory*, I: 364.

31. Ramage Oral History, 108–9; Blair, *Silent Victory*, I: 364.

32. Ramage Oral History, 111–14; Blair, *Silent Victory*, I: 364–65.

33. Ramage Oral History, 119.

34. Ibid., 119.

35. Ibid., 120.

36. Ray Karr to Bob Hall, 16 August 2004.

37. Dave Green to Hall, 10 November 1997.

38. Ramage Oral History, 120.

39. Erwin, *My Navy Story*, 1–2.

40. Ibid., 3–14.

41. Ibid., 15–18.

42. Ibid., 20.

43. Ramage Oral History, 122–24; Ramage 1987 videotaped interview with Robert Hall and Joseph Caruso.

44. Erwin, *My Navy Story*, 20–21.

45. Ramage to Barbara Ramage, undated letter circa January 1944. Personal papers of Vice Admiral Ramage provided by his son, James Ramage.

46. Erwin, *My Navy Story*, 22–23.

47. Ibid., 24–25.

48. Ramage 1987 videotaped interview with Hall and Caruso.

49. Karr to Hall, 16 November 2001.

50. Ramage 1987 videotaped interview with Hall and Caruso.

51. Erwin, *My Navy Story*, 26–27; Ramage 1987 videotaped interview with Hall and Caruso.

52. Knoblock, *Black Submariners,* 311.

53. Erwin, *My Navy Story*, 26.

54. Ibid., 28.

55. Ramage 1987 videotaped interview with Hall and Caruso.

56. Smith, Steven Trent. *Wolf Pack. The American Submarine Strategy That Helped Defeat Japan.* Hoboken, N.J.: John Wiley & Sons, Inc., 2003, 56–59.

57. Ibid., 61.

58. Erwin, *My Navy Story*, 29.

## CHAPTER 2: THE *PARCHE* CREW

Primary sources for this chapter are interviews with Campbell, Casassa, Erwin, Robert A. Hall, David F. Hussey, Charles W. Gooden, Myron W. Grover, Karr, Kimmons, Corwin M. Maupin, Roberts, Staggs, and Donald E. Walters.

1. Blair, *Silent Victory*, I: 570.
2. Smith, *Wolf Pack*, 143.
3. Ramage Oral History, 125.
4. Erwin, *My Navy Story*, 31.
5. Ibid., 31–32.
6. LaVO, Carl. *Back From the Deep. The Strange Story of the Sister Subs Squalus and Sculpin*. Annapolis: Naval Institute Press, 1994, 15–17; McLeod, Grover S. *Sub Duty*. Birmingham, Al.: Manchester Press, 1986, 2–23.
7. *United States Submarine Veterans of World War II. A History of the Veterans of the United States Naval Submarine Fleet*. Dallas: Taylor Publishing Company, 1984–1990, III: 239.
8. Ibid., IV: 115.
9. Karr to Hall, 16 November 2001.
10. Silvis, Robert and Robert Hall (editors). *Parche SS 384*. Monroe, Wi.: New Life Press, 2002, 9.
11. *United States Submarine Veterans of World War II*, I: 406.
12. Ibid., I: 281.
13. Ibid.
14. Ibid., I: 259; Ramage 1987 videotaped interview with Hall and Caruso.
15. *United States Submarine Veterans of World War II*, I: 280.
16. Hawn, Richard G., "A Wonderful War," 3. Ten-page submarine service memoirs, courtesy of Mrs. R. G. Hawn.
17. Ibid., 9.
18. Ramage Oral History, 120; Ramage 1987 videotaped interview with Hall and Caruso.
19. Karr to Hall, 16 August 2004.
20. Ibid.
21. Ramage 1987 video with Caruso and Hall.
22. *United States Submarine Veterans of World War II*, I: 222.
23. Hughes to Hall, 3 December 1992.
24. Smith, *Wolf Pack*, 144.
25. *United States Submarine Veterans of World War II*, I: 413.
26. Ramage Oral History, 126.
27. Erwin, *My Navy Story*, 33.

**CHAPTER 3: FIRST ACTION**
Primary sources for this chapter are interviews with Campbell, Casassa, Erwin, Hall, Hussey, Gooden, Grover, Karr, Kimmons, Maupin, Roberts, Staggs, and Walters.
1. Allcorn, Frank W., III. Manuscript notes from unfinished memoir, courtesy of his son Frank W. "Skip" Allcorn IV.
2. Erwin, *My Navy Story*, 35.
3. Ibid., 35–36.
4. Ibid., 49.
5. Ramage Oral History, 127.
6. Erwin, *My Navy Story*, 37.

7. Ibid., 36.
8. Ibid., 37.
9. Smith, *Wolf Pack*, 145–47; Alden, Cdr. John D, USN (Ret). *U.S. Submarine Attacks During World War II.* Annapolis: Naval Institute Press, 1989, 96.
10. Hawn, "A Wonderful War," 18.
11. Erwin, *My Navy Story*, 8.
12. Ibid., 41.
13. O'Kane, Rear Adm. Richard H., USN (Ret.). *Clear the Bridge! The War Patrols of the U.S.S. Tang.* Chicago: Rand McNally & Company, 1977, 40; Ramage 1987 videotaped interview with Hall and Caruso.
14. Erwin, *My Navy Story,* 41.

## Chapter 4: Convoy Killers

Primary sources for this chapter are interviews with Campbell, Casassa, Erwin, Gooden, Grover, Hall, Hussey, Karr, Kimmons, Maupin, Roberts, Staggs, and Walters.

1. Erwin, *My Navy Story*, 43.
2. "IJN Minelayer *Maeshima*: Tabular Record of Movement." © 2008–2009 Bob Hackett, Sander Kingsepp, and Peter Cundall. Accessed http://www.combined fleet.com/Maeshima_t.htm on 4 December 2009.
3. Smith, *Wolf Pack,* 150.
4. Alden, *United States and Allied Submarine Successes in the Pacific and Far East During World War II,* D-137. JANAC's postwar credit gave *Parche*'s torpedo victims as the 6,475-ton freighter *Shoryu Maru* and 5,244-ton *Taiyoku Maru,* but the JANAC researchers did not have access to some of the Japanese sources reviewed by John Alden in recent years.
5. Ibid.
6. Ramage Oral History, 131.
7. Ibid., 132.
8. Erwin, *My Navy Story*, 45.
9. Ibid.
10. Knoblock, *Black Submariners*, 310.
11. Erwin, *My Navy Story*, 47.
12. Ibid., 47–48.
13. Ibid., 48.
14. Ibid., 95.
15. Ibid., 48.
16. Ibid., 49.

## Chapter 5: Parks' Pirates

Primary sources for this chapter are interviews with Campbell, Casassa, Erwin, Paul W. Gilcher, Gooden, Grover, Hall, Hussey, Karr, Kimmons, Maupin, Charles C. McNutt, Glenn W. Meise, Edward C. Mokos, Edward A. Rauscher, Roberts, Walters, Charles E. Welton, and Ronald E. Williams.

1. Hawn, "A Wonderful War," 3–5.

2. Erwin, *My Navy Story*, 52; excerpt from William "Lonnie" Hughes wartime diary, courtesy of Lonni M. Martin.
3. Ibid., 53.
4. Ibid., 54.
5. Ibid., 55.
6. Ramage Oral History, 137–39.
7. Smith, *Wolf Pack*, 180–82.
8. Ibid., 182.
9. Ramage Oral History, 140.
10. Ibid., 134.
11. Smith, *Wolf Pack*, 183; Erwin, *My Navy Story*, 56.
12. Erwin, *My Navy Story*, 56.
13. Meise, Glenn W. "WWII Tidbits," unpublished recollections, 1.
14. Ibid., 2.
15. McNutt to author, 9 September 2009.
16. Smith, *Wolf Pack*, 187–88.
17. Meise, "WWII Tidbits," 3.
18. McNutt, Charles C. Untitled Navy memoirs, collection of short stories involving life on *Parche*. "Man Overboard," 17.
19. Erwin, *My Navy Story*, 57.
20. Ibid.
21. Ramage Oral History, 141.
22. Ibid.
23. Ibid., 142.
24. Smith, *Wolf Pack*, 189.
25. Erwin, *My Navy Story*, 59.
26. Allcorn to Bob Hall, 14 November 2001, courtesy of Skip Allcorn.
27. Ramage Oral History, 144.

**CHAPTER 6: "A PERFECT DREAM"**

Primary sources for this chapter are interviews with Campbell, Casassa, Erwin, Gilcher, Gooden, Grover, Hall, Hussey, Karr, Kimmons, Maupin, McNutt, Meise, Mokos, Rauscher, Roberts, Walters, Welton, and Williams.

1. Meise, "World War II Tidbits," 3.
2. Erwin, *My Navy Story*, 60.
3. Ramage Oral History, 145.
4. Ibid.
5. Erwin, *My Navy Story*, 60.
6. McNutt to Ramage, 15 September 1987.
7. Ramage to McNutt, 5 October 1987.
8. Erwin, *My Navy Story*, 61.
9. Ibid., 61.
10. Ibid., 62.
11. Tully, Anthony, "IJN *Kaiyo*: Tabular Record of Movement." Accessed http://www.combinedfleet.com/Kaiyo.htm on 8 December 2009.
12. Hughes diary; Meise, "World War II Tidbits," 3–4.

13. Erwin, *My Navy Story*, 63.
14. Ibid., 64.
15. Ibid.
16. Ibid.
17. Smith, *Wolf Pack,* 193.
18. Ramage Oral History, 147.
19. Ibid.
20. Ibid.
21. Smith, *Wolf Pack,* 193.
22. Ramage Oral History, 149.

## CHAPTER 7: RED'S RAMPAGE: "I GOT MAD"

Primary sources for this chapter are interviews with Campbell, Casassa, Erwin, Gilcher, Gooden, Grover, Hall, Hussey, Karr, Kimmons, Maupin, McNutt, Meise, Mokos, Rauscher, Roberts, Walters, Welton, and Williams.

1. Smith, *Wolf Pack*, 194–96.
2. Ibid.
3. Ibid., 198.
4. Erwin, *My Navy Story*, 67.
5. Smith, *Wolf Pack*, 199.
6. Ibid., 200.
7. Ibid.
8. Ibid.
9. Ramage Oral History, 150.
10. Ibid.
11. Ibid.
12. Allcorn manuscript notes.
13. Smith, *Wolf Pack*, 201–202.
14. Erwin, *My Navy Story*, 68.
15. Ramage Oral History, 151.
16. Allcorn manuscript notes.
17. Ramage Oral History, 152; Meise, "World War II Tidbits," 5.
18. Smith, *Wolf Pack*, 203.
19. Ibid.; Allcorn manuscript notes.
20. Meise, "World War II Tidbits," 5.
21. Smith, *Wolf Pack*, 204.
22. Ibid.
23. Allcorn manuscript notes.
24. Smith, *Wolf Pack*, 208.
25. Ibid., 204.
26. Ibid., 205.
27. Ramage Oral History, 156.
28. It is fair to note that there has been some disagreement over the years about how many men remained topside on *Parche*'s bridge after Ramage cleared the deck. Clearly, Quartermaster George Plume remained, as he was given the Silver Star later for his actions this night. Jim Campbell and Ed Rauscher were

still topside until *Parche* was nearly rammed moments later. Rauscher was then ordered below, while Campbell maintains that he remained topside with Plume and Ramage throughout the remaining minutes of the attack. Plotting officer Bob Erwin confirms that Campbell did not come down. Skip Allcorn produced a radio interview transcript from 11 January 1945 in which Red Ramage's statements about his Medal of Honor night were quoted: "Things got so hot, though, that I ordered all hands below and stayed topside with two of my crew to direct the fight."

29. Ramage Oral History, 154.
30. Allcorn manuscript notes.
31. If this tanker was indeed *Ogura Maru*, author Steve Smith's reconstruction of the Convoy MI-11 attacks shows that she was not fatally damaged by *Parche*'s torpedoes. Trying to reconstruct the results of such a confused action make it difficult at best to determine just which ship *Parche*'s torpedoes might have finished off at this moment.
32. Smith, *Wolf Pack*, 205.
33. Karr to Hall, 16 November 2001.
34. Ibid.
35. Knoblock, *Black Submariners*, 311.
36. Smith, *Wolf Pack*, 206.
37. Allcorn to Steve Smith, 29 May 2002, courtesy of Skip Allcorn.
38. Allcorn manuscript notes.

## CHAPTER 8: "THE GOOD LORD HAD BEEN WITH US"

Primary sources for this chapter are interviews with Campbell, Casassa, Erwin, Gilcher, Gooden, Grover, Hall, Hussey, Karr, Kimmons, Maupin, McNutt, Meise, Mokos, Rauscher, Roberts, Walters, Welton, and Williams.

1. Smith, *Wolf Pack*, 207–9.
2. Ibid., 209.
3. Ramage Oral History, 157.
4. Ibid., 158; Hughes diary.
5. Erwin, *My Navy Story*, 75.
6. Ramage Oral History, 160.
7. Hughes diary.
8. McNutt, Charles C. Untitled Navy memoirs, collection of short stories involving life on *Parche*. "Bootlegging," 24.
9. Erwin, *My Navy Story*, 75.
10. Allcorn memoir notes; Ramage Oral History, 160.
11. Blair, *Silent Victory*, II: 654.
12. Alden, *United States and Allied Submarine Successes in the Pacific and Far East During World War II*, D-173–4.
13. Smith, *Wolf Pack*, 213.
14. Ibid., 214.
15. Ramage to Clay Blair Jr. for *Silent Victory*; Smith, *Wolf Pack*, 208.

**CHAPTER 9: "A CALCULATED RISK"**
Primary sources for this chapter are interviews with Campbell, Casassa, Hurschel M. Chambers Jr., Erwin, Gilcher, Gooden, Grover, Hall, Hussey, Karr, Kimmons, Joseph D. Leiching, Maupin, McNutt, Meise, Mokos, Rauscher, Roberts, George G. Tubb, Walters, Welton, and Williams.

1. Hawn, "A Wonderful War," 5–6.
2. Green to Hall, 10 November 1997.
3. McNutt memoirs, "Bootlegging," 24.
4. Erwin, *My Navy Story*, 76.
5. Ibid.
6. Ibid.
7. Jim Hawkey to Bob Hall, 3 January 2000.
8. Lonnie Hughes to Bob Hall, 7 October 1993.
9. Erwin, *My Navy Story*, 79.
10. Tubb, George G. "My Silent Service Days. A Personal Narrative." Wartime memoir compiled in 2000, 1.
11. Ibid., 2.
12. Ibid., 2–4.
13. Ibid., 5.
14. Ibid.
15. Ramage Oral History, 165–66.
16. Ramage 1987 videotaped interview with Hall and Caruso.
17. Erwin, *My Navy Story*, 80.
18. Ibid., 80–81.
19. Tubb, "My Silent Service Days," 6–7.
20. Ibid., 7–8.
21. Ramage 1987 videotaped interview with Hall and Caruso.
22. Erwin, *My Navy Story*, 81–82.
23. Ibid., 82.
24. Ibid., 82–83.
25. LaVO, *Back From the Deep*, 174–75.
26. Erwin, *My Navy Story*, 84.
27. Ramage Oral History, 169.
28. Erwin, *My Navy Story*, 84.
29. Tubb, "My Silent Service Days," 9.
30. Ramage 1987 videotaped interview with Hall and Caruso.

**CHAPTER 10: "THE BENDIX LOG BLEW UP"**
Primary sources for this chapter are interviews with Campbell, Casassa, Chambers, Erwin, Gilcher, Gooden, Grover, Hall, Benjamin Harrison, Hussey, Karr, Alden L. Lawrence, Leiching, Maupin, McNutt, Meise, Mokos, Roberts, Tubb, Walters, Welton, and Williams.

1. *United States Submarine Veterans of World War II*, I: 252.
2. Goodson to Hall, 3 December 1992.
3. Ramage Oral History, 174.
4. Knoblock, *Black Submariners*, 82.

5. Hawn, "A Wonderful War," 18.
6. Ibid., 18–19.
7. Ibid., 19.
8. Jasper Hill to Hall, 24 May 1989.
9. Lawson Ramage to Charles McNutt, 5 October 1987; Ramage Oral History, 175.
10. Erwin, *My Navy Story*, 85.
11. Hawn, "A Wonderful War," 19.
12. Erwin, *My Navy Story*, 88.
13. Ramage Oral History, 177.
14. Meise, "World War II Tidbits," 3.
15. Erwin, *My Navy Story*, 86–87.
16. Hawn to Hall, 7 October 1993.
17. Erwin, *My Navy Story*, 95.
18. Hughes diary.
19. Erwin, *My Navy Story*, 88.
20. Ibid., 89.
21. Hughes diary.

## CHAPTER 11: TRAGEDY AT SEA

Primary sources for this chapter are interviews with Campbell, Casassa, Erwin, David A. Forbes, Richard J. Frank, Henry G. Gay Jr., Gilcher, Grover, Hall, Thornton H. Hamlin Jr., Harrison, Karr, Lawrence, Leiching, Maupin, McNutt, Meise, Mokos, Roberts, Robert T. Silvis, Robert H. Swanson, Tubb, Walters, Welton, and Williams.

1. Goodson to Hall, 3 December 1992.
2. Knoblock, *Black Submariners*, 311; Kimmons to Hall, 19 December 1997.
3. Erwin, *My Navy Story*, 91; Karr to Hall, 16 November 2001.
4. Erwin, *My Navy Story*, 92.
5. Ibid., 91.
6. Watkins to Ramage, 10 November 1944, Ramage personal papers, courtesy of James Ramage.
7. Barbara to Red Ramage, 2 May 1946.
8. Ramage Oral History, 162–3, 180.
9. Wright, Capt. Richard M., USN (Ret.). Oral History Interview No. 202. East Carolina University, J. Y. Joyner Library, Manuscript Collection, 1–8.
10. Hughes to Hall, 30 October 1998.
11. *United States Submarine Veterans of World War II*, IV: 131.
12. *United States Submarine Veterans of World War II*, I: 234; Frank memoir, 8–9.
13. Silvis, *Parche SS 384,* 50.
14. Ibid., 51.
15. Tubb, "My Silent Service Days," 11.
16. Ibid., 15.
17. Ibid., 15–16.
18. Hughes to Hall, 3 December 1992.

19. Erwin, *My Navy Story*, 96; Hughes diary.
20. Ibid.
21. Tubb, "My Silent Service Days," 16.
22. Erwin, *My Navy Story*, 97.
23. Wright Oral History, 15–16.
24. Erwin, *My Navy Story*, 97.
25. Hughes diary.
26. Karr recollections to Hall, 16 August 2004.
27. Williams to Hall, 22 December 2004.
28. Tubb, "My Silent Service Days," 17.
29. Ibid.
30. Hughes diary.
31. Erwin, *My Navy Story*, 99–100.
32. Alden, *United States and Allied Submarine Successes in the Pacific and Far East During World War II,* D-263.
33. Jarco to Hall, undated 1993 letter.
34. Tubb, "My Silent Service Days," 15.
35. Schiefer to Hall, undated 1993 letter.
36. Erwin, *My Navy Story*, 100.
37. Hughes diary.

**CHAPTER 12: "THAT SHIP WAS GONE"**

Primary sources for this chapter are interviews with Roland E. Burker, Campbell, Casassa, Erwin, Frank, Gay, Gilcher, Ralph Giordano, Grover, Hall, Hamlin, Karr, August L. Kulick, Lawrence, Leiching, Maupin, McNutt, Meise, Carl J. Meyer, Mokos, Frederick A. Richards, Roberts, Silvis, Swanson, Tubb, Walters, Williams, and Carl J. Zeller.

1. Tubb, "My Silent Service Days," 11.
 2. Williams to Hall, 22 December 2004.
 3. Tubb, "My Silent Service Days," 18.
 4. Erwin, *My Navy Story,* 103.
 5. Giberson, Art. *Century of War.* Pensacola, Fl.: iUniverse Incorporated, 2002, 86.
 6. *United States Submarine Veterans of World War II*, I: 301.
 7. Ibid., I: 286.
 8. Erwin, *My Navy Story,* 104–105.
 9. Ibid., 104.
10. Karr to Hall, 16 December 1992.
11. Dale M. Mielke diary, courtesy of Charles Hinman, USS *Bowfin Museum.* Mielke's diary entries often vary from the dates *Parche* was keeping on this side of the equator by one day.
12. Hughes diary.
13. Mielke diary.
14. Hughes to Hall, 12 May 1997.
15. Erwin, *My Navy Story,* 106.
16. Mielke diary.

17. Ibid.

18. Ibid.

19. Ibid.

20. Erwin, *My Navy Story,* 107.

21. Mielke diary.

22. Ibid.

23. Erwin, *My Navy Story,* 107; Meise, "World War II Tidbits," 4.

24. Paul Kuter journal. Wartime notes/journal kept on *Parche*, provided by his son, David Kuter.

25. Mielke diary.

26. Alden, *United States and Allied Submarine Successes in the Pacific and Far East During World War II,* D-282. In its postwar assessment, JANAC listed *W-3* as 615 tons. Erwin, *My Navy Story,* 108.

27. Giberson, *Century of War*, 88.

28. Mielke diary.

29. Ibid.

30. Ibid.

31. Alden, *United States and Allied Submarine Successes in the Pacific and Far East During World War II,* D-283. In his previous edition, Alden had originally listed this gun action victim as *Togo Maru*.

32. Mielke diary.

33. Hughes to Hall, 12 May 1997; Erwin, *My Navy Story,* 109.

34. Kuter journal.

35. Giberson, *Century of War*, 86.

36. Alden, *United States and Allied Submarine Successes in the Pacific and Far East During World War II,* D-283.

37. Mielke diary.

38. Hughes diary.

39. Ibid.

40. Ibid.

41. Mielke diary.

42. Ibid.

43. Alden, *United States and Allied Submarine Successes in the Pacific and Far East During World War II,* D-284.

44. Hughes diary.

45. Alden, *United States and Allied Submarine Successes in the Pacific and Far East During World War II,* D-284.

46. Hughes diary.

47. Mielke diary.

48. Erwin, *My Navy Story,* 111.

49. Hughes diary.

50. Ibid.

51. Mielke diary.

52. Ibid.

53. Kuter journal.

54. Erwin, *My Navy Story,* 111.
55. Mielke diary.
56. Ibid.
57. Ibid.
58. Erwin, *My Navy Story,* 112.
59. Blair, *Silent Victory*, II: 818–19.
60. Mielke diary.
61. Hughes diary.
62. Alden, *United States and Allied Submarine Successes in the Pacific and Far East During World War II,* D-286.
63. Hughes diary.
64. Mielke diary.
65. Kuter journal.
66. Erwin, *My Navy Story,* 113.
67. Mielke diary.
68. Ibid.
69. Erwin, *My Navy Story,* 114.
70. Mielke diary.
71. Erwin, *My Navy Story,* 114.
72. Mielke diary.

### CHAPTER 13: LIFEGUARD LEAGUE

Primary sources for this chapter are interviews with Burker, Campbell, Casassa, William F. Coleman, Erwin, Frank, Gay, Gilcher, Giordano, Grover, Hall, Hamlin, Kulick, Lawrence, Leiching, Maupin, McNutt, Meise, Meyer, Mokos, Richards, Roberts, Silvis, Swanson, Carl W. Vozniak, Walters, Williams, and Zeller.

1. Erwin, *My Navy Story,* 115.
2. Knoblock, *Black Submariners*, 290.
3. Erwin, *My Navy Story,* 117.
4. Mielke diary.
5. Ibid.
6. McNutt memoirs, "Restricted to Dry Dock," 22.
7. Mielke diary.
8. Lockwood, Charles A., Vice Adm., USN (Ret.), and Hans Christian Adamson, Col., USAF (Ret.). *Zoomies, Subs and Zeroes. Heroic Rescues in World War II by the Submarine Lifeguard League.* Philadelphia: Chilton Company, 1956, 87–92.
9. Hyams, Joe. *Flight of the Avenger: George Bush at War.* San Diego: Harcourt Brace Jovanovich, Publishers, 1991, 114–23.
10. Giberson, *Century of War*, 88.
11. Mielke diary.
12. Alden, *United States and Allied Submarine Successes in the Pacific and Far East During World War II,* D-304.
13. Mielke diary.

## CHAPTER 14: "ONE HELL OF A BEATING"

Primary sources for this chapter are interviews with Burker, Campbell, Casassa, Coleman, Frank, Gay, Gilcher, Giordano, Grover, Hall, Hamlin, Kulick, Lawrence, Leiching, McNutt, Meise, Meyer, Mokos, Richards, Roberts, Silvis, Swanson, Vozniak, Walters, Williams, and Zeller.

1. Silvis, *Parche SS 384,* 33.
2. Ibid.
3. Mielke diary.
4. Ibid.
5. Ibid.
6. Ibid.
7. Ibid.
8. Hackett, Bob, Sander Kingsepp, and Peter Cundall, "IJN Subchaser *CH-51*: Tabular Record of Movement." Accessed http://www.combinedfleet.com/Shisaka_t.htm on 21 August 2009. See also Alden, *United States and Allied Submarine Successes in the Pacific and Far East During World War II,* D-306.
9. Ibid.
10. Ibid.
11. Giberson, *Century of War*, 87.
12. Meise, "WWII Tidbits," 4.
13. Mielke diary.
14. McNutt memoirs, "Depth Charging," 18.
15. Ibid., "Navy Photographer," 19.
16. Giberson, *Century of War*, 88.
17. Ibid.
18. Silvis, *Parche SS 384,* 34.
19. Mielke diary.
20. Ibid.
21. Ibid.
22. Ibid.
23. Ibid.
24. Ibid.
25. Ibid.
26. Ibid.

## CHAPTER 15: EPILOGUE

1. Giberson, *Century of War*, 89.
2. Ibid.
3. Erwin, *My Navy Story*, 101.
4. Harry Slajer to his mother, 20 May 1946; Reaves to Hall, 21 November 1996. Letters from collection of Robert Hall.
5. Slajer to Patricia Jean Slajer, 17 June 1946.
6. Reaves to Hall, 21 November 1996.
7. Silvis, *Parche* SS 384, 38–39.
8. Slajer to mother, 4 July 1946.
9. Reaves to Hall, 21 November 1996.

10. Ibid.
11. Silvis, *Parche* SS 384, 40–41.
12. Ibid., 42–43.
13. Reaves to Hall, 21 November 1996.
14. Ibid.
15. Blair, *Silent Victory*, I: 858.
16. Green to Hall, 10 November 1997.
17. Knoblock, *Black Submariners*, 314.
18. Ibid., 290.
19. *United States Submarine Veterans of World War II*, III: 240.
20. Ibid., IV: 115.
21. Ibid., IV: 131.
22. Ibid., I: 281.
23. Ibid., I: 301.
24. Ibid., I: 259.
25. Ibid., I: 405.
26. Ibid., I: 155, 287.
27. Ibid., I: 222.
28. Ibid., I: 406.
29. Ibid., I: 234.
30. Ibid., I: 281.
31. Ibid., I: 252.
32. Ibid., I: 253.
33. Silvis, *Parche* SS 384, 47.
34. Hall to author, 10 January 2010.

# Bibliography

**CORRESPONDENCE, TELEPHONE INTERVIEWS**

Barnett, Stephen (son of the late Percy Barnett). Telephone interview with author 11 October 2009.

Brown, Walter E., Jr. Telephone interview with Maury Martin 29 July 2009.

Buckner, Grace (wife of the late Orvail Buckner). Telephone interview with author 7 September 2009.

Burker, Roland E. Telephone interviews with author 25 August and 10 October 2009.

Burton, Lowell (formerly Brodsky). Telephone interview with author 17 August 2009.

Campbell, Churchill J. Telephone interview with author 5 August, 14 August, 3 September, and 25 November 2009. Additional correspondence and e-mails during this period.

Casassa, Nicholas M. Telephone interview with author 8 August 2009.

Chambers, Hurschel M., Jr. Telephone interview with author 2 September 2009.

Christy, William (son of the late Desmond A. Christy). Telephone interview with author 24 October 2009.

Coleman, William F. Telephone interview with author 10 August 2009.

DeSola, Joseph, Jr. (son of the late Joseph E. DeSola). Telephone interview with author 10 October 2009 and subsequent e-mail correspondence and personal meetings.

Dillon, Mary (wife of the late Robert E. Dillon). Telephone interview with author 10 October 2009.

Ernest, Robert, and Howard G. Ernest (sons of the late Howard E. Ernest). Telephone interviews with author 15 October 2009.

Erwin, Robert. Telephone interviews with author 23 July and 9 August 2009. Additional audiotaped interview sesssions between Erwin and Dave Hall from 15 November 2009. Subsequent e-mail and mail correspondence and personal interview 20 January 2010.

Forbes, David A. Telephone interview with author 9 August 2009.

Fournier, Genny (wife of the late Nelson Fournier). Telephone interview with author 1 October 2009.

Frank, Richard. Telephone interview with author 25 August 2009.

Gadd, Mike (son of Francis O. Gadd). Telephone interview 14 August 2009.

Gay, Henry G., Jr. Telephone interview with author 3 September 2009.

Gilcher, Paul W. Various e-mail correspondence 15–18 August 2009.

Giordano, Ralph. Telephone interview with author 8 August 2009.

Gomes, Nancy K. (daughter of the late Charles G. Keenan, Jr.). Email and correspondence of October 2010.

Gooden, Charles W. Telephone interview with author 29 July and 31 October 2009.

Grover, Myron W. Telephone interview with author 7 September 2009.

Haba, Eugene E. Telephone interview with author 20 January 2010.

Hall, Robert A. Telephone interview with author 5 August 2009. Subsequent follow-up calls and letters with author and 1 September 2010 round-table interview.

Hamlin, Thornton H., Jr. Telephone interview with author 3 August 2009.

Harrison, Benjamin (on sailing lists as Benjamin H. Couture during war-time). Telephone interview with author 5 August 2009.

Hawn, Emme (wife of the late Richard G. Hawn). Telephone interview with author 28 September 2009 and correspondence.

Holleran, Ruth (wife of the late John M. Holleran). Telephone interview with author 6 August 2009.

Hussey, David F. Telephone interviews with author 1 August and 10 October 2009.

Karr, Raymond W. Telephone interviews with author 2 August and 15 October 2009 and subsequent correspondence.

Kimmons, Carl E. Telephone interviews with author 2 August and 7 September 2009.

Kulick, August L. Telephone interviews with author 14 August and 10 October 2009.

Kuter, Richard, and David Kuter (sons of the late Paul Kuter). E-mail correspondence in October 2009 concerning stories from their father. Diary/journal of Kuter supplied by his son David and other recollections from Paul's daughter Susan Reed.

Larsen, Donald (nephew of the late Hollis Larsen). Telephone interview with author 11 October 2009.

Lawrence, Alden L. Interviews from January–September 2009 conducted and compiled by his son, Keith A. Lawrence.

Leiching, Joseph D. Telephone interviews with author 23 August and 11 October 2009.

Lutz, Claude, Jr. (son of the late Claude Lutz). Telephone interview 1 November 2009, plus follow-up correspondence and e-mail.

Manns, Norma (wife of the late David Manns). Telephone interview with author 28 September 2009.

Martin, Lonni M. (daughter of the late William A. Hughes). Telephone interview with author 21 January 2010. Diary of William "Lonnie" Hughes supplied by his daughter, along with photos and various papers.

Maupin, Corwin. Telephone interview with author 29 July 2009. Subsequent follow-up calls with author and 1 September 2010 round-table interview.

McNutt, Charles C. Telephone interviews with author 28 July, 10 October and 15 October 2009 and various correspondence.

Meise, Glenn W. Interviewed by his daughter Wahneta Meise Goon during December 2009 with questions from author. Additional five-page World War II testimonial, "WWII Tidbits," written by Meise 10 January 2003, supplied by Rex and Wahneta Goon.

Meyer, Carl J. Telephone interview with author 11 August 2009.

Mokos, Edward. Telephone interviews with author 27 July and 14 November 2009.

Payne, Eugene (nephew of Vice Admiral McCrory). Telephone interview with author 7 September 2009 and additional e-mail and correspondence.

Payne, Ozro V., Jr. Telephone interview with author 1 August 2009.

Ramage, Lawson P. Videotaped interview with shipmates Robert Hall and Joseph Caruso from 1987 courtesy of Dave Hall. Other papers, videos, and wartime letters of Admiral Ramage were furnished by his son, James Ramage.

Rauscher, Edward A. Telephone interview with author 6 August 2009.

Richards, Frederick A. Telephone interviews with author 8 August and 4 October 2009, subsequent e-mail correspondence with author, and 1 September 2010 round-table interview.

Roberts, Samuel R. Telephone interview with author 1 August 2009.

Satterfield, Margaret (wife of the late Charles Satterfield). Telephone interview with author 24 October 2009.

Silvis, Robert T. Telephone interview with author 8 August 2009.

Staggs, Harold. Telephone interview with Maury Martin 29 July 2009 and with author 24 October 2009. Subsequent follow-up calls with author and 1 September 2010 round-table interview.

St. Denny, Pat (wife of the late Ralph B. St. Denny). Telephone interview with author 28 September and 16 October 2009.

Swanson, Robert H. Telephone interview with Maury Martin 29 July 2009 and with author 11 October 2009.

Tubb, George G. Telephone interviews with author 5 August and 10 Ocotber 2009 and various correspondence.

Vogedes, Cecile (wife of the late Frederick Z. Vogedes). Telephone interview with author 15 September 2009.

Vozniak, Carl. Telephone interviews with author 25 July 2009 and 20 January 2010, and 1 September 2010 round-table interview.

Walters, Donald E. Telephone interviews with author 8 August 2009 and 22 February 2010.

Welton, Charles E. Telephone interview with author 12 October 2009.

Williams, Ronald E. Telephone interviews with author 6 August and 14 August 2009 and 19 January 2010, and 1 September 2010 round-table interview.

Zeller, Carl J. Telephone interview with author 3 September 2009.

## ARTICLES / MEMOIRS / REPORTS

Allcorn, Frank W., III. Notes from unpublished memoir, courtesy of his son, Frank W. "Skip" Allcorn IV.

Frank, Richard. Unpublished memoirs.

Hackett, Bob, Sander Kingsepp and Peter Cundall, "IJN Subchaser *CH-51*: Tabular Record of Movement." Accessed http://www.combinedfleet. com/Shisaka_t.htm on 21 August 2009.

Hawn, Richard G. "A Wonderful War." Ten-page submarine service memoirs, courtesy of Mrs. R. G. Hawn.

Hughes, William A. "Lonnie." Wartime diary, courtesy of his daughter, Lonni M. Martin.

"IJN Minelayer *Maeshima*: Tabular Record of Movement." © 2008–2009 Bob Hackett, Sander Kingsepp, and Peter Cundall. Accessed http:// www.combinedfleet.com/Maeshima_t.htm on 4 December 2009.

Karr, Raymond. Untitled Navy memoirs, family history, and written recollections of service on board *Parche*.

McNutt, Charles C. Untitled Navy memoirs, collection of short stories involving life on *Parche*.

Mielke, Dale M. Personal diary kept on board USS *Parche*, courtesy of Charles Hinman, USS *Bowfin* Museum.

Meise, Glenn W. "World War II Tidbits." Unpublished recollections.

Ramage, Lawson P. "Reminiscences of Vice Admiral Lawson P. Ramage, U. S. Navy (Retired)." Interview by John T. Mason Jr. for the Oral History Project of the U.S. Naval Institute. Annapolis: U.S. Naval Institute, June 1975.

———. Personal papers and correspondence provided by his son, James Ramage.

Submarine Force Museum Archives. Groton, Connecticut. Wendy S. Gulley, archivist. Various *Parche* articles and images supplied in August 2009.

"Sub *Parche* Sank 5 Jap Ships in 46-Minute Scrap." *Atlanta Constitution*, 6 June 1945, 1–2.

Tubb, George G. "My Silent Service Days. A Personal Narrative." Wartime memoir compiled in 2000.

Tully, Anthony, "IJN *Kaiyo*: Tabular Record of Movement." Accessed http://www.combinedfleet.com/Kaiyo.htm on 8 December 2009.

Various correspondence to *Parche* newsletter editor Robert Hall from his shipmates (as cited in Notes).

War patrol reports, USS *Parche* and USS *Trout*.

Wright, Capt. Richard M., USN (Ret.). Oral History Interview No. 202. East Carolina University, J. Y. Joyner Library, Manuscript Collection.

## BOOKS

Alden, Cdr. John D., USN (Ret.) *U.S. Submarine Attacks During World War II*. Annapolis: Naval Institute Press, 1989.

————. *United States and Allied Submarine Successes in the Pacific and Far East During World War II. Chronological Listing*. Pleasantville, NY: Self-published, second edition, October 1999.

Blair, Clay, Jr. *Silent Victory. The U.S. Submarine War Against Japan*. Philadelphia: J. B. Lippincott Company, 1975. Reprint.

DeRose, James F. *Unrestricted Warfare. How a New Breed of Officers Led the Submarine Force to Victory in World War II*. New York: John Wiley & Sons, Inc., 2000.

Erwin, Lt. Robert L., USNR. *My Navy Story*. Privately published, December 2001.

Giberson, Art. *Century of War*. Pensacola, Fl.: iUniverse Incorporated, 2002.

Hinkle, David Randall (ed.). *United States Submarines*. New York: Barnes and Noble Books, 2002.

Holmes, Harry. *The Last Patrol*. Shrewsbury, Eng.: Airlife Publishing Ltd., 1994.

Hyams, Joe. *Flight of the Avenger: George Bush at War*. San Diego: Harcourt Brace Jovanovich, Publishers, 1991.

Kimmett, Larry, and Margaret Regis. *U.S. Submarines in World War II. An Illustrated History*. Seattle: Navigator Publishing, 1996.

Knoblock, Glenn A. *Black Submariners in the United States Navy, 1940–1975*. Jefferson, N.C.: McFarland & Company, 2005.

LaVO, Carl. *Back From the Deep. The Strange Story of the Sister Subs Squalus and Sculpin*. Annapolis: Naval Institute Press, 1994.

Lockwood, Charles A., Vice Adm., USN (Ret.), and Hans Christian Adamson, Col., USAF (Ret.). *Zoomies, Subs and Zeroes. Heroic Rescues in World War II by the Submarine Lifeguard League*. Philadelphia: Chilton Company, 1956.

McLeod, Grover S. *Sub Duty.* Birmingham, Al.: Manchester Press, 1986.

Newpower, Anthony. *Iron Men and Tin Fish: The Race to Build a Better Torpedo During World War II.* Westport, Conn.: Praeger Security International, 2006.

O'Kane, Rear Adm. Richard H., USN (Ret.). *Clear the Bridge! The War Patrols of the U.S.S. Tang.* Chicago: Rand McNally & Company, 1977.

Roberts, Bruce, and Ray Jones. *Steel Ships and Iron Men.* Chester, Conn.: The Globe Pequot Press, 1991.

Roscoe, Theodore. *United States Submarine Operations in World War II.* Annapolis: Naval Institute Press, 1949.

Silvis, Robert and Robert Hall (editors). *Parche SS 384.* Monroe, Wi.: New Life Press, 2002.

Smith, Steven Trent. *Wolf Pack. The American Submarine Strategy That Helped Defeat Japan.* Hoboken, N.J.: John Wiley & Sons, Inc., 2003.

*United States Submarine Veterans of World War II. A History of the Veterans of the United States Naval Submarine Fleet.* Four volumes. Dallas: Taylor Publishing Company, 1984–1990.

Wheeler, Keith. *War Under the Pacific.* Alexandria, Va.: Time-Life Books, 1980.

# Index

Fenno, Frank W., 277
*Finback* (SS-230), 14, 23, 51, 248
Fisher, "LC" (Leo), 242, 247, 288
Fisk, William Arthur, 73
Flack, Robert Francis, 144, 146, 155, 173, 185–186, 194
Flanagan, Robert Edward, 241, 277
*Florikan* (ASR-9), 277
Folse, John Stephen, 49
Forbes, David Allen, 174, 194
Fournier, Nelson Carl, 49, 157, 200, 277
Frank, David, 46
Frank, Richard John, 174–175, 178, 186, 189, 191, 195, 241, 254, 261, 264, 292
Frederick, "LB" (Freddy), 21, 46, 65, 133, 197, 200, 241
Frye, Edward Seely, 195
*Fukuju Maru No. 3* (Japanese freighter), 88
*Fulton* (AS-11), 150–151, 153–154, 196, 206, 279, 287
*Fuso Maru* (Japanese transport), 101, 119, 129

Gabik, Francis Norman, 275
Gadd, Francis Oliver, 203, 209, 213, 218, 225, 233, 241, 243, 256, 267, 275–277, 287
Gallaher, Anton Renki (Tony), 27, 54–55
Ganyard, Bricker McDonald, 200, 203, 207, 225, 232, 234
*Gar* (SS-206), 127
*Gato* (SS-212), 31, 74
Gay, Henry Grady, Jr., 174–175, 182, 241, 260, 292
Geier, Max, 194, 223, 241, 251
Gilcher, Paul William (Bill), 81–83, 95, 110, 118, 127, 135, 184
*Gilliam* (APA-57), 280
Gilmore, Howard Walter, 131–132
Giordano, Ralph, 212, 234, 241, 257, 291
Goding, Mark Alden, 25, 41, 75, 78, 138, 143, 151, 153
Gooden, Charles William (Chuck), 31, 48, 63, 74, 110–111, 133, 139, 151, 153
Goodson, Allan Douglas, Jr., 153–155, 167–168, 293
Gormley, Morris William, 151
*Grampus* (SS-207), 48
Gray, John Campbell, Jr., 24, 49, 53, 55–56, 58, 62–63, 66, 71, 104–105, 107, 109–110, 117, 121, 131, 144,

156–157, 171–172, 174, 182, 184, 194, 198, 200, 203, 212, 241, 243, 275
*Grayback* (SS-208), 35
Green, David Hepburn, 13–14, 16–18, 22, 28–29, 34, 47, 56, 61, 67, 74, 77–78, 89, 93, 100, 103–104, 124–125, 127, 133, 136, 142, 146, 148, 151, 154–155, 158, 162, 173, 286
Green, Donald Nelson, 65, 137, 168
Green, Nancy, 18
*Greenlet* (ASR-10), 76
*Grenadier* (SS-210), 7, 38
Grenfell, Elton W., 192
*Grouper* (SS-214), 127, 151
Grover, Myron Woodard, 49, 102, 134–135, 174, 182, 185, 200, 235, 260, 266, 273, 276, 291
*Growler* (SS-215), 131–132
*Guardfish* (SS-217), 30, 153, 155
Gubaney, Robert Edward, 23, 46, 75, 77

Haba, Eugene Edward, 277–281, 283
*Haddo* (SS-255), 38
*Halfbeak* (SS-352), 285
Hall, Bobby Coy, 151, 155, 216, 241, 251–253, 290, 292
Hall, Judy, 293–294
Hall, Robert Ames (Bob), 39–40, 46, 48, 67–68, 80, 116, 124, 135, 143, 147, 151, 155, 159, 161–162, 167, 174, 176–177, 186, 191, 193, 195, 200, 204–205, 210, 241, 289, 293–298
Halsey, William F. (Bull), 144, 149
Hamlin, Thornton Huntington, Jr., 181, 194, 229, 257, 262, 287
*Hammerhead* (SS-364), 76, 79–81, 85, 89, 91–92, 95–96, 100–103, 169
Hansen, Arne Christopher, 244
Harris, Caleb Seymore, Jr., 206
Hawkey, Robert James (Jim), 31–32, 85, 110, 137, 148, 155, 196, 200, 212, 216, 241, 277, 279, 283, 288
Hawn, Richard Gatling, 41–44, 43, 55, 73, 75, 78, 133, 156–158, 178, 188, 195, 293
Hayes, Daniel Edward, 40, 67, 73, 75, 287, 290
Hayes, Thomas Wallace, 232, 241
Heaton, Harry Lee, Jr., 242, 246, 253, 262–264
Hennessy, John Harold, Jr. (Spike), 173, 179, 185, 192, 203, 208, 210–211,

342 | Index

# About the Author

Stephen L. Moore, a sixth-generation Texan, is the author of thirteen previous books on World War II and Texas history. His previous Naval Institute Press release, *Presumed Lost* (2009), follows the survivors of seven U.S. submarine crews who were captured by the Japanese during World War II. His Texas history titles include *Savage Frontier*, a four-volume chronology of the early Texas Rangers, and *Eighteen Minutes: The Battle of San Jacinto and the Texas Independence Campaign* (2004). Moore is a frequent speaker at Texas book events and conferences and writes for local historical journals. He, his wife Cindy, and their three children live north of Dallas in Lantana, Texas.